Psychiatry and the Humanities, Volume 4

The Literary Freud:
Mechanisms of Defense
and the Poetic Will

Assistant Editor
Gloria H. Parloff

Editorial Aides
Katherine S. Henry
Eve Nelson Shapiro

Published under the auspices of the
Forum on Psychiatry and the Humanities
The Washington School of Psychiatry

Psychiatry and the Humanities

VOLUME 4

The Literary Freud: Mechanisms of Defense and the Poetic Will

Editor
Joseph H. Smith, M.D.

New Haven and London   Yale University Press

1980

Designed by John O. C. McCrillis
Set in VIP Baskerville type.
Printed in the United States of America by
The Vail-Ballou Press, Inc., Binghamton, N.Y.

Published in Great Britain, Europe, Africa, and
Asia (except Japan) by Yale University Press,
Ltd., London. Distributed in Australia and
New Zealand by Book & Film Services, Artarmon,
N.S.W., Australia; and in Japan by Harper & Row,
Publishers, Tokyo Office.

Library of Congress Cataloging in Publication Data

Main entry under title:

The Literary Freud.

　　(Psychiatry and the humanisties; v. 4)
　　Includes bibliographies and index.
　　1. Psychoanalysis and literature—Addresses,
essays, lectures. I. Smith, Joseph H., 1927–
II. Series.
RC321.P943 vol. 4 [PN56.P92] 616.8′9′008s [801′.92]
ISBN 0-300-02405-3　　79-19104

Contributors

Harold Bloom, Ph.D. Professor of Humanities, Yale University

Leslie Brisman, Ph.D. Associate Professor of English, Yale University

Susan Hawk Brisman, Ph.D. Associate Professor of English, Vassar College

Morris Dickstein, Ph.D. Professor of English, Queens College, City University of New York

Marshall Edelson, M.D., Ph.D. Professor of Psychiatry, Yale University School of Medicine; Member, Western New England Institute for Psychoanalysis

Shoshana Felman, Ph.D. Associate Professor of French, Yale University

Margaret Ferguson, Ph.D. Assistant Professor of English and Literature, Yale University

David Gordon, Ph.D. Professor of English, Hunter College and City University of New York Graduate Center

Geoffrey Hartman, Ph.D. Professor of English and Comparative Literature, Yale University; Past Coordinator, Mark and Viva Kanzer Fund for Psychoanalytic Studies in the Humanities, Yale University

John T. Irwin, Ph.D. Professor and Chairman, The Writing Seminars, Johns Hopkins University

William Kerrigan, Ph.D. Associate Professor of English, University of Virginia

Humphrey Morris, M.D. Resident in Psychiatry, McLean Hospital, Belmont, Massachusetts

Meredith Anne Skura, Ph.D. Assistant Professor of English, Rice University; has taught English at Yale University and the University of Bridgeport; formerly candidate in training, Western New England Institute for Psychoanalysis, New Haven, Connecticut

Contents

Introduction
by Joseph H. Smith   ix

1   Freud's Concepts of Defense and the Poetic Will
     by Harold Bloom   1

2   Lies against Solitude: Symbolic, Imaginary, and Real
     by Susan Hawk Brisman and Leslie Brisman   29

3   The Price of Experience: Blake's Reading of Freud
     by Morris Dickstein   67

4   Two Questions about Psychoanalysis and Poetry
     by Marshall Edelson   113

5   On Reading Poetry: Reflections on the Limits and
Possibilities of Psychoanalytical Approaches
     by Shoshana Felman   119

6   Border Territories of Defense: Freud and Defenses
of Poetry
     by Margaret W. Ferguson   149

7   Literature and Repression: The Case of Shavian
Drama
     by David J. Gordon   181

8   Diction and Defense in Wordsworth
     by Geoffrey Hartman   205

9   Figurations of the Writer's Death: Freud and Hart
Crane
     by John T. Irwin   217

10   The Articulation of the Ego in the English
Renaissance
     by William Kerrigan   261

11   The Need to Connect: Representations of Freud's
Psychical Apparatus
     by Humphrey Morris   309

12   Revisions and Rereadings in Dreams and Allegories
        by Meredith Anne Skura   345

Index   381

Introduction

The poet or the religious genius does not first renounce the things of this world for that which he already intuits as higher; he first recoils out of special attunement to the equation of things of this world and death and then is compelled to find if he can or forge if he must that which he can hold as life. He cannot simply accept what society offers as the good life, but neither can he simply accept the figurations of life previously forged by even those few and most loved similarly attuned precursors. It is these figurations, not the conventional good life, that would be his real temptation. But the mode of temptation implies a struggle already in motion and, for the genius, an agon through which his own figuration of life can be wrought.

Harold Bloom is the foremost chronicler of this struggle in the genius as poet. He has outlined "a catastrophe theory of creativity" (1978) not unrelated to a reading of Freud as verging upon the idea that "to be human is a catastrophic condition" (1978, p. 367).

In *Beyond the Pleasure Principle* Freud wrote:

> The attributes of life were at some time evoked in inanimate matter by the action of a force of whose nature we can form no conception. It may perhaps have been a process similar in type to that which later caused the development of consciousness in a particular stratum of living matter. The tension which then arose in what had hitherto been an inanimate substance endeavoured to cancel itself out. In this way the first instinct came into being: the instinct to return to the inanimate state. [p. 38]

Departing from the letter for what Bloom (1978, p. 360) takes as the spirit of the Freudian text, a third sentence could be inserted paraphrasing the second, to read, "It may perhaps have been a process similar in type to that which later caused the development of creativity in a particular stratum of consciousness."

As explication of the nature of the poetic will and of such an evocative force, Bloom wrote:

> the creative . . . "moment" is a negative moment . . . [that] tends to rise out of an encounter with someone else's prior moment of negation. . . . "Creativity" is thus always a mode of repetition *and* of memory and also of what Nietzsche called the will's revenge against . . . time's statement of: "It was." What links repetition and revenge is the psychic operation that Freud named "defense." . . . [1978, p. 361]

Let us allow Freud to 'comment' on this passage as follows:

> Every modification which is . . . imposed upon the course of the organism's life is accepted by the conservative organic instincts and stored up for further repetition. Those instincts are therefore bound to give a deceptive appearance of being forces tending towards change and progress, whilst in fact they are merely seeking to reach an ancient goal by paths alike old and new. . . . It would be in contradiction to the conservative nature of the instincts if the goal of life were a state of things which had never yet been attained. On the contrary, it must be an *old* state of things, an initial state from which the living entity has at one time or another departed and to which it is striving to return by the circuitous paths along which its development leads. [Freud, 1920, p. 38]

By "beyond the pleasure principle" Freud meant to mean the repetition compulsion as manifestation of the death instinct. But a consistent reading of the text reveals that he there (and elsewhere) interpreted the pleasure principle as equivalent to both, in the sense of being the regulatory principle of the repetition compulsion and of the death instinct. These are not beyond the pleasure principle but beyond pleasure seeking

(Smith, 1977), but so also is Eros, not according to Freud's title but, again, in accord with a consistent reading of his text. Eros, Thanatos, and the reality principle—none is beyond the pleasure principle; all are beyond mere pleasure seeking. The pleasure principle does not refer to phenomenal pleasure but asserts that life is ultimately interpretable by reason of a dynamic coherency. As such, reality does not alter the principle, but life itself.

In sum, in the difficult text of *Beyond the Pleasure Principle* the new assertion is not that Thanatos is beyond the pleasure principle, but that Eros is. It is the latter assertion which Bloom interprets, at least according to my interpretation of Bloom, as a lapse in the Freudian project of demythologization. For Bloom, Freud's Eros—other than in Bloom's interpretation as figurative meaning versus death as literal meaning, that is, short of Freud's passage into the Sublime—is a deus ex machina, a too-easy out from the sterner Freudian passages on death as the aim of life quoted above. Possibly, if Freud, never one to cater to humanity's needs for an upbeat philosophy, could now witness the readiness with which his Eros is embraced and the almost universal rejection of his Thanatos, he might be inclined to side with Bloom.

But let us not pre- (or post-) judge the matter in such ultimate terms. Freud saw that repetition could be constructive and celebrative of life, as, for example, in the play and daydreaming of children; but he also saw that repetition could, as in the wake of overwhelming trauma, become a compulsive emblem of death. In "Creative Writers and Day-dreaming" (Freud, 1908), he seems to have placed the poetic stance more nearly in the locus of the former than the latter. Although he thought himself to be extolling the value of art and only derogating the neurosis of religion, the tendency of his move there was to trivialize one as much as the other. Here, uncharacteristically, he seems to have occupied the place of Kierkegaard's reviewer rather than that of Kierkegaard's poet:

> What is a poet? An unhappy man who in his heart harbors a deep anguish, but whose lips are so fashioned that the

moans and cries which pass over them are transformed
into ravishing music. His fate is like that of the unfortunate victims whom the tyrant Phalaris imprisoned in a brazen bull, and slowly tortured over a steady fire; their cries
could not reach the tyrant's ears so as to strike terror into
his heart; when they reached his ears they sounded like
sweet music. And men crowd about the poet and say to
him, "Sing for us soon again"—which is as much as to say,
"May new sufferings torment your soul, but may your lips
be fashioned as before; for the cries would only distress us,
but the music, the music, is delightful." And the critics
come forward and say, "That is perfectly done—just as it
should be, according to the rules of aesthetics." Now it is
understood that a critic resembles a poet to a hair; he only
lacks the anguish in his heart and the music upon his lips. I
tell you, I would rather be a swineherd, understood by the
swine, than a poet misunderstood by men. [Kierkegaard,
1959, p. 19]

Bloom, as a critic forever stung by this Kierkegaard passage,
will make no such mistake. Instead he has found within Freud's
work the materials for constructing a profoundly antithetical
dynamic of the poetic will.

It should be noted that a reading of Bloom's chronicle of the
poet's struggle with his precursor as an oedipal one in merely
the ordinary understanding of that term would inevitably be a
weak misreading. A strong misreading in those terms would,
on the other hand, inevitably alter one's understanding of what
constitutes an oedipal struggle. Oedipal identifications are ordinarily understood as referring to the internalization as a
superego feature of aspects of the relationship with a parent or
parental surrogate. Bloom's assertion that the precursor is internalized into the poet's id is a radical misreading of the Freudian text. What could it mean?

It can be taken that in a crisis, and in the event of a critical
identification, there is not some addition to the superficies of
an otherwise stable structure but a shaking of the foundations
and a pervasive change. The poet as poet is taken over by a

power with which he has chosen to wrestle. It is not essentially
a matter of passivity. The experience of a negative moment
that coincides with the negative moment of a precursor is to be
understood as an achieved catastrophe. It reaches beyond the
ordinary understanding of oedipal identification to those primal internalizations which are and yet cannot be because no
boundary is yet set across which anything could be said to be
internalized. They are, rather, boundary-establishing phenomena which presuppose the possibility of internalization proper.
But who is to say that there is not such a reestablishment of
boundaries even in oedipal identifications?

In "Freud and the Poetic Sublime" (1978), Bloom locates the
Tasso *Gerusalemme Liberata* passage in Freud (1920, p. 22),
where Tancred unwittingly slays his beloved Clorinda only to
wound yet again her imprisoned soul, as marking the point of
Freud's passage into the Sublime. Freud is drawn parallel with
Tancred, as follows:

> When Freud writes (and the italics are his): *"It seems, then,
> that a drive is an urge inherent in organic life to restore an earlier
> state of things,"* then he slays his beloved trope of "drive" by
> disguising it in the armor of his enemy, mythology. But
> when he writes (and again the italics are his): *"the aim of all
> life is death,"* then he wounds his figuration of "drive" in a
> truly Sublime or "uncanny" fashion. [Bloom, 1978, p. 368]

The interpretation is the prelude to reading *"death equals literal meaning"* and *"Eros equals figurative meaning"* (Bloom, 1978,
p. 368). Bloom would agree (1978, p. 360) that the spirit of
Freud himself, whose dominant self-concept was that of strong
scientist rather than strong poet, might at this point be much
more likely to be heard saying "Et tu, Harold?" than "Right on,
Bloom!" but there can be no doubt that it is a bold and fascinating reading.

In Bloom's interpretation as set forth in this volume, Freudian defense and drive each informs and contaminates the
other, but so also do Eros and Thanatos (p. 21). What Bloom
calls Freud's problematic trope of flight is itself antithetical, involving a polarization in which flight is always simultaneously

both flight away from and flight toward—away from tension and toward discharge; away from the object of danger and toward the object of desire. The objects of danger and desire become known, determinate—actually constituted as such—as the individual achieves separateness from the mother/child unity. With experience and development, objects of danger and of desire change. What remains constant is that whatever is interpreted as danger evokes the tendency to distance or destroy, the motive force Freud conceptualized as Thanatos, and whatever is interpreted as an object of desire evokes the tendency to approach, integrate, or sustain, the motive force Freud conceptualized as Eros.

The accent in a particular flight might be clearly a fleeing from danger or toward the object of desire, or even a soaring above such poles to find them anew at another level. But the fundamental mental turning away from or turning toward is, according to Bloom, to trope or is strictly analogous with troping and therefore "To defend poetry . . . to defend trope . . . is to defend defense" (this volume, p. 2).

Primal turning away, primal repression, refers to an innate tendency to turn from—as a danger—the tension at the source of need and toward the object of satisfaction, prior to the time when either need or object is yet known. It is *by* the turning, and by the action pattern which satisfies the need, that first the object of satisfaction and later the need come to be known. To turn away from tension as danger is to go toward death in the sense of going toward tension reduction, but it is simultaneously to go toward life as a turning toward the object of desire. Pleasure and unpleasure mediate (regulate) but are not the objects or poles of these turnings. The essential poles are the objects of danger and the objects of desire.

Presumably, consciousness is evoked by tension, but the content and focus of consciousness are first toward the to-be-known object of satisfaction. It is in this context that danger and desire, Thanatos and Eros, can be seen as polarities of absence and presence, with each pole having a certain kind of priority. Danger institutes consciousness, but consciousness comes into being in the shape of the image of the object. However,

while it can be interesting and not trivial to trace the place and
relative emphasis given to absence or presence in the work of a
writer or even in an entire cultural era, to debate the fundamental priority of absence or presence is idle. One is not
prior to the other; each can only be in the light of the other.
One does not found or give or lead to the other; they are mutually given, mutually constitutive. But of course humans are
capable of negation. One can be asserted as a cover, as a denial
for the other. And the paradox of negation may be that it is ultimately the only access to both. A strong figuration of absence
covers and encloses the presence that counts; a strong figuration of presence covers and encloses an equally crucial absence.

Danger and desire, Thanatos and Eros, inform and contaminate each other, both in the sense of polarities which define
and ultimately constitute each other and in the sense that the
motive force of 'away from' is also the motive force of 'toward.'
This is the great problem of the economic point of view taken,
as it were, out of context, that is, emphasized to the relative
exclusion of the other metapsychological points of view: energy
is energy, which explains everything and nothing. It is this
dimension of identity which tends to undermine Freud's
rigorously maintained dualism. However, it is an identity that
could only undermine a concept of dual drives as au-
tochthonous forces which enter into experience as already
given opposites and find in experience merely a scene in which
to struggle against each other. This concept of drives derives
from the reading of drives as mythological entities; by way, that
is, of forgetting the sense in which abstractions are 'mythological entities'—a forgetting that entails the reification and anthro-
pomorphization of concepts which then indeed become mythological entities.

As stated, the latter way of reading could be the basis of only
bad science and weak poetry. But is it not also at least akin to
the preliminary imaginative grasp of both strong science and
strong poetry in which the genuinely real or symbolic aspects
of the world and of the human order are prefigured, those
aspects which a narrow scientism or weak poetry would never
bring to light? Furthermore, might not such an imagination be,

not only the preliminary basis for either strong conceptualization or strong figuration, but the necessary continuing mediator between conceptualization and figuration in either the strong scientist or the strong poet?

The subject matter of this volume is joined in those lines of Stevens' "An Ordinary Evening in New Haven" taken by Bloom as preface for The Anxiety of Influence:

> . . . A more severe,
> More harassing master would extemporize
> Subtler, more urgent proof that the theory
> Of poetry is the theory of life,
> As it is, in the intricate evasions of as . . .

The last line of that prefatory quote presages the poem's conclusion:

> It is not in the premise that reality
> Is a solid. It may be a shade that traverses
> A dust, a force that traverses a shade.
> [Stevens, 1972, pp. 349 and 351]

The question is that if, as Hölderlin (Heidegger, 1971, p. 213; Richardson, 1963, pp. 463–64; Ricoeur, 1974, p. 467) asserted, "Poetically man dwells . . . ," what would a strong science of man himself be?

The literary Freud arising from the essays presented here, and from the various prior interpretations of Lacan, Derrida, and Bloom, is a Freud at once beyond defense and nothing but defense. Defense, for Bloom, is the fundamental concept of psychoanalysis, the center of Freud's vision of man. But if the drives, as Bloom sees them, are also defenses; if to trope is to defend; if the literal is a defense against life and the figurative a defense against death—that is, if language in its entirety is defense—then everything, save the poetic will, is defense, and the necessity for refracting the Bloomian white light of defense into its many-colored components becomes indeed imperative. But to see all as defense, to see the defending trope as defending against another or other defending tropes, one negative

moment as defending against another negative moment, is to
see the nothingness which defense ultimately defends against,
and in that sense to be beyond defense. A *no* is said to defense
as nay-saying; defense as undoing is itself undone.

But what of the poetic will? For Bloom it is the ego of the
poet not as man but of the poet as poet, and a vision of the
will's limits and of the will's desire beyond limits as creative
revenge against time and time's "It was." Rather than suggesting a status for the poetic drive or will alongside the Freudian
death-drive and Eros, Bloom suggests that the creative will or
poetic drive reveals the Freudian drives as being themselves
defenses. For poets as poets, drive is the quest for priority, the
urge for immortality (this volume, pp. 6, 26, 27), and is "just
as mythological an entity, no more and no less, as libido or the
death-drive" (p. 8)—and just as problematic, with its own
"contamination of drive and defense" (pp. 20, 25).

In a passage leading to a conceptualization of primal defenses and defenses proper, Bloom continues: "From a normative Jewish or Christian point of view, catastrophe is allied to
the abyss, and creation is associated with an order imposed
upon the abyss. But from a Gnostic perspective, catastrophe is
true creation because it restores the abyss, while any order that
steals its materials from the abyss is only a sickening to a false
creation" (p. 20).

Notwithstanding the different treatment by each, Bloom
must here be placed with Freud, Heidegger, Lacan, and Derrida in the emphasis given to absence, negativity, death—an
emphasis which I have elsewhere elaborated as follows:

> In the infant, prior to the differentiation of self and object,
> the experience of need (from the adult point of view, the
> experience of the absence of the object of need) is the void
> in which consciousness appears and, eventually, the void in
> which language, and thus a world, is given. With the ad-
> vent of ideation and language, primitive blank need be-
> comes demand or desire in the face of situations which
> have come to be differentially interpreted as absence, loss,
> privation, or finitude. But originally there is only the void,

the abyss, with no ideational or linguistic means of dif-
ferentiating this from the plenitude of the absolute unity
of mother and child which is the ground of experiencing
absence. But at the point of original need, the void/pleni-
tude is felt and marked as a beginning of selfhood and
world, in such a way that the human both flees from and is
drawn back to it as his ownmost origin and destiny, while
in some way knowing that neither flight nor approach is
possible because the void is omnipresent as ground of all
that is. However, such knowledge, like the death-instinct, is
largely silent—it is knowledge of the self mediated primarily by mood rather than by ideation or thought. It is
silent awareness—at the heart of manic-depressive psychosis it is silent but desperately acute awareness—of the
ground of consciousness rather than the content of consciousness. [Smith, 1976, pp. 404–05]

This is the silent knowledge at the heart of manic-depressive
psychosis—the disease at the border of nothingness and being,
the disease par excellence of the fundamental turning toward a
stance of one's own—and, I would suggest, also the silent
knowledge at the heart of the poetic will.

REFERENCES

Bloom, H. *The Anxiety of Influence*. New York: Oxford University Press,
1973.
———. *A Map of Misreading*. New York: Oxford University Press,
1975.
———. "Freud and the Poetic Sublime." *Antaeus* 30/31 (1978):
355–76.
Freud, S. *Standard Edition of the Complete Psychological Works*. London:
Hogarth, 1953–74. "Creative Writers and Day-dreaming" (1908),
vol. 9. *Beyond the Pleasure Principle* (1920), vol. 18.
Heidegger, M. *Poetry, Language, Thought*. Translations and introduc-
tion by A. Hofstadter. New York: Harper Colophon Books, 1971.
Kierkegaard, S. *Either/Or*, vol. 1. Translated by D. Swenson and L.
Swenson with revisions and a foreword by H. Johnson. New York:
Doubleday Anchor Books, 1959.

Lacan, J. "Seminar on 'The Purloined Letter.' " *Yale French Studies* 48 (1972) : 39–72.
Richardson, W. *Heidegger—Through Phenomenology to Thought.* The Hague: Nijhoff, 1963.
Ricoeur, P. *The Conflict of Interpretations: Essays in Hermeneutics.* Edited by D. Ihde. Evanston, Ill.: Northwestern University Press, 1974.
Smith, J. Review of E. Bär, *Semiotic Approaches to Psychotherapy,* and M. Edelson, *Language and Interpretation in Psychoanalysis. Psychiatry* 39 (1976) : 404–09.
———. "The Pleasure Principle." *International Journal of Psycho-Analysis* 58 (1977) : 1–10.
Stevens, W. *The Palm at the End of the Mind.* Edited by Holly Stevens. New York: Random House Vintage Books, 1972.

1

Freud's Concepts of Defense and the Poetic Will

HAROLD BLOOM

A person tropes in order to tell many-colored rather than white lies to himself. The same person utilizes the fantasies or mechanisms of defense in order to ward off unpleasant truths concerning dangers from within, so that he sees only what Freud once called an imperfect and travestied picture of the id.[1] Troping and defending may be much the same process, which is hardly a comfort if we then are compelled to think that tropes, like defenses, are necessarily infantilisms, travesties that substitute for more truly mature perceptions. The potential power of trope necessarily dismisses all such pseudocompulsion. Yet the analytical tendency in any lover of poetry ought to keep him vulnerable to the audacity of the wit of Thomas Love Peacock, who in *The Four Ages of Poetry* saw poetic trope as a "wallowing in the rubbish of departed ignorance, and raking up the ashes of dead savages to find gewgaws and rattles for the grown babies of the age."[2]

Defense in poetry then called up Shelley's reply, *A Defense of Poetry*, where amid so much magnificence, Shelley gave us the finest trope of critical transumption (or troping upon a previous trope) that I know. Speaking of the errors and sins of the men who were the great poets, Shelley grandly adds: "they

1. *Standard Edition of the Complete Psychological Works* 23 : 237. Hereafter referred to as *S.E.*
2. H. F. B. Brett-Smith, ed., *Peacock's Four Ages of Poetry, Shelley's Defence, etc.* (Oxford: Basil Blackwell, 1953), p. 15.

1

have been washed in the blood of the mediator and redeemer, time."[3] The reader is thus reminded that the infantilism of the grown baby is of that sort to which Shelley leaps, transcending Christian tropes of salvation and subtly recalling a marvelous figuration by the dark Heraclitus:

> Time is a child playing draughts; the lordship is to the child.[4]

If that is infantilism, then we need not fear a yielding to it. But clearly it is something else, something we want to call poetry, and to whose defense we spring. To defend poetry, which is to say, to defend trope, in my judgment is to defend defense itself. And to discuss Freud's concepts of defense is to discuss also what in Romantic or belated poetry is the poetic will itself, the ego of the poet not as man, but of the poet as poet. Freud's triumph, in an aesthetic rather than a scientific sense, is that the reverse seems more and more true also. To discuss the poetic will without referring to the ego's defenses is less and less interesting.

But I must begin by defining, as best I can, the poetic will, taking Nietzsche as inescapable point of origin. One day when Nietzsche's Zarathustra crosses over a bridge, he is surrounded by a crowd of cripples. A hunchback, with admirable irony, utters a great challenge to the prophet:

> You can heal the blind and make the lame walk; and from him who has too much behind him you could perhaps take away a little.[5]

Zarathustra refuses, saying that to take away the hump from the hunchback is to rob him of his spirit. Yet in his meditation upon redemption that follows, Zarathustra transcends the hunchback's irony and proceeds to dream a great dream of the will. All of us have too much behind us, and the prophet, though poignantly calling himself "a cripple at this bridge,"

3. Ibid., p. 57.
4. John Burnet, *Early Greek Philosophy* (New York: Meridian Books Reprint, 1957), p. 139.
5. *The Portable Nietzsche*, p. 249.

gives us a vision of the will's limits and of the will's desire
beyond limits:

> To redeem those who lived in the past and to recreate all
> 'it was' into a 'thus I willed it'—that alone should I call
> redemption. Will—that is the name of the liberator and
> joy-bringer; thus I taught you, my friends. But now learn
> this too: the will itself is still a prisoner. Willing liberates;
> but what is it that puts even the liberator himself in fetters?
> 'It was'—that is the name of the will's gnashing of teeth
> and most secret melancholy. Powerless against what has
> been done, he is an angry spectator of all that is past. The
> will cannot will backwards; and that he cannot break time
> and time's covetousness, that is the will's loneliest melan-
> choly.[6]

A little further on, Zarathustra sums up this wisdom for us:

> This, indeed this alone, is what *revenge* is: the will's resent-
> ment against time and time's 'it was'.[7]

Nietzsche does not mean that this will is itself the poetic or
creative will, but the burden here must be taken on by the poet
above all persons, since earlier in the second part of *Zarathustra*
Nietzsche twice attacks the poets, meaning Goethe in particular. In the rhapsody "Upon the Blessed Isles," we are warned
that the poets lie too much, and yet the creative will is exalted.
Out of the poets, if they cease to lie, will come "ascetics of the
spirit," as Zarathustra will later prophesy.

But *can* they cease to lie, and particularly *against* time's "it
was"? What is the poetic drive, or instinct to make what can reverse time? Freud ended with a vision of two drives only,
death-drive and Eros or sexual drive, but he posited only a
single energy, libido. The poetic drive or will is neither masked
death-drive nor sublimated sexual drive, and yet I would not
assert for it a status alongside the two Freudian drives. Instead
I will suggest that the creative will or poetic drive puts the
Freudian drives into question, by showing that those drives

6. Ibid., p. 251.
7. Ibid., p. 252.

4 FREUD'S CONCEPTS OF DEFENSE AND POETIC WILL

themselves are defenses, or are so contaminated by defenses as to be indistinguishable from the resistances they supposedly provoke.[8]

It isn't possible to ask coherently what Freud meant to mean by defense," without deciding first what he meant to mean by a "drive" (*Trieb*). The drive or urge (setting aside the weak translation, "instinct") is a dynamic movement that puts pressure upon a person toward some object. Your body and mind are stimulated, whether sexually and toward self-preservation, or toward aggression and death, and your body and mind therefore become tense. This tension needs resolution, and so the drive or urge moves upon some object so as to end tension. That Freud cannot be talking about merely biological impulses always should have been clear, long before the drives become overtly cosmological and hence mythological in *Beyond the Pleasure Principle*. Freud postulates that the psyche indeed has bodily intentions, or as he finally put it in his *Outline of Psycho-Analysis*, drives are "the somatic demands upon the mind" (*S.E.* 23 : 148). Since psyche and body are conceived as a radical dualism, Freud is justified in seeing the drive as a frontier concept, neither truly mental nor truly physical. A drive is thus a dialectical term. Philip Rieff expressed this nicely when he wrote that the drive, to Freud, is "just that element which makes any response inadequate."[9] A dialectical concept necessarily is subject to "vicissitudes," and if it invokes the will, we can be sure that a shadow or blocking-agent will threaten the will, that anteriority will make a stand against desire.

Yet defense, in Freud, is a far less mythological concept than the drive, and also is less dialectical. No one has ever demonstrated to us that drives even exist, but no hour of our lives

8. I am using "contaminated" in its strictly rhetorical sense of the ancient *Contaminatio*, which is a kind of interlacing. See "A Note on Contaminatio," pp. 100–04 of William Beare's *The Roman Stage* (London: Cambridge University Press, 1950): "A character in a play, when removed from his setting, ceases to exist; everything he said in his original context, at least when related to that context, would be meaningless in a *different* context. [Hence] the part would have to be rewritten afresh. The dramatist would have to write the new words himself. This is not borrowing, but original composition" (p. 103).
9. Philip Rieff, *Freud: The Mind of the Moralist* (1961), p. 32.

goes by without reminding us painfully that the entire range of
defense mechanisms can be at work unceasingly. Jacques Lacan
has insisted that the four fundamental concepts of psychoanalysis are the unconscious, the compulsion to repeat, the transference, and the drive.[10] I am not a psychoanalyst, but as an
amateur speculator I would ask whether defense is not *the* most
fundamental concept of psychoanalysis, and also the most em-
pirically grounded of all Freud's pathbreaking ideas. Repression is the center of Freud's vision of man, and when a revised
theory of defense broke open the white light of repression into
the multicolored auras of the whole range of defenses, then
Freud had perfected an instrument that even psychoanalysis
scarcely has begun to exploit. The theory of defense is now essentially where Freud left it, and it seems to me startling that
ego psychology should have done so little to develop what
might have been its main resource. Yet it may be inevitable that
so agonistic a concept as defense should make Freud's followers
wary of entering upon a struggle in which the founder is
doomed always to win.

Freud's earliest notion of defense was very simple; defense
was what put an idea out of the range of consciousness. But
even that simple a concept is a trope, since the flight or distancing of an idea, putting it out of range, is hardly literal language
(whatever *that* may be). And though this first concept of defense was intellectually simple, its figuration was very complex.
A sustained meditation upon Freud's rhetoric would have to
engage the highly problematic troping of flight as the prime
image of repression throughout his work, a troping that he
shares with Milton, whether we think of Satan exploring the
abyss, Eve's dream of flight, or Milton's own stance in his in-
vocations.

Why Freud, in 1894, chose the word *Abwehr* for this most
crucial of all his concepts I do not know, but the choice was in
some respects a misleading one. Freud's *Abwehr* is set against
change; it is in the first place, then, a stabilizing mechanism.
Defense, in war or in sport, seeks more than stability; it seeks

10. Jacques Lacan, *The Four Fundamental Concepts of Psycho-Analysis* (1978).

victory or the annihilation of change. Perhaps Freud selected the word *Abwehr* because he intuited even then, back in 1894, that the ego's pleasure in defense is both active and passive, and so an ambiguous concept of ego required a more ambiguous process than mere stabilization in its operations against internal excitations.

Defense, though it be against drive, in actuality works against representations of the drive, and these can be only fantasies, memories, signals, unless a particular situation is interpreted by the ego as fantasy or signal. But defense is so contaminated by drive, that defense also becomes fantasy or signal. I merely state the clinical evidence that everyone encounters every day, but this leads to the particular difficulty or inadequacy of Freud's concepts of defense, both early and late. Defense is unique among all central Freudian formulations in that its weaknesses are entirely theoretical, and not at all practical or empirical. Why is there psychic defense anyway? Why should an urge arising from the drive cause unpleasure to any ego whatsoever? I do not believe that Freud ever found a single clear answer to these questions. Later I shall suggest that this failing is what compelled Freud to his mythological speculations in *Beyond the Pleasure Principle.*

Defense, for poets, always has been trope, and always has been directed against prior tropes. Drive, for poets, is the urge for immortality, and can be called the largest of all poetic tropes, since it makes even of death—literal death, our death— a figuration rather than a reality. But here I return to the problematic of the poetic will, in order to explore that analogue of the mutual contamination of drive and defense in the Freudian vision.

Following Nietzsche, I have suggested that the poetic will is an argument against time, revengefully seeking to substitute "It is" for "It was." Yet this argument always splits in two, because the poetic will needs to make another outrageous substitution, of "I am" for "It is." Both parts of the argument are quests for priority, and Freud takes his place in a tradition that goes from Vico to Emerson and Nietzsche whenever the founder of psychoanalysis speculates upon priority, which is so frequent an undersong throughout his writings.

The psyche, the image or trope of the self, has an invariable priority, for Freud, over reality or the object-world. Rieff expresses this rhetorical priority of mind over reality in Freud by returning us to the most fundamental of Western synecdoches, man as microcosm and the cosmos as macrocosm: "The self was no alien from the natural world; we were conscious of being not only subjects but objects of nature among other natural objects."[11] The dominant influence upon Freud, here as elsewhere, as noted by so many exegetes from Rank to Rieff, is certainly Schopenhauer, a presence difficult to evade in Freud's Vienna.

Schopenhauer's account of repression emphasized only the derangements of memory, but in his theory of the Sublime the philosopher more authentically can be judged Freud's precursor. If we substitute for Schopenhauer's conscious turning-away Freud's unconsciously purposeful forgetting, then Schopenhauer's story of how the will is made poetic and Sublime becomes Freud's story of repression:

> But these very objects, whose significant forms invite us to a pure contemplation of them, may have a hostile relation to the human will in general, as manifested in its objectivity, the human body. They may be opposed to it; they may threaten it by their might that eliminates all resistance, or their immeasurable greatness may reduce it to nought. Nevertheless, the beholder may not direct his attention to this relation to his will which is so pressing and hostile, but, although he perceives and acknowledges it, he may consciously turn away from it, forcibly tear himself from his will and its relations, and, giving himself entirely up to knowledge, may quietly contemplate, as pure, will-less subject of knowing, those very objects so terrible to the will . . . he is then filled with the feeling of the *sublime*. . . .[12]

Repression, like the movement to the Sublime, is a turning operation, away from the drive and toward the heaping up of the unconscious. Pragmatically, repression, like Schopenhauer's

11. Philip Rieff, "Introduction," in *Freud, General Psychological Theory* (1963), p. 9.
12. Arthur Schopenhauer, *The World as Will and Representation*, p. 201.

Sublime, exalts mind over reality, over the hostile object-world, though in Freud's valorization this exaltation is highly dialectical. The unconscious mind is rhetorically an oxymoron, and the augmentation of the unconscious, though it cuts away much of the domain of the object-world, is covertly a parody-version of Schopenhauer's contemplation.

I have been following a circuitous path to a declaration that the poetic will, or urge to the Sublime, is just as mythological an entity, no more and no less, as libido or the death-drive. The chiasmus that Laplanche isolates as the rhetorical figure for the relation of Eros to Thanatos appears again in the relation of trope to the poetic will.[13] Freud's concepts of defense are themselves drives, and his difficult notion of the drive itself is a defense. Against what? Lacan, in his lecture on "The Deconstruction of the Drive," calls the drive a fundamental fiction, in Bentham's sense of a "fiction," and so Lacan is able to speak of a constant force, beyond biology: "it has no day or night, no spring or autumn, no rise and fall" (1978, p. 165). Lacan even speaks of the drive as *montage,* meaning that every drive must be partial, and also that the scopic drive becomes the true model for understanding. As Lacan says, in one of his superb breakthroughs: "What one looks at is what cannot be seen" (p. 182). Drive is ambiguous, a synecdoche for that aspect of every ego "who, alternately, reveals himself and conceals himself by means of the pulsation of the unconscious" (p. 188). Whatever Lacan intends here, I read him as interpreting the Freudian synecdoche as being at once the partial drive and its defensive vicissitudes. Drive therefore defends against its own incompleteness, its own need to look at what cannot be seen.

But perhaps what Freud always defended against, until *Beyond the Pleasure Principle,* was the possibility that a monistic vision of human aggression would crowd out the dualistic vision of human sexuality. If this speculation were wholly correct, then the mythology of drives was a perpetual defense against a Nietzschean nihilism, against seeing the will to power as the true center of mankind. It seems clear today that the full

13. Jean Laplanche, *Life and Death in Psychoanalysis* (1976), p. 124.

range of defenses elaborated by Anna Freud are perfectly coherent entities in the context of aggression, without any necessary recourse to sexual neuroses. As I read the great epilogue-
essay "Analysis Terminable and Interminable," it is Freud's
belated valorization of the castration complex, a final attempt
to give the theory of sexuality equal privilege with the theory of
aggressivity's valorization of the death-drive.

Freud, in my judgment, wrote two texts which truly are High
Romantic crisis-poems, "On Narcissism: An Introduction" and
Beyond the Pleasure Principle. I am going to give a full reading
here only to the latter, strictly following the paradigm of the
crisis-lyric as I have developed it in some previous books. But
to account for the full range of psychic tropes or verbal defenses in *Beyond the Pleasure Principle*, and to illustrate further
the mutual contamination of the concepts of drive and defense
in Freud, I turn first to the essay, really the prose rhapsody, on
narcissism. Though I will dissent implicitly from much that
Laplanche says, my reading of this essay is indebted to the
fourth chapter of *Life and Death in Psychoanalysis*. The binary
rhetoric of Lacan and Laplanche, with its reductive reliance
upon Jakobson's metaphor/metonymy pseudodialectic, accounts for my principal unhappiness with "the French reading"
of Freud, but that is an argument to be conducted elsewhere.[14]

The concept of narcissism, as we ought never to forget, was
the actual engine of change in Freud's theory. In the crisis-year
of 1914, Freud's theory at first seemed complete, but the vehement burst of inspiration in Rome, during "seventeen delicious
days" with Minna Bernays, changed all that. If Minna was the
Muse, the Sublime antagonist was the treacherous Gentile son,
Jung, whose appropriation of Freud's earlier version of the ego
helped provoke a severe clinamen away from that ego. The
earlier ego was a kind of Virgilian logos, dependent upon repression of the drive, upon the tropological flight of images,
memories, thoughts permeated by the ambivalences of drive.
This ego is still vulnerable to the devastating critique of J. H.
Van den Berg, that: "the theory of repression . . . is closely

14. See my essay, "The Breaking of Form," in *Deconstruction and Criticism*, by
Bloom et al. (1979).

related to the thesis that there is sense in everything, which in turn implies that everything is past and there is nothing new."[15] Van den Berg might well be criticizing Virgil but not Ovid, and I would venture that the later Freudian ego, the narcissistic ego, is an Ovidian image. The simplistic conflict of drives—ego drives against sexual drives—is over, because the narcissistic ego is not at all an agent directing itself against a sexual drive, an Aeneas defending himself from a Dido of Carthage. From the ambiguous cosmos of the drive we have moved to an Ovidian, flowing world of desire and wish, a cosmos where a more radical dualism lurks, the cosmos of Eros and Thanatos, as it will prove to be.

It is always worth recalling that Freud initially followed Ovid, in 1910, when he used the term *narcissism* for the first time to refer to homosexuals taking themselves as their own sexual object (*S.E.* 7 : 145 n.). In the wavering interplay between the ego-libido of self-preservation and object-love, Freud found a more powerful trope for his earlier balancings of the drive as taking place between mind and reality. Captivated by its own bodily image, the Ovidian ego confines libido within the floodgates of the psychic microcosm, a confinement that allowed Lacan his prime heresy of the mirror-stage.

After 1920, with his second theory of the psyche, Freud was to espouse a more primal heresy, almost a gnosis, in the absolute dualism that set against all object relations a primary narcissism, a true First Idea, glorying in priority and solipsistically free of objects, as in Schopenhauer's Sublime. There is no distinction between id and ego, precursor and Ovidian poet, in the curiously sleeplike vision of primary narcissism. The Stevensian image of a child asleep in its own life is precisely applicable to Freud at this single moment. As in Whitman's *Song of Myself,* the distinction between autoeroticism and narcissism wavers and those two states of the psyche uneasily merge.

Lacan and Laplanche, in their different but complementary ways, have shown that Freud placed his concept of libido in a more coherent context, after 1914, by hinting that psychic en-

15. J. H. Van den Berg, *The Changing Nature of Man,* trans. H. F. Croes (New York: Norton, 1961), p. 176.

ergy truly derives from the "narcissistic passion," and also that the essay "On Narcissism: An Introduction" was able to tie together the two previously disjunctive notions of psychic topography and the theory of drives. Laplanche brilliantly reads the essay's dialectic as: narcissism is a love of the self; narcissism is a love of the ego; this investment of self-love actually *constitutes* the otherwise elusive ego (1976, pp. 70, 73–74).

At the least, Lacan and Laplanche help explain why the breakthrough of the "On Narcissism" essay led Freud on to the writing of *Beyond the Pleasure Principle*. The dialectics of aggression, so long evaded by Freud, follow the realization that narcissistic self-esteem, once badly wounded, must *defend* itself by aggression. Aggression rising up as a defense against the narcissistic scar that everyone suffers during infancy, is still the most persuasive account we have for why human aggressivity develops so early. With this link between the theory of narcissism and the aggressive drive kept firmly in mind, I turn now to a full reading of *Beyond the Pleasure Principle*. A revisionary text like *Beyond* . . . should be susceptible to an analysis on the scheme of my "revisionary ratios," if they are to be of any general use in reading difficult works that turn upon issues of crisis and catastrophe.[16]

Beyond the Pleasure Principle is divided into seven chapters, of which the last is very brief and clearly serves as a coda. I will interpret the book here as a dialectical lyric—indeed, as a post-Romantic crisis-lyric. Such an interpretation must be willing to risk outrageousness. Jacques Derrida warns against any premature classification of *Beyond* . . . as a literary text, but I intend to experiment with such a premature reading anyway.[17] A text self-revisionist to this degree is almost definitive of one central stigma of the literary.

Freud's darkest precursor in *Beyond the Pleasure Principle* is necessarily himself, but chapter 1 performs a double clinamen, an ironic swerve away both from the pre-1919 Freud, and from the visions of Schopenhauer and Nietzsche. What looks like

16. For a full account of my "revisionary ratios," refer to my books, *The Anxiety of Influence* (1973) and *A Map of Misreading* (1975).

17. Jacques Derrida, "Speculations—On Freud" (1978), p. 79.

self-contradiction in chapter 1 is an irony or allegory, in which Freud says one thing and means another. What he says is that the pleasure principle has priority over the principle of constancy. What he means is that the psychoanalyst need not base his speculations upon the empirical groundings of late nineteenth-century biology and physics.

The concept of the pleasure principle never changed in Freud, but its hierarchial status in regard to other principles was always unstable. Evidently this resulted from the economic nature of the pleasure principle, which is defined dualistically as a drive that seeks to attain a reduction in the quantity of excitation, while fleeing any increase in such excitation. The reductive quest and the repressive flight are not tropes easily assimilated to one another. Something of a similar rhetorical difficulty appears in the images that define the principle of constancy. The psyche is described as maintaining the quantity of excitation in itself at as low and constant a level as can be achieved. But this level is reached by strikingly mixed images: excessive energy must be discharged, while any further augmentation of excitement must be evaded. If it cannot be evaded, then it must be repressed. Thus both principles—pleasure and constancy—require descriptions antithetical *in themselves but not to one another*. The rhetorical pattern of the two principles is much the same, which may be why Freud begins *Beyond* . . . with the apparently self-contradictory notion that the constancy principle "is only another way of stating the pleasure principle" (*S.E.* 18 : 9). But Freud's own dominant trope here is an irony. Only the repressive element in the two principles verges upon an identity. The active element in the pleasure principle is a reductive nay-saying to every stimulus, but in the constancy principle it is an eruption, a volcanic release. By assigning priority to the negative, Freud prepares for his second topology, his final mapping of the mind. I suggest now that a defensive operation, a reaction-formation, is at work in Freud in this revisionary preparation, which culminates in *The Ego and the Id* (1923) and in *Inhibitions, Symptoms and Anxiety* (1926). Anna Freud remarks that "reaction-formation secures the ego against the return of repressed impulses from within"

(1946, p. 190), and the repressed impulse here is nothing less than Freud's own scientism. I quote from my own *A Map of Misreading*: "dialectical images of presence and absence, when manifested in a poem rather than a person, convey a saving atmosphere of freshness, however intense or bewildering the loss of meaning" (p. 97).

I would apply this to *Beyond the Pleasure Principle*'s first chapter by saying that its dialectical image of presence is the pleasure principle, and of absence the constancy principle. In order to break with his first topology, Freud will bewilder us by reorienting his dualisms. Against his own drive for scientific authority, he now swerves into a purely speculative authority. Against the dualism of Schopenhauer, which set up the Will or thing-in-itself in opposition to the objective world, the world as representation, Freud now opts for a more drastic dualism, or at least what he must have regarded as the most thoroughgoing of dualisms. Beyond the pleasure principle lies not the world as representation, but what Milton had called the universe of death.

Between the first two chapters of *Beyond . . . ,* Freud negotiates what I have called a Crossing of Election, a disjunctive awareness of his own revisionary crisis as founder of psychoanalysis.[18] The crisis-question is not: "Am I still a psychoanalyst when I am at my most speculative?" but rather, "Is not psychoanalysis the only true mode of speculation?" To this question, the text of *Beyond . . .* will render a triumphant and affirmative answer, whether or not the reader is prepared to yield to its authority. But this answer is deferred, and chapter 2 instances a new defensive strategy, Freud's own playing-out of the vicissitudes of reversal and of turning against one's own self.

Not only is there a disjunctive gap between chapters 1 and 2, but chapter 2 is highly disjunctive in itself. Its two subjects—traumatic neurosis and children's play—are not only antithetical in regard to one another, but Freud emphasizes their overt disjunction by his extremely abrupt and arbitrary transi-

18. For my theory of three Crossings or crisis-points in a strong text, see my *Wallace Stevens: The Poems of Our Climate* (1977), pp. 400–06.

tion between them. Their true connection is rhetorical, by way of Freud's highly characteristic synecdoche of neurosis as mutilated part and psychic health as macrocosmic unity. Rieff has priority in having described this accurately as Freud's master trope (1961, p. 47). A neurotic's dreams are seen as belated efforts to master trauma *after* the shock has been inflicted. With the keenest element in his genius, which can be called nothing but uncanny, Freud intuits that the crux here is repetition, and in an addition to the text of *Beyond* . . . made in 1921, he hints that masochism informs this repetition (*S.E.* 18 : 13–14, 14 n. 1). Suddenly we are given the narrative concerning Freud's infant grandson, with his ingenious game of the *'fort-da.'* Whereas the neurotic repeated his trauma in nightmare, the healthy baby repeated a distressing experience as a game. Rhetorically, by synecdoche, traumatic nightmare is a failed game, because it lacks the joyful restitution of a *'da.'* But Freud does not make the rhetorical interpretation. Games *and* art, he says, are not his concern. In the higher speculation that is psychoanalysis, the quarry must be "the operation of tendencies *beyond* the pleasure principle, that is, of tendencies more primitive than it and independent of it" (*S.E.* 18 : 17).

In my reading, chapter 2 is a *tessera,* an antithetical completion that fails to complete and that leaves Freud exposed to the literary equivalent of the vicissitudes of drive, that is, to a certain cognitive and imagistic reversal that is self-wounding. The repetition compulsion is itself a synecdoche for the wounded condition of Freud's earlier hypotheses when he confronts them in the postwar atmosphere of 1919. He had been repeating only a part of psychoanalysis, he now believes, under the delusion that he had mastered the whole of it. Tacitly, and perhaps unknowingly, his text lets us understand that his own earlier synecdoches were incomplete.

With chapter 3 we have what I would call Freud's *kenosis,* an emptying-out of his prior stances (pre-1919) which manifests the one repetitive defense to which he was subject: isolation. Too strong a psyche to suffer regression or undoing, he nevertheless shares with the strongest poets the metonymic defense that burns away context. Isolation separates thoughts from all

other thoughts, usually by destroying or injuring temporality.
Even as we see Stevens, in *The Auroras of Autumn*, defend his
poetic self by an undoing metonymic movement, so in chapter
3 we can observe Freud defending his psychoanalytic strength
by isolating too rigorously a crucial element in his praxis: the
transference (Bloom, 1977, p. 266). What is emptied out of its
earlier, hoped-for fullness in chapter 3 is precisely an idealized
transference, and the first product of this kenosis is what Freud
grimly calls a "fresh, 'transference neurosis' " (*S.E.* 18 : 18).
Something intense, which I surmise is his isolating compulsion
to repeat, fixates Freud to the frustrating difficulties of transference throughout chapter 3. What ought to have been an exposition of repetition itself becomes an eloquent lament that
repeats the noble sorrows of the analyst as he struggles on
against the transference neurosis.

The frightening trope of the "narcissistic scar" conveys
overtly the infant's first failure in sexual love. Does it covertly
carry some sense of Freud's more exalted wound of triumph in
his agon with all prior speculations, his own included? The
"daemonic" power that psychoanalysis reduces as repetition-
compulsion is cited by Freud as being present in what he calls
the lives of normal people. Is he, Freud, the first listed of those
"whose human relationships have the same outcome"? Whose
career is it that is summed up in "the benefactor who is abandoned in anger after a time by each of of his *protégés*, however
much they may otherwise differ from one another, and who
thus seems doomed to taste all the bitterness of ingratitude"?
(*S.E.*, 18 : 22).

It would seem, then, that it is the reign of the pleasure principle "over the course of the processes of excitation in mental
life" (*S.E.* 18 : 23) that is truly emptied out in chapter 3. In an
earlier essay I have interpreted Freud's use of Tasso here as an
allegory of the founder's Sublime wounding of his fundamental concept of the drive (1978, esp. pp. 367–68). But nearly
every paragraph in chapter 3 voids something that Freud had
posited earlier. Very much in the mode of the Sublime poet,
Freud comes up to what I have called a Crossing of Solipsism
(1977, pp. 400–06) in the gap between the end of chapter 3

and the start of chapter 4. The question becomes, not the poetic one of the possibility of love for others, but the psychoanalytic one of affective investment (cathexis) in Freud's earlier self and its conceptualizations. Enormous strength flows in again with the *daemonization* of chapter 4, as Freud begins to open himself more fully to his own darkest and most powerful speculations.

Yet this is a strength of Freud's own repression, of his flight from vexing memories—indeed, even from memories of chapter 1 of the very book he is writing! Chapter 4 is an indeliberate exercise in the Grotesque, with much of its rhetoric a curious litotes, and with its argument colored by images of depth. Freud represses his new freedom from scientism, and the repression allows a certain bathos its moment in the text:

> Let us picture a living organism in its most simplified possible form as an undifferentiated vesicle of a substance that is susceptible to stimulation. . . . This little fragment of living substance is suspended in the middle of an external world charged with the most powerful energies; and it would be killed by the stimulation emanating from these if it were not provided with a protective shield against stimuli. . . . *Protection against* stimuli is an almost more important function for the living organism than *reception of* stimuli. . . . [*S.E.* 18 : 26–27]

Supposedly owing this model to embryology, Freud actually owes it to his own defense against biologism, the biologism that he embraced consciously and never could bear to disavow. This grotesque organism is a kind of time-machine, because its "protective shield" precisely does the work of Nietzsche's revengeful will, substituting a temporality that does not destroy for one that would, if mortal time were not warded off. The repressed movement from scientism to speculation here achieves a curious triumph and allows Freud to revise fully his views of dreams that occur in traumatic neuroses, or dreams recalling childhood traumas that rise during the course of a psychoanalysis. Here are the accents of rhetorical triumph, as Freud acquires a new, more Sublime confidence in the fusion of his speculative powers and psychic realities:

> If there is a 'beyond the pleasure principle', it is only consistent to grant that there was also a time before the purpose of dreams was the fulfilment of wishes. This would imply no denial of their later function. But if once this general rule has been broken, a further question arises. May not dreams which, with a view to the psychical binding of traumatic impressions, obey the compulsion to repeat—may not such dreams occur *outside* analysis as well? And the reply can only be a decided affirmative. [*S.E.* 18 : 33]

What fascinates me here is Freud's astonishing rhetorical authority. In response to so scrupulous, so knowing, so rational a voice, even the wariest reader must yield, though the reader yields only to the author's revisions and reversals of earlier formulations. It is fitting that chapter 5, which follows, should be a sublimation or *askesis* of the crucial and invariably problematic theory of the drives. *How*, Freud asks, is the predicate of being *Triebhaft* related to repetition-compulsion? The answer is a definition of drive that sublimates Freud's earlier account of drive, metaphorically substituting "drive" for the defenses of repetition: undoing, isolating, regressing:

> At this point we cannot escape a suspicion that we may have come upon the track of a universal attribute of instincts and perhaps of organic life in general which has not hitherto been clearly recognized. *It seems, then, that an instinct is an urge inherent in organic life to restore an earlier state of things* which the living entity has been obliged to abandon under the pressure of external disturbing forces. . . . [*S.E.* 18 : 36]

Where once we encountered a drive only by embodying defenses against it, now we experience a drive as a regressive defense. But against what? Against life itself would seem to be the answer, or at least against animation. Drives are *détours*, in

Freud's new metaphor, "circuitous paths to death." They are
not instances of self-destructiveness, which has been the influential but weak misreading popularized by Norman O. Brown.
Rather, they remain dialectical and mythological entities, which
cannot be reduced to clinical examples. In some sense, the
"paths to death" prelude Freud's own Crossing of Identification (Bloom, 1977, pp. 400–06), his willingness to confront
death, his own death. Certainly he wished to die and did die
only in his own fashion; he followed his own path to death, but
only after two more decades of productive life.

The disjunctive gap between chapters 5 and 6 can be seen
better if we omit the last, brief paragraph of chapter 5, which
was added in 1923 (S.E. 18 : 43, n. 1). We would then pass directly from a long final paragraph in 5 that bitterly rejects the
notion that there is a drive toward perfection in human beings,
to an almost equally long opening paragraph in 6 that actually
asserts a desire to be wrong about an "opposition between the
ego or death instincts and the sexual or life instincts" (S.E.
18 : 44). If the hidden burden at the end of 5 is Freud's own
rare drive toward perfection of the work, then the equally hidden burden at the start of 6 is Freud's anxiety that his own final
formulations make any drive toward perfection of the life impossible. But *that* is Freud's Crossing, to choose perfection of
the work, and so he moves on in chapter 6 to project or cast out
a specious immortality and to introject the sublime necessity of
dying. This makes of 6 that final movement I have named by
the ratio of *apophrades*, which in rhetoric is the mode of transumption, and in poetry is manifested through images of earliness and lateness (Bloom, 1975, pp. 73–74, 101–03, 125–43).
Freud's own belatedness is elegantly shrugged off with the remark that: "We have unwittingly steered our course into the
harbour of Schopenhauer's philosophy" (S.E.. 18 : 49–50). But
Freud's more crucial earliness, his originality which transcends
that of any other modern speculator, is masterfully traced in an
extraordinary narrative history of the theory of the drives. In
this history, as I have remarked elsewhere (1978, pp. 368–69),
the monistic libido theory of Jung is accurately dismissed as lit-
eralistic reductiveness, and Freud's own thoroughgoing dua-

lism is rightly appraised as a figuration that allows him to anticipate future theory, even in the absence of clinical evidence:

> I do not dispute the fact that the third step in the theory of
> the instincts, which I have taken here, cannot lay claim to
> the same degree of certainty as the two earlier ones—the
> extension of the concept of sexuality and the hypothesis of
> narcissism. [S.E. 18 : 59]

As Freud remarks, his own observational evidence for his
speculative third step is repetition-compulsion, and there is a
prodigious leap from that to the death-drive. But even physiological or chemical language is figurative, as he goes on to remind us; and how, then, should depth psychology presume to a
language other than trope? The brief and beautiful coda that is
chapter 7 extends the transumption, and gives us the hidden
Freudian metalepsis that I have summarized elsewhere in this
formula: literal meaning equals anteriority equals an earlier
state of meaning equals an earlier state of things equals death
(1978, p. 368). Literal meaning, by a metaleptic leap, is therefore death, while figurative meaning is Eros. Reverse this
Freudian formula and you have part of the context in which
the poetic will must operate. Death, time's "it was," is literal
meaning; Eros or figuration becomes the will's revenge against
time.

How shall we sum up the revisionary pattern of *Beyond the
Pleasure Principle,* its own individual troping of the tradition of
crisis-lyric and catastrophe-creation? Laplanche eloquently sees
the text as granting fantasy an absolute priority, since it
mythologizes "a kind of antilife as sexuality, frenetic enjoyment, the negative, repetition-compulsion" (1976, p. 124).
But Laplanche need not have been startled, nor should he expect us to be surprised. Rieff long ago pointed out that the idea
of the Primal Scene also grants the priority to fantasy (1961, p.
53), and we can add that primal repression or originary fixation must have a fantasy basis also, since it posits repression
before there is anything to be repressed. The peculiar achievement
and textual originality of *Beyond . . . ,* among Freud's works,
must be found elsewhere.

The originality, still unsettling, remains Freud's initial clinamen or irony in *Beyond* . . ., which is that the principle of constancy, like the pleasure principle, is transcended by a Schopenhauerian drive to Nirvana. This is Freud's actual "beyonding,"
as it were, and though it is outrageously speculative, it is *not* in
the fantasy mode of the various primal formulations. Catastrophe is, alas, not a fantasy but is the macrocosmic synecdoche of
which masochism and sadism form microcosmic parts. It is not
self-destruction that energizes the death-drive but rather the
turning of aggression against the self. Freud's astonishing originality is that, in *Beyond* . . ., he sees catastrophe as being itself
a defense, and I would add that catastrophe-creation is thus a
defense also. To answer again the question: Defense against
what? is to return to everything problematic about the poetic
will, with its own mutual contaminations of drive and defense.

From a normative Jewish or Christian point of view, catastrophe is allied to the abyss, and creation is associated with an
order imposed upon the abyss. But from a Gnostic perspective,
catastrophe is true creation because it restores the abyss, while
any order that steals its materials from the abyss is only a sickening to a false creation.[19] Freud's materialistic perspective is
obviously neither that of normative theism nor of gnosis, yet
his catastrophe theories unknowingly border upon gnosis. For
what is the origin of Freud's two final drives, Eros and Thanatos, if it is not catastrophe? Why should there be urges innate
in us to restore an earlier condition unless somehow we had
fallen or broken away out of or from that condition? The urges
or drives act as our defenses against our belated condition; but
these defenses are gains (however equivocal) through change,
whereas defenses proper, against the drives, are losses through
change, or we might speak of losses that fear further change.
Change is the key term, and every cosmic origin of change is
seen by Freud as having been catastrophe.

The origin of defense proper, for Freud, is primal fixation,
an initial catastrophic origin of drives. Can we account for this
very curious speculative principle in Freud, in which there is

19. See Hans Jonas, *The Gnostic Religion* (Boston: Beacon Press, 1963), pp.
190 ff.

flight from the drive before the drive has been instituted? The pattern is: defense, followed by catastrophe, followed by drive, or as I would trope this triad: limitation or contraction, followed by substitution, followed by representation or restitution (Bloom, 1975b, pp. 5–6). I do not for a moment believe that Freud was following, even unconsciously, a Gnostic or Kabbalistic paradigm, but I certainly do believe that he was following, perhaps unconsciously, a similar metaphysical model from Schopenhauer.

Granting that I merely seem to be playing with figurations, permit me to extend the play for a space. What might it mean to say that defense is a movement of limitation or withdrawal, and that the drive is a contrary movement of representation or restitution? Since I have shown defense and drive as contaminating one another anyway, the distinction of contraries here could only be relative. Thus, one could speak of Thanatos as a limiting drive and Eros as a restituting one, but the chiasmic linkage of the two drives (as Laplanche maps it) also brings about a crossing-over of their functions. Again, one could say that reaction-formation, the repetition compulsions, and sublimation are defenses or tropes of limitation, while turning against the self, repression, and the negation that mingles projection and introjection are more nearly defenses of restitution. It is suggestive that Thanatos as a drive thus would be more closely allied to reaction-formations, compulsions to repeat, and the "cultural" defense of sublimation, whereas sadomasochism, repression, and introjection become the fantasies of Eros, the losses engendered by its drive.

Freud, during a few weeks in July and August of 1938, wrote his unfinished *An Outline of Psycho-Analysis*. The little book is difficult and rewarding, and has the peculiar authority of being Freud's last writing of any length. Perhaps because of the aggressive stance signaled by Freud's "Introductory Note," the dualism of the drives is stated with a singular and positive harshness. Both drives are called conservative—indeed, almost regressive—forces, and deeply contaminate one another, as when Freud bluntly remarks that "the sexual act is an act of aggression with the purpose of the most intimate union" (*S.E.*

23 : 149). The darkness of this final vision of the drives emerges most clearly when both aggression against the self, or the death-drive, and libido, or Eros, become outriders on our way to oblivion, allegorical and ironic guides to the last things:

> Some portion of self-destructiveness remains within . . . till at last it succeeds in killing the individual, not, perhaps, until his libido has been used up or fixated in a disadvantageous way. [*S.E.* 23 : 150]

What begins to be clear is that the drives and the defenses are modeled upon poetic rhetoric, whether or not one believes that the unconscious is somehow structured like a language. Eros or libido *is* figurative meaning: the death-drive *is* literal meaning.[20] The defenses *are* tropes, and thus constitute the contaminating aspects of both Eros and the death drive. Eros and Thanatos take the shape of a chiasmus, but this is because the relation between figurative and literal meaning in language is always a crossing-over.

It is a curious truth that figurative meaning or Eros is "more conspicuous and accessible to study" than literal meaning or the death-drive. If my analogue holds at all, then sadism and masochism are overliteralizations of meaning, failures in Eros and so in the possibilities of figurative language. Or perhaps we might speak of a "regression of libido," a fall into metonymizing, as being due to a loss of faith in the mind's capacity to accept the burden of figuration. Sexual "union" is after all nothing but figurative, since the joining involved is merely a yoking in act and not in essence. The act, in what we want to call normal sexuality, is a figuration for the unattainable essence. Sadomasochism, as a furious literalism, denies the figurative representation of essence by act.

Freud concluded "that the death drives are by their nature mute and that the clamour of life proceeds for the most part from Eros." Can we interpret this as meaning that wounded narcissism becomes physical aggression because the loss in self-esteem is also a loss in the language of Eros? Wounded narcis-

20. I am aware that these identifications need further comment, which I hope to provide in a later work.

sism is at the origins of poetry also, but in poetry the blow to self-esteem strengthens the language of Eros, which defends the poetic will through all the resources of troping. Lacking poetry, the sadomasochist yields to the literalism of the death-drive precisely out of a rage against literal meaning. When figuration and sadomasochism are identified, as in Swinburne or Robinson Jeffers, then we find always the obsession with poetic *belatedness* risen to a terrible intensity that plays out the poetic will's revenge against time by the unhappy substitution of the body, another's body or one's own, *for* time. Raging against time, forgetting that only Eros or figuration is a true revenge against time, the sadomasochist overliteralizes his revenge and so yields to the death-drive.

In my reading of *Beyond . . .*'s chapter 5 as Freud's *askesis,* his own sublimation, I implicitly questioned the coherence of the defense of sublimation even as I centered upon the hidden metaphor I named a contamination.[21] I return to that metaphor of contamination for my conclusion. When drive is viewed as defense, then drive becomes trope or myth, cosmological rhetoric rather than biological instinct. Yet Freud had not waited until 1919, or even until "On Narcissism" in 1915, to reveal this mutual contamination of drive and defense. At least as early as the essay on "Taboo and Emotional Ambivalence" in 1912, which was to become the second chapter of *Totem and Taboo,* he had recognized that his fundamental concepts necessarily had contaminated one another by what he called a "mutual inhibition":

> As a result of the repression which has been enforced and which involves a loss of memory—an amnesia—the motives for the prohibition (which is conscious) remain unknown; and all attempts at disposing of it by intellectual processes must fail, since they cannot find any basis of attack. The prohibition owes its strength and its obsessive character precisely to its unconscious opponent, the concealed and undiminished desire—that is to say, to an internal necessity

21. For a critique of sublimation, in the context of poetry, see my *Poetry and Repression,* pp. 253–54 and passim.

inaccessible to conscious inspection. The ease with which the prohibition can be transferred and extended reflects a process which falls in with the unconscious desire and is greatly facilitated by the psychological conditions that prevail in the unconscious. The instinctual desire is constantly shifting in order to escape from the *impasse* and endeavours to find substitutes—substitute objects and substitute acts—in place of the prohibited ones. In consequence of this, the prohibition itself shifts about as well, and extends to any new aims which the forbidden impulse may adopt. Any fresh advance made by the repressed libido is answered by a fresh sharpening of the prohibition. The mutual inhibition of the two conflicting forces produces a need for discharge, for reducing the prevailing tension; and to this may be attributed the reason for the performance of obsessive acts. [*S.E.* 13 : 30]

Here the defense of repression and the drive of Eros are so deeply interlocked as to produce taboo, which is the masterpiece of emotional ambivalence, and is the foundation of all literary allegory or irony. Angus Fletcher, in his seminal study of allegory, relates the poetic will's quest to overcome taboo to the trope of transumption (1964, pp. 233–42, esp. 241 n. 33), which I have shown to be the ancient rhetorical equivalent of Freud's *Verneinung*, that negation which mingles the defenses of projection and introjection. I shall conclude here by comparing the introjective aspect of the Freudian negation to its parallel in the poet's transumptive will.

Freudian negation and poetic transumption both are instances of psychical duplicity, and both ultimately depend upon a metaphysical dualism. The Freudian *Verneinung* involves the formulation of a previously repressed feeling, desire, or thought, which returns into consciousness only by being affectively disowned, so that defense continues. To carry the truth into the light while still denying it means that one introjects the truth cognitively while projecting it emotionally. Few insights, even in Freud, are so profound as this vision of negation, for no other theoretical statement at once succeeds as well in trac-

ing the epistemological faculty convincingly to so primitive an
origin, or accounts nearly so well for the path by which thought
sometimes can be liberated from its sexual past. Since the ego is
always a bodily ego, the defenses of swallowing-up and spitting-
out, through fantasies, still acknowledge cognitively the ultimate authority of the fact.

I want to contrast to Freud's negation the equivalent process
in Vico, for Vico is the great precursory theoretician of the poetic will and of its revisionary ratio that I have called transumption (following Fletcher). What Freud calls the drives, Vico calls
"ignorance" or "not understanding the things." Here is Vico on
the mingled process of projection and introjection, an ambivalence which for him rises out of the bodily ego, out of a situation in which the ego is ignorant of origins and of the relation between cause and effect:

> man in his ignorance makes himself the rule of the uni-
> verse, for in the examples cited he has made of himself an
> entire world. So that, as rational metaphysics teaches that
> man becomes all things by understanding them, this imagi-
> native metaphysics shows that man becomes all things by
> *not* understanding them; and perhaps the latter proposi-
> tion is truer than the former, for when man understands
> he extends his mind and takes in the things, but when he
> does not understand he makes the things out of himself
> and becomes them by transforming himself into
> them. . . .[22]

Extending the ego to take in the things is not introjection but
projection, while the imaginative metaphysics of negation, making "the things out of himself," is a mode of identification, just
as introjection is. Not to understand is to suffer drives, and the
mind's response is the transformation of defense into a negation that provokes thought. The mutual contamination of drive
and defense, of poetic will, with its interplay between literal
and figurative, and trope, with its interplay of substitutes, is the
common feature linking the speculations of Vico and Freud.

22. *The New Science of Giambattista Vico,* trans. T. G. Bergin and M. H. Fisch
(Ithaca, N.Y.: Cornell University Press, 1968), pp. 129–30.

Wallace Stevens, in the closing cantos of his superb crisis-poem *The Auroras of Autumn,* provides me with a coda to my investigation of Freud's own poetic will, which took its revenge against time precisely by contaminating the concepts of defense and of the drive. The trope of transumption, as I have expounded it elsewhere (1976, p. 20), is the ultimate poetic resource in the will's revenge against time, because transumption undoes the poet's belatedness, the Freudian *nachträglichkeit.* Stevens, having suffered the anxieties of death-in-life when he first confronted the beautiful menace of the aurora borealis, transumes the northern lights and returns to a vision of earliness, to a Nietzschean and Whitmanian trope of earth's innocence which is *not* a regression, but a true Freudian negation:

> So, then, these lights are not a spell of light,
> A saying out of a cloud, but innocence.
> An innocence of the earth and no false sign
>
> Or symbol of malice. That we partake thereof,
> Lie down like children in this holiness,
> As if, awake, we lay in the quiet of sleep,
>
> As if the innocent mother sang in the dark. . . .[23]

Stevens projects what Freud would have called the drive of Eros figurated by the auroras, its serpentine malice, and simultaneously introjects its literal autumnal aspect, the death-drive, final form of serpentine change. The effect is precisely that of chapters 6 and 7 of *Beyond the Pleasure Principle.* A final sublimity is achieved and though literal death is accepted, the figurative promise of a poetic immortality returns even as the figurative appears to be cast out. That Freud, more passionately even than the poets, shared in this figurative promise we know from many passages in his works, but never more revealingly than from some belated remarks he added to an interleaved copy of the 1904 edition of *The Psychopathology of Everyday Life:*

---

[23]. The text is from *The Palm at the End of the Mind,* ed. Holly Stevens (New York: Knopf, 1971), p. 314. See my commentary in *Wallace Stevens: The Poems of Our Climate,* pp. 277–78.

Rage, anger and consequently a murderous impulse is the source of superstition in obsessional neurotics: a sadistic component, which is attached to love and is therefore directed against the loved person and repressed precisely because of this link and because of its intensity.—My own superstition has its roots in suppressed ambition (immortality) and in my case takes the place of that anxiety about death which springs from the normal uncertainty of life. [*S.E.* 6 : 260 n. 3]

Against the literalism and repetition of the death-drive, Freud sets, so early on, the high figuration of his poetic will to an immortality. Perhaps someday that may seem the truest definition of the Freudian Eros: the will's revenge against time's "it was" is to be carried out by the mind's drive to surpass all earlier achievements. Only the strongest of the poets, and Sigmund Freud, are capable of so luminous a vision of Eros.

REFERENCES

Bloom, H. *The Anxiety of Influence.* New York: Oxford University Press, 1973.
———. *A Map of Misreading.* New York: Oxford University Press, 1975.
———. *Poetry and Repression.* New Haven: Yale University Press, 1976.
———. *Wallace Stevens: The Poems of Our Climate.* Ithaca, N.Y.: Cornell University Press, 1977.
———. "Freud and the Poetic Sublime: A Catastrophe Theory of Creativity." *Antaeus,* no. 30/31 (Spring 1978) : 355–77.
Bloom, H.; de Man, P.; Derrida, J.; Hartman, G.; and Miller, J. H. *Deconstruction and Criticism.* New York: Seabury Press, 1979.
Derrida, J. "Speculations—on Freud," translated by I. McLeod. *Oxford Literary Review* 3, no. 2 (1978).
Fletcher, A. *Allegory: The Theory of a Symbolic Mode.* Ithaca, N.Y.: Cornell University Press, 1964.
Freud, A. *The Ego and the Mechanisms of Defense.* Translated by C. Baines. New York: International Universities Press, 1946.
Freud, S. *The Standard Edition of the Complete Psychological Works.* London: Hogarth, 1953–74.
  The Psychopathology of Everyday Life (1901), vol. 6.

Three Essays on the Theory of Sexuality (1905), vol. 7.
Totem and Taboo (1913), vol. 13.
Beyond the Pleasure Principle (1920), vol. 18.
An Outline of Psycho-Analysis (1940 [1938]), vol. 23.
"Analysis Terminable and Interminable" (1937), vol. 23.
Lacan, J. *The Four Fundamental Concepts of Psycho-Analysis.* Edited by
    J. A. Miller, translated by A. Sheridan. New York: Norton, 1978.
Laplanche, J. *Life and Death in Psychoanalysis.* Translated by J. Mehl-
    man. Baltimore: Johns Hopkins University Press, 1976.
Nietzsche, F. *The Portable Nietzsche.* Translated by W. Kaufmann. New
    York: Viking Press, 1954.
Rieff, P. *Freud: The Mind of the Moralist.* New York: Anchor Books,
    1961.
————. "Introduction." In S. Freud, *General Psychological Theory.* New
    York: Collier Books, 1963.
Schopenhauer, A. *The World as Will and Representation.* Vol. 1, trans-
    lated by E. F. J. Payne. New York: Dover, 1966.

2

Lies against Solitude:
Symbolic, Imaginary, and Real

SUSAN HAWK BRISMAN AND LESLIE BRISMAN

In the poem "Of Mere Being," Wallace Stevens pictures a golden bird singing "without human meaning, / Without human feeling, a foreign song." This image provokes an insight coincident with the poet's awareness of an addressee:

> You know then that it is not the reason
> That makes us happy or unhappy.
> The bird sings. Its feathers shine.

> The palm stands on the edge of space.
> The wind moves slowly in the branches.
> The bird's fire-fangled feathers dangle down.

So matter of fact is the poet's tone in presenting the images of the last four lines that we cannot say there is any joy in the images as such. There is instead a cold serenity about the act of placing in time and space the deconstructive awareness that happiness is not a function of the reason. Perhaps this serenity could nonetheless be thought a kind of happiness, a psychoanalytic happiness, insofar as the turn to images of what Stevens calls "mere being" involves the pleasure of release from the tension of a previously unrecognized source of anxiety (about human meaning) rather than a positive fulfillment of an instinctual drive.

Emphasizing the need to make unconscious elements conscious, Freud directs us to the joint revelation of the *itness* of things and the landscape of the id at moments of recognition

like Stevens' "then." Defining happiness as the postponed gratification of an infantile wish,[1] Freud also offers a general direc-
tive for exploring, beyond admiration for felicitous phrases,
the pleasures of poetry dependent on postponed satisfaction,
like the delayed discovery in this poem that Stevens is addressing himself to and being assimilated into the company of his
great precursors in the tradition of the sublime. If we approach
poetry looking for expressions of a postponed infantile wish,
and keep in mind Jacques Lacan's insistence that the primary
desire is the desire for recognition,[2] we are directed to the
poet's conjured "you"—the addressee who is sometimes general
(like the third-person "one") but sometimes as much a presence
in a poem as Stevens' "you" heading the passage quoted above.

What is the relationship between the primordial desire for
recognition (by another person) and the acts of recognition
(coming to awareness) privileged in poetry and psychotherapy?
Poetic discourse, like the discourse of the analysand, is predi-
cated on lies against the solitude of a speaker in need of recognition in both senses. Though poems have readers and analy-
sands have analysts, these actual addressees are to be
distinguished from the idealized or hypothesized addressees
who bring speakers recognition and *to* recognition. In transference, however, the distinction is repressed, and the analysand
treats his or her analyst as though the analyst *were* a wholly
responsive parent or a lover capable of satisfying the dialogic
and extradialogic needs for relationship. For therapy's sake the
transference must be approached as one more resistance to be
conquered; but it can also prove to be a process through which
the analysand gains power over his or her emotional needs.
Something like transference occurs in poetry, and it is closely
related to the power of poetic voice. The purpose of this essay

    1. "Happiness is the deferred fulfillment of a prehistoric wish. That is why
wealth brings so little happiness; money is not an infantile wish." Sigmund
Freud, *The Origins of Psycho-Analysis: Letters to Wilhelm Fliess, Drafts and Notes:
1877–1902*, p. 242 (letter of 16 January 1898). We are indebted to Dr. Stanley
A. Leavy for this reference.
    2. "The first object of desire is to be recognized by the other." Jacques
Lacan, "Symbol and Language," in *The Language of the Self*, p. 31.

is to explore, with the help of a psychoanalytic distinction about the kind of presences we invent or find, the methods and achievements of poets that belie the solitude of their speakers.

Original Presence

Poems about an idealized past in childhood, individual preexistence, or mythic prehistory remind us that in positing an infantile wish for recognition we also imagine an original state of wholeness in which self and other were not so distinguished. Milton pictures God teasing Adam about God's own solitude before the creation of angels and men, and Marvell playfully conjectures, in "The Garden," that "Two paradises 'twere in one / To live in paradise alone." What poets conceive in terms of mythic prehistory, psychologists conceive in terms of individual infancy and the (fabricated) memory that the self was originally continuous with the surrounding world.

If we keep in mind Freud's definition of an instinct as an urge inherent in organic life to restore an earlier state of things (1920, p. 36), we may regard the wish for recognition as characteristic of a second stage, like that of paradise with Adam aware of his solitude. There are two infantile stages comparable to the two stages in mythic prehistory. The label *autoeroticism* is sometimes attached by psychologists to the first stage, in which an infant receives pleasurable sensations from his own body without recourse to another person or, more important, without any awareness of another person as different from and outside himself. Pleasurable sensations are registered anarchically, independent of an image of a unified body. The second stage is identified with *narcissism,* and here the ego in its entirety, rather than an isolated sensation or body-part, is taken as love-object. Adult narcissism, like adult autoeroticism, indicates a fixation at the corresponding stage in childhood. But in its original form, childhood narcissism defines the time in which the child, engaged in the process of synthesizing his own ego, simultaneously forms and shapes his idea of another self with whom he identifies. Lacan calls this the *stade du miroir,* because of the crucial role played by the child's identification with the mirror-image of himself or the image of another child perceived as an integrated whole.[3] Modeling himself on this projected, mirrored, or actual counterpart, the child pieces together a sense of himself.

For Wordsworth, there is no break between the self continuous with the world (the autoerotic self) and the self involved in its imaginary counterpart (the narcissistic self). For him the essential mirroring consists in the simultaneous synthesis of one's own ego and the combining into the form of "one beloved Presence" the various impressions of the mother perceived as another self. The child,

> when his soul
> Claims manifest kindred with an earthly soul,
> Doth gather passion from his Mother's eye!
> Such feelings pass into his torpid life
> Like an awakening breeze, and hence his mind
> Even [in the first trial of its powers]
> Is prompt and watchful, eager to combine
> In one appearance, all the elements
> And parts of the same object, else detach'd
> And loth to coalesce.
>
> [1805, *Prelude* II.241–50]

This state is paradisal (anterior to solitude) for "no outcast he, bewilder'd and depress'd," the child senses this beloved Presence exalting "All objects through all intercourse of sense," the way Adam might be thought to have sensed all objects exalted in paradise because of the single beloved Presence of God.

The biblical paradise, the Wordsworthian "one beloved Presence," and the Lacanian *stade du miroir* are three lies against solitude that exclude a competing myth of original alienation and assert the primacy of the awareness of a benevolent Presence. Adam does not mature outside paradise and then come to know God and a better place. Unlike begotten mortals, for whom the idea of God and the possibility of romantic love are late arrivals on the scene of consciousness (if they come at all),

3. "The Mirror Stage as Formative of the Function of the I," in *Écrits*, pp. 1–7.

he has the awareness of his Creator given to him as his first thought, and likewise the want of a mate is quickly supplied by God when "for the man there was not found a helper fit for him" (Genesis 2 : 20). Wordsworth leaps over the earliest stage of sleeping or unconscious infancy to the stage where the individual mind can be imagined to be making "first trial of its powers" and synthesizing the figure of the mother as it begins to synthesize its concept of itself. Lacan similarly preempts the possibility of alienation and imagines the mirror stage to be very early—six to eighteen months.[4] Watching another person or watching himself in a mirror, the infant is imagined to anticipate, to look ahead past his present stage of motor incoordination, and to identify with the counterpart who seems already to have gotten things together, to have constituted an integrated self.

In different ways these myths of a primordial state can explain the function and mechanism of poetic lies against solitude. In terms of the biblical paradigm, poetic discourse— whether or not in the form of overt prayer—marks a return from a state of alienation to a state of Divine Presence. After the Fall, Adam and Eve hear the Lord God walking in the cool of the day and hide themselves from His Presence. Every lyric, as an act of self-definition, may be regarded as a response to God's call, "Where are you?" But as appeals to the original, responsive nature of paradise, where to be was to be heard, lyric speakers—whether in love poems, devotional poems, or poems about alienation from nature, society, or the past—may be said to address the Original Presence, who has absented Himself, and thus to turn the question around: "Where are *you* that *I* should be alone?" Lyrics express self-recognition as well as desire, but as expressions of desire they implicitly (sometimes explicitly) appeal to a supremely responsive auditor and so give priority to the desire for recognition by an Other over the desire for a specific object or state. Lacan relates the desire for recognition to the master-slave dialectic in Hegel's *Phenome-*

4. Ibid., p. 2. The dating of the literal mirror-stage is discussed by Anthony Wilden in Lacan's *The Language of the Self*, pp. 173–74.

nology,[5] and the inevitable inequality of poet and Presence confirms, in poem after poem, the centrality of the desire for recognition.

It can be said that parents brooding over their child protect him from the truth of his own solitude, or alternatively that the child in brooding over himself—in figuring to himself an Other brooding over him—protects himself from his own solitude. Choosing the more self-reflexive version of this lie, Wordsworth in the Intimations Ode raises it to the status of a supreme fiction, which substitutes for the Original Presence of God. The poet addresses the child:

> Thou, over whom thy Immortality
> Broods like the Day, a Master o'er a Slave,
> A Presence which is not to be put by.

It is significant that this stanza should address the child directly, restoring to the poet a sense of presence inadequately evoked earlier when he called, "Thou child of joy / Shout round me, let me hear thy shouts, thou happy Shepherd-boy." Many interpreters of the Intimations Ode have recognized the inadequacy of that earlier attempt to turn the feeling of absence (loss of the visionary gleam) into presence (into a responsive rather than an artificial pastoral scene). They have located a truer voice of feeling a stanza later in the ode, when the poet says, "But there's a Tree, of many, one." Wordsworth finds, as Martin Buber noted, that a man cannot say "thou" to a tree; but a poet can, in recognizing how poetic discourse itself recapitulates the condition of primary desire, say "thou" to a little child, recognizing the self in that Other. For many readers— and ultimately for the poet himself—the new form of direct address ("Thou little child" in stanza 8) sounds an even falser note than the attempted address to the pastoral "child of joy" in stanza 3. But if it does not prove the final solution to the problem of solitude—the feeling of being cast out "From God, who is our home"—the vision of the child brooded over by the abstraction, "Thy Immortality," may substitute an image of a

5. See "Interpretation and Temporality," in *The Language of the Self,* pp. 79–80.

Presence no less awesome than the one who nurtured to independence in His garden the "Full soon" fallen Adam. Like the biblical and Wordsworthian paradigms of an Original Presence, the Lacanian notion of a mirror stage allows the happy recollection of an Imaginary Other to be absorbed into the id rather than the superego. The child, Lacan says, develops an ego through identification with an ideal image—a mirror-image or an abstract ideal based on the child's interaction with other children. Because these ideal images seem to exist already, while the ego is yet to be constituted, the feeling of solitude must be a rather belated feeling, dependent on having already synthesized a self that can stand alone. Calling the id or unconscious "the discourse of the Other,"[6] Lacan finds that an awareness of self-as-other precedes an awareness of the self-as-self. Though the ego can come to stand alone, it is buttressed by the recollection of its essentially communing and communal nature. The most sublime moment in Wordsworth's ode confirms this view:

> Hence in a season of calm weather
> Though inland far we be,
> Our Souls have sight of that immortal sea
> Which brought us hither,
> Can in a moment travel thither,
> And see the Children sport upon the shore,
> And hear the mighty waters rolling evermore.

Hence (as we may imagine a Lacanian reading of Wordsworth's ode to run), though inland far we be—though we develop further and further interiority—we can always return to the mirror stage and recollect that we came to recognize our own identity by seeing other children or images of ourselves sporting on the shore; we came into our own voice by hearing the discourse of the ocean, the sound of the prevenient and eternal Other.

At this point it may be worth recalling that the mirror stage is as much a myth as the biblical paradise or the Wordsworthian vision of "one dear Presence." That is to say, we need not posit

6. See *The Language of the Self*, pp. 27, 106–07, and *The Four Fundamental Concepts of Psycho-Analysis*, p. 131.

the historicity of any of these states in order to accept them as
models of what goes on in either psychoanalytic or poetic discourse. Yeats, in *Among School Children,* questioned how historical, how fabricated are all myths of presence:

> Both nuns and mothers worship images
> But those the candles light are not as those
> That animate a mother's reveries,
> But keep a marble or a bronze repose.
> And yet they too break hearts—O Presences
> That passion, piety or affection knows,
> And that all heavenly glory symbolize—
> O self-born mockers of man's enterprise. . . .

This stanza begins with a desire to distinguish religious images
from memories related to parents and children, just as one
might distinguish the biblical myth of God's presence in Eden
from the psychoanalytic myth of a certain stage in the child's
development. Yet the two kinds of "Presences" come to seem
alike. The ambiguous line, "And that all heavenly glory symbolize," means either that a mother's memories and the church's
icons point alike to the true glory of heavenly things, or that
earthly presences contain all the glory that men have displaced
onto heaven. Yeats seems to favor the second alternative, for
he places himself among the worshipers of images; recollected
"passion" has evoked and "known" all too painfully the Presence of Maud Gonne in the first part of the poem.

Because Yeats's Presences were never actualized in historical
reality but derived from the past through complex interweav-
ings of memory and desire, the poet can call them "self-born"
and make them symbols as well as products of the au-
tochthonous imagination. In simplest terms, man creates in his
own image the God whose Presence fills Eden. More important,
the Presences are self-born in the sense that they seem to be
generated right here in poetic discourse, just as the patient in
conversation with his analyst creates the images he substitutes
for the persons of his father, mother, and analyst. The recognition of this difference may seem to undermine poetic discourse, just as—if prematurely brought to light—it may under-

mine the discourse of psychoanalysis. But ultimately the concept of Original Presence is not rendered useless by the recognition that such originality is really the product of later invention. Because the poet cannot detach the experience of poetic discourse from the implied auditor or reader any more than the analyst can detach his patient's talk from the situation of analyst as auditor, poets and analysts touch on what Lacan calls "the simple fact that Language, before signifying *something*, signifies for someone" (1968, pp. 76–77). This "before" constitutes a new priority and makes of every sense of presence actualized in poetic discourse a sign of or substitute for the Original Presence of God, mother, or imaginary counterpart.

The Analyst and the Absent Addressee

Though poets may lie against solitude by seeking to restore something like a sense of Original Presence, they can also cast a skeptical eye on such myths and turn to more specific forms of address in the predicate that there is not—and never was—anything else. A single text can offer a spectrum of attitudes toward the idea of Original Presence and a range of relationships between a new addressee and an idealized, original *Thou*.

Consider Coleridge's *Dejection: An Ode*, first written as a verse letter to Sara Hutchinson and six months later published in *The Morning Post* on Wordsworth's wedding day. The facts about publication suggest a range of lies against solitude: a poet bares his soul to his actual beloved (Sara), to an idealized, responsive listener ("O Lady" and in one earlier version "O Edmund"), to the circle of his closest friends on whose presence and opinion his own ego seems to depend (symbolized by Wordsworth the man and his bride Mary); or, transforming and transcending a core of "viper thoughts, that coil around [his] mind," he addresses public figures (Wordsworth as poet), or the public at large (the newspaper's audience), or something like an idealized public (a Platonic idea of a literary audience to whose company the act of writing a sublime ode constitutes a rite of passage). In itself this range of auditors could suggest the essential solitude of the poet, who like his own ancient mariner can stop one of three but can only yearn, as an outsider, for the kind of community of men and God imaged in walking "to the kirk / With a goodly company." On the other hand, the same ability freely to turn from one kind of addressee to another can suggest a self growing strong enough in its own right to transcend any particular encounter and the sense of desperate solitude which makes one force oneself on an unwitting wedding guest. This developing sense of the poetic ego's strength is like the developing ability of the analysand to recathect libido and make emotional investments in the past and future more subject to rational control. But our exposition of the poetic parallel to therapy beyond the stage of transference is best postponed.

Not the least remarkable thing about the Dejection Ode is the way overt rejection of a myth of Original Presence becomes hard to distinguish from tranquil restoration of something very much like it. From one standpoint, the most powerful lie against solitude comes in the opening word of the poem, "Well!" which, in announcing a freedom to speak in a conversational tone, anticipates and perhaps undermines any subsequent attempt either to withdraw into more private melancholy or to break the intimacy of the opening address by turning to the wind, the world outside, or any higher addressee. But unlike some twentieth-century poets who seek above all to maintain the conversational tone, Coleridge finds the lie that one is conversing, not just talking to oneself, too hard to bear. We can glimpse his need and his power to establish a stronger lie against solitude by juxtaposing two poetic passages:

> To me alone there came a thought of grief:
> A timely utterance gave that thought relief,
>   And I again am strong.

> A grief without a pang, void, dark and drear,
> A stifled, drowsy, unimpassioned grief,
> Which finds no natural outlet, no relief,
>   In word, or sigh, or tear.

The first passage is Wordsworth's, announcing what seems, both from the perspective of the rest of his ode and more especially from the perspective of Coleridge's ode, too easy an answer to the problem of solitude. Critics have debated just what that "timely utterance" is—even whose it is (nature's or the poet's)—but looking back on it from the later perspective of the same ode and Coleridge's, one wonders if the important thing about that timely utterance isn't precisely that it marks a point where the burden of solitude was not yet sufficiently felt—a point where it didn't seem to matter who spoke what to whom. In contrast, Coleridge's "grief without a pang" is unuttered and unrelieved; a sentence fragment unable to complete itself, his four lines stand for all the reservations one could have about the salutary power of "timely utterance."

If Wordsworth's lines could be said to describe an early resistance to psychoanalytic discourse (the notion that one can say quickly and definitively all there is to say), Coleridge's lines could describe the resistance even to free association encountered in the transference. Before pursuing the parallel to the analytic situation, however, we need to say something about the choice of the analyst-figure. Like people, there are poems that appear to be shopping around for analysts of a particular personality and intelligence; and the change in addressee within a poem can sometimes be like a change in doctor. But far more important for the progress of a literary analysis or psychoanalysis are the changes in the relationship of the speaker and his projected addressee to the Presences of the past. It is possible to regard every poet as engaged, in however complex a way, with the resolution of his oedipal problems with previous literary history. Despite academic resistance to this notion (something like the early resistance to Freud on the grounds that he reduced man to a copulating ape), we could say that this concept of literary influence no more restricts the subject matter of poetry than privileging sexuality restricts the range of human personality. Yet because specific poetic precursors are, unlike biological parents, chosen figures in relation to whom the poetic ego comes into its own, we can regard a poet's involvement with a specific precursor as being more like an analysand's involvement with his analyst than with his parents.

Our example here may seem peculiarly unpromising, because Wordsworth was never as absent or silent for Coleridge as we like our analysts to be. But if it is the business of the analyst to bring to light elements of the analysand's unconscious, then we may have a special insight into Coleridge's unconscious, his "discourse of the Other," through the actual discourse of the actual Other—the poems written by Wordsworth. We know that Coleridge wrote the Dejection Ode after hearing Wordsworth recite to him the first four stanzas of the Intimations Ode. Wordsworth confronted Coleridge with what Coleridge passionately wished to be: the poet who could write like that, who could write *that*.

Though Coleridge never addresses Wordsworth by name in the final version of the poem (he canceled an earlier apostrophe, "O William"), Wordsworth does emerge as a symbolic addressee, a figure on whom Coleridge recathects his poetic admiration and love. But we need to give the term *symbolic* a more precise definition and place it in the context of a range of addressees to consider in reading poems. Like an analysand, a poetic speaker may belie the reality of his solitude by invoking an Original Presence (God or idealized parent) or some person or image, like the sea, that represents a fully idealized Presence. He may substitute for the Original Presence a counterpart self, either a deficient double, like Eliot's "hypocrite lecteur," or a version of the self so idealized—like Blake's "friend with whom he lived benevolent"—that the other figure is addressed without reference to an absent parent or higher authority. (Some would point out, however, that since the "friend" in Blake is ultimately revealed as Jesus, the counterpart self really is an Original Presence.) Finally, a poet may implicitly or explicitly reject both the Original Presence and the counterpart self as vain idealizations, and substitute his own conversational tone and his intention to address real people in ordinary language for what he takes to be "a mere fiction of what never was."

These three possibilities might be given the Lacanian names, the Symbolic, the Imaginary, and the Real, however much we may distort Lacan's shiftier use of the terms, which generally refer to states rather than to species of the Other. For Lacan the unconscious is structured like a language in that both involve a preestablished symbolic order. For the sake of literary criticism in particular, and more generally for psychoanalytic technique relying heavily on secrets encoded in a nonparaphrasable verbal surface, the oft-repeated Lacanian dictum that the unconscious is structured *like* a language could be conveniently rewritten as the revisionary idea that the unconscious is structured *by* language, by actual words or the symbol-making faculty first exercised during an individual's acquisition of language. Lacan himself may only occasionally, only playfully, intend the rewritten form of this hypothesis about language; but the force of Lacan's revision of Freud (implicit in the thought that the unconscious is structured at all) leads to the blurring of the boundaries between id and ego and between primary and secondary process. Increasingly we are learning that desire is not a welter of preverbal impulses but an unconscious structured around language, an unconscious into which previous Symbolic forms are assimilated. For Freud, or for Freud as he has been misunderstood by those against whom Lacan argues, the unconscious is an unstructured amalgam of repressed instincts; but for Lacan, or Lacan's Freud, the unconscious is structured by repressed representations or symbols, and the symbolic order of these signifiers has priority over the actualizations of their significances in an individual's personal history.

For the religious poet this symbolic order—or the actual words of Scripture—is God's order, and if "in the beginning was the Word," then subsequent words of postscriptural poets must attempt to recapture or acknowledge the ultimate signified, God himself (Lacan might say the "symbolic father," or the "Name of the Father").[7] The tradition of addressing a muse likewise returns us to the identity of the Original Presence and the symbolic order of language. Since the order which the poet seeks to enter is one he takes to be established before his birth, it is symbolic in the sense that its referent, its significance, is always prevenient. We might call Petrarch's Laura and Dante's Beatrice Symbolic addressees (almost identical to muses or

7. *The Four Fundamental Concepts*, pp. 113, 281–82; *Écrits*, p. 67.

God) in whom the element of the Imaginary has been radically curtailed. No less than Whitman's or Hart Crane's poems to the sea, poems addressed to muse-figures may provide opportunities for expressing what Freud called "the oceanic feeling" (1930, pp. 64, 65), and the desire for recognition by or reunion with the Symbolic Other may be the most civilized sublimation of an instinct more elementary than the sexual, an instinct to restore an earlier state of tranquil union with one's world.

The order of the Imaginary never loses its mediate and unstable position, for, retrospectively, the personal experience apprehended in the Imaginary can shade into the Symbolic, as when a father is remembered as Law Incarnate or a mother as Benevolent Presence; on the other hand, the Imaginary in its immediacy (in the poetic illusion of "presence") seems indistinguishable from the Real. Lacan, who generally regards only the idealized father-figure as a Symbolic Other, regards the imago of the mother as Imaginary and the whole state of the Imaginary as something to be transcended in socialization and maturation of the ego. (Lacan would presumably have no hesitation in analyzing the Blest Babe passage of Wordsworth's *Prelude*, cited above, as a description of the Imaginary mirror stage; unlike the symbolic father, in whose presence or under whose aegis the child learns language and the whole order of the Symbolic, the *actual* mother, or nurse, functions as a mirror-self or Imaginary Other.)

Lacan's devaluation of the Imaginary as something to be outgrown or "decentered" also serves the cause of his polemic against normative American ego psychology, a polemic energized by the mysterious belief that the Symbolic has priority in time as well as importance. In the analysis of poetry, both aspects of the devaluation of the Imaginary find their parallels: the maturation of the poetic ego may be measured by a demystification of illusions about the Imaginary and a turn to the Real; and the ambition to transcend the limits of the human, the ambition of the sublime, can find fulfillment in the collapse of the Imaginary in face of the Symbolic. Lacan himself would probably say that to treat the Symbolic as a person to talk to is to mistake the Imaginary for the Symbolic; but if this is a mistake, it is one not only at the heart of traditional religion (which depends on the idea of the Wholly Other as a person who can be addressed in prayer), but a mistake close to the human heart of everyone who remembers actual parents or an idealized childhood as though there were to be found in those parents or at that time not just particular Imaginary figures but a wholly responsive, benevolent Presence, a Symbolic Other. For a given poet the idea of a Symbolic Other as a person to be addressed may or may not be a fiction; but the transitions by which the fictionality of the Symbolic Other or the insufficiency of an Imaginary Other are realized, are transitions that have a certain authenticity beyond that of the addressees themselves.

Defining the Real as a "plenum,"[8] Lacan warns against confusing it with *real* in the ordinary sense of "actual" because one's actual state is more often than not a state of deprivation. Fredric Jameson has usefully suggested that we define the Real as History with a capital *H;*[9] while he means by "History" anything but the career of the individual ego, we may define the Real as the potential career of the ego beyond the situation of psychoanalysis. Lacan's own use of the term varies; he sometimes means an abstract or symbolic reality hard to tell from the Symbolic, and sometimes seems to mean something like "actual" rather than "imaginary." We shall use the term to refer to the analysand's life outside the analytic situation insofar as it provides for the actualization of desires uncovered in analysis. Like a Symbolic or Imaginary addressee, a Real addressee is not actually "there"; but, whereas the Symbolic is a refiguration (or prefiguration) of one's actual, personal past, the Real lies ahead in the future opened to the analysand by disentangling him from his attachments to the past. For the purposes of literary analysis we may use the term *Real* to refer to the audience a

8. *Écrits,* p. x; *Four Fundamental Concepts,* pp. 53–55; *Language of the Self,* pp. 187, 271.

9. Fredric Jameson, "Imaginary and Symbolic in Lacan: Marxism, Psychoanalytic Criticism, and the Problem of the Subject," p. 384. For Jameson's description and dismissal of mainstream literary criticism as tracings of the career of the poetic ego, see p. 379. For a fine demonstration of the personal and psychoanalytic idea of the Real, see Thomas Weiskel, *The Romantic Sublime: Studies in the Structure and Psychology of Transcendence.*

speaker would wish to have outside a poem, whether that means a contemporary (a friend of the poet or a monarch) or a future public like the world that Shelley, at the end of "To a Skylark," claims "should listen then."

We may assume that a given poet actually composed in solitude, but we can define his desire to touch the ears of actual friends and readers as an ambition to turn Imaginary discourse into the Real. Addressing Coleridge in *The Prelude,* Wordsworth usually addresses an Imaginary brother, an idealized counterpart not wholly reconcilable with "poor Coleridge," as Wordsworth's sister called him. But in such moments of uncertainty about his own fictions as the one which prefaces the Blest Babe passage in Book 2, Wordsworth looks beyond the fiction of a friend who is a constant presence and seems to be addressing the Real Coleridge. Discourse with a Real addressee is always technically beyond a poem, though less distant at some moments of poems than at others. Wordsworth addressing Dorothy at the close of *Tintern Abbey* turns away from memory and the Miltonic sublime to conversation with his beloved sister and prayer for its continuity. As opposed to the sublime, which may prove (or has just proven) a vain belief, the sister discovered to be beside him and suddenly addressed seems to be just what Lacan calls the Real: a plenum, an unknowable fullness of Presence beyond the soul's constructions and reconstructions.

One purpose that can be served by the distinction between Symbolic, Imaginary, and Real addressees, however uncertain these terms may seem in themselves, is to remind us of the inconstant status of a poetic addressee and to direct our attention to significant changes. The question of whether a religious poet is addressing a Symbolic Other, an Imaginary counterpart created by the poet in his own image, or a Real and living God may be less a matter of a critic's choice of vocabulary than of the essential turns in poetic discourse. Even a verse letter overtly written by one person to another (as Coleridge's Dejection Ode was originally addressed to Sara Hutchinson) undergoes changes in the Symbolic component of its addressee

and in the relation of its particular apostrophes to its more ambitious fictions of an auditor. For some poems the moments
when the addressee seems most composite are specially privileged.

In *The Triumph of Life* Shelley uses as an Imaginary counterpart, Rousseau, though at points Wordsworthian language contributes startlingly to the Symbolic dimension of this composite
precursor. Perhaps the most magical moment of Browning's
Sordello, for which the entire poem prepares, concerns the
transformation of the poet Eglamor from a parodic counterpart self to a figuration of Original Presence. When William
Collins, in the *Ode on the Poetical Character,* turns to "thou, thou
rich-haired Youth of Morn," he creates a figure simultaneously
incarnating Original Presence (the Son) and a counterpart self
(the Poet). When Milton addresses Adam in *Paradise Lost,* or
when Marvell addresses Cromwell in his "Horatian Ode," the
poet makes of his addressee a composite of the Symbolic godlike hero, the Imaginary counterpart, and the Real individual
half perceived in and half created from history. When Pope's
Belinda is raped of a lock of hair and addressed by Clarissa,
she remains in part the moralist's deficient double or Imaginary alter ego; but she also emerges, beyond identification with
the actual Arabella Fermor, as a Real lady who might, by exercising good social sense, chase away the greatest evil of old age,
solitude.

Sometimes changes in the order of being of the addressee
are so prominent that the poem, like an analysand questioned
and pressed by the analyst, seems addressed to those changes—
which in turn half reflect, half impel changes in the ego behind
the poem. These effects are noteworthy in some love poems,
for example, in a turn from narcissistic involvement with an
Imaginary Other to what emerges by comparison as a genuine
gesture—to a real person—of persuasion to love. Changes in
the order of being of the addressee are even more important in
poems directly involved with precursor texts or poets. Let us
return to Coleridge's Dejection Ode and examine the stanza
with the strongest overt turn in addressee:

Hence, viper thoughts, that coil around my mind,
  Reality's dark dream!
I turn from you, and listen to the wind,
  Which long has raved unnoticed. What a scream
Of agony by torture lengthened out
That lute sent forth! Thou Wind, that rav'st without,
  Bare crag, or mountain tairn, or blasted tree,
Or pine-grove whither woodman never clomb,
Or lonely house, long held the witches' home,
  Methinks were fitter instruments for thee,
Mad Lutanist! who in this month of showers,
Of dark-brown gardens, and of peeping flowers,
Makest Devils' yule, with worse than wintry song,
The blossoms, buds, and timorous leaves among.
  Thou Actor, perfect in all tragic sounds!
Thou mighty Poet, e'en to frenzy bold!
  What tellest thou now about?
  'Tis of the rushing of an host in rout,
  With groans, of trampled men, with smarting wounds—
At once they groan with pain, and shudder with the cold!
But hush! there is a pause of deepest silence!
  And all that noise, as of a rushing crowd,
With groans, and tremulous shudderings—all is over—
  It tells another tale, with sounds less deep and loud!
    A tale of less affright,
    And tempered with delight,
  As Otway's self had framed the tender lay,—
  'Tis of a little child
  Upon a lonesome wild,
Not far from home, but she hath lost her way:
And now moans low in bitter grief and fear,
And now screams loud, and hopes to make her mother hear.

The opening lines of the stanza appear to be announcing the kind of moment in a psychoanalytic session when attention is drawn from viper thoughts of the past to some present reality like the sound of the wind outside the consulting room. In *Group Psychology and the Analysis of the Ego* (1921, p. 126), Freud uses the example of the view from the window, among others, to indicate the sort of thing an analysand will mention, if pressed, at the moment when his resistance has made him silent: "Then one knows at once that he has gone off into the transference and that he is engaged upon what are still unconscious thoughts relating to the physician." Before specifying why we may regard Wordsworth as the physician-figure in this poem, we might sketch some implications of this identification: the turn from the poet's viper thoughts to the wind may be seen as no mere flight of free association from one poetic figure to another but a special crossing-point between the poet's involvement with the more nebulous presences of his own past and past literary history, on the one hand, and on the other, his unconscious thoughts cathected on his contemporary, Wordsworth. On the surface (in terms of explicit addressee), there is a turn from the Imaginary (the viper thoughts) to the actual wind, and that turn itself seems to bring relief from the pressure of scrutinizing those viper thoughts. But the wind is no sooner noticed than it is figured as the Imaginary Other which, in raving and producing screams of agony, exactly mirrors the speaker's earlier wish to "startle [his] dull pain, and make it move and live." Insofar as the tale-telling of the wind "that raves without" resembles the discourse of a freed unconscious and is imagined as giving better expression to a complex series of emotions than the speaker could, the wind addressed as *thou* becomes the poet's Imaginary counterpart. At the same time, however, if Coleridge has "gone off into the transference," then his implicit addressee has assumed the status of a Symbolic Other the way an analyst in transference has cathected on him emotions associated with an Original Presence.

Though a certain amount of psychic energy is taken up, during the stage of transference, with the analysand's present relationship to his analyst, the subject of discourse continues to be the history of the analysand's psyche. Noting how the wind changes from "tragic sounds" to "tender lay," we may be tempted to ask which wind represents the outcry in dejection of Coleridge himself; but we should be guided, by the indefiniteness of the Imaginary, past the vain attempt to seize on any one guise, and spurred to consider how all the various winds in this stanza figure the poet's psychic history. Did Coleridge's cry of dejection sound at some point like a wind making devils' yule? Can we locate a point at which his voice was hushed? Can we mark in his history a turn from a cry like a host in rout to a less discordant, more poetic form of outcry? If we remember the central poetic trope of the wind as inspiration, then the concept of transference can guide us to the possibility of substituting a poet's literary history for his psychic history.

Turning to the wind, Coleridge turns to nature; but if Homer and nature are the same, the turn to nature is actually a turn to literary history. Coleridge finds himself disclaiming as an image of self-release what comes to him as the ravings of a "mad lutanist." This loud, hellish clamor seems to belong to an older poetic tradition, a tradition of the Miltonic sublime, in contrast to the homelier tonality of himself as dejected man and poet. Rejecting the wind's loud uproar as something closer to his poetic ancestors than to his melancholy self, Coleridge suggests that his conversational tone can supersede the tradition of the sublime and restore something like the intimacy of an Original Presence. Milton himself often represented the routing of the old gods with all their sound and fury. Banishing a melancholy associated with superstition in *L'Allegro,* he turned to a purer melancholy closer to spirituality or imagination itself in the companion poem *Il Penseroso.* This much literary history Coleridge can recapitulate. He finds his own expression of melancholy in the wind making devils' yule to be a false "companionable form" (his phrase in *Frost at Midnight*), a rehearser of tragic sounds that seem to belong to an older generation, an alien style.

For Coleridge no "pause of deepest silence" in the course of literary history was as definitive as that between the eighteenth-century style he and Wordsworth inherited and the new mode they announced with their publication of *Lyrical Ballads.* We know that Coleridge originally wrote "William" in place of "Otway," and that William Wordsworth's poem *Lucy Gray* offers a situation like the tale "tempered with delight" here. We might regard "Otway" as a kind of belated screen-memory, a defen-

sive substitution of an earlier literary memory for a later, potentially more traumatic threat to Coleridge's poetic powers.
Alternatively, it has been suggested that Coleridge's choice of
"Otway" may have been influenced less by anything actually
written by Thomas Otway, the Restoration dramatist, than by
the proximity in sound of "Otway" to Ottery St. Mary,
Coleridge's birthplace.[10] Imagining the tender lay to be the
river Otter's, the *Otter's way* of binding the child to his past,
Coleridge could triumph over biographical facts of loss or separation from an Original Presence through the invention of a
fiction comparable to Wordsworth's memory of one, "the
fairest of all rivers, [which] loved / To blend his murmurs with
my nurse's song" (*Prelude* I, 270–71). But whatever the source
or the strength of the defensive substitution of Otway for William, we may return to Wordsworth's poem *Lucy Gray* with
some conviction that in doing so we are moving not outside
Coleridge but toward the center of his unconscious. If, as
Lacan insists, "the unconscious is the sum of the effects of
speech on a subject" (1978, p. 126), then the literary critic's
turning to precursor texts resembles less the analyst's vain attempt to find the true, extrapsychological history of a trauma
than it does the attempt to uncover the poet's unconscious, into
which a precursor, a precursor's *words*, have been absorbed.

Let us focus, then, on the situation in Wordsworth's poem as
the crucial trope for Coleridge's final reworking in this stanza
of his own dejection and solitude. The stanza concludes open-
endedly with a nightmare vision of solitude: as we leave the lost
child we hear her *now* as she "screams loud, and hopes to make
her mother hear." One critic has described this situation as the
runaway-child syndrome; the child experiences ambivalent
feelings of yearning for and wariness of the mother-figure.[11] A
stanza that abandons the story with the plea to "hear" and
leaves the girl unable to conjure her mother represents the
primary desire for recognition and the general situation of the

10. We are very much indebted to Dr. Stephen Weissman of the Washington
School of Psychiatry for this point.
11. Beverly Fields, *Reality's Dark Dream: Dejection in Coleridge*, pp. 18–23, 146.

poet able to write any words he desires, but unable to restore, through solitary discourse, the Original Presence.

What the poet can do is re-present the order of being of the Other and convince us that his power of re-presentation can substitute for, or even transcend, a vision of Original Presence. The speaker of Wordsworth's *Lucy Gray* proposed, somewhat impersonally, that Lucy yet survives as a spirit of place, a nymphal creature haunting the borderland between the human and the natural. Her survival involves, moreover, an identification between her "solitary song" and the wind:

> —Yet some maintain that to this day
> She is a living child;
> That you may see sweet Lucy Gray
> Upon the lonesome wild.
>
> O'er rough and smooth she trips along,
> And never looks behind;
> And sings a solitary song
> That whistles in the wind.

Apparently appropriating Wordsworth's fiction, Coleridge actually dissolves the artistry implied by a "solitary song" and makes a more primitive identification between the moans and screams of the wind and the moans and screams of the lost child. The wind Coleridge now hears renders her living, original voice before Wordsworth transformed her suffering to song and kept her free from death.

By revising Wordsworth's poem and restoring to the story of Lucy Gray a more "natural" ending, Coleridge not only clears a space for his own fiction of the eddying soul, but finds a more convincing alternative to death in the very turns of thought which characterize the stanza as a whole. Has he not represented the turn from the Miltonic to the Wordsworthian tale as his own turn, and one as natural as a change in the wind? Here is the essential psychoanalytic cure and its poetic analogue: addressing oneself not to the specters of the past but to the negotiated crossings between them, one discovers in oneself a strength one can call one's own.

Though his victory over the viper thoughts of the past comes through identifying with Wordsworth's "tale of less affright," we cannot say that Milton has represented the Imaginary Other, Wordsworth the Real addressee. On the contrary, the turn to the Wordsworthian alternative is apprehended as a turn that helps form the poet's true, conversational self in the very process of recognizing his Imaginary Other that "rav[es] without." While the wind becomes the counterself represented in the conscious order of the Imaginary, Wordsworth, behind the façade of "Otway's self," tacitly becomes a representative of what Lacan calls the unconscious order of the Symbolic, the structure comprised less by interpersonal relations with actual other people in one's personal past than by interpoetic relations with the discourse of the Other poet. Most important, since the crossings or rewritings do not involve the simple substitution of one Imaginary Other for another, the desired excursive power (the ability to substitute one addressee for another) cannot be mistaken for shallowness in the heart's affections or the experiential failure to substitute one object of desire for another (one Sara for another, or either for Coleridge's mother). Beyond both fickleness on the one hand and fixation on the other is the ability to move between Symbolic, Imaginary, and Real addressees and to reconstitute the ego as the self capable of—and actually performing—these transitions in a poem.

The transitions among the Miltonic, Wordsworthian, and "natively" Coleridgean elements within the poem do not simply represent in miniature a larger pattern perceivable in text after text; an allusion to *Lucy Gray,* taken alone, has no intrinsic link with a preestablished order of literary history. Yet if we see that allusion as part of a turn from sublime energy (significantly unfocused in the suggestion of "ravings") to the conversational mode of telling tales, then the little girl proves less a lost child than a found symbol for the poet's unconscious—a symbol for the simple, homey desire for recognition at the core of the id. Assimilating poetic precursors into the id and re-presenting the order of the Symbolic through the figure of the child, Coleridge triumphs over the particulars of his personal, Imaginary past.

Yet he does not wipe away personality, which is a function not of basic desires but of the way we symbolize and resymbolize them. Since the image of the child represents a *domesticated* sublime, a *diminished* solipsism, the turn to the child allows a self-recognition of his own manner that guards against an onslaught from the id and the impersonality of the Symbolic order. A mode of self-recognition replaces the desire for recognition by others all the more surely because, in hearing the wind as indistinguishable from the child's cry, Coleridge makes his own perception part of the image and its history; putting himself there, he puts ego where id (and the range of precursors there) used to be. He modifies our understanding of the Coleridgean ego, defined now less by the drives that frustrate it than by its capable imaginative refigurations of the situation of desire.

The route just outlined may seem excessively complicated and somewhat arbitrary. For some readers, Coleridge's ability to re-present the primary desire for recognition as the screaming child's unfulfilled hope of making her mother hear is an imaginative triumph in its own right and a moving emblem of the restored health of the mind exercising its excursive power and moving from trope to trope. For other readers the representation of a traumatic situation at the close of this stanza assumes its significance only in relation to the crossing-over to the next stanza, where Coleridge is less the lost child than the comforting mother guarding Sara from a similar trauma by declaring his desire to be a Real Other in her life or to figure "gentle Sleep" as a Symbolic Other invoked in prayer or lullaby. But we do better to imagine these points of view not as alternative readings *of* Coleridge's poem but alternate readings or rereadings *in* the poem. No poem—and no analysis—can, as such, restore an idealized parent or provide a real lover and addressee; but like a psychoanalysis, a poem can challenge the potentially overwhelming power of the past by relocating what Wordsworth called the "hiding places" of power in the turns and transformations of addressee. In a letter "To a Junior Soph, at Cambridge," Coleridge wrote, "All activity is in itself pleasure; and according to the nature, powers, and previous habits of the sufferer, the activity of the fancy will call the other faculties of the soul into action."[12] Though in psychotherapy transference is resistance, not cure, in poetry the activity of the mind freely transferring libido from an Imaginary Other to a Symbolic or a Real Other is a kind of cure. For Lacan, "the transference is the enaction of the unconscious" (1978, pp. 267, 146), a gnomic phrase in which the neologism itself can represent the *activity* of refiguration. Such psychic activity is, in Coleridge's words, "a new and unfailing source of employment, the best and surest nepenthe of solitary pain."

The Conversational Tone and the Daemonic Sublime

Because conversation depends upon the responsive presence of a Real addressee, it remains technically outside the province of both poetic and psychoanalytic discourse, though the achievement of both can be marked by the demystification of Symbolic or Imaginary shadows. In Coleridge's Dejection Ode, the case with which an addressee is evoked or altered makes the conversational mode itself appear to be a sign of supreme power. Though in the middle of stanza 7 "there is a pause of deepest silence," talk continues past the mention of such silence. Even the extremes of desolation and death are, in poetry, "tempered with delight" by the sheer power of verse to go on and subsume any pause. The more conversational it is—the easier the mode of moving from one point to another—the more poetry fosters the gentle illusion that no silence, and no solitude, is definitive. On the other hand, certain breaks and changes in addressee (even the same breaks viewed differently) accrue to themselves a power representative of an ultimate power creative of life and death. The pause of deepest silence is like the pause in Milton's Nativity Ode where the world is hushed for the death of the old self and the birth of Christ, or like that "unusual stop of sudden silence" in *Comus* where Thyrsis hears a song that ravishes Silence and makes her wish to "Deny her nature, and be never more, / Still to be so displaced." We may call *conversational* the power of poetry to lie

12. For this and the following Coleridge phrase, see *The Complete Works of Samuel Taylor Coleridge*, 4 : 432.

against solitude by fostering the illusion of community and continuity; like a drawing room filled with guests, a poem can suggest an imaginary society in which a speaker may turn from one addressee to another without worrying about his or their sudden "excuse me's."

We need a name for the contrasting power by which the poet seems to create his auditor rather than casually accept one as given or retreat into silence or solipsism. Terms like *creative* or *divine* are too general and belie the individual and often unorthodox use of such power. Let us appropriate the term *daemonic,* which refers to the Greek semideities sometimes associated with spirits of the dead, sometimes taken to be supernatural agents controlling personal destiny, and sometimes understood as personifications of the individual's creative energy. Though the word may be confused with *demonic,* that association is often unfortunate. Sometimes evil, as when Milton's Satan creates Sin out of his own brain, daemonic power can be innocent, like the Lady's song in *Comus* that "might create a soul / Under the ribs of Death."

If we compare with the daemonic power that brings a poet to voice, the power of the transference in psychoanalysis, we can sometimes compare the conversational tone in poetry to the therapeutic goals that lie beyond transference. Discussing the difficulty of the transference neurosis in *The Question of Lay Analysis* (1926, p. 227), Freud remarks that breaking off analysis when the specter of the transference rears its head "would be as though one had conjured up spirits and run away from them as soon as they appeared." Some poems, like Blake's *The Tyger* (discussed below) do something like that, while others recapitulate the turn from the daemonic to the conversational voice as though that in itself were therapy or release. Consider this anonymous lyric:

> Westron wind, when will thou blow?
> The small rain down can rain:
> Christ, if my love were in my arms
> And I in my bed again!

How does one talk about such a poem? One might broach the lyric by noting that nothing is more ordinary than talk about the weather; "it's raining" the second line says ("can" means "does"), and that ordinary observation fills in the gap between two expressions of desire: would that Zephyrus were blowing outside; would that I and my love were in bed together. One gets further, however, by identifying a distinction between the lies against solitude in the first and third lines. The first line addresses the west wind the way Shelley does in his great ode; whether as spring wind or wild west wind, Zephyrus is invoked as a daemonic Other. The third line does not quite constitute a prayer. "If" means "if only," not "please help me, Lord," and so one cannot say that Christ is a daemonic Other, only that the speaker turns inward and expresses to himself his heartfelt desire. Moving from daemonic addressee to self-address—and to the expression of a wish really oblivious of an auditor—the speaker moves conversationally. The poem is remarkable for the ease and rapidity of that change in address, and for the way the second line, that most ordinary piece of language, is transformed from an observation about gloomy weather to performative language making of the weather a mediator between outside and inside, daemonic Other and innermost feelings. By recognizing and giving a name to the sublime language the first line exemplifies, we are more likely to see the change as domesticating, or making ordinary and conscious, feelings previously repressed.

In many poems the daemonic and conversational elements are not easily separable, though the extent of and reasons for that fact may be well worth discussing. Coleridge's Dejection Ode restores the gentle voice of the conversational mode after the tumultuous and climactic seventh stanza; the sign of redemption from the "lonesome wild" is the poet's ability to turn with ease from one addressee to another. He says "Visit her, gentle Sleep!" and then a few lines later addresses the lady directly. But this little night music, in which the interior monologuist slides easily from a Symbolic addressee to one who seems by comparison Real, tells only half the story. One could also concentrate on the daemonic power of invocation in the last lines, as the lady becomes not just another auditor but—as though she had never been addressed before—an auditor summoned into being: "O simple spirit, guarded from above, / Dear Lady! friend devoutest of my choice." Her devotion constitutes her divine power, and she seems no longer Sara but an epiphany of the Original Presence coming, in a modern version of the deus ex machina, as a sign of the ultimate redemption of the Romantic quester. His final prayer to her, "Thus mayest thou ever, evermore rejoice," wafts speaker and addressee into what Milton calls "the blest kingdoms meek of joy and love."

In approaching other poems, one might ask at any point whether the conversational or the daemonic lie is being fostered, or whether one rests at a point where a speaker might define his personality by the way he negotiates the crossing between the two modes. Sometimes transition is so subtle that it is hard to tell whether the poet belies his solitude by genially treating the addressee as near or hopelessly remote. So Dryden opens his poem in memory of Mr. Oldham, "Farewell, too little, and too lately known, / Whom I began to think and call my own." Because their acquaintance was just developing—just now, as it were—Oldham seems almost present, as a friend might be, at the same time that he is not just dead but idealized and permanently distanced. Like many poems in a lighter vein, Pope's *To a Lady: Of the Characters of Women* opens with a lie against solitude wholly in the conversational realm: "Nothing so true as what you once let fall, / 'Most women have no characters at all.' " The social charm of addressing such a poem to a lady proves a magic charm under whose influence the solitude of the poet—and even the extrapoetic problem of Pope's remove from womankind—seem illusions that fade, while the enduring graciousness of the relationship between speaker and auditor becomes a poetic reality. Yet as Pope turns from one portrait to another, an abyss opens beneath the circle of informal conversation, and we stare into a region, like that at the border of Milton's hell, where "nature breeds / Perverse":

> See Sin in state, majestically drunk;
> Proud as a peeress, prouder as a punk;
> Chaste to her husband, frank to all besides,
> A teeming mistress, but a barren bride.

A remarkable achievement in tone, the passage superimposes on a conversational mode the sublime creation by poetic fiat of the giant forms we are asked to behold.

Unlike Pope's *To a Lady,* many later eighteenth-century poems wholly abandon the conversational framework and address abstractions of their own creation. But it would be misleading to try to distinguish one literary age from another on the basis of the prominence of one of these powers over the other. Daemonic power is not an invention of the pre-Romantic poet nor a prerogative of the Romantic. True both to Victorian sensibility and an ongoing religious tradition, Hopkins begins his sonnet *Carrion Comfort* by addressing Despair and comes to see from a distance "That night, that year / Of now done darkness I wretch lay wrestling with (my God!) my God." For once "my God!" has the force of apostrophe rather than vain exclamation; the moment of present recognition interrupts the history of that night the way the epiphany of a God interrupts history. A Renaissance poem like Donne's Holy Sonnet "Batter my heart, three-personed God" seems to create the personage of a ravishing deity, while leaving no doubt that Donne's is the energy behind the challenge, "o'erthrow me, and bend / Your force, to break, blow, burn, and make me new."

Like love poems, religious lyrics can exhibit the conversational power of addressing God as an intimate or near-at-hand overhearer of one's intimate thoughts; or they can exhibit the daemonic power of calling into being a deity the sudden recognition of whom comes like a new creation. In Herbert's *The Collar,* what begins as the speaker's energy of protest ("I struck the board, and cry'd, No more") itself calls into being an answering voice:

> But as I rav'd and grew more fierce and wilde
>   At every word,
> Me thoughts I heard one calling, *Child!:*
>   And I reply'd, *My Lord.*

In a startling way, God's single word, *Child!,* can remind us that while the order of the Imaginary can only be dimly recalled in a poem, the order of the Symbolic (insofar as it is constituted

by the discourse of the Other rather than personal representatives of law or language like one's actual parents) can seem to
have real presence in a poem. God seems to have written *Child!*
before the speaker of the poem could speak his protest.
Though the poem dramatically represents the speaker coming
upon (coming up to) God's discourse, the poet represents the
priority of the Symbolic order over both the Imaginary past
and the more recent awareness of its absence. As a believer,
Herbert knows God is there before man protests; as an onlooker to the process of fiction-making, the reader knows that
the answering voice the speaker thought he heard is not really
another voice, the voice of God, but the voice of the speaker's
own reservations about his attitude of rebelliousness. But both
of these truths seem irrelevant to this poem of daemonic
power, where the voice of conscience—the voice of corrective
consciousness—*is* the voice of God, and where, in the end, the
poet restores the proper sequence of God calling and man
coming to find an answering voice: "And I reply'd, *My Lord.*"
From the perspective of the poem as a unified speech, the
words *My Lord* illustrate the daemonic power of the poet who
seems to call his addressee into being. On the other hand, the
speaker does move from vain invocation (like "Call in thy
deaths head there" four lines earlier) to an awareness of true
calling, and the illusion in "Me thoughts I heard one calling"
emerges as the higher truth that God calls, man responds. Herbert's poem thus illustrates a tendency of the religious imagination to regard the conversational and daemonic as initially or
superficially antagonistic but ultimately coextensive. The dialogue in which one is called *Child* and responds *My Lord* represents the archetypal religious conversation. There may remain
a distinction between a conversational and an awesome tone,
but ultimately the only conversation occurs when one addresses
a Creator or another creature with a *thou* direct enough to appear to bring forth a presence out of the objective world.

In his *Songs of Innocence and of Experience,* Blake offers
an unusual critique of the religious imagination and its *thou*-
saying. In general, the *Songs of Innocence* illustrate the gentle
fiction of conversation, while the *Songs of Experience* exemplify

the more terrifying power of the daemonic imagination. Perhaps the most polarized pair are *The Lamb* and *The Tyger*. The first is a poem where innocence is marked by the speaker's freedom to converse with an animal as though it, and the whole order of creation, were responsive to poetic voice. The opening stanza reaches its climax with the question addressed to the lamb about its own power of voice: "Dost thou know who . . . / Gave thee such a tender voice, / Making all the vales rejoice!" As the lamb is imagined to hear the speaker, so the vales are imagined to hear the lamb. The final two lines repeat the opening two exactly, because in this world of innocence poetic echo serves as an emblem of the responsiveness of nature: "Little Lamb who made thee / Dost thou know who made thee." The first time round these lines ask a question; the second time the lines themselves constitute an answering voice.

In the second stanza Blake purifies the conversational imagination until the innocence regained seems that of an essential, pristine Christianity:

> Little Lamb I'll tell thee,
> Little Lamb I'll tell thee!
> He is called by thy name,
> For he calls himself a Lamb:
> He is meek & he is mild,
> He became a little child:
> I a child & thou a lamb,
> We are called by his name.
> Little Lamb God bless thee.
> Little Lamb God bless thee.

To reimagine this song as a song of experience one has only to conceive of the second stanza ending as the first did with an exact repetition of the opening two lines. Setting a heavy stamp of spiritual authority on his doctrine, the speaker would thus shatter rather than safeguard this dream of communication. Instead, by altering "Little Lamb I'll tell thee!" to "Little Lamb God bless thee," Blake lets the fiction of a child catechizing a lamb express the ambition to realize an ultimate voice in the Word of God descending on the lamb. Between the opening

and concluding lines of refrain, the equality presupposed by
the conversational mode is first disturbed by the proclamation
of religious truth and then reestablished in the discovery of a
higher religious truth.

Even the first truth is not simple, however. The speaker
could have announced that God made the lamb and that this is
all we know on earth and all we need to know. Instead he answers the question of the identity of the lamb's creator by announcing, more than a name, a miraculously compressed dis-
quisition on the integrity of the Creator and his relation to his
creatures: "He is called by thy name, / For he calls himself a
Lamb." By itself "He is called by thy name" means that calling
God a Lamb acknowledges the meekness and mildness of the
Son. Yet together the lines make of the identity of what God is
called and what he calls himself an exemplum of divine self-
sufficiency and divine mercy. God's greatest gift to man is his
incarnation as the lamblike Son; man's greatest gift to God is
his acknowledgment of his redeemer in calling him the Lamb
of God. This reciprocal relation between God and man is the
highest truth (the most profound lie against solitude), in relation to which the conversational equality, "I a child & thou a
lamb," is a repetition in a lesser mode.

All this, however, is part of the speaker's authoritative declaration. What follows is a conversational reassertion of equality
in face of a higher truth: "I a child & thou a lamb, / We are
called by his name." Even if an I-Thou relationship between a
child and a lamb is a fragile fiction, it seems a real repetition in
a finite mode of the infinite I-Thou relationship between God
and His creatures, who are named and addressed by Him.
Though the lamb represents an Imaginary Other for the child,
God incarnate in the lamb is the Symbolic Other and the ultimate addressee of the poem. If the concluding refrain dismisses the lamb with a blessing on its head, here is no high
priest of the imagination pronouncing a final benediction on a
member of his flock, but one communicant sharing with another the feeling that if Symbolic authority is actualized above
rather than between us, "Everything we look upon is blessed."

Like *The Lamb*, *The Tyger* poses questions about creature and creator and the act of naming that relates them. In *The Tyger*, however, the speaker holds no reserve of knowledge to share with the creature he addresses:

> Tyger, Tyger, burning bright,
> In the forests of the night;
> What immortal hand or eye
> Could frame thy fearful symmetry?

One way of measuring how far these lines are from the conversational mode of *The Lamb* is by trying to substitute "Dost thou know the hand or eye?" for "What immortal hand or eye." In *The Lamb* the speaker moves so easily from a question about what the lamb knows to a question about a creator that the presence and potential responsiveness of the addressee seem things taken for granted: "Little Lamb who made thee / Dost thou know who made thee." The speaker of *The Tyger* can manage no such transition from a question about the animal as an object of creation to a question that makes the animal a conversational *Thou*. This speaker's energy of inquiry burns through the ostensible addressee and kindles the tiger with a purely daemonic power.

When a child addresses a lamb, his lie against solitude forms a gentle fiction, a dalliance with what Milton, acknowledging in *Lycidas* the limits of his imagination, called "false surmise." But there is nothing gentle about the fiction of addressing this tiger, however gentle the tiger Blake drew in the accompanying illustration. Some readers have seen in the tiger a figure of liberty calling forth terror from the agents of sexual and political repression, and fervid awe from all who welcome political or visionary change. To those who thus read the poem prophetically, the tiger is an Imaginary Other whose integrated being is a model for the speaker building his ego in this dazzling recreation of a *stade du miroir;* when that personal and social integration is as fully achieved as is the tiger's form from his assembled bodyparts, the Imaginary will become the Real. To those who read the poem as a nightmare of deluded consciousness, the tiger is also an Imaginary Other, but one standing in the way of the neurotic speaker's exploration of the forests of his

own night; the Creator as Symbolic Other is the absent addressee behind the tiger, and the speaker, who will not be cured,
is forever directed back to an Original Presence from involvement with whom one must emerge to be healthy and whole.

Whether we regard the speaker of this poem as anxiety incarnate or a figure of the poet looking forward to a revolution
in the organization of both the body politic and the self, we can
see in his incessant questions the daemonic effort to call forth
the Symbolic Other he does not find. For the structural anthropologist, distant cousin to the Lacanian psychoanalyst, the
order of the Symbolic means the basic laws of exchange on
which a social structure is based. For the speaker of this poem,
the structuralist's dream of recreating complex structures from
a simpler grammar of exchanges would find its fulfillment if
the speaker's own awe were matched by an awesome series of
answers or questions thrown back at him, the way God manifests Himself to Job.

If there is no answering voice in this poem, however, there is
something that takes its place: the tiger itself is like the Le-
viathan and Behemoth of which God speaks in Job, and the
awesome thoughts that come to the speaker take the place of
thoughts articulated by a voice in a whirlwind. There may be
no dialogic symmetry of talking and listening, no symmetry of
exchanges between creature and Creator; but the fearful symmetry of the tiger evokes from the speaker a response to this
Imaginary counterpart like that he desires to have from a Symbolic Other.

Can the reimagination of a primal scene of creation displace
the primacy of the desire for recognition from a Creator? As
the speaker's questioning continues, he substitutes for the desired recognition the desire to know the original components of
creation: "And when thy heart began to beat, / What dread
hand? & what dread feet?" Though altered in ink to "What
dread hand formd thy dread feet?" in a late copy, the line as
received leaves unspecified whether the dreaded feet are those
of the Creator or his creature. In place of innocent synecdoches, which stand in *The Lamb* for a responsive universe in
which creature and Creator are linked by love and trust, such

highly compressed figures oddly dismember both the tiger and his hypothesized Creator and leave in the hands of the re-imaginer of those early scenes the power to create them anew. The very question, "Did he who made the Lamb make thee?" gives articulate form at last to the speaker's binary astonishment (his nervous demands for a *this* to complement a *that*) and compensates for his inability to accept the hexameral symmetry of God's making the tiger and seeing that it was good.

Like a personal past as it is reconstructed in analysis, the hexameral creation may never have taken place. There may never have been Promethean feats of benevolence like seizing fire, nor angels throwing down their spears and weeping, whether in joy and victory or in contrition and defeat. But there is nothing mythic about transferring onto the maker of the tiger emotions once associated with the ultimate parent, the maker of the lamb. Were the speaker able to confront in the tiger's maker a Real Other, then a revolution—whether in religious, social, or psychoanalytic terms—would indeed take place. But halted at the stage of transference, the speaker of *The Tyger* is at once a characteristic victim of illusions about the Creator and a prophetic emblem of the therapy that is possible, that must be possible, through and beyond the transference.

"It is possible, possible, possible. It must / Be possible." So Wallace Stevens, at a climactic point in *Notes toward a Supreme Fiction,* imagines being freed of illusions and facing the reality of bare earth:

> It must be that in time
> The real will from its crude compoundings come,
>
> Seeming, at first, a beast disgorged, unlike,
> Warmed by a desperate milk. To find the real,
> To be stripped of every fiction except one,
>
> The fiction of an absolute.

If it is a goal of poetic discourse, like psychoanalysis, to transcend our bondage to forms of the Imaginary and Symbolic Other and "to find the real," it is to the credit of a poet like Stevens that he recognizes the indomitable quality of our instinct for recognition by an Other who yet survives all our deconstruction of illusions about a responsive world. At just this point in Stevens' poem, he turns to apostrophize the Canon Aspirin with an ultimate appeal to be heard and recognized as a poet:

> Angel,
> Be silent in your luminous cloud and hear
> The luminous melody of proper sound.

In part, the Canon Aspirin is Stevens' Imaginary Other, a model of poetic freedom in recognition of whom the poet develops his own ego and comes to say, "as I am, I am." But the Canon is also compounded from the literary canon—from Milton, from the Romantic tradition of regarding Milton's skyvaulting Satan as a model of the poet, and in particular from Browning's *Pauline,* where the imagination is "a very angel, coming not / In fitful visions but beside me ever / And never failing me." Like the "you" heading the quotation that introduces this essay, Stevens' addressee here is a Symbolic Other, a venerable figure of the past as we would have it present and responsive to us. Recathecting onto this Canon Aspirin, this learned doctor, a desire for recognition once directed toward the figures of the religious and literary past, Stevens stands with and for all poets who have attempted the daemonic sublime and have discovered in their capacity for transference the source of poetic power.

REFERENCES

Coleridge, S. T. *The Complete Works of Samuel Taylor Coleridge.* Edited by W. G. Shedd. New York: Harper, 1864.

Fields, B. *Reality's Dark Dream: Dejection in Coleridge.* Kent, Ohio: Kent State University Press, 1967.

Freud, S. *The Origins of Psycho-Analysis: Letters to Wilhelm Fliess, Drafts and Notes: 1877–1902.* Edited by Marie Bonaparte et al. New York: Basic Books, 1954.

————. *The Standard Edition of the Complete Psychological Works.* London: Hogarth, 1953–74.

Beyond the Pleasure Principle (1920), vol. 18.
Group Psychology and the Analysis of the Ego (1921), vol. 18.
The Question of Lay Analysis (1926), vol. 20.
Civilization and its Discontents (1930), vol. 21.
Jameson, F. "Imaginary and Symbolic in Lacan: Marxism, Psychoana-
lytic Criticism, and the Problem of the Subject." In *Literature and Psy-
choanalysis: The Question of Reading: Otherwise,* edited by S. Felman.
Yale French Studies, no. 55/56 (1977).
Lacan, J. *The Language of the Self.* Translated by A. Wilden. Baltimore:
Johns Hopkins University Press, 1968.
———. *Écrits.* Translated by A. Sheridan. New York: Norton, 1977.
———. *The Four Fundamental Concepts of Psycho-Analysis.* Edited by
J.-A. Miller. Translated by A. Sheridan. New York: Norton, 1978.
Weiskel, T. *The Romantic Sublime: Studies in the Structure and Psychology
of Transcendence.* Baltimore: Johns Hopkins University Press, 1976.

3

The Price of Experience:
Blake's Reading of Freud

MORRIS DICKSTEIN

> This Angel, who is now become a Devil, is my particular
> friend: we often read the Bible together in its infernal or
> diabolical sense. . . .
> —*The Marriage of Heaven and Hell*

> If I cannot bend the Higher Powers, I will move the Infer-
> nal Regions.
> —Epigraph to *The Interpretation of Dreams*

What follows is not primarily intended as an essay on the relation of psychoanalysis to literature, still less as a psychocritical
study of poetic origins, valuable as that can be (though it also
entails the risk of reducing art to neurosis, motivation to a system, or criticism to biography). My purpose, apart from practical criticism, is to inquire into the startling modernity of one
English poet, born in 1757 but almost unknown in his time,
whose psychological acuity we could easily ignore, for it accords
more with our image of a modern novelist than an eighteenth-
century poet. To an age which has witnessed what Philip Rieff
calls "the emergence of psychological man," Blake is an an-
achronism, our double, our brother, our wittily diabolical contemporary. In so many words let me try to say why.

The study of influence has been anxiously debated in recent
critical theory, but it is far from being a new approach to literature. The quest for sources and analogues was a staple of the

old historical and philological scholarship, which was gradually
routed by the New Criticism but still leads a shadowy half-life
in the lower depths of the caves of academe. The attention of
the New Critics was largely directed toward individual works,
but there is a world of difference between the artificial isolation
of single poems in Cleanth Brooks's *The Well Wrought Urn*
(1947) and the close exegesis of sample passages in an exactly
contemporary European work, Erich Auerbach's *Mimesis*
(1946). Brooks objectifies and quarantines separate works at
the behest of a formalist theory of poetic unity. He examines
poems in isolation to avoid contaminating them with ideology,
from the explicit ideas of the author to the ideological orientation of the critic and his contemporaries. Like a scientist who
needs a controlled medium for his experiments, Brooks isolates
separate specimens to probe their stresses and tensions, neg-
lecting comparable examples and even ignoring family resemblances within the author's own work, at the behest of
Coleridge's principle that the work of art must "contain in itself
the reason why it is so, and not otherwise."

Auerbach, on the other hand, was very much the flower of
European historical and philological tradition, and his specimen passages, for all his rigorous attention to style, serve as
synecdoches for the entire work, for the author's sense of reality, and sometimes for the whole epoch. While pretending to
extract what he learns from only a few sentences, Auerbach
implicitly brings to bear everything he already knows as a matrix for the act of explication. Though beautifully attuned to
the concrete literary voice, *Mimesis* is a work of *Geistesgeschichte*
whose vehicle is stylistic analysis; it shows how the verbal medium embodies the writer's sense of reality, and ultimately the
spirit of the age. What Auerbach finally demonstrates is that a
work of art is not an intricate object but a way of seeing that
fills the whole space between the social and philosophical
macrocosm and the linguistic and narrative microcosm. This
amplitude of vision is finally what justifies the pretense and
keeps *Mimesis* fresh and alive, where *The Well Wrought Urn* has
come to seem pinched, constricted. Brooks is an intelligent man
who has willfully simplified himself, a keen reader whose

method is finally convenient for pedagogy but deadening for criticism—which, like medicine, has no business amputating healthy limbs or murdering to dissect.

The eclectic turns of recent American criticism can be catalogued in terms of the exclusions and prohibitions of the New Critics. Each of the "fallacies" of the last generation fathered busy critical schools in the present one. The biographical fallacy issued in a rich revival of literary biography, in books which have begun to take on the scale of the massive Victorian "life and letters." Along with the intentional fallacy, it has also given much impetus to psychoanalytic criticism, in which the life and work are shown to interact in ways uninteresting to a formalist. The modern bias against the sociological treatment of literature—a common enough approach in the nineteenth century, especially in the aftermath of Taine and his followers, but which Wellek and Warren in *Theory of Literature* labeled an "extrinsic approach"—has not yet fertilized a viable Marxist criticism. But it has given rise to a new cultural history, in which the transformations of literature, the arts, and popular culture can be examined in the context of social and cultural change. (It has also immensely increased the prestige of older historical critics like Auerbach, Wilson, and Trilling, who swam against the New Critical tide, moving freely between literature and society in ways that were by no means extrinsic to literature or lacking in critical sophistication.)

In much the same way declining sanctions of the affective fallacy let loose a wave of reader-oriented criticism which turned the text from an intricately wrought object impaled in analytic space to a temporal happening unfolding in the mind of the individual reader. From this new subjectivity flows the mischievous idea of indeterminacy in interpretation, with criticism as a metaphor for the act of reading and every reading a fictive construct, a projection upon an indefinitely variable text. (This happy anarchic relativism promises to become an even bigger boon for the literature industry than New Critical explication, which worked well on only a handful of poets, and not at all well on most fiction.)

Finally, the New Critical emphasis on the isolated text has led to the recent interest in "intertextuality" and influence, a concern with the way different works interact and interanimate each other. In the hands of Harold Bloom, this approach eschews both source-study and stylistic influence, nor does it concern itself with the intellectual background of literary works, as older scholars frequently did. Bloom's focus lies somewhere between "voice" and the phenomenological structure of perception. He is concerned with a writer's fundamental rhythms of apprehension as revealed in his most intensely imagined moments. For the positivist scholar influence is what can be isolated, labeled, and identified. It certainly involves no anxiety for either poet or critic, any more than Northrop Frye's archetypes do. For the dialectical Bloom this kind of mechanical transaction, in which something hard and fast changes hands, is replaced by something mercurial and impalpable, an agon between texts which unfolds under the metaphoric banners of psychic processes—anxiety, repression, defense.

Increasingly in later books Bloom has insisted that the contest is between tropes, not between minds or persons, but his own tone always reveals the intensity of his personal agon with poets as a critic, interpreter, and theorist. Criticism always involves some will to mastery, like literature itself, no matter how eloquent the tribute it pays *to* literature; Bloom has been reviled by high-minded idealists for coming clean on this competitive secret and making this agon the core of a theoretical drama. Just as Freud felt that psychoanalysis had delivered the third great blow to human pride after Copernicus and Darwin, Bloom's work has evidently been a sore trial for idealized visions of the literary process, upon which he brings to bear what he has learned not only from the skepticism of Freud but from the corrosive irony of Nietzsche and the insidious donnish wit of Borges.

Like the New Critics, Bloom has little interest in the historicity of literature, the place of authors in time or in their own times. If Eliot imagined all the great poets seated around a heavenly table called Culture, all shoving over a bit as each new one arrives on the scene, Bloom imagines the poets in an increasingly crowded battle royal, with each latecomer having to jostle for space. Like Eliot and Borges he believes that the con-figuration of the canon changes with every new arrival, and hence he adapts from Borges the witty notion that writers may influence their precursors was well as their successors. In "Kafka and His Precursors" Borges writes: "The fact is that each writer *creates* his precursors. His work modifies our con-ception of the past, as it will modify the future" (1966, p. 113). Borges' list of Kafka's precursors is a whimsical one, but there are passages in Kleist, Dickens, and Hawthorne that we cannot resist calling Kafkaesque today. Kafka is the grid through which we perceive these authors and acknowledge their moder-nity. ("We feel, in reading *The Witch of Atlas,*" says Bloom, "that Shelley has read too deeply in Yeats. . . . The hugely idiosyn-cratic Milton shows the influence, in places, of Wordsworth; Wordsworth and Keats both have a tinge of Stevens; the Shel-ley of *The Cenci* derives from Browning; Whitman appears at times too enraptured by Hart Crane" [1973, pp. 153–54].) While ahistorical in some ways, this nice conceit is also impli-citly historicist, since it presumes the privileged point of view of a later observer, the contemporary reader or critic, the order-ing mind to whom all past writing is simultaneously present,[1] and who is therefore in a unique position to become conscious (as the writers themselves do not) of the undertows or counter-currents of "influence."

My subject in this essay is the lyric poetry of Blake, especially his *Songs of Experience,* and in the tolerant spirit of intertextual hindsight my aim is to show how these poems were influenced by Freud and the ideas of psychoanalysis. But I am acutely aware of the pitfalls of this retrospective wisdom. As Eliot re-marked, we know much more than the writers of the past be-cause "they are that which we know."[2] Especially in recent years, as the call for relevance has been heard in the universi-ties, and as the empirical bias of American criticism has given

1. "The historical sense involves a perception, not only of the pastness of the past, but of its presence. . . . This historical sense . . . is a sense of the timeless as well as the temporal." T. S. Eliot, "Tradition and the Individual Talent," in *Selected Essays* (1951), p. 14.
2. Ibid., p. 16.

way to a theoretical interest in language, psychiatry, and the
social sciences, one way of insisting that a merely literary work,
written by someone quite dead, has something timely to say to
us, is by associating it with the name of a distinguished modern
master—a Marx, a Freud, a Nietzsche—whose truths are cer-
tifiably contemporary and even fashionable, whose very name
has become a talisman for advanced thinking. I am also mindful of the many syntheses and revisions of these thinkers we
have read in recent years, few of which respect the excrucia-
tingly hard work of becoming Marx or becoming Freud, the
empirical caution which validates the speculative daring.

Freud painstakingly revised his ideas all through his life,
but he shunned all merely philosophical adjustments of
psychoanalysis, as he watched schismatic followers retreat from
sex and biology into the mists of religion, idealism, and the
power of positive thinking. If only Freud had read more Marx,
more Nietzsche, more Saussure, if only. . . . Freud was particularly sensitive on the score of Nietzsche, whom he recognized as
a precursor and a genius, and therefore avoided. I am tempted
to add my curiosity about what Freud might have thought of
Blake, particularly in the light of his remarkable discussion of
the German fantasist E. T. A. Hoffman in his paper on "The
Uncanny." But in any case he was always tolerant toward literary precursors, whom he found less threatening and more per-
cipient than rival theoretical systems. On his seventieth birthday Freud generously attributed the discovery of the
unconscious to the poets, claiming for psychoanalysis only a scientific method by which the unconscious could be studied. Less
well known is his sharp distinction, near the end of *The Interpretation of Dreams,* of the "unconscious of the philosophers" from
" 'our' unconscious":

> By them the term is used merely to indicate a contrast with
> the conscious: the thesis which they dispute with so much
> heat and defend with so much energy is the thesis that
> apart from conscious there are also unconscious psychical
> processes. Lipps carries things further with his assertion
> that the whole of what is psychical exists unconsciously and

that a part of it also exists consciously. But it is not in order to establish *this* thesis that we have summoned up the phenomena of dreams and of the formation of hysterical symptoms; the observation of normal waking life would by itself suffice to prove it beyond any doubt. The new discovery that we have been taught by the analysis of psychopathological structures and of the first member of that class—the dream—lies in the fact that the unconscious (that is, the psychical) is found as a function of two separate systems and that this is the case in normal as well as in pathological life. [1900–01, p. 614]

The first system, the unconscious or *Ucs.*, contains not what is unconscious in the loose sense, but what is "inadmissible to consciousness," what cannot be reached voluntarily, without the stratagems of analysis. The second system, the preconscious or *Pcs.*, can be admitted to consciousness, though not without passing through censorship and perhaps distortion.

But the looser sense of the unconscious, which includes both systems, survives from pre-Freudian psychology into present-day common usage. As David J. Gordon points out in his valuable study *Literary Art and the Unconscious,* even sophisticated critics tend to use the term in the "less strict sense, to denote mental events that are merely removed rather than barred from awareness, that are not fully conscious but capable of becoming so without much resistance."[3] Ruth L. Munroe makes a similar distinction in discussing the mechanism of repression, which is surely the key to the concept of the unconscious. (Freud: "it is possible to take Repression as a center and to bring all the elements of psychoanalytic theory into relation with it.")[4] As Munroe writes in her discussion of defense mechanisms: "Repression means, in essence, thorough dismissal from consciousness. It should not be confused with voluntary

3. David J. Gordon, *Literary Art and the Unconscious* (1976), p. xiv. This penetrating book establishes a firmer and less reductive ground for psychoanalytic criticism than anything else I have read.
4. Quoted by William Healy et al. in *The Structure and Meaning of Psychoanalysis* (1930), p. 219.

refusal to act upon impulse, often called suppression. When a person counts to ten and refrains from punching somebody in the nose, he is controlling his anger, not repressing it. In repression he does not feel angry at the person at all" (1955, p. 245). Freud himself makes the same point with his customary lucidity and precision in the nineteenth of his *Introductory Lectures* (1915–17, pp. 294–96).

In discussing the "influence" of Freud on Blake, and the key role of both repression and unconscious motivation in Blake's conception of the psyche, I have no intention of arguing that he anticipated the technical nuances of Freud's systematic thinking, which Freud himself claimed as his major advance over the intuitions of the poets and the discoveries of the philosophers. But neither do I wish merely to invoke Freud's name as a magical charm. Blake, too, was a formidable systematic thinker in his later poems, as Northrop Frye's extraordinary *Fearful Symmetry* (1947) long ago demonstrated. "I must Create a System, or be enslav'd by another Mans," Blake once wrote;[5] I see no need to impose on him the enslavement his work successfully eluded, especially now that Freud's system has come to seem to us less a direct description of what is simply real and more a fascinating series of metaphors, a powerfully organized but contingent vision of the dynamics of the mind—contingent above all, as he insisted, on new data, new metaphors, new advances in other sciences. Freud particularly anticipated advances in our understanding of the chemistry of brain functions; with his resolute materialism, he was not upset that psychiatry might one day return to the neurological fold, to become the truly "scientific psychology" he had tried to project in the 1890s.

Despite Freud's reduction in status from the cartographer of the mind to one of its visionary philosophers, the absence of Freud's name in the literature on Blake is truly surprising. Those who try to relate Blake's system to occultism and the

5. *Jerusalem* 10 : 20. *The Poetry and Prose of William Blake*, ed. David V. Erdman (1965), p. 151. All my quotations from Blake are from this edition (hereafter cited in parentheses within the text), which faithfully reproduces the oddities of Blake's spelling and punctuation.

"perennial philosophy," of course, have much more recourse to Jung,[6] especially after Blake's principal critic, Frye, became a major theorist of "the archetypes of literature." Even those who take Blake's system on its own terms, as Frye himself and Harold Bloom do, tend to subsume some of his most direct and simple early lyrics to the four phases of existence which he exfoliated so ingeniously in his longer prophetic books. I myself don't find even the lyrics of his teen-age years simple, but I find the complexity of the *Songs of Innocence and of Experience* in their psychology rather than their hints of metaphysics. In general our advance in understanding his system has worked against our immediate grasp of his psychological acuity. It was Eliot in 1920, who was so snobbish and condescending toward Blake's "philosophy" (which he compared to "an ingenious piece of home-made furniture: we admire the man who has put it together out of odds and ends about the house"), who described the lyrics as "the poems of a man with a profound interest in human emotions, and a profound knowledge of them."[7]

Eliot's judgment was revived and revised only recently by F. R. Leavis, in a book that tried to remobilize Blake as a social visionary and proleptic critic of industrial society: "Blake's genius was to be, in the sense in which a great novelist necessarily is, a profound psychologist. That is apparent not only in the lyrics, but, for all the confusion and the elements of unsuccess from which none of them is free, in the longer poems. He presents with clairvoyant penetration and compelling actuality the state—or rather the interacting energies, the disharmonies, the conflicts and the transmutations—of humanity as it is" (1972, p. 17). Despite the deep affinities between Blake and Lawrence, whose mantle as social prophet and outcast Leavis had come by the end of his life to assume for himself, this is a surprising comment from the seventy-seven-year-old critic, analogous to his celebrated turnabout on Dickens. Leavis had never written about Blake at any length; he had no affinity for

6. The main psychological study of Blake is a Jungian one, W. P. Witcutt, *Blake: A Psychological Study* (1946).

7. T. S. Eliot, "William Blake," *Selected Essays*, pp. 321, 319.

the Miltonic and allegorical traditions to which Blake's longer poems pertain; and he had often pilloried poets whose appeal seemed thematic or ideological rather than aesthetic, disinterested. Certainly his qualified praise of the longer poems seems as much a self-revision as a revision of Eliot.[8]

But though Leavis' comment is accurate as far as it goes, it's too general in a way that begs the very questions it raises. The handful of references to Freud in the critical literature are even more general in character, such as Auden's sweeping assertion that "the whole of Freud's teaching may be found in *The Marriage of Heaven and Hell*"[9] and Mark Schorer's comment on "Infant Sorrow" that "the infant who learns to 'sulk' immediately is a creature not out of Lavater's psychology but out of Freud's" (1959, p. 204). When a more specific and sophisticated debate about Blake's lyrics developed in the early 1960s, it tended to lose hold of Eliot's insight into Blake as a psychologist; such an emphasis presumably belonged to the bad old days when the longer poems were considered incoherent gibberish with splendid purple patches—bad poetry and bad thinking—and Blake's basic sanity was still in question, as it had been in his own lifetime. In the hands of systematic critics like Frye, Bloom, and Hazard Adams, Blake's lyrics were accorded their niche in the overall system, like statuary in a cathedral; their figures were subdued to the architecture of the whole, the characters treated as prototypes of Orc or Urizen, denizens of Beulah or Generation. Critics like E. D. Hirsch, Jr., and Martin Price reacted by insisting that Blake evolved and changed, that his thinking went through a series of transformations from the Christian pastoral mode of the *Songs of Innocence* to the revolutionary antinomianism of *The Marriage of Heaven and Hell,* the hopes for political change embodied in the early

8. This is no doubt confirmed by his dedicating the book to his students at the University of York, "who gave me a new Blake with clean margins to write in."

9. W. H. Auden, "Psychoanalysis and Art To-day" (1935), reprinted in *The English Auden,* ed. Edward Mendelson, p. 339. Auden's essay, though more ragged and amateurish than Lionel Trilling's later "Freud and Literature," is still worth reading. Its few references to Blake are only parenthetical, but it gives a surprisingly Blakean accent to Freud's whole system.

prophetic books, the ardent feminism of *Visions of the Daughters of Albion,* the sexual vitalism and bitter social criticism of the songs in the Rossetti manuscript and the *Songs of Experience,* and so on.

That Blake did grow and change seems incontrovertible. After all, the early 1790s were among the most turbulent and unstable years in European history, and his poems show how closely attuned he was to the revolutionary ferment in France and England.[10] It is also evident that his mythology developed piecemeal and gradually, since we can see its rudest beginnings in poems like *Tiriel* (1788), whose Lear-like hero foreshadows the tyrannical Urizen, and "A Song of Liberty" (probably 1790), which anticipates the conflict, which dominated several of the early prophetic books, between the Jehovah-like Urizen, the repressive spirit of the Old Regime, and the fiery young Orc, the "new born terror" who embodies revolution in religion, politics, and morals. As the Revolution turns into the Terror and Blake's hopes for real political progress in England abate, the insurgency of Orc gives way to the futility of the Orc cycle, and Orc gives way to Los, the artist, who becomes the protagonist of the larger drama. In a shift that can also be traced in Wordsworth, Coleridge, and other ardent young sympathizers with the French Revolution, the initial hopes for political change shift to a faith in art and imagination, a turn in consciousness that must prepare the ground for a new politics, for which England had shown itself unready. Another distinct shift occurs in the depiction of female characters. Oothoon, the heroine of the *Visions of the Daughters of Albion,* is a liberated woman in the spirit of the Rossetti lyrics of 1793; though the two men in the poem view her as a fallen woman, she has put aside self-tormenting guilt and speaks openly for frank and shameless love and "the lineaments of Gratified desire." By 1794, in *Europe: A Prophecy,* however, Blake begins a series of portraits of feminine jealousy and possessiveness, the manipu-

10. Both David V. Erdman's study of Blake's politics, *Blake: Prophet Against Empire* (1954), and E. P. Thompson's illuminating account of the culture of the artisan underclass in the 1790s in *The Making of the English Working Class* (1963) situate Blake concretely in the political currents of his age.

lations of the "female will"—a stunning change that seems
rooted less in politics than in the nearly unknown terrain of
Blake's personal life. (We may get a glimpse of that terrain in
the love triangle and ensuing jealousy portrayed in a little lyric
called "My Pretty Rose Tree," as J. Middleton Murray specu-
lated [1933, pp. 45–46]. This is perhaps related to the legend
that Blake invited another woman to join his menage, much to
the horror of Catherine Blake, whose personal feelings perhaps fell short of their mutual principles.)

The problem with evolutionist critics of Blake, especially
when they deal with earlier poems like the *Songs of Innocence,* is
that they are forced to ignore his complex irony, as if that were
a later by-product of the French Revolution. Both Price and
Hirsch are subtle readers, and Hirsch is particularly cogent on
the overall theme of guardianship in the *Songs of Innocence,* but
implicitly they try to wean at least part of Blake away from antinomianism and even recoup him for Christianity.[11] Of the
"Holy Thursday" of *Innocence* Price says, "The last line seems
pat and inadequate to those who are on the watch for irony"
(1965, p. 394). Well, the last line *is* pat and inadequate, a moralistic truism which scarcely resolves the issues raised by the
poem. The same can be said of the last lines of "The Chimney
Sweeper" and "The Little Black Boy"—indeed, of much else in
those two poems before the last lines. In fact, the false resolution is one of the key techniques of the *Songs of Innocence,* the
enticing platitude that represents common thinking and gives
us the illusion of having done with a problem, enabling us to
put it aside without dealing with it or even thinking about it.
This makes a direct bridge to the *Songs of Experience,* which
frequently throws the veil of irony aside and deals directly with
the ruinous results of this false consciousness.

This is why "The Chimney Sweeper" and "Holy Thursday"
of *Experience* are much simpler than their counterparts in *Innocence;* they are poems of outright denunciation and prophetic
wrath. Irony always embodies a double consciousness: at one

11. Recently even Leavis endorsed that general view of J. G. Davies that, far
from being "the great heresiarch," his doctrines "fall within the general tradition of Christianity" (*Nor Shall My Sword,* p. 13).

level the literal meaning of the words and the cast of mind of those who believe them, at another level the real truth of the situation, which language, ideology, and self-delusion conspire to conceal. "The Chimney Sweeper" and "The Little Black Boy" portray characters who preach and believe in Christian resignation in the face of slavery and the murderous abuse of children, who take refuge in the thought of an afterlife, which pacifies them yet provides them with genuine consolation. Each of the poems contains guardian figures who tell their suffering charges that they must be patient and yielding, for there is a world elsewhere, where suffering is rewarded as virtue, where the hierarchies of earth are inverted, its horrors redeemed.

> Theres little Tom Dacre, who cried when his head
> That curl'd like a lambs back, was shav'd, so I said,
> Hush Tom never mind it, for when your head's bare,
> You know that the soot cannot spoil your white hair.
>
> [E 10]

The lamb's back is the very image of shorn innocence and of Christ himself, whose own resignation nevertheless dissolved into despair at the moment of crucifixion. The suffering Christ appears in person in "On Another's Sorrow," where he tries to give consolation for human griefs he has no power to alter or alleviate. Like the guardian angels in "Night," who are unable to keep the wolves and tigers from descending on the flock, he can only promise redemption, not offer protection:

> But if they rush dreadful;
> The angels most heedful,
> Recieve each mild spirit,
> New worlds to inherit.
>
> [E 14]

In "The Chimney Sweeper" Tom Dacre dreams of another angel who amplifies the older sweep's advice of "hush" and "never mind it":

> And the Angel told Tom if he'd be a good boy,
> He'd have God for his father & never want joy.

The result of all this encouragement is that Tom, who is not yet inured to the mortifications of the sweeper's short life, who cried when his head was first shaved, gives up all resistance and accepts his lot with a fatal but consoling sense of resignation:

> And so Tom awoke and we rose in the dark
> And got with our bags & our brushes to work.
> Tho' the morning was cold, Tom was happy & warm,
> So if all do their duty, they need not fear harm.

To choose between the literal and the ironic reading of these lines is a futile exercise, for the poem occupies the embattled space between them, signaling both readings, favoring neither; its meaning, if not indeterminate, is doubled over upon itself. Just as the chimney sweepers sustain a fine balance between inner grace and outer horror, the whole poem is balanced between a visionary faith in the fortifying strength of innocence and a devastating satire on the psychology of quietistic acceptance and complicity with oppression. Should we doubt the power of innocence to fortify us against misery without fundamentally altering it, we can read Blake's Shakespearean "Song by an Old Shepherd":

> Blow, boisterous wind, stern winter frown,
> Innocence is a winter's gown;
> So clad, we'll abide life's pelting storm
> That makes our limbs quake, if our hearts be warm.
>
> [E 457]

One of the signal strengths of Blake's vision of innocence is the absence of euphoria or idealization. Neither Christ nor the angels can suspend the laws of nature in "On Another's Sorrow" and "Night"; the "Ecchoing Green" of daylight and children's play will inevitably turn into the "darkening Green" of evening and adulthood; the beautiful chain of guardianship and mutual care in "A Dream" must overcome anxiety, separation, and the threat of despair. In the world of Innocence those who lose parents find surrogate parents, but innocence also fosters dependency and prolongs it. Wise guardians, like the nurse in "Nurse's Song" and the parent in "Infant Joy," yield to the wisdom of the child, for they recognize that in some matters the child is closer to the source, as Wordsworth insisted in his Intimations Ode. Dependency can buck up our inner resources, but in the face of a larger threat it can damage our chances of survival. The evidence indicates that the life expectancy of chimney sweepers could hardly have been much better than for inmates of a concentration camp.[12] When Tom Dacre finally accepts his lot, he enjoys for the first time the warmth of community and of illusory hope, but what he joins is a community of the condemned, where

> thousands of sweepers Dick, Joe Ned & Jack
> Were all of them lock'd up in coffins of black.

The angel dispels this vision but it's a true one, for the literal chimney foreshadowed the probable coffin. Yet the temporary consolation is real: "Tho' the morning was cold, Tom was happy and warm."

Up until this point there is nothing particularly Freudian about Blake's psychology. What links Freud to the *Songs of Innocence* is only what links him as well to other Romantic writers like Wordsworth and Rousseau: an emphasis on the formative importance of childhood, as part of a larger dialectic between nature and culture. For Blake, in both *Innocence* and *Experience,* what society does to its children is an index to its own mental health and communal humaneness. In *Experience,* instead of yielding to the child, the supposed guardians regiment and manipulate him; aside from harming the child, this shows them at war with their own natures, cut off from the vital energies that are not yet warped and thwarted in the child. In his book on Freud, Philip Rieff, though he does not mention Blake, tries in vain to separate Freud from the Romantic "cult of the child" which he sees in Wordsworth and Coleridge. For Rieff, the Romantics are primitivists and utopian irrationalists (somewhat like the young people of the 1960s, whom he would later find such an apocalyptic threat to culture). Freud, on the other

---

12. See Martin K. Nurmi, "Fact and Symbol in 'The Chimney Sweeper' of Blake's *Songs of Innocence,*" in *Blake: A Collection of Critical Essays,* ed. Northrop Frye (1966), pp. 15–22.

hand, is a "tough-minded" moralist who would demonstrate
that children are anything but innocent (Rieff, 1959, pp.
100–01).

In that sense neither were Blake's nor Wordsworth's children
"innocent." The child in the early books of *The Prelude* and
related poems like "Nutting," far from being in any simple con-
cord with "Nature," grows and changes through quasi-sexual
acts of violating nature; the infant at the mother's breast in the
famous passage of the second book of *The Prelude* receives nurture and security in a process of sensual and libidinous interchange. Like the great breakthrough Freud made in the
1890s, the whole of *The Prelude* is a kind of self-analysis, in
which a blocked writer seeks the origins of his predicament in
his formative experiences and earliest memories.

In the *Songs of Innocence* the key word for childhood is *joy,* a
sort of benign life-force which we suppress at our own peril.
But it is not yet differentiated into the more explicitly sexual
"delight" of the *Songs of Experience.* Nor has it yet become the
lusty pleasure and appetite of the *Visions of the Daughters of Albion,* whose message is

> Take thy bliss O Man!
> And sweet shall be thy taste & sweet thy infant joys renew!
> Infancy, fearless, lustful, happy! nestling for delight
> In laps of pleasure; Innocence! honest, open, seeking
> The vigorous joys of morning light; open to virgin bliss.
>
> [*E* 48]

This is a far cry, yet not utterly different, from the earlier "Infant Joy" in the *Songs of Innocence,* in which a complaisant
parent, instead of giving a two-day-old child an arbitrary name,
which would amount to a premature social identity, allows the
infant to "name" itself, and calls it Joy, a name identical to its
essence.

By the time of the *Visions,* Blake is ready to argue that this
benign interchange can be replicated in later life, that infant
joy can find its fulfillment in adult sexuality, unless its current
has been turned awry by repression, guilt, and secrecy: "Who

taught thee modesty, subtil modesty! child of night & sleep.
. . . hypocrite modesty! / This knowing, artful, secret, fearful,
cautious, trembling hypocrite." The presexual, beatific vision of
infant joy in the *Songs of Innocence* has turned into a conception
of infant sexuality as both source and metaphor for the undis-
torted erotic life of the adult. In the interim Blake seems to
have read a good deal of Freud, or more plausibly, to have
read the French Revolution as Wordsworth and Coleridge first
did, not simply as a promise of political change but as an apocalyptic redemption of human nature and the five senses. Oothoon speaks for his sexual utopianism while the obtuse pair of
men in the poem are products of the skepticism and pessimism
with which he already greeted his own vision. For Bromion, the
rapist, sex is power and possession; his tool is his "signet," his
brand of imperial conquest. For Theotormon, tormented by his
theology, isolated in almost psychotic depression and jealousy,
sex has become fundamentally autoerotic, a doleful ecstasy of
religious masochism:

> the youth shut up from
> The lustful joy, shall forget to generate. & create an amorous
>   image
> In the shadows of his curtains and in the folds of his silent
>   pillow.
> Are not these the places of religion? the rewards of continence?
> The self enjoyings of self denial?

The religion of continence is polluted by masturbatory fantasies. Theotormon has become a kind of spectre, "a solitary
shadow wailing on the margin of non-entity," a creature (like
Thel in *The Book of Thel*) who resists embodiment, who both
fears and envies the generative world and takes refuge from
life in a jealousy fueled by conventional morality. Such a man,
says Oothoon, even if married, can only become the detached
voyeur of his own relations, a spectator in the theater of his
narcissism:

> Can that be Love, that drinks another as a sponge drinks
>   water?

That clouds with jealousy his nights, with weepings all the day:
To spin a web of age around him, grey and hoary! dark!
Till his eyes sicken at the fruit that hangs before his sight.
Such is self-love that envies all! a creeping skeleton
With lamplike eyes watching around the frozen marriage bed.

[E 49]

In Blake, premature and sudden aging usually symbolizes blocked sexuality and thwarted nature. This blocking or repression is Blake's key Freudian idea; as in Freud, it is closely linked to a notion of the unconscious, an insistence that we all have powerful wishes that undergo mutation, deflection, and distortion before expressing themselves, that even our vaunted self-awareness can become a screen that shields us from our deepest needs and desires.

The symbiosis of repressive morality, asceticism, and covert eroticism is scarcely a modern discovery; superficially, at least, it was a subject of Voltairean raillery all through the Enlightenment, as in Diderot's *La Religieuse* and *Supplement to Bougainville's "Voyage."* But it would be hard to find a more Freudian (or Nietzschean) comment on the ethics of repression than Blake's brilliantly compacted phrase "the self enjoyings of self denial." Nietzsche analyzed Christian morality as the tyranny of the weak over the strong. Blake goes further: in his view continence is not only rooted in masochism, providing a perverse sexual kick, but also in narcissism, the inability of the self to progress toward an object outside itself—unless, Blake adds in a neat feminist twist, it can assert power over the object and assimilate it to itself: "Can that be Love, that drinks another as the sponge drinks water?"

The roots of this psychology can be found, as Auden indicates, in Blake's key post-Revolutionary manifesto, *The Marriage of Heaven and Hell,* a good part of which may date from 1790, though completed in 1792–93. What foreshadows the theme of repression which would be developed in the lyrics of the Rossetti manuscript and the *Songs of Experience* is the dialectic of desire and restraint, Energy and Reason. In the *Marriage,* the visionary yet natural joy that was a fundamental life-force in

the *Songs of Innocence* has been sexualized into libido, into desire and Energy. As opposed to the orthodox religious and
philosophical dualism, which separates body from soul, which
subjects matter to the dominion of Spirit and insists "that God
will torment man in Eternity for following his Energies," Blake
asserts that "Man has no body distinct from his Soul" and "Energy is the only life and is from the Body."

Blake's *Marriage* is an essay in what we would today call revisionism, but its philosophical and theological components need
not detain us here. Blake is opposed to the moralistic dualism
which pits spirit against matter, gives primacy to ideas, and
identifies energy and desire with the evils of the fallen body.
His main theme, in fact, is a burlesque and an inversion of the
Christian notion of the Fall. In Blake's view, which has links to
a long Christian heretical tradition (of which Norman O.
Brown is one modern oracle, as his frequent citations of Blake
emphasize), our fall was not a fall into sexuality and embodiment but into crippled sexuality and murderous self-division.
In Blake's fundamental myth, our "enlarged & numerous
senses" of former times have decayed under the attacks of a
repressive morality, and through internal conflict, so that "man
has closed himself up, till he sees all things thro' narrow chinks
of his cavern." Blake's *Songs of Experience* will be virtually a catalogue of the ways this closing up occurs, though it will be more
reticent and uncertain about *why* it occurs.

Blake's mythological system is also based on the fall from
wholeness to partiality and self-division. The four Zoas, though
to some extent they are "real" characters enacting fragments of
personal drama, on another level represent man's warring faculties—head, heart, and so on—and they, in turn, are divided
from their emanations or female halves. This corresponds to
Freud's assumption, confirmed by modern endocrinology, that
male and female are relative points on a spectrum rather than
static alternatives. Blake dramatizes in poem after poem how
characters like Urizen become caricatures of unfeeling mascu-
linity and ratiocination when they cast out their own more
tender "female" qualities. The same process accounts for the
distortions of cunning and possessiveness that make up the

"female will." The apocalyptic scenario of Blake's long poems is a mythic action whose utopian terminus is self-reconciliation, the reconstruction of the whole man.

This reconciliation is also the exuberant hope of the *Marriage*, whose recurrent theme of fall and millennial redemption sketches out in terse aphoristic terms what is enlarged into mythic drama in Blake's longer epics. The Devil, Blake's antinomian spokesman, tells us that "Energy is the only life and is from the Body and Reason is the bound or outward circumference of Energy." Blake neither accepts the Christian/Cartesian dualism which gives primacy to Reason, nor casts out reason entirely, in the manner of his later surrealist admirers. As a draughtsman and engraver, despite the dreamlike and fantasy quality of many of his images, Blake is particularly insistent on clarity and definition of form, on what he calls the "wiry & bounding line," and hostile to all romantic vagueness, such as the shadowy and suggestive chiaroscuro of Rembrandt. Though Blake detests the academic classicism of Joshua Reynolds and his school, he is himself a classicist of the sublime, who believes that evocations of imaginative and spiritual afflatus can and must achieve precise incarnation, as they do in the prophetic poetry and crisp narrative line of the Old Testament. The only Christian myth that deeply attracts him is that of the Incarnation, the idea of God or spirit taking on real circumference or "human form divine." For the artist, as for the man, form alone realizes the link between the human and the divine—the divine in man, since "All deities reside in the human breast." By giving it form, body, and outline, Reason enables Energy to incarnate itself, to ascend like Jesus from amorphous impalpability to fleshly actualization.

This reconciliation is what happens ideally. What we are more likely to see in the world as we know it, Blake finds, is Reason at war with desire, sapping its force:

> Those who restrain desire, do so because theirs is weak enough to be restrained; and the restrainer or reason usurps its place & governs the unwilling.

And being restrained it by degrees becomes passive till it
is only the shadow of desire.

[E 34]

The sovereignty of reason and self-control is an illusion, a
ghastly victory which reduces the desiring self, like Theotormon, to a spectre wailing at the margins of nonentity. Yet desire, instinct, says Blake, is the primary force, which reason can
only steal and sublimate. This Blake asserts by reading *Paradise
Lost* "in its infernal or diabolical sense":

It indeed appear'd to Reason as if Desire was cast out,
But the Devils account is, that the Messiah fell. & formed a
heaven of what he stole from the Abyss
This is shewn in the Gospel, where he prays to the Fa-
ther to send the comforter or Desire that Reason may have
Ideas to build on. . . .

[E 34–35]

This is Blake at his wittiest and most paradoxical, acting as a
tongue-in-cheek collector and reviser of our cultural and religious myths, yet in the process slyly propounding, almost
seriously, a theology and psychology of his own. The expulsion
of Satan from heaven—the official reading of Milton's poem—
implies, in Blake's view, an idealist psychology in which the
"nether" impulses, the infernal energies of desire, constitute a
fallen deviation (or derivation) from a primary spiritual norm.
Instead, Blake insists, reason is a derivative of desire, which
goes amiss by turning in revulsion upon its infernal origins in
the "lower" faculties. In the brilliantly epigrammatic section of
the *Marriage* called Proverbs of Hell, Blake repeatedly asserts
the unhealthy consequences of this self-revulsion:

He who desires but acts not, breeds pestilence.

Sooner murder an infant in its cradle than nurse unacted
desires.

[E 35, 37]

A complementary group of proverbs praises excess and over-
flow, sometimes as the only way of finding natural limits, the
true boundary or circumference of need, feeling, and behavior,
free from arbitrary constraint:

> The road of excess leads to the palace of wisdom.

> If the fool would persist in his folly he would become wise.

> You never know what is enough unless you know what is
> more than enough.

This praise of excess is connected with the idea of self-fulfill-
ment and individual genius: "No bird soars too high. if he soars
with his own wings."

Blake is never a naturalist in Wordsworth's sense, for he
grants no independent value or priority to the life of nature
("Where man is not nature is barren"). Though Blake has little
feeling for inanimate nature except as it serves man, he devotes
the first forty-odd lines of his late "Auguries of Innocence"
(1818) to the mistreatment of birds and animals as an index of
man's social degradation and spiritual impoverishment. Combining natural piety and a modern ecological humility, he contrasts the brutalization of nature into an instrument for man
with an ideal respect for nature as a correlative to man's own
freedom, his respect for himself:

> A Robin Red breast in a Cage
> Puts all Heaven in a Rage. . . .
> A dog starvd at his Masters Gate
> Predicts the ruin of the State. . . .
> Each outcry of the hunted Hare
> A fibre from the Brain does tear. . . .
> The Game Cock clipd & armd for fight
> Does the Rising Sun affright. . . .
> The wild deer wandring here & there
> Keeps the Human Soul from Care. . . .
>
> [E 481]

But in the early 1790s Blake's stress is on the stunting and
constricting of *human* nature, for which our treatment of na-

ture itself provides constant analogies. In "The School Boy," a very simple poem, which originally appeared in *Innocence* but eventually migrated to the *Songs of Experience,* Blake compares the happiness and spontaneity of the boy in nature to his self-dramatizing misery, his feeling of imprisonment, at school. The second half of the poem is an appeal from a restrictive society to the freedom of nature, phrased as a series of questions, a gentle challenge:

> How can the bird that is born for joy,
> Sit in a cage and sing.
> How can a child when fears annoy,
> But droop his tender wing,
> And forget his youthful spring.
>
> O! father & mother, if buds are nip'd,
> And blossoms blown away,
> And if the tender plants are strip'd
> Of their youth in the springing day,
> By sorrow and cares dismay,
>
> How shall the summer arise in joy
> Or the summer fruits appear
> Or how shall we gather what griefs destroy
> Or bless the mellowing year,
> When the blasts of winter appear.
>
> [*E* 31]

The anticipation of summer and the inevitability of winter are characteristic of the realism of *Innocence*, which is always aware of itself as a transitional state foreshadowing growth and change and hedged by the threat of adversity. But the natural analogy is a very limiting one, since human growth isn't really similar to the cycle of the seasons or to natural fruition. The poem's elemental naturalism links it to some of Wordsworth's more pristine *Lyrical Ballads,* composed only a few years later, such as "The Reverie of Poor Susan" (in which a young girl is also compared to a caged songbird), "To My Sister," "Expostulation and Reply," and "The Tables Turned" (poems that

praise "a wise passiveness" and "impulses from a vernal wood"
as against "our meddling intellect").

Within the *Songs of Experience*, "The School Boy" settles in at
the most primitive end of the book's spectrum, where repression is entirely external to the individual himself, an imposition
by unsympathetic parent-figures who practice bad nurture and
enforce rigid precepts. (Only the poem's stress on the formative importance of childhood—the relation of spring buds to
summer fruits—keeps it, like other Songs of Innocence, from
being entirely pre-Freudian.) Before looking at the spectrum of
repression in the *Songs of Experience,* we must glance at Blake's
1793 notebook, usually called the Rossetti manuscript, which
contains first drafts of many of the songs, and numerous others
he finally chose not to engrave. The poems in this workshop
link up closely with the Freudian themes of *The Marriage of
Heaven and Hell* and *Visions of the Daughters of Albion,* and lead
us directly into *Experience.* Blake's notebook frequently shows
him in a militant and didactic mood. He preaches openness
and respect for nature even, as we see later, at the cost of self-
consumption.

> Abstinence sows sands all over
> The ruddy limbs & flaming hair
> But Desire Gratified
> Plants fruits of life & beauty there
>   *
> In a wife I would desire
> What in whores is always found
> The lineaments of Gratified desire.

>   [*E* 465]

As in the *Marriage* and *Visions,* the innocent naturalism of a
poem like "The School Boy" has here been pervasively sexualized and takes on a harsh and scabrous tone. The world of
the notebook is a bleak and bitter one, in which deceit, jealousy,
and hypocrisy threaten to poison all relationships, unless the
countervalues of Blake-Oothoon prevail. In a poem called
"How to know Love from Deceit," Blake, in typically dialectical
fashion, diagrams the contrast as starkly as possible:

> Love to faults is always blind
> Always is to joy inclind
> Lawless wingd & unconfind
> And breaks all chains from every mind
>
> Deceit to secresy confind
> Lawful cautious & refind
> To everything but interest blind
> And forges fetters for the mind
>
> [E 463]

This is partly a metrical experiment, in which Blake tries to use
as many of the same rhyme-words as possible. (If he took his
own message of liberation more literally he could only write
free verse.) What is special about Blake's theme is not simply
his savage burlesque of respectablity, calculation, and interest,
but his effort to found a Promethean psychology of exuberance
on revolutionary politics, his comparison of the mind in fetters
and the mind unchained. Many of the poems praise daylight—
especially lovemaking in daylight—over darkness and secrecy,
the children of repression.

But the result is no Nirvana, for Blake is also willing to project the sinister side of mental liberation. Desire Gratified is also
desire used up, exhausted, and consuming others. Nature is
synonymous with transience ·and flux. One rarely noticed
notebook poem is called "Soft Snow":

> I walked abroad in a snowy day
> I askd the soft snow with me to play
> She playd & she melted in all her prime
> And the winter calld it a dreadful crime
>
> [E 464]

Here the child from the world of Innocence consumes the
snow with his new sexual heat. As in Renaissance poems, her
orgasm, her climax, is a "little death," at once fulfillment and
destruction, consummation and consumption. With some justice, a feminist might object to this as a stereotyped view of the
melting sexuality of women, and their dispensability, like
Kleenex, in serving male needs. But Blake is eager to combat

the stereotype that women don't feel or enjoy sex except as
neurasthenic emotion and romantic fantasy. Instead Blake's
woman plays (gambles, gambols) and melts (comes, dies), in
line with her basic nature. Fixity has no place in human relations, only in the sandy, rocky realm of laws and fetters; eternity can be glimpsed only through the acceptance of process, of
what is fleeting:

> He who binds to himself a joy
> Doth the winged life destroy
> But he who kisses the joy as it flies
> Lives in Eternitys sun rise
>
> [E 465]

Like fixity and possessiveness, self-constraint is a formula for
natural blight. Aggression must as surely be ventilated as sexual
need. The alternative is not simply conscious hypocrisy—what
obsesses Hamlet, "that a man can smile and smile and be a
villain"—but emotional sterility, an invisible poisoning of the
whole landscape of feeling, growth, and fruition:

> I feared the fury of my wind
> Would blight all blossoms fair & true
> And my sun it shind & shind
> And my wind it never blew
>
> But a blossom fair or true
> Was not found on any tree
> For all blossoms grew & grew
> Fruitless false tho fair to see
>
> [E 458]

The structure of this poem is beautifully circular. The very
"blossoms fair & true," that he wishes to preserve lose their
mettle through his unnatural respect for them. They suffer
worse than the blight he fears: they become coldly respectable,
luxuriantly sterile and deceitful—all mere appearance, like so
much of the society Blake sees around him in 1793. As nature
needs both wind and sun for hardy growth and true fruition,
human nature dare not cap its own furies, sexual and aggres-

sive, until they have exploded to excess and found their own
shape and limit. This is the early Freud, beloved of Reich and
R. D. Laing, the anti-Victorian spokesman for sexual enlightenment, whose horizons would only gradually darken (as they did
rather differently for Blake in the later epics) into the stoic pessimism of *Civilization and Its Discontents* and "Analysis Terminable and Interminable." Yet neither Blake nor Freud ever approached the sin of believing in Original Sin, what Randall
Jarrell once described as "the ignoble truth of man's deprav-
ity," so dear to modern Christian writers, especially South-
erners. "Most of us know, now," said Jarrell, "that Rousseau
was wrong; that man, when you knock his chains off, sets up
the death camps. Soon we shall know everything the eighteenth
century didn't know, and nothing it did, and [it] will be hard to
live with us."[13]

In his own way Blake was a man of the eighteenth century
for all his imagined antipathy to Rousseau and Voltaire, whom
he unfairly conflated as scoffers and skeptics. Had he read
Rousseau more carefully he might have recognized not the
credulous delusions about human nature we still project upon
his name, but a reflection of his own prophetic bitterness. Blake
might even have recognized his own acerbic tone, despite manifest differences, in the slashing and vehement lines of Randall
Jarrell. But Jarrell's prose reminds me of Blake in quite another way. By simplifying the doctrine of Original Sin into
something so sweeping that it seems facile and fatuous, he approaches self-caricature and his lines gradually turn upon
themselves. What first seems like testimony to Original Sin finally testifies to its absurdity, as Jarrell slips imperceptibly from
ideologue to satirist. This is where the method of the *Songs of
Experience* rejoins the *Songs of Innocence* and departs from the
Rossetti poems out of which it emerges.

Recall the ambiguity of "The Chimney Sweeper" of *Innocence,* how it occupies an indeterminate space of meaning between two possible interpretations, two opposite but equally
real psychic states, one of consolation, the other a culpable

13. Quoted by Alfred Kazin in *Bright Book of Life* (1973), pp. 38–39.

complicity with oppression, a self-destroying passivity. In "The
Black Boy" and "The Chimney Sweeper" Blake is commenting
on the power of myths to console and delude us with their genuine warmth, especially when we associate them with seemingly
beneficent guardian figures. The philosophical revisionism of
the Proverbs of Hell erects this universal credulity into a Freudian principle: "Every thing possible to be believ'd is an image
of truth" (*E* 36). This was a key principle that Freud applied to
everything from delusions and dreams to slips of the tongue.
Error is an image of truth, Freud insisted; the unconscious
does not lie, but merely speaks to us in language distorted by
repression:

> the data of consciousness have a very large number of gaps
> in them; in healthy and in sick people psychical acts often
> occur which can be explained only be presupposing other
> acts, of which, nevertheless, consciousness affords no evi-
> dence. These not only include parapraxes and dreams in
> healthy people, and everything described as a psychical
> symptom or an obsession in the sick; our most personal
> daily experience acquaints us with ideas that come into our
> head we do not know from where, and with intellectual
> conclusions arrived at we do not know how. [1915b, pp.
> 166–67]

Many of the best of Blake's *Songs of Experience* are studies in
delusion, in which Blake dramatizes the language and actions
through which the unconscious speaks. We can see how this
begins in "I feared the fury of my wind." All the other Rossetti
poems I have cited so far are powerful credos which make
strong ethical and ideological statements. In that poem, however, the speaker is very much *not* William Blake, unless it is
Blake in a dark confessional mood, for the speaker has fallen
into precisely the behavior castigated in the other poems. While
the directly ideological poems were left behind in the notebook,
many of the *Songs of Experience* have personae as categorical as
Randall Jarrell, who are perfect specimens of what Henry
James would later call "the unreliable narrator."
     In the *Songs of Experience* the momentary verbal ironies we

observed in *Innocence* give way to sustained dramatic ironies that satirize a whole cast of mind into which the reader himself is often enticed, entrapped. Poems like "A Poison Tree" are dramatic monologues whose speakers are Swiftian personae, case studies, exemplary spokesmen for defective attitudes. But Blake has little interest in verbal tics and nuances of "personality" à la Browning. Instead of giving us individual characterizations, the poems offer highly condensed metaphors for malign moral stances and psychological states: not personal idiosyncrasies but, as Blake's subtitle puts it, "States of the Human Soul." Like the Poison Tree itself, which is a highly charged literary symbol, this lyric as a whole, to which I'll soon return in detail, is poetically compressed rather than novelistic, expansive, or realistic: a crystallization of a plausible but pernicious cast of mind. There are many ways in which Blake was likely to have found the work of Swift uncongenial, but this technique is reminiscent of the cruelly brilliant narrative masks of the earlier satirist.

Except for its greatest poem, "London," in which a prophetic outcast very much like Blake records what he hears, sees, or imagines in the streets of the great city, the *Songs of Experience* are less effective when they speak directly in the poet's own voice than when they are dramatic and oblique. This must be why Harold Bloom described "The Garden of Love" as a poem that "might perhaps have been better left in the notebook" (1963, p. 149). Like so many of the other poems, it is about repression, but mainly in the political sense rather than the Freudian one. Like the speaker in "The School Boy" but without his ingratiating charm, the voice we hear in "The Garden of Love" thinks of repression in terms of a very simple etiology: *They* have done it to him, the Others who inscribed "Thou shalt not" over the Chapel of Love:

> And Priests in black gowns, were walking their rounds,
> And binding with briars, my joys & desires.
>
> [*E* 26]

We can imagine a poem in which this belief would itself be taken as a delusion or projection, but here Blake does not treat it that way. The speaker's attitudes are too consistent with what Blake himself says in moods of angry polemical simplification.

The relative weakness of "The Garden of Love," its self-righteousness, shows itself in this absence of irony. A slight example of how Blake exploits the ironic mode can be found in the notebook draft of "The Lilly." In its final version in *Experience,* this slight quatrain reads almost like a Song of Innocence:

> The modest Rose puts forth a thorn:
> The humble Sheep, a threatening horn:
> While the Lilly white, shall in Love delight,
> Nor a thorn nor a threat stain her beauty bright.
>
> [E 25]

The two pairs of lines read like emblems for Oothoon before and after she sloughs off the guilt attendant upon her fall into sexuality. The surprise in the draft is to find that before "modest" Blake first characterized the rose as "envious" and then "lustful," while the "humble" sheep was first designated "coward." Blake first intended a direct denunciation of hypocrisy, an Oothoon-like attack on abstinence and humility as expressions of prurience and a fear of life. Instead of such a direct Freudian analysis, he decided to implicate by irony the reader's own lax approbation of the Christian virtues. It takes time for us to realize that "modest" and "humble" are ironic rather than honorific, that the poem identifies purity not with chastity and defensiveness but with love. Before we recognize we've been had—our prejudices implicated—the poem has closed around us like a silken net.

To this day many readers remain entrapped in a similar but more famous poem, "Ah! Sun-Flower."

> Ah Sun-flower! weary of time,
> Who countest the steps of the Sun:
> Seeking after that sweet golden clime
> Where the travellers journey is done.
>
> Where the Youth pined away with desire,
> And the pale Virgin shrouded in snow:

> Arise from their graves and aspire,
> Where my Sun-flower wishes to go.
>
> [E 25]

Our instinctive tendency is to trust the narrator of the poem, and therefore to read the situation as he does, as an evocation of the most poignant romantic *Sehnsucht*. What could be more "poetic" than the flower's unrequited love for the sun, or the premature death of the unfulfilled youth and the pale virgin, who look to heaven to reward their continence. (It must be those priests in black gowns who've been at it again.) But our romantic sympathy ensnares us in the delusions of the sun-flower, the youth, and the virgin—and the narrator—concerning the "sweet golden clime / Where the travellers journey is done." Like them we ignore the fact that we are bound to the earth and doomed to redescend to it. Like "The Lilly," engraved on the same plate, the poem is partly a burlesque of Innocence, in this case the utopian visions which, however lovely as fables, can prove destructive when they keep us from living a full life. Like "The Little Black Boy" and "The Chimney Sweeper" of *Innocence,* the poem is about the relation between consolation and delusion. But the incipient irony of the earlier poems has woven itself into a tender trap; we are caught out by the transcendental illogic of our own sentimentality.

Entrapment is the central theme of one of the most powerful of the *Songs of Experience,* "A Poison Tree."

> I was angry with my friend;
> I told my wrath, my wrath did end.
> I was angry with my foe:
> I told it not, my wrath did grow.
>
> And I waterd it in fears,
> Night & morning with my tears:
> And I sunned it with smiles,
> And with soft deceitful wiles.
>
> And it grew both day and night.
> Till it bore an apple bright.

And my foe beheld it shine.
And he knew that it was mine.

And into my garden stole,
When the night had veild the pole;
In the morning glad I see;
My foe outstretched beneath the tree.

[*E* 28]

The narrator tells us this black little tale of revenge—revenge for what? no reason given—like a hotshot entrepreneur gloating over a deal that decimated his competitors. This is Blake's more complex and macabre version of "I feard the fury of my wind," but the speaker has mobilized his restraint into aggression, his sunny smiles into cunning and deceit. His cunning is firmly grounded in an acute understanding of his avaricious opponent ("And my foe beheld it shine. / And he knew that it was mine."), who can be tempted to seize what belongs to another, while the narrator, a more spiritual type, remains superior to mere material acquisitiveness. The scent of the hunt is what interests him most, though he is also proud of his catch: a creature of night and darkness like himself.

The notebook includes one incendiary touch of irony that Blake prudently altered, a Nietzschean title, "Christian Forbearance." Of course, the substitute title, "A Poison Tree," is a more complex and oblique allusion to Christianity. The narrator and his foe enact a parody of the Christian vision of the fall of man: the foe succumbs to fleshly acquisitiveness while the narrator, the tempter, plays God and also plays his Satanic agent, the serpent. But just as Satan and the serpent are distorted versions of once-resplendent Orcian forms, so the narrator is a repressed and distorted model of the ideal of conduct he let slip in the first two lines. His forthright treatment of his friend, which exorcises his anger, tips us off to the self-destructive character of the clever duplicity by which he tempts and entraps his "Foe." What he presents proudly as a masterpiece of strategy we can read only as a triumph over himself. The crucial second stanza shows us the process by which his personality is warped and twisted into something lethal and serpentine. To make poison he must become poison, and the poison destroys him. Whether, strictly speaking, we characterize the narrator's anger as suppressed or repressed, Freud has many eloquent passages on how repressed material proliferates rather than languishes by being cut off from conscious expression. In *Inhibitions, Symptoms and Anxiety,* Freud writes:

> If the ego succeeds in protecting itself from a dangerous instinctual impulse, through, for instance, the process of repression, it has certainly inhibited and damaged the particular part of the id concerned; but has at the same time given it some independence and has renounced some of its own sovereignty. This is inevitable from the nature of repression, which is, fundamentally, an attempt at flight. The repressed is now, as it were, an outlaw; it is excluded from the great organization of the ego and is subject only to the laws which govern the realm of the unconscious. [1926, p. 153]

Freud's metaphor here is political: sovereignty, insurrection, flight, outlawry. Bad government without a broad consensus provokes pockets of resistance which flourish underground and to which the polity, the self, will prove vulnerable when they surface again in strength. In his 1915 paper on repression, Freud uses a metaphor even more apposite to "A Poison Tree," when he says that "the instinctual representative develops with less interference and more profusely if it is withdrawn by repression from conscious influence. It proliferates [*wuchert*] in the dark, as it were, and takes on extreme forms of expression" (1915a, p. 149). *Wuchern* suggests rank and luxuriant growth, like that of a weed or fungus.

Immediately preceding "A Poison Tree" are the last lines of "Infant Sorrow," the poem loosely linked to "Infant Joy" in *Innocence:*

> Struggling in my fathers hands:
> Striving against my swadling bands:

Bound and weary I thought best
To sulk upon my mothers breast.

[*E* 28]

We are tempted to identify this ominous infant with Orc, the
figure of revolutionary vengeance, the "new born terror" of the
Song of Liberty and the early prophetic books. But this unholy
terror turns sly and calculating, in a way that associates him
with the protagonist of "A Poison Tree" rather than the howl-
ing Orc. In the draft this short poem proceeds for many more
stanzas, beginning:

When I saw that rage was vain
And to sulk would nothing gain
Turning many a trick & wile
I began to soothe and smile

[*E* 720]

And the poem ends with the same combination of violence and
self-deterioration we find in "A Poison Tree." All this is foreshadowed in the engraved lines by the word *sulk,* a wonderful
play on *suck* and a word rich with connotations of duplicity and
postponed aggression.

None of the other protagonists of the *Songs of Experience*
displays the same capacity to transform self-repression into a
fist of violence. More often they take out their aggressions entirely on themselves, or suffer passively at the hands of social
and parental powers which like to claim a monopoly on violence. In one poem, "A Little Boy Lost," a child is even burned
alive for some mild religious heterodoxy. In "The Chimney
Sweeper" and "Holy Thursday" the torture and executions are
slower and more subtle, the poet's protest equally impassioned.
The proto-Marxian theme of social repression and exploitation
runs through the book at an angle to the proto-Freudian theme
of psychological repression, until the two lines meet in "London," the summation of all the poems. What joins the two
themes together is the emphasis on childhood taken over from
the *Songs of Innocence;* childhood remains the test of what is natural and potentially redemptive in both the psyche and society.

Except for "London," however, the social poems are flattened
into prophetic wrath compared either to their counterparts in
Innocence or to the rich psychological studies in *Experience*. As
Harold Bloom remarks, "two contrary readings of the first *Holy
Thursday* were equally true, but from the stance of Experience
only one reading is possible" (1963, p. 142).

This is slightly less true of "The Chimney Sweeper" of *Experience*, where psychological perverseness plays almost as important a role as social exploitation.

> A little black thing among the snow:
> Crying weep, weep, in notes of woe!
> Where are thy father & mother? say?
> They are both gone up to the church to pray.
>
> Because I was happy upon the heath,
> And smil'd among the winters snow:
> They clothed me in the clothes of death,
> And taught me to sing the notes of woe.
>
> And because I am happy, & dance & sing,
> They think they have done me no injury:
> They are gone to praise God & his Priest & King
> Who make up a heaven of our misery.
>
> [*E* 22–23]

There is no ambivalence here, as in the first "Chimney
Sweeper," no thought of consolation or redemption. On the
contrary, that very vision of redemption is coldly satirized in
the final lines, which set up a Marxian constellation of religion
as an anodyne of the masses and the promise of an afterlife as
an ideological prop of exploitation in this life. The rather pe-
remptory liberal reformer who confronts the sweep in the first
three lines looks down on the grimy child as a "case" of parental neglect: a dehumanized and pathetic black dot on the frigid
social horizon. But the sweep himself, when he speaks in line
four, takes the poem beyond such pathos and subtle condescension. "Pity would be no more, / If we did not make somebody Poor: / And Mercy no more could be, / If all were as
happy as we," says Blake in "The Human Abstract" (*E* 27). The

Christian virtues themselves ratify the evils they contemplate so passively. This is brought home in the double meaning of the poem's last line. Priest and King build their wealth and power on our suffering, our labor, but they also build their theology out of our misery.

But the real linch-pin is the psychological note introduced by the reiterated word *because*. The sweep tells his interrogator that he is no victim of neglect; indeed, his parents are pious and self-righteous—free of any sense of guilt. Yet he insists that they have acted not out of poverty but out of perverseness. As with the embittered nurse in the "Nurse's Song" of *Experience,* which follows directly, it is precisely the child's happiness that incites them, for it rankles and challenges their own repressed being. The benign guardians of *Innocence* have turned envious and resentful of their charges, for they are not satisfied with their own lives. Blake has leavened his Marx with a touch of Dostoevsky.

All through the *Songs of Experience* we see the brutal side of guardianship and the debilitating effects of dependency—both of which had been so nurturing in the child's world of *Innocence.* "My Pretty Rose Tree" (engraved on the same plate as "Ah! Sun-Flower" and "The Lilly") is one of Blake's little psychological studies, like the "Nurse's Song" and "A Poison Tree," in which the speaker doesn't really understand the story he's telling us because he doesn't see what's happening to him: in Freud's sense of repression, it is "inadmissible to consciousness." He has turned down a lovely flower, a sexual offer, and returns to boast about it to his pretty rose-tree, who refuses to be grateful for his righteous self-abnegation.

> Then I went to my Pretty Rose-tree;
> To tend her by day and by night.
> But my Rose turnd away with jealousy:
> And her thorns were my only delight.
>
> [*E* 25]

"To tend her by day and night" echoes the formula Blake used for the growth of the poison tree. It suggests something poisonous in the relationship between the pretty rose and the gar-

dener-spouse, a vegetative dependency that preceded the intervention of the other flower. The speaker sees himself only as
the victim of injustice and feminine irrationality. Without even
enjoying a little dalliance he is blamed for infidelity; for owning
up to the incident he is punished for his honesty.

The final line is the kicker; it brings to mind "the self enjoyings of self denial," which Blake also dramatizes in the covert,
onanistic sexuality of "The Sick Rose." In confessing to the
rose-tree the speaker sought not only moral credit for his self-
denial but also a masochistic pleasure in becoming a victim.
The balance of dependency has shifted but the relation remains unequal. The rose's thorns prove more delightful than
her petals, more delightful even than an interlude with the
flower, and without the attendant guilt. Blake turns a mere incident of seeming morality into a study in repression and self-
deception. Flaunting his virtues and revealing his injuries, the
speaker succeeds only in exposing himself. We have come far
from "The Garden of Love," where only an external source of
repression could be acknowledged, and even from "A Poison
Tree," where the speaker consciously remade himself into the
warped agent of his own bottled-up anger. In "My Pretty Rose
Tree" the speaker is the victim not of a malevolent Other but
of a psychological process he doesn't begin to understand.

After 1926 Freud, followed by Anna Freud, generally substituted the term *defense* for *repression* in describing this process.[14]
One of Blake's key psychological lyrics actually centers on the
metaphor of defense. Blake's most striking treatment of repression is this neglected little masterpiece, "The Angel," which is
tenuously linked with that most delicate and charming of the
Songs of Innocence, "A Dream." In "A Dream," as in so many *Innocence* poems, the world of Experience casts its tragic shadow
in the threat of separation between parent and child, a shadow
so ominous that Blake briefly transferred the poem to *Experience*. A mother ant has lost her way in a dark wood of traditional allegory, whose bewildering entanglements may also
apply syntactically to the mind of the human dreamer who tells

14. Freud, *Inhibitions, Symptoms and Anxiety*, pp. 163–64; Anna Freud, *The Ego
and the Mechanisms of Defense* (1936, 1966).

the story. Thinking only of the torments of the husband and children who await her, the mother ant remains lost until the dreamer herself sheds a tear of pity. At this point, as if conjured up by the dreamer's own breakthrough into sympathy, a slightly pompous glow-worm, "watchman of the night," and a convenient beetle come to guide the wanderer home. In her "Angel-guarded bed" the dreamer has justified her dependency by learning to support the dependency of others. As E. D. Hirsch has shown (pp. 203–05), a beautiful chain of guardianship is established, which runs from the angel and the dreamer down to the glow-worm, the beetle, and the little ants. Each creature feels implicated in the fate of another, as in John Donne's famous seventeenth Meditation, and this alone overcomes the threat of separation and loss.

When Blake comes to write "The Angel," the spirit of dependency has taken on an entirely different cast, akin to that in "My Pretty Rose Tree":

> I Dreamt a Dream! What can it mean?
> And that I was a maiden Queen:
> Guarded by an Angel mild;
> Witless woe, was ne'er beguil'd!
>
> And I wept both night and day
> And he wip'd my tears away
> And I wept both day and night
> And hid from him my hearts delight
>
> So he took his wings and fled:
> Then the morn blush'd rosy red:
> I dried my tears & armd my fears,
> With ten thousand shields and spears.
>
> Soon my Angel came again:
> I was arm'd, he came in vain:
> For the time of youth was fled
> And grey hairs were on my head.
>
> [E 24]

This is armed innocence, virtue militant, but as Blake believed that "war is energy enslaved" this is also his most cunning study in repression. The guardian angel of the earlier poem has become a suitor, but this dreamer feels betrayed by any intimation of sexual maturity, her own as well as his. She hides from him both the treasures of her body and her own reciprocal emotion and desire, like the Sick Rose who hides and luxuriates in her own "bed / Of crimson joy," until she is "found out." She clings to the contradictory vision of herself as a childlike ward and a Virgin Queen. She has an image of the Angel as he *ought* to be, mild and unthreatening; like the speaker in "My Pretty Rose Tree," she treasures a sense of injured innocence. The repeated formula of "night and day," "day and night," shows how she empties desire into sentimentality, emotion into self-pity, gradually becoming the substitute guardian of her own isolated but well-defended self. In what can only be a direct satire on the *Songs of Innocence*, Blake underlines the sinister and delusive side of dependency. He shows how it can stunt development and arm the psyche against experience.

In his paper "On Narcissism," Freud describes how the formation of an idealized self-image can be a way of clinging to the narcissistic satisfactions of childhood:

> For the ego the formation of an ideal would be the conditioning factor of repression.
>
>   This ideal ego is now the target of the self-love which was enjoyed in childhood. . . . As always where the libido is concerned, man has here again shown himself incapable of giving up a satisfaction he had once enjoyed. [1914, p. 94]

Writing in what was still an age which idealized femininity, Freud also argued that women were more prone to narcissism, and better able to entice the other sex into collaborating with their own self-love (1914, pp. 88–90). When the dreamer in "The Angel" fails to achieve this, she retreats into a self-image of unfathomable victimization, "witless woe," which Blake no doubt wishes us to read ironically as "mindless misery," bereft of all self-awareness. Her image of helplessness is hardly consistent with the strength of the "ten thousand shields and spears" with which she fends off her suitor and her own feelings. By the last two lines of the poem, her vigilant resistance has hardened into the armor of habit, and the feelings themselves have atrophied into a premature old age. No poem could better illustrate Freud's motto that "The interpretation of dreams is the royal road to a knowledge of the unconscious activities of the mind" (1900–01, p. 608).

Even apart from the recitation of dreams, note the similarity between these monologues and analytic speech. What's missing on Blake's couch is only the transference, the speaker's projection of fantasies and reactions onto the silent analyst. Literary characters sometimes approximate this by addressing the reader as a passive interlocutor, as the hyperconscious narrator does in the first part of Dostoevsky's *Notes from Underground,* a monologue which is really a frenetic dialogue with only one speaker. In Blake's lyrics the irony within the poem and in its relation to linked and overlapping poems provides a substitute for transference and for the interventions of the analyst.

Finally, in "London," Blake goes one step further, to merge dream and reality in daringly compressed poetic language. The speaker in that poem has usually been described as a walker in the city. But if we consider the poem's feverish, hallucinatory atmosphere, we can just as easily depict him as a vivid dreamer, a tormented visionary whose dream is a kaleidoscope of the real city, but heightened, impacted, intensified.[15] This ambience Blake builds up through repetition, incantatory language, and a technique of telescoping or condensation which dreams share with the language of poetry. As Lionel Trilling argued in "Freud and Literature," "Freud discovered in the very organization of the mind those mechanisms by which art makes its effects, such devices as the condensations of meanings and the displacement of accent" (1950, p. 53). Nowhere is this better demonstrated than in the middle stanzas of "London":

> In every cry of every Man
> In every Infants cry of fear,

15. T. S. Eliot praised Blake's "gift of hallucinated vision." *Selected Essays,* p. 322.

> In every voice: in every ban
> The mind-forg'd manacles I hear
>
> How the Chimney-sweepers cry
> Every blackning Church appalls,
> And the hapless Soldiers sigh,
> Runs in blood down Palace walls
>
> [E 27]

The subtle repetitions of "charter'd" and "marks" in the first stanza lead here to incantatory variations on "every cry" and "every Man," which develop into a summation of the key theme of *Innocence and Experience:* the nature of a society that warps and torments its young. The infant already cries in anticipation of the life before it, which has already put its mark on the father, entrapped the chimney-sweeper, and maimed the soldier. The social and psychological themes of *Experience* merge in Blake's vision of the "marks of weakness, marks of woe" on "every face." The cacophonous sounds of the city unite not simply into a portrait of fear and pain but into a prophecy of apocalyptic vengeance. The blackening churches of London, which have tolerated the abuse of children as chimney-sweepers, betray their grimy moral essence. The palace which bloodies its soldiers in endless wars shows *its* bloody nature, as in a dream which is also a foretelling of revenge.

The effect is like that of a Fritz Lang movie, in which an atmosphere of fatality casts its shadow from the beginning over an already stylized landscape. By a foreshortening even more dramatic than the end of "The Angel"—a dazzling condensation of language and significance—Blake strips the veil of hypocrisy from pious but poisonous social goals, just as he unmasks the self-deceptions of repressive virtue in his psychological studies. The synthesis of "London" is enough to keep us from isolating the themes of psychological and social repression, or subordinating one to the other. What condemns society in the *Songs of Experience* is its palpable effect on the lives and minds of individuals, whose own "mind-forg'd manacles" its values help to shape and tighten.

Blake is akin to both Marx and Freud in his depiction of the psyche and society in terms of a dynamic of internal conflict. Blake had a systematic and dialectical mind, as they did: "Without Contraries is no progression," he writes in *The Marriage of Heaven and Hell.* "Attraction and Repulsion, Reason and Energy, Love and Hate, are necessary to Human existence" (*E* 34). This joins him to poets as far back as Homer, Euripides, and Catullus, but it connects with few of the models of mind available to him in his own time. His model is not based on the association of ideas or on a mechanical process of stimulus and response, tension and release. It abjures the Enlightenment materialism of *L'homme Machine* as it attacks the dualism of Christianity and of Descartes. It refuses to idealize the mind as a separate spiritual realm, or to degrade it to a mere function of physical stimulus. For Blake, as for Freud, the way down was the way up. ("If I cannot bend the Higher Powers, I will move the Infernal Regions," read Freud's Latin epigraph to *The Interpretation of Dreams.*) As a psychologist Blake's closest precedent in the eighteenth century is the novelist Samuel Richardson, whom Diderot accurately praised for illuminating the dark cave of the unconscious mind, and whose influence can be felt most immediately in Rousseau's *La Nouvelle Hélöise.* But where Richardson is Proustian in his minute analysis of motivation and feeling, Blake is Freudian in his emphasis on sexuality, repression, and the formative importance of childhood, beginning with the first days of infancy.

Here is the heart of Blake's modernity and perhaps the key to the neglect he experienced in his own time. Though his personal mythology is unique, Blake's revolutionary political attitudes were at least as close to a main current of his age as they are to ours, when we tend to assimilate them to the energizing platitudes of sentimental radicalism. But Blake's psychology, especially as it centers on sexuality, never fails to stagger undergraduates when they first encounter his work (though the platitudes of sexual liberation can be just as muddled as the slogans of revolution). Though children read Blake's lyrics with as much pleasure as he hoped they would, his poetry speaks with exceptional force to the conflicts and confusions of adolescence, when the passage from Innocence to Experience is just

taking place, when the clash between the impositions of authority and the anarchy of individual will is being felt most vividly,
when sex and repression are in constant and immediate
struggle.

It is scarcely an accident that the gradual discovery of Blake
in the twentieth century parallels the gradual ascendancy of
Freud. "Beware when the great God lets loose a thinker on this
planet," said Emerson. "The very hopes of man, the thoughts
of his heart, the religion of nations, the manners and morals of
mankind are all at the mercy of a new generalization." Our
brightest flashes of self-recognition in the mirror of Blake's poetry belonged to the period, not yet over, when middle-class
culture, especially in America, became pervasively Freudian,
when the ubiquity of sex and the belief in unconscious motivation crystallized in new approaches in every sphere, from child-
rearing to history-writing, from criminal justice to advertising.
(Books like James Agee's *Let Us Now Praise Famous Men*, with its
whole pages of Blake quotations, and other works of the 1920s
and 1930s, show how Blake's work, abetted by Lawrence, became for some members of the avant-garde more of a secular
religion than a body of literature.) As the cultural prestige of
Freud declines, as psychoanalysis loses ground to other models
of mind, Blake too may well descend, as Wordsworth did by
the end of the nineteenth century, from the status of an exemplary moralist to a ready niche in the academic pantheon as an
English Romantic poet.

REFERENCES

Auden, W. H. "Psychoanalysis and Art Today" (1935). In *The English
  Auden*. Edited by E. Mendelson. New York: Random House, 1977.
Auerbach, E. *Mimesis*. Bern: A. Francke, 1946. [*Mimesis*. Translated by
  W. Trask. Princeton, N.J.: Princeton University Press, 1953.]
Blake, W. *The Poetry and Prose of William Blake*. Edited by D. V. Erd-
  man. Garden City, N.Y.: Doubleday, 1965.
Bloom, H. *Blake's Apocalypse* (1963). Garden City, N.Y.: Anchor, 1965.
————. *The Anxiety of Influence: A Theory of Poetry*. New York: Oxford
  University Press, 1973.

Borges, J. L. *Other Inquisitions 1937–1952*. New York: Washington Square Press, 1966.

Brooks, C. *The Well Wrought Urn*. New York: Harcourt, Brace, 1947.

Eliot, T. S. *Selected Essays*. London: Faber and Faber, 1951.

Erdman, D. V. *Blake: Prophet Against Empire*. Princeton, N.J.: Princeton University Press, 1954.

Freud, A. *The Ego and the Mechanisms of Defense*. Rev. ed. New York: International Universities Press, 1966.

Freud, S. *Standard Edition of the Complete Psychological Works*. London: Hogarth, 1953–74.

    The Interpretation of Dreams (1900–01), vols. 4, 5.

    "On Narcissism: An Introduction" (1914), vol. 14.

    "Repression" (1915a), vol. 14.

    "The Unconscious" (1915b), vol. 14.

    Introductory Lectures on Psycho-Analysis (1915–17), vols. 15, 16.

    "The 'Uncanny' " (1919), vol. 17.

    Inhibitions, Symptoms and Anxiety (1926), vol. 20.

    Civilization and Its Discontents (1930), vol. 21.

    "Analysis Terminable and Interminable" (1937), vol. 23.

Frye, N. *Fearful Symmetry*. Princeton, N.J.: Princeton University Press, 1947.

Gordon, D. J. *Literary Art and the Unconscious*. Baton Rouge: Louisiana State University Press, 1976.

Healy, W.; Bronner, A. F.; and Bowers, A. M. *The Structure and Meaning of Psychoanalysis*. New York: Knopf, 1930.

Hirsch, E. D., Jr. *Innocence and Experience: An Introduction to Blake*. New Haven: Yale University Press, 1964.

Kazin, A. *Bright Book of Life*. Boston: Little, Brown, 1973.

Leavis, F. R. *Nor Shall My Sword*. New York: Barnes & Noble, 1972.

Munroe, R. L. *Schools of Psychoanalytic Thought*. New York: Henry Holt, 1955.

Murry, J. M. *William Blake* (1933). New York: McGraw-Hill, 1964.

Nurmi, M. K. "Fact and Symbol in 'The Chimney Sweeper' of Blake's *Songs of Innocence*." In N. Frye, ed. *Blake: A Collection of Critical Essays*. Englewood Cliffs, N.J.: Prentice-Hall, 1966.

Price, M. *To the Palace of Wisdom* (1964). Garden City, N.Y.: Anchor, 1965.

Rieff, P. *Freud: The Mind of the Moralist* (1959). Garden City, N.Y.: Anchor, 1961.

Schorer, M. *William Blake: The Politics of Vision* (1946). New York: Vintage, 1959.

Thompson, E. P. *The Making of the English Working Class.* London:
    Gollancz, 1963.
Trilling, L. "Freud and Literature," *The Liberal Imagination.* New York:
    Viking Press, 1950.
Witcutt, W. P. *Blake: A Psychological Study.* London: Hollis & Carter,
    1946. [Reprint. Port Washington, N.Y.: Kennikat Press, 1966.]

4

Two Questions about Psychoanalysis
and Poetry

Marshall Edelson

My first question is: Why should the psychoanalyst qua psycho-analyst pay any special attention to poetry?

First, because language is the source of the primary data of psychoanalysis. The psychoanalyst may turn to poetry, as I have (Edelson, 1975), for examples of an intensely concentrated exploitation of the many resources of language. In poetry, the psychoanalyst becomes aware of hypersemanticity, of the way in which different but related meanings intersect or converge upon a word or phrase. In poetry, he discovers patterns of sounds supporting semantic structures as a chordal progression underlies a melody or a tone of voice illuminates a discourse. These patterns, together with syntactic forms, provide emphasis, create tension, and arouse anticipations and expectations. Sounds by their own qualities, and in the context of the semantic structures in which they are embedded, symbolize conceptions of affect and attitude. Syntactic forms, similarly, present rather than represent meanings by exemplifying and thereby alluding to the very properties of a syntactic form itself. The probability is that each use of language the psychoanalyst encounters in poetry has found or will find its way into the psychoanalytic situation. Theoretical and research interests aside, it is always possible that by reading poetry with pleasure and care the psychoanalyst enhances his readiness to hear and respond to such uses of language in his clinical work.

Second, because poetry is a product of the mind, the same

mind that produces to some extent in much the same way dreams, symptoms, and parapraxes. Poetry constrains the psychoanalyst to construct a theory of the mind that is consistent with the mind's production of the former as well as the latter. Poetry informs the psychoanalyst that operations such as condensation and displacement are involved in the most disciplined and integrated, as well as in the most wayward and pathological, creations of man (Edelson 1975, p. 187).

Third, because poetry instigates acts of interpretation by literary critics, as the verbal productions of the analysand instigate acts of interpretation by the psychoanalyst. There are questions here worth investigating. In what ways are the "acts of interpretation" carried out by one importantly alike and in what ways importantly unlike the "acts of interpretation" carried out by the other? What is the difference between understanding a poem and interpreting it, between understanding what the analysand says and interpreting it? What is the difference between explaining a poem and interpreting it, between explaining what the analysand says and interpreting it (Edelson, 1975, part 1)? What are the events that provide occasions for or instigate acts of interpretation, and to what extent are they similar or dissimilar in the two cases? Such events may include apparent senselessness when one expects or assumes sense; ambiguities—syntactic, semantic, phonological, and logical; deviance; disjunctions, sudden changes in content or style, abrupt breaks in continuity, a felt lack of relatedness; tropes or figures of speech (Edelson, 1975, 1978). To what extent are the aims and the context of acts of interpretation by literary critic and psychoanalyst congruent?

With regard to the last question, a few comments are in order. The psychoanalyst's principal skill lies not in making interpretations but in creating a situation in which his acts of interpretation are mutative (that is, affect the analysand). Interpretation in psychoanalysis is a three-termed predicate; it is a relation requiring three terms for its expression. It involves a joint effort by psychoanalyst and analysand to enable the analysand to make sense out of what appears senseless—a dream, a neurotic symptom, a parapraxis. However, interpretation as it is carried out by the literary critic is often discussed as if it were a two-termed predicate. What is emphasized is interpretation of a text and the difficulties in the relationship between interpreter and text—rather than interpretation of a text for someone else (a reader, an audience) to whom the text is problematic and whose relation to the text may be affected by the interpretation. Little is said about the vicissitudes of the relationship between interpreter and reader, and usually interest in this relationship is aroused only when the literary critic is also a teacher.

There is a major flaw here in the application of psychoanalysis. For either the writer of the text is regarded as a patient, although he cannot join the literary critic in, or contribute to, the effort to interpret the text—a crucial part of any process we call psychoanalytic—or the literary critic is regarded as a patient conducting a self-analysis, whose unconscious mental processes, reactions to the text, and attitudes toward the writer of the text, constitute both an obstacle to interpretation and the means that make interpretation possible. Surely, however, if there is an analogy to psychoanalytic interpretation, then the relation between a text that is apparently senseless and someone else—a reader—for whom it should make sense and who is to be altered by interpretation is also important. The literary critic somehow has to find ways to affect some reader. The literary critic's skill is ultimately to be evaluated in terms of some change brought about in at least one reader's capacity to comprehend, appreciate, or respond to a poem. One could, of course, respond to the last three sentences: (1) by denying that there is an analogy between psychoanalytic interpretation (as defined in the previous paragraph) and literary interpretation of a text; or (2) by rejecting one or another aspect of the definition of psychoanalytic interpretation here given (for example, that psychoanalytic interpretation always involves an effort to make sense out of what appears to be senseless).

Fourth, the psychoanalyst qua psychoanalyst should pay special attention to poetry, because the reader's response to poetry is a phenomenon which, like many another, calls for psychoanalytic investigation. I. A. Richards (1929) once reported a study

of the obstacles within readers that led to their misreading poetry. Certainly, his list of obstacles would be enriched if the psychoanalyst were to bring to bear upon such a problem the psychoanalytic theory of the mind and its account of primary and
secondary mental processes; a consideration of the difference
between motivated disguises and the apparent senselessness
brought about by a particular mode of representation of meaning; and the study of defenses against impulses and affects and
resistance to the apprehension of images or ideas that will un-
leash or arouse these. A psychoanalyst who focused upon this
one problem might shed a good deal of additional light on the
interaction between modes of representation, motivational
structures, and cognitive functioning.

Not only the creation of poetry, but also the satisfaction it
brings, are as much mysteries of the mind as the creation of
music and the satisfaction it brings. Stone (1961) writes of the
mother-of-separation, the mother who is in contact not physically but through acts of speech, as the primal transference figure in psychoanalysis. Surely, the intense response to voice
alone, regardless of content, to patterns of sound, to linkages
between sound and sense, has something to do in both the
reader of poetry and the analysand with the relation to the
mother-of-separation and her quintessentially linguistic presence. Here, poetry and psychoanalysis may share a common
foundation, and the connection between the response to poetry
and the response to the psychoanalyst's voice cries for psychoanalytic investigation.

Similarly, the intense response to condensations and verbal
communications in poetry may have its source in a recognition
and enjoyment of a mode of mental functioning. This phenomenon is also observed in the psychoanalytic situation. Here, the
analysand may, for example, fear, but often as well delight and
take pride in, the dreams he creates and the operations he discovers which have entered into his construction of his dreams.
Psychoanalytic investigation of the connection between these
phenomena should yield important information about the
human capacity for observing and taking pleasure in one's own
modes of mental functioning.

My second question is: What assumptions are made in some uses of psychoanalysis in literary criticism, which call for examination by the psychoanalyst? The ones that come to mind especially are assumptions about the relation between tropes or figures of speech and mechanisms of defense.

First, the assumption may be made that literal language is not possible, that language is ineluctably figurative, and that in a fundamental (that is, literal!) sense, any use of language is, in part at least, tropological. (I have discussed this assumption in passing in Edelson, 1978.) This assumption requires examination in the light of psychoanalytic theorems about different modes of ego functioning; the relation between language and cognition; and the extent to which and the circumstances in which uses of language can be purely cognitive and, therefore, at least relatively drive-autonomous and affect-autonomous.

Second, the assumption may be made that all figurative language (and, therefore, under the previous assumption, any use of language) is always, in part at least, defensive; that is, whatever functions it serves, it serves defense as well. Defense is regarded as a ubiquitous aspect of human action. This assumption requires examination in the light of psychoanalytic theorems about ego-autonomous functions, which are presumed to have origins neither in drive nor in defense.

Third, the assumption may be made that each trope or figure of speech expresses, serves, or is connected with a specific mechanism of defense. This assumption requires examination in the light of psychoanalytic theorems about the nature of defense. To what extent is it useful to conceive of defenses as abstract mechanisms and to what extent as, rather, kinds of fantasies (for example, of turning away or shutting one's eyes, of swallowing or taking in an object, of changing the image of one's self)? Are defenses essentially linguistic? Can they be defined solely in terms of linguistic operations (Edelson, 1972, 1975)? Are specific defenses and tropes regularly associated or correlated? Are defenses and specific figurative ways of using language connected by virtue of the relation of each to some third factor such as innate style of cognition (Shapiro, 1965)?

I have no comment to make about these assumptions here.

They do require further discussion but, even more important, they are suitable for empirical study by the psychoanalyst in the psychoanalytic situation itself.

REFERENCES

Edelson, M. "Language and Dreams: *The Interpretation of Dreams* Revisited." *Psychoanalytic Study of the Child* 27 (1972) : 203–82.
———. *Language and Interpretation in Psychoanalysis.* New Haven: Yale University Press, 1975.
———. "What Is the Psychoanalyst Talking About?" In J. H. Smith, ed., *Psychoanalysis and Language,* vol. 3 of *Psychiatry and the Humanities.* New Haven: Yale University Press, 1978.
Richards, I. A. *Practical Criticism.* New York: Harvest Book, 1929.
Shapiro, D. *Neurotic Styles.* New York: Basic Books, 1965.
Stone, L. *The Psychoanalytic Situation.* New York: International Universities Press, 1961.

5

On Reading Poetry:
Reflections on the Limits
and Possibilities
of Psychoanalytical Approaches

SHOSHANA FELMAN

To account for poetry in psychoanalytical terms has traditionally meant to analyze poetry as a symptom of a particular poet. I would here like to reverse this approach, and to analyze a particular poet as a symptom of poetry.

No poet, perhaps, has been as highly acclaimed and, at the same time, as violently disclaimed as Edgar Allan Poe. The most controversial figure on the American literary scene, "perhaps the most thoroughly misunderstood of all American writers,"[1] "a stumbling block for the judicial critic,"[2] Edgar Allan Poe has had the peculiar fortune of being at once the most admired and the most decried of American poets. In the history of literary criticism, no other poet has engendered as much disagreement and as many critical contradictions. It is my

1. "Although Poe was not the social outcast Baudelaire conceived him to be, he was, and still is, perhaps the most thoroughly misunderstood of all American writers. . . . I have no quarrel with those who dislike Poe's work so long as they understand it. . . . I am persuaded that much of the criticism of Poe in this century, whether favorable or unfavorable, has been done by people who have not taken the trouble to understand his work." Floyd Stovall, *Edgar Poe the Poet. Essays New and Old on the Man and His Work.*

2. T. S. Eliot's famous statement on Poe in his study, "From Poe to Valéry," *Hudson Review,* Autumn 1949; reprinted in *The Recognition of Edgar Allan Poe: Selected Criticism Since 1829,* ed. Eric W. Carlson, p. 205. This collection of critical essays will hereafter be cited as *Recognition.*

contention that this critical disagreement is itself symptomatic of a *poetic effect,* and that the critical contradictions to which Poe's poetry has given rise are themselves indirectly significant of the nature of poetry.

THE POE-ETIC EFFECT: A LITERARY CASE HISTORY

No other poet has been so often referred to as a "genius," in a sort of common consensus shared even by his detractors. Joseph Wood Krutch, whose study of Poe tends to belittle Poe's stature and to disparage the value of his artistic achievement, nevertheless entitles his monograph *Edgar Allan Poe: A Study in Genius.* So do many other critics, who acknowledge and assert Poe's "genius" in the very titles of their essays, and thus propose to study "The Genius of Poe" (J. M. S. Robertson),[3] *Le Génie d'Edgar Poe* (Camille Mauclair, Paris, 1925), *Edgar Allan Poe: His Genius and His Character* (John Dillon, New York, 1911), *The Genius and Character of Edgar Allan Poe* (John R. Thompson, privately printed, 1929), *Genius and Disaster: Studies in Drugs and Genius* (Jeannet A. Marks, New York, 1925), "Affidavits of Genius: French Essays on Poe" (Jean A. Alexander).[4] "It happens to us but few times in our lives," writes Thomas W. Higginson, "to come consciously into the presence of that extraordinary miracle we call genius. Among the many literary persons whom I have happened to meet, . . . there are not half a dozen who have left an irresistible sense of this rare quality; and among these few, Poe."[5] For Constance M. Rourke, "Poe has become a symbol for the type of genius which rises clear from its time;"[6] the English poet A. Charles Swinburne speaks of "the special quality of [Poe's] strong and delicate genius;"[7] the French poet Mallarmé describes his translations of Poe as "a monument to the genius who . . . exercised his influ-

---

3. *Modern Quarterly* 3 (1926) : 274–84; 4 (1927) : 60–72.
4. *Dissertation Abstracts* 22, no. 3 (September 1961) : 866.
5. Thomas Wentworth Higginson, "Poe" (1879), in *Recognition,* p. 67.
6. "Edgar Allan Poe," from *American Humor: A Study of the National Character* (1931); reprinted in *Recognition,* p. 167.
7. Letter to Sara Sigourney Rice, Nov. 9, 1975; in *Recognition,* p. 63.

ence in our country;"[8] and the American poet James Russell
Lowell, one of Poe's harshest critics, who, in his notorious ver-
sified verdict, judged Poe's poetry to include "two fifths sheer
fudge," nonetheless asserts: "Mr. Poe has that indescribable
something which men have agreed to call *genius*. . . . Let talent
writhe and contort itself as it may, it has no such magnetism.
Larger of bone and sinew it may be, but the wings are wanting.[9]

However suspicious and unromantic the critical reader might
wish to be with respect to "that indescribable something which
men have agreed to call genius," it is clear that Poe's poetry
produces, in a uniquely striking and undeniable manner, what
might be called a *genius-effect:* the impression of some un-
definable but compelling *force* to which the reader is subjected.
To describe "this power, *which is felt,*"[10] as one reader puts it,
Lowell speaks of "magnetism"; other critics speak of "magic."
"Poe," writes Bernard Shaw, "constantly and inevitably *produced
magic* where his greatest contemporaries produced only
beauty."[11] T. S. Eliot quite reluctantly agrees: "Poe had, to an
exceptional degree, the feeling for the incantatory element in
poetry, of that which may, in the most nearly literal sense, be
called 'the *magic* of verse.' "[12]

Poe's "magic" is thus ascribed to the ingenuity of his ver-
sification, to his exceptional technical virtuosity. And yet, the
word *magic,* "in the most nearly literal sense," means much
more than just the intellectual acknowledgment of an outstanding technical skill; it connotes the effective action of something
which exceeds both the understanding and the control of the

8. Mallarmé, "Scolies," in *Oeuvres complètes,* ed. H. Mondor and G. Jean-
Aubry (Paris: Pléiade, 1945), p. 223; my translation.

9. James Russell Lowell, "Edgar Allan Poe," first version (1845); *Recognition,*
p. 11.

10. P. Pendleton Cooke, quoting Elizabeth Barrett, in "Edgar A. Poe," in
Recognition, p. 23. Original italics.

11. George Bernard Shaw, "Edgar Allan Poe" (1909), in *Recognition,* p. 98.
Italics mine. As a rule, henceforth, only authors' italics will be indicated; all
other italics mine.

12. T. S. Eliot, "From Poe to Valéry," *Recognition,* p. 209.

person who is subjected to it; it connotes a force to which the reader has no choice but to submit. "No one could tell us what it is," writes Lowell, still in reference to Poe's genius, "and yet there is none who is not *inevitably aware* of . . . its power."[13] "Poe," said Bernard Shaw, *"inevitably* produced magic." There is something about Poe's poetry which, like fate, is experienced as *inevitable,* unavoidable (and not just as irresistible). What is more, once this poetry is read, its inevitability is there to stay; it becomes lastingly inevitable: "it will *stick to the memory* of every one who reads it," writes P. Pendleton Cooke.[14] And T. S. Eliot: "Poe is the author of a few . . . short poems . . . which do somehow *stick in the memory."*[15]

This is why Poe's poetry can be defined, and indeed has been, as a poetry of *influence* par excellence, in the sense emphasized by Harold Bloom: "to inflow" = to have power over another. The case of Poe in literary history could in fact be accounted for as one of the most extreme and most complex cases of "the anxiety of influence," of the anxiety unwittingly provoked by the "influence" irresistibly emanating from this poetry. What is unique, however, about Poe's influence, as about the "magic" of his verse, is the extent to which its action is unaccountably insidious, exceeding the control, the will, and the awareness of those who are subjected to it. "Poe's influence," writes T. S. Eliot, "is . . . puzzling":

> In France the influence of his poetry and of his poetic theories has been immense. In England and America it seems almost negligible. . . . And yet one cannot be sure that one's own writing has *not* been influenced by Poe. [*Recognition,* p. 205; Eliot's italics]

Studying Poe's influence on Baudelaire, Mallarmé, and Valéry, Eliot goes on to comment:

> Here are three literary generations, representing almost exactly a century of French poetry. Of course, these are

13. "Edgar Allan Poe," p. 11.
14. "Edgar A. Poe," p. 23.
15. "From Poe to Valéry," pp. 207–08.

poets very different from each other. . . . But I think we can trace the development and descent of one particular theory of the nature of poetry through these three poets and it is a theory which takes its origin in the theory . . . of Edgar Poe. And the impression we get of the influence of Poe is the more impressive, because of the fact that Mallarmé, and Valéry in turn, did not merely derive from Poe through Baudelaire: each of them subjected himself to that influence directly, and has left convincing evidence of the value which he attached to the theory and practice of Poe himself. . . .

I find that by trying to look at Poe through the eyes of Baudelaire, Mallarmé and Valéry, I become more thoroughly convinced of his importance, of the importance of his *work* as a whole. [*Recognition,* pp. 206, 219; Eliot's italics]

Curiously enough, while Poe's worldwide importance and effective influence is beyond question, critics nonetheless continue to protest and to proclaim, as loudly as they can, that Poe is *un*important, that Poe is *not* a major poet. In an essay entitled "Vulgarity in Literature" (1931) and taxing Poe with "vulgarity," Aldous Huxley argues:

Was Edgar Allan Poe a major poet? It would surely never occur to any English-speaking critic to say so. And yet, in France, from 1850 till the present time, the best poets of each generation—yes, and the best critics, too; for, like most excellent poets, Baudelaire, Mallarmé, Paul Valéry are also admirable critics—have gone out of their way to praise him. . . . We who are speakers of English . . . , we can only say, with all due respect, that Baudelaire, Mallarmé, and Valéry were wrong and that *Poe is not one of our major poets.* [*Recognition,* p. 160]

Poe's detractors seem to be unaware, however, of the paradox that underlies their enterprise: it is by no means clear why anyone should take the trouble to write—at length—about a writer of no importance. Poe's most systematic denouncer, Ivor Winters, thus writes:

> *The menace* lies not, primarily, in his impressionistic
> admirers among literary people of whom he still has some,
> even in England and in America, where a familiarity with
> his language ought to render his crudity obvious, for these
> individuals in the main do not make themselves perma-
> nently very effective; *it lies rather in the impressive body of
> scholarship*. . . . When a writer is supported by a sufficient
> body of such scholarship, a very little philosophical eluci-
> dation will suffice to establish him in the scholarly world as
> a writer whose greatness is self-evident.[16]

The irony which here escapes the author is that, in writing his
attack on Poe, what the attacker is in fact doing is adding still
another study to the bulk of "the impressive body of scholarship" in which, in his own terms, "the menace lies"; so that,
paradoxically enough, through Ivor Winters' study, "the menace"—that is, the possibility of taking Poe's "greatness as a
writer" as "self-evident"—will indeed increase. I shall here precisely argue that, regardless of the value-judgment it may pass
on Poe, this impressive bulk of Poe scholarship, the very quantity of the critical literature to which Poe's poetry has given rise,
is itself an indication of its effective poetic power, of the
strength with which it drives the reader to an *action*, compels
him to a *reading-act*. The elaborate written denials of Poe's
value, the loud and lengthy negations of his importance, are
therefore very like psychoanalytical negations. It is clear that if
Poe's text in effect were unimportant, it would not seem so important to proclaim, argue, and prove that he is unimportant.
The fact that it so much *matters* to proclaim that Poe *does not
matter* is but evidence of the extent to which Poe's poetry is, in
effect, a *poetry that matters*.

Poe might thus be said to have a *literary case history*, most
revealing in that it incarnates, in its controversial forms, the
paradoxical nature of a strong *poetic effect:* the very poetry
which, more than any other, is experienced as *irresistible* has
also proved to be, in literary history, the poetry most *resisted,*

16. Ivor Winters, "Edgar Allan Poe: A Crisis in American Obscurantism"
(1937), in *Recognition,* p. 177.

the one that, more than any other, has provoked resistances.

This apparent contradiction, which makes of Poe's poetry a unique case in literary history, clearly partakes of the paradoxical nature of an *analytical effect*. The enigma it presents us with is the enigma of "the analytical" par excellence, as stated by Poe himself, whose amazing intuitions of the nature of what he calls "analysis" are strikingly similar to the later findings of psychoanalysis:

> The mental features discoursed of as the analytical are, in themselves, but little susceptible of analysis. *We appreciate them only in their effects.* [17]

Because of the very nature of its strong "effects," of the reading-*acts* that it provokes, Poe's text (and not just Poe's biography or his personal neurosis) is clearly an analytical case in the history of literary criticism, a case that suggests something crucial to understand in psychoanalytic terms. It is therefore not surprising that Poe, more than any other poet, has been repeatedly singled out for psychoanalytical research, has persistently attracted the attention of psychoanalytic critics.

THE PSYCHOANALYTICAL APPROACHES

The best known and most influential psychoanalytic studies of Poe are the 1926 study by Joseph Wood Krutch, *Edgar Allan Poe: A Study in Genius*, and the 1933 study by Marie Bonaparte, *Edgar Poe: Étude psychanalytique*,[18] later to appear in English as the *Life and Works of Edgar Allan Poe*.[19] More recently, Jacques Lacan has published a more limited study of one tale by Poe, "The Seminar on *The Purloined Letter*," first published in 1966.[20]

17. "The Murders in the Rue Morgue," in *Edgar Allan Poe: Selected Writings*, ed. David Galloway, p. 189. Hereafter cited as Poe.

18. Paris: Denoel et Steele.

19. Translated by John Rodker. All references to Marie Bonaparte will be to this edition.

20. "Le Séminaire sur La Lettre volée," in *Écrits* (Paris: Seuil, 1966). First translated by Jeffrey Mehlman in *French Freud, Yale French Studies*, vol. 48 (1972). A more comprehensive translation of Lacan's text has been recently published in Jacques Lacan, *Écrits: A Selection*, trans. Alan Sheridan (New York: Norton, 1977). All references here to "The Seminar on *The Purloined Letter*" are to the *Yale French Studies* translation.

Joseph Wood Krutch: Ideological Psychology, or the Approach of Normative Evaluation

For Joseph Wood Krutch, Poe's text is nothing other than an accurate transcription of a severe neurosis, a neurosis whose importance and significance for "healthy" people is admittedly unclear in Krutch's mind. Poe's "position as the first of the great neurotics has never been questioned" (p. 208), writes Krutch ambiguously. And less ambiguously, in reply to some admiring French definitions of that position: "Poe 'first inaugurated the poetic conscience' only if there is no true poetry except the poetry of morbid sensibility" (p. 210). "He must stand or fall with that whole body of neurotic literature of which his works furnish the earliest complete example" (p. 212). Since Poe's works, according to Krutch, "bear no conceivable relation . . . to the life of any people, and it is impossible to account for them on the basis of any social or intellectual tendencies or as the expression of the spirit of any age," the only possible approach is a biographical one, and "any true understanding" (p. 210) of the work is contingent upon a diagnosis of Poe's nervous malady. Krutch thus diagnoses in Poe a pathological condition of sexual impotence, the result of a "fixation" on his mother, and explains Poe's literary drive as a desire to compensate for, on the one hand, the loss of social position of which his foster father had deprived him, through the acquisition of literary fame, and on the other hand, his incapacity to have normal sexual relations, through the creation of a fictional world of horror and destruction in which he found refuge. Poe's fascination with logic would thus be merely an attempt to prove himself rational when he felt he was going insane; and his critical theory merely an attempt to justify his peculiar artistic practice.

The obvious limitations of such a psychoanalytic approach were very sharply and very accurately pointed out by Edmund Wilson in his essay "Poe at Home and Abroad."[21] Krutch, argues Wilson, seriously misunderstands and undervalues Poe's writings, in

21. In *Recognition*, pp. 142–51.

complacently caricaturing them—as the *modern school of social psychological biography,* of which Mr. Krutch is a typical representative, *seems inevitably to tend to caricature the personalities of its subjects.* We are nowadays being edified by the spectacle of some of the principal ornaments of the human race exhibited exclusively in terms of their most ridiculous manias, their most disquieting neurosis, and their most humiliating failures. [*Recognition,* p. 144; italics mine]

It is, in other words, the reductionist, stereotypical simplification under which Krutch subsumes the complexities of Poe's art and life that renders this approach inadequate:

> Mr Krutch quotes with disapproval the statement of President Hadley of Yale, in explaining the refusal of the Hall of Fame to accept Poe among its immortals: "Poe wrote like a drunkard and a man who is not accustomed to pay his debts"; and yet Mr. Krutch himself . . . is almost as unperceptive when he tells us, in effect, that Poe wrote like a dispossessed Southern gentleman and a man with a fixation on his mother. [Wilson, *Recognition,* p. 145]

Subscribing to Wilson's criticism, I would like to indicate briefly some further limitations in this type of psychoanalytic approach to literature. Krutch himself, in fact, points out some of the limits of his method, in his conclusion:

> We have, then, traced Poe's art to an abnormal condition of the nerves and his critical ideas to a rationalized defense of the limitations of his own taste. . . . The question whether or not the case of Poe represents an exaggerated example of the process by which all creation is performed is at best an open question. The extent to which all imaginative works are the result of the unfulfilled desires which spring from either idiosyncratic or universally human maladjustments to life is only beginning to be investigated, and with it is linked the related question of the extent to which all critical principles are at bottom the systematized and rationalized expression of instinctive tastes which are conditioned by causes often unknown to those whom they

affect. The problem of finding an answer to these questions . . . is the one distinctly new problem which the critic
of today is called upon to consider. He must, in a word, endeavor to find *the relationship which exists between psychology
and aesthetics.* [pp. 234–35; italics mine]

This, indeed, is the real question, the real challenge which Poe
as poet (and not as psychotic) presents to the psychoanalytic
critic. But this is precisely the very question which is bracketed,
never dealt with, in Krutch's study. Krutch discards the question by saying that "the present state of knowledge is not such
as to enable" us to give any answers. This remark, however,
presupposes—I think mistakenly—that the realm of "aesthetics," of literature and art, might not itself contain some
"knowledge" about, precisely, "the relationship between psychology and aesthetics"; it presupposes knowledge as a *given,*
external to the literary object and imported into it, and not as a
result of a reading-process, that is, of the critic's work upon
and with the literary text. It presupposes, furthermore, that a
critic's task is not to question but to answer, and that a question
that cannot be answered, can also therefore not be asked; that
to raise a question, to articulate its thinking power, is not itself
a fruitful step which takes some work, some doing, into which
the critic could perhaps be guided by the text.

   Thus, in claiming that he has traced "Poe's art to an abnor-
mal condition of the nerves," and that Poe's "criticism falls
short of psychological truth," Krutch believes that his own work
is opposed to Poe's as health is opposed to sickness, as "normality" is opposed to "abnormality," as truth is opposed to delusion. But this ideologically determined, clear-cut opposition between health and sickness is precisely one that Freud's
discovery fundamentally unsettles, deconstructs. In tracing
Poe's "critical ideas to a rationalized defense of the limitations
of his own taste," Krutch is unsuspicious of the fact that his *own*
critical ideas about Poe could equally be traced to "a rationalized defense of the limitations of his own taste"; that his doctrine, were it to be true, could equally apply to his own critical

enterprise; that if psychoanalysis indeed puts rationality as such in question, it also by the same token puts *itself* in question.

Krutch, in other words, reduces not just Poe but analysis itself into an ideologically biased and psychologically opinionated caricature, missing totally (as is most often the case with "Freudian" critics) the *radicality* of Freud's psychoanalytic insights: their self-critical potential, their power to return upon themselves and to unseat the critic from any condescending, guaranteed, authoritative stance of truth. Krutch's approach does not, then, make sophisticated use of psychoanalytic insights, nor does it address the crucial question of "the relationship between psychology and aesthetics," nor does it see that the crux of this question is not so much in the interrogation of whether or not all artists are necessarily pathological, but of what it is that makes of *art*—not of the artist—an object of *desire* for the public; of what it is that makes for art's *effect*, for the compelling power of Poe's poetry over its readers. The question of what makes poetry lies, indeed, not so much in what it was that made Poe write, but in what it is that *makes us read him*[22] and that ceaselessly drives so many people to *write about him.*

Marie Bonaparte: The Approach of Clinical Diagnosis

In contrast to Krutch's claim that Poe's works, as a literal transcription of his sickness, are only meaningful as the expression of morbidity, bearing "no conceivable relation . . . to the life of any people," Marie Bonaparte, although in turn treating Poe's works as nothing other than the recreations of his neuroses, tries to address the question of Poe's power over his readers through her didactic explanation of the relevancy, on the contrary, of Poe's pathology to "normal" people: the pathological tendencies to which Poe's text gives expression are an exaggerated version of drives and instincts universally human, but which "normal" people have simply repressed more suc-

---

22. Cf. Edmund Wilson: "The recent revival of interest in Poe has brought to light a good deal of new information and supplied us for the first time with a serious interpretation of his personal career, but it has so far entirely neglected to explain why we should still want to read him" (*Recognition*, p. 142).

cessfully in their childhood. What fascinates readers in Poe's texts is precisely the unthinkable and unacknowledged but strongly felt *community* of these human—all too human—sexual drives.[23]

If Marie Bonaparte, unlike Krutch, thus treats Poe with human sympathy, suspending the traditional puritan condemnation and refraining, at least explicitly, from passing judgment on his "sickness," she nonetheless, like Krutch, sets out primarily to diagnose that "sickness" and trace the poetry to it. Like Krutch, she comes up with a clinical "portrait of the artist" which, in claiming to account for the poetry, once again verges on caricature and cannot help but make us smile.

> If Poe was fundamentally necrophilist, as we saw, Baudelaire is revealed as a declared sadist; the former preferred dead prey or prey mortally wounded . . . ; the latter preferred live prey and killing. . . .
>
> How was it then, that despite these different sex lives, Baudelaire the sadist recognised a brother in the necrophilist Poe? . . .
>
> This particular problem raises that of the general relation of sadism to necrophilia and cannot be resolved except by an excursus into the theory of instincts. [Bonaparte, p. 680]

Can poetry thus be clinically diagnosed? In setting out to expose didactically the methods of psychoanalytic interpretation, Bonaparte's pioneering book at the same time exemplifies the very naïveté of competence, the distinctive *professional* crudity of what has come to be the classical psychoanalytic treatment of literary texts. Eager to point out the *resemblances* between psychoanalysis and literature, Bonaparte, like most psychoanalytic critics, is totally unaware of the *differences* between the two: unaware of the fact that the differences are as important and as significant for understanding the meeting-ground as are the resemblances, and that those differences also have to be accounted for if poetry is to be understood in its own right. Set-

23. Cf. chapter 45, "Literature: Its Function and Elaboration," and chapter 46, "Poe's Message to Others" (pp. 639–97).

ting out to study literary texts through the application of
psychoanalytic methods, Bonaparte, paradoxically enough but
in a manner symptomatic of the whole tradition of applied psychoanalysis, thus remains entirely blind to the very specificity of
the object of her research.

It is not surprising that this blind nondifferentiation or confusion of the poetic and the psychotic has unsettled sensitive
readers, and that various critics have, in various ways, protested
against this all too crude equation of poetry with sickness. The
protestations, however, most often fall into the same ideological
trap as the psychoanalytical studies they oppose: accepting (taking for granted) the polarity of sickness versus health, of normality versus abnormality, they simply trace Poe's art (in opposition, so they think, to the psychoanalytic claim) to
normality as opposed to abnormality, to sanity as opposed to
insanity, to the history of ideas rather than that of sexual
drives, to a conscious project as opposed to an unconscious
one. Camille Mauclair insists upon the fact that Poe's texts are
"constructed objectively by a will absolutely in control of itself,"
and that genius of that kind is "always sane."[24] For Allen Tate,

> The actual emphases Poe gives the perversions are richer
> in philosophical implication than his psychoanalytic critics
> have been prepared to see. . . . Poe's symbols refer to a
> known tradition of thought, an intelligible order, apart
> from what he was as a man, and are not merely the index
> to a compulsive neurosis . . . the symbols . . . point to-
> wards a larger philosophical dimension.[25]

For Floyd Stovall, the psychoanalytic studies "are not literary
critiques at all, but clinical studies of a supposed psychopathic
personality" (p. 182):

> I believe the critic should look within the poem or tale for
> its meaning, and that he should not, in any case, suspect
> the betrayal of the author's unconscious self until he has
> understood all that his conscious self has contributed. To

24. Camille Mauclair, *Le Génie d'Edgar Poe.* Quoted in Poe, p. 24.
25. *Recognition,* p. 239.

affirm that a work of imagination is only a report of the unconscious is to degrade the creative artist to the level of an amanuensis.

I am convinced that all of Poe's poems were composed with conscious art. [p. 183]

"The Raven", and with certain necessary individual differences every other poem Poe wrote, was the product of conscious effort by a healthy and alert intelligence. [p. 186]

It is obvious that this conception of the mutual exclusiveness, of the clear-cut opposition between "conscious art" and the unconscious, is itself naïve and oversimplified. Nonetheless, Stovall's critique of applied psychoanalysis is relevant to the extent that the psychoanalytic explanation, in pointing exclusively to the author's unconscious sexual fantasies, indeed does not account for Poe's outstanding "conscious art," for his unusual poetic mastery and his ingenious technical and structural self-control. As do its opponents, so does applied psychoanalysis itself fail precisely to account for the dynamic *interaction* between the *unconscious* and the *conscious* elements of art.

If the thrust of the discourse of applied psychoanalysis is, indeed, in tracing poetry to a clinical reality, to *reduce* the poetic to a "cause" outside itself, the crucial limitation of this process of reduction is, however, that the cause, while it may be *necessary*, is by no means a *sufficient* one. "Modern psychiatry," judiciously writes David Galloway, "may greatly aid the critic of literature, but . . . it cannot thus far explain why other men, suffering from deprivations or fears or obsessions similar to Poe's, failed to demonstrate his particular creative talent. Though no doubt Marie Bonaparte was correct in seeing Poe's own art as a defense against madness, we must be wary of identifying the *necessity* for this defense, in terms of Poe's own life, with the *success* of this defense, which can only be measured in his art."[26]

That the discourse of applied psychoanalysis is limited precisely in that it does not account for Poe's poetic *genius* is in fact the crucial point made by Freud himself in his prefatory note to Marie Bonaparte's study:

26. "Introduction" to Poe, pp. 24–25.

Foreword

In this book my friend and pupil, Marie Bonaparte, has shown the light of psychoanalysis on the life and work of a great writer with pathologic trends.

Thanks to her interpretative effort, we now realize how many of the characteristics of Poe's works were conditioned by his personality, and can see how that personality derived from intense emotional fixations and painful infantile experiences. *Investigations such as this do not claim to explain creative genius,* but they do reveal the factors which awake it and the sort of subject matter it is destined to choose. . . .

Sigm. Freud

No doubt, Freud's remarkable superiority over some (most) of his disciples—including Marie Bonaparte—proceeds from his acute *awareness* of the very *limitations* of his method, an awareness that in his followers seems most often not to exist.

I would like here to raise a question which, springing out of this limitation of applied psychoanalysis, has, amazingly enough, never been asked as a serious question: is there a way *around* Freud's perspicacious reservation, warning us that studies like those of Bonaparte "do not claim to explain creative genius"? Is there, in other words, a way—a different way—in which psychoanalysis *can* help us to account for poetic genius? Is there an alternative to applied psychoanalysis?—an alternative that would be capable of touching, in a psychoanalytic manner, upon the very specificity of that which constitutes the poetic?

Before endeavoring to articulate the way in which this question might be answered, I would like to examine still another manner in which Poe's text has been psychoanalytically approached: Jacques Lacan's "Seminar" on Poe's short story, "The Purloined Letter."

Jacques Lacan: The Approach of Textual Problematization

"The Purloined Letter," as is well known, is the story of the double theft of a compromising letter, originally sent to the queen. Surprised by the unexpected entrance of the king, the queen leaves the letter on the table in full view of any visitor, where it is least likely to appear suspicious and therefore to attract the king's attention. Enters the Minister D., who, observing the queen's anxiety and the play of glances between her and the unsuspicious king, analyzes the situation, figures out, recognizing the addressor's handwriting, what the letter is about, and steals it—by substituting for it another letter which he takes from his pocket—under the very eyes of the challenged queen, who can do nothing to prevent the theft without provoking the king's suspicions, and who is therefore reduced to silence. The queen then asks the prefect of police to search the minister's apartment and person, so as to find the letter and restore it to her. The prefect uses every conceivable secret-police technique to search every conceivable hiding place on the minister's premises, but to no avail: the letter remains undiscovered.

Having exhausted his resources, the prefect consults Auguste Dupin, the famous "analyst," as Poe calls him (i.e., an amateur detective who excels in solving problems by means of deductive logic), to whom he tells the whole story. (It is, in fact, from this narration of the prefect of police to Dupin and in turn reported by the first-person narrator, Dupin's friend, who is also present, that we, the readers, learn the story.)

On a second encounter between the prefect of police and Dupin, the latter, to the great surprise of the prefect and of the narrator, produces the purloined letter out of his drawer and hands it to the prefect in return for a large amount of money. The prefect leaves, and Dupin explains to the narrator how he came into possession of the letter: he had deduced that the minister, knowing that his premises would be thoroughly combed by the police, had concluded that the best principle of concealment would be to leave the letter in the open, in full view: in that way the police, searching for hidden secret drawers, would be outwitted, and the letter would not be discovered precisely because it would be too self-evident. On this assumption, Dupin called on the minister in his apartment and, glancing around, soon located the letter most carelessly hanging from the mantelpiece in a card-rack. A little later, a disturbance in the street provoked by a man in Dupin's employ drew the minister to the window, at which moment Dupin quickly replaced the letter with a facsimile, having slipped the real one into his pocket.

I will not enter here into the complexity of the psychoanalytic issues involved in Lacan's "The Seminar on *The Purloined Letter*," nor will I try to deal exhaustively with the nuanced sophistication of the seminar's rhetoric and theoretical propositions;[27] I will confine myself to a few specific points that bear upon the methodological issue of Lacan's psychoanalytic treatment of the literary material.

What Lacan is concerned with at this point of his research is the psychoanalytic problematics of the "repetition-compulsion," as elaborated in Freud's speculative text, *Beyond the Pleasure Principle*. The thrust of Lacan's endeavor, with respect to Poe, is thus to point out—so as to elucidate the nature of Freudian repetition—the way in which the story's plot, its sequence of events (as, for Freud, the sequence of events in a life-story), is entirely contingent on, overdetermined by, a principle of repetition that governs it and inadvertently structures its dramatic and ironic impact. "There are two scenes," remarks Lacan, "the first of which we shall straightway designate the primal scene, . . . since the second may be considered its repetition in the very sense we are considering today" (p. 41). The "primal scene" takes place in the queen's boudoir: it is the theft of the letter from the queen by the minister; the second scene—its repetition—is the theft of the letter from the minister by Dupin, in the minister's hotel.

What constitutes repetition for Lacan, however, is not the mere thematic resemblance of the double *theft*, but the whole structural situation in which the repeated theft takes place: in each case, the theft is the outcome of an intersubjective relationship between three terms; in the first scene, the three participants are the king, the queen, and the minister; in the second, the three participants are the police, the minister, and

27. For a remarkable analysis of these issues, see Barbara Johnson's essay, "The Frame of Reference: Poe, Lacan, Derrida," in *Literature and Psychoanalysis: The Question of Reading—Otherwise, Yale French Studies*, no. 55/56 (1977).

Dupin. In much the same way as Dupin takes the place of the minister in the first scene (the place of the letter's robber), the minister in the second scene takes the place of the queen in the first (the dispossessed possessor of the letter); whereas the police, for whom the letter remains invisible, take the place formerly occupied by the king. The two scenes thus mirror each other, in that they dramatize the repeated exchange of "three glances, borne by three subjects, incarnated each time by different characters" (p. 44). What is repeated, in other words, is not a psychological act committed as a function of the individual psychology of a character, but three functional *positions in a structure* which, determining three different *viewpoints*, embody three different relations to the act of seeing—of seeing, specifically, the purloined letter.

The first is a glance that sees nothing: the King and the Police.

The second, a glance which sees that the first sees nothing and deludes itself as to the secrecy of what it hides: the Queen, then the Minister.

The third sees that the first two glances leave what should be hidden exposed to whomever would seize it: the Minister, and finally Dupin. [p. 44]

Lacan's analysis can be schematized in the following figure:

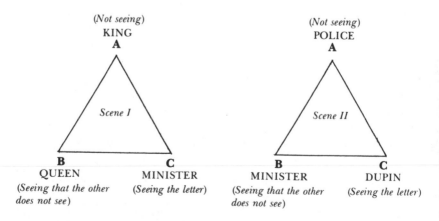

(Not seeing)
KING
A

Scene I

B
QUEEN
(Seeing that the other does not see)

C
MINISTER
(Seeing the letter)

(Not seeing)
POLICE
A

Scene II

B
MINISTER
(Seeing that the other does not see)

C
DUPIN
(Seeing the letter)

Although Lacan does not elaborate upon the possible further ramifications of the above structure, the diagram is open to a number of illuminating terminological translations, reinterpreting it in the light of Freudian and Lacanian concepts. Here are two such possible translations:

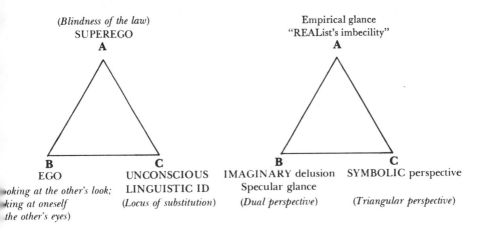

(Blindness of the law)
SUPEREGO
A

B   C
EGO   UNCONSCIOUS
oking at the other's look;   LINGUISTIC ID
king at oneself   *(Locus of substitution)*
the other's eyes)

Empirical glance
"REAList's imbecility"
A

B   C
IMAGINARY delusion   SYMBOLIC perspective
Specular glance
(Dual perspective)   *(Triangular perspective)*

"What interests us today," insists Lacan,

> is the manner in which the subjects relay each other in their displacement during the intersubjective repetition.
>   We shall see that their displacement is determined by the place which a pure signifier—the purloined letter—comes to occupy in their trio. And that is what will confirm for us its status as repetition automatism. [p. 45]

The purloined letter, in other words, becomes itself—through its insistence in the structure—a symbol or a signifier of the *unconscious,* to the extent that it "is destined . . . to signify the annulment of what it signifies" (p. 63)—the necessity of its own *repression,* of the repression of its message: "It is not only the meaning but the text of the message which it would be dangerous to place in circulation" (p. 56). But in much the

same way as the repressed *returns* in the *symptom,* which is its repetitive symbolic substitute, the purloined letter ceaselessly returns in the tale—as a signifier of the repressed—through its
repetitive displacements and replacements. "This is indeed
what happens in the repetition compulsion," says Lacan (p. 60).
Unconscious desire, once repressed, survives in displaced symbolic media which govern the subject's life and actions without
his ever being aware of their meaning or of the repetitive pattern they structure:

> If what Freud discovered and rediscovers with a perpet-
> ually increasing sense of shock has a meaning, it is that the
> displacement of the signifier determines the subjects in
> their acts, in their destiny, in their refusals, in their blind-
> nesses, in their end and in their fate, their innate gifts and
> social acquisitions notwithstanding, without regard for
> character or sex, and that, willingly or not, everything that
> might be considered the stuff of psychology, kit and ca-
> boodle, will follow the path of the signifier. [p. 60]

In what sense, then, does the second scene in Poe's tale, while
repeating the first scene, nonetheless differ from it? In the
sense, precisely, that the second scene, through the repetition,
allows for an understanding, for an *analysis* of the first. This
analysis through repetition is to become, in Lacan's ingenious
reading, no less than an *allegory of psychoanalysis.* The intervention of Dupin, who restores the letter to the queen, is thus compared, in Lacan's interpretation, to the intervention of the analyst, who rids the patient of the symptom. The analyst's
effectiveness, however, does not spring from his intellectual
strength but—insists Lacan—from his position in the (repetitive) structure. By virtue of his occupying the third position—
that is, the *locus* of the unconscious of the subject as a place of
substitution of letter for letter (of signifier for signifier)—the
analyst, through transference, allows at once for a repetition of
the trauma, and for a symbolic substitution, and thus effects
the drama's denouement.

It is instructive to compare Lacan's study of the psychoanalytical repetition compulsion in Poe's text to Marie Bonaparte's

study of Poe's repetition compulsion through his text. Although the two analysts study the same author and focus on the same psychoanalytic concept, their approaches are strikingly different. To the extent that Bonaparte's study of Poe has become a classic, a model of applied psychoanalysis which illustrates and embodies the most common understanding of what a psychoanalytic reading of a literary text might be, I would like, in pointing out the differences in Lacan's approach, to suggest the way in which those differences at once put in question the traditional approach and offer an alternative to it.

1. *What does a repetition compulsion repeat? Interpretation of difference as opposed to interpretation of identity*

For Marie Bonaparte, what is compulsively repeated through the variety of Poe's texts is *the same* unconscious fantasy: Poe's (sadonecrophiliac) desire for his dead mother. For Lacan, what is repeated in the text is not the content of a fantasy but the symbolic displacement of a signifier through the insistence of a signifying chain; repetition is not of *sameness* but of *difference*, not of independent terms or of analogous themes but of a structure of differential interrelationships,[28] in which what *returns* is always *other*. Thus, the triangular structure repeats itself only through the *difference* of the characters who successively come to occupy the three positions; its structural significance is perceived only *through* this difference. Likewise, the significance of the letter is situated in its *displacement*, that is, in its repetitive movements toward a *different* place. And the sec-

---

28. Cf.: "Need we emphasize the similarity of these two sequences? Yes, for the resemblance we have in mind is *not a simple collection of traits chosen only in order to delete their difference. And it would not be enough to retain those common traits at the expense of the others for the slightest truth to result.* It is rather the intersubjectivity in which the two actions are motivated that we wish to bring into relief, as well as the three terms through which it structures them.

"The special status of these terms results from their corresponding simultaneously to the three logical moments through which the decision is precipitated and to the three places it assigns to the subjects among whom it constitutes a choice. . . . Thus three moments, structuring three glances, borne by three sujects, incarnated each time by different characters." ("The Seminar on *The Purloined Letter,*" pp. 43–44.)

ond scene, being, for Lacan, an allegory of analysis, is important not just in that it *repeats* the first scene, but in the way this
repetition (like the transferential repetition of a psychoanalytical experience) *makes a difference:* brings about a solution to
the problem. Thus, whereas Marie Bonaparte analyzes repetition as the insistence of identity, for Lacan, any possible insight
into the reality of the unconscious is contingent upon a perception of repetition, not as a confirmation of identity, but as the
insistence of the indelibility of a difference.

2. *An analysis of the signifier as opposed to an analysis of the signified*

   In the light of Lacan's reading of Poe's tale as itself an allegory of the psychoanalytic reading, it might be illuminating to
define the difference in approach between Lacan and Bonaparte in terms of the story. If the purloined letter can be said to
be a sign of the unconscious, for Marie Bonaparte the analyst's
task is to uncover the letter's *content,* which she believes—as do
the police—to be *hidden* somewhere in the real, in some secret
biographical *depth.* For Lacan, on the other hand, the analyst's
task is not to read the letter's hidden referential content, but to
situate the superficial indication of its textual movement, to
analyze the paradoxically invisible symbolic evidence of its displacement, its structural insistence, in a signifying chain.
"There is such a thing," writes Poe, "as being too profound.
Truth is not always in a well. In fact, as regards the most important knowledge, I do believe she is invariably superficial." [29]
Espousing Poe's insight, Lacan makes the principle of symbolic
evidence the guideline for an analysis not of the signified but of
the signifier—for an analysis of the unconscious (the repressed)
not as hidden but on the contrary as *exposed*—in language—
through a significant (rhetorical) displacement.

   This analysis of the signifier, the model of which can be
found in Freud's interpretation of dreams, is nonetheless a radical reversal of the traditional expectations and presuppositions
involved in the common psychoanalytical approach to literature, and its invariable search for hidden meanings. Indeed,

29. "The Murders in the Rue Morgue," in Poe, p. 204.

not only is Lacan's reading of "The Purloined Letter" subversive of the traditional model of psychoanalytical reading; it is, in general, a type of reading that is methodologically unprecedented in the whole history of literary criticism. The history of reading has accustomed us to the assumption—usually unquestioned—that reading is finding meaning, that interpretation—of whatever method—can dwell but on the meaningful. Lacan's analysis of the signifier opens up a radically new assumption, an assumption which is nonetheless nothing but an insightful logical and methodological consequence of Freud's discovery: that what *can* be read (and perhaps what *should* be read) is not just meaning, but the lack of meaning; that significance lies not just in consciousness, but, specifically, in its disruption; that the signifier can be analyzed in its effects without its signified being known; that the lack of meaning—the discontinuity in conscious understanding—can and should be interpreted as such, without necessarily being transformed into meaning. "Let's take a look," writes Lacan:

> We shall find illumination in what at first seems to obscure matters: the fact that the tale leaves us in virtually total ignorance of the sender, no less than of the contents, of the letter. [p. 57]
>
> The signifier is not functional. . . . We might even admit that the letter has an entirely different (if no more urgent) meaning for the Queen than the one understood by the Minister. The sequence of events would not be noticeably affected, not even if it were strictly incomprehensible to an uninformed reader. [p. 56]
>
> But that this is the very effect of the unconscious in the precise sense that we teach that the unconscious means that man is inhabited by the signifier. [p. 66]

Thus, for Lacan, what is analytical par excellence is not (as is the case for Bonaparte) the *readable,* but the *unreadable,* and the *effects* of the unreadable. What calls for analysis is the insistence of the unreadable in the text.

Poe, of course, had said it all in his insightful comment, previously quoted, on the nature of what he too—amazingly enough, before the fact—called "the analytical":

> The mental features discoursed of as the analytical are, in themselves, but little susceptible of analysis. We appreciate them only in their effects. [p. 189]

But, oddly enough, what Poe himself had said so strikingly and so explicitly about "the analytical" had itself remained totally unanalyzed, indeed unnoticed, by psychoanalytic scholars before Lacan, perhaps because it, too, according to its own (analytical) logic, had been "a little too self-evident" to be perceived.

3. *A textual as opposed to a biographical approach*

The analysis of the signifier implies a theory of textuality for which Poe's biography, or his so-called sickness, or his hypothetical personal psychoanalysis, become irrelevant. The presupposition—governing enterprises like that of Marie Bonaparte—that poetry can be interpreted only as autobiography is obviously limiting and limited. Lacan's textual analysis for the first time offers a psychoanalytical alternative to the previously unquestioned and thus seemingly exclusive biographical approach.

4. *The analyst/author relation: a subversion of the master/slave pattern and of the doctor/patient opposition*

Let us remember how many readers were unsettled by the humiliating and sometimes condescending psychoanalytic emphasis on Poe's "sickness," as well as by an explanation equating the poetic with the psychotic. There seemed to be no doubt in the minds of psychoanalytic readers that if the reading situation could be assimilated to the psychoanalytic situation, the poet was to be equated with the (sick) patient, with the analysand on the couch. Lacan's analysis, however, radically subverts not just this clinical status of the poet, but along with it the "bedside" security of the interpreter. If Lacan is not concerned with Poe's sickness, he is quite concerned, nonetheless, with the *figure of the poet* in the tale, and with the hypotheses made about his specific competence and incompetence. Let us not forget that both the minister and Dupin are said to be poets, and that it is their *poetic* reasoning that the prefect fails to understand and which thus enables both to outsmart the police. "D——, I presume, is not altogether a fool," comments Dupin early in the story, to which the prefect of police replies:

> "Not altogether a fool, . . . but then he's a poet, which I take to be only one remove from a fool."
> "True," said Dupin, after a long and thoughtful whiff from his meerchaum, "although I have been guilty of certain doggerel myself." [p. 334]

A question Lacan does not address could here be raised by emphasizing still another point that would normally tend to pass unnoticed, since, once again, it is at once so explicit and so ostentatiously insignificant: why does Dupin say that he too is *guilty* of poetry? In what way does the status of the poet involve guilt? In what sense can we understand *the guilt of poetry*? [30]

Dupin, then, draws our attention to the fact that both he and the minister are poets, a qualification with respect to which the prefect feels that he can but be condescending. Later, when Dupin explains to the narrator the prefect's defeat as opposed to his own success in finding the letter, he again insists upon the prefect's blindness to a logic or to a "principle of concealment" which has to do with poets and thus (it might be assumed) is specifically *poetic:*

> This functionary [the prefect] has been thoroughly mystified; and the remote source of his defeat lies in the supposition that the Minister is a *fool,* because he has acquired renown as a *poet.* All fools are poets; this the Prefect *feels;* and he is merely guilty of a *non distributio medii* in thence inferring that all poets are fools. [pp. 341–42]

In Baudelaire's translation of Poe's tale into French, the word *fool* is rendered, in its strong, archaic sense, as: *fou,* "mad." Here, then, is Lacan's paraphrase of this passage in the story:

30. The scope of the present essay does not allow me to pursue this question further, but I intend to return to it in the (forthcoming) extended version of this study (see n. 33 below).

> After which, a moment of derision [on Dupin's part] at
> the Prefect's error in deducing that because the Minister is
> a poet, he is not far from being mad, an error, it is argued,
> which would consist, . . . simply in a false distribution of
> the middle term, since it is far from following from the
> fact that all madmen are poets.
> Yes indeed. But we ourselves are left in the dark as to
> the poet's superiority in the art of concealment. [p. 52]

Both this passage in the story and this comment by Lacan seem
to be marginal, incidental. Yet the hypothetical *relationship between poetry and madness* is significantly relevant to the case of
Poe and to the other psychoanalytical approaches we have been
considering. Could it not be said that the error of Marie Bonaparte (who, like the prefect, engages in a search for *hidden*
meaning) lies precisely in the fact that, like the prefect once
again, she simplistically *equates* the poetic with the psychotic,
and so, blinded by what she takes to be the poetic *incompetence,*
fails to see or understand the specificity of poetic *competence?*
Many psychoanalytic investigations diagnosing the poet's
sickness and looking for his poetic secret on (or in) his person
(as do the prefect's men) are indeed very like police investigations; and like the police in Poe's story, they fail to find the letter, fail to see the textuality of the text.

Lacan, of course, does not say all this—this is not what is at
stake in his analysis. All he does is open up still another question where we have believed we have come in possession of
some sort of answer:

> Yes indeed. But we ourselves are left in the dark as to the
> poet's superiority in the art of concealment. [p. 52]

This seemingly lateral question, asked in passing and left un-
answered, suggests, however, the possibility of a whole different focus or perspective of interpretation in the story. If
"The Purloined Letter" is specifically the story of "the poet's superiority in the art of concealment," then it is not just an allegory of psychoanalysis but also, at the same time, an allegory of
poetic writing. And Lacan is himself a poet to the extent that a

thought about poetry is what is superiorly concealed in his "Seminar."

In Lacan's interpretation, however, "the poet's superiority" can only be understood as the structural superiority of the third position with respect to the letter: the minister in the first scene, Dupin in the second, both, indeed, poets. But the third position is also—this is the main point of Lacan's analysis—the position of the analyst. It follows that, in Lacan's approach, the status of the poet is no longer that of the (sick) patient but, if anything, that of the analyst. If the poet is still the object of the accusation of being a "fool," his folly—if in fact it does exist (which remains an open question)—would at the same time be the folly of the analyst. The clear-cut opposition between madness and health, or between doctor and patient, is unsettled by the odd functioning of the purloined letter of the unconscious, which no one can possess or master. "There is no metalanguage," says Lacan: there is no language in which interpretation can itself escape the effects of the unconscious; the interpreter is not more immune than the poet to unconscious delusions and errors.

5. *Implication, as opposed to application, of psychoanalytic theory*

Lacan's approach no longer falls into the category of what has been called "applied psychoanalysis," since the concept of "application" implies a relation of *exteriority* between the applied science and the field which it is supposed, unilaterally, to inform. Since, in Lacan's analysis, Poe's text serves to *re-interpret Freud* just as Freud's text serves serves to interpret Poe; since psychoanalytic theory and the literary text mutually inform—and displace—each other; since the very position of the interpreter—of the analyst—turns out to be not *outside*, but *inside* the text, there is no longer a clear-cut opposition or a well-defined border between literature and psychoanalysis: psychoanalysis could be intraliterary just as much as literature is intrapsychoanalytic. The methodological stake is no longer that of the *application* of psychoanalysis *to* literature, but rather, of their *interimplication in* each other.

If I have dealt at length with Lacan's innovative contribution and with the different methodological example of his approach, it is not so much to set this example up as a new model for imitation, but rather to indicate the way in which it suggestively invites us to go beyond itself (as it takes Freud beyond itself), the way in which it opens up a whole new range of as yet untried possibilities for the enterprise of reading. Lacan's importance in my eyes does not, in other words, lie specifically in the new dogma his "school" proposes, but in his outstanding demonstration that *there is more than one way* to implicate psychoanalysis in literature; that *how to* implicate psychoanalysis in literature is itself a question for interpretation, a challenge to the ingenuity and insight of the interpreter, and not a *given* that can be taken in any way for granted; that what is of analytical relevance in a text is not necessarily and not exclusively "the unconscious of the poet," let alone his sickness or his problems in life; that to situate in a text the analytical as such—to situate the object of analysis or the textual point of its implication—is not necessarily to recognize a *known*, to find an answer, but also, and perhaps more challengingly, to locate an *unknown*, to find a question.

THE POE-ETIC ANALYTICAL

Let us now return to the crucial question we left in suspension earlier, after having raised it by reversing Freud's reservation concerning Marie Bonaparte's type of research: *can* psychoanalysis give us an insight into the specificity of the poetic? We can now supplement this question with a second one: where can we situate the analytical with respect to Poe's poetry?

The answers to these questions, I would suggest, might be sought in two directions. (1) In a direct reading of a poetic text by Poe, trying to locate in the poem itself a signifier of poeticity and to analyze its functioning and its effects; to analyze—in other words—how poetry as such works through signifiers (to the extent that signifiers, as opposed to meanings, are always signifiers of the unconscious). (2) In an analytically informed reading of literary history itself, inasmuch as its treatment of Poe obviously constitutes a (literary) *case history.* Such a reading has never, to my knowledge, been undertaken with respect to any writer: never has literary history itself been viewed as an analytical object, as a subject for a psychoanalytic interpretation.[31] And yet it is overwhelmingly obvious, in a case like Poe's, that the discourse of literary history itself points to some unconscious determinations which structure it but of which it is not aware. What is the unconscious of literary history? Can the question of *the guilt of poetry* be relevant to that unconscious? Could literary history be in any way considered a repetitive unconscious *transference* of the guilt of poetry?

Literary history, or more precisely, the critical discourse surrounding Poe, is indeed one of the most visible ("self-evident") *effects* of Poe's poetic signifier, of his text. Now, how can the question of the peculiar effect of Poe be dealt with analytically? My suggestion is: by locating what seems to be unreadable or incomprehensible in this effect; by situating the most prominent discrepancies or discontinuities in the overall critical discourse concerning Poe, the most puzzling critical contradictions, and by trying to interpret those contradictions as symptomatic of the unsettling specificity of the Poe-etic effect, as well as of the necessary contingence of such an effect on the unconscious.

Before setting out to explore and to illustrate these two directions for research, I would like to recapitulate the primary historical contradictions analyzed at the opening of this study as a first indication of the nature of the poetic. According to its readers' contradictory testimonies, Poe's poetry, let it be recalled, seemed to be at once the most *irresistible* and the most *resisted* poetry in literary history. Poe is felt to be at once the most unequaled master of "conscious art" *and* the most tortuous unconscious case, as such doomed to remain "the perennial victim of the *idée fixe,* and of amateur psychoanalysis."[32] Poetry, I would thus argue, is precisely the effect of a deadly

31. I have attempted, however, an elementary exploration of such an approach with respect to Henry James in my essay, "Turning the Screw of Interpretation," in *Literature and Psychoanalysis: The Question of Reading—Otherwise,* *Yale French Studies* 55/56 (1977) : 94–138.

32. The formula is David Galloway's (Poe, p. 24).

struggle between consciousness and the unconscious; it has to do with resistance and with what can neither be resisted nor escaped. Poe is a symptom of poetry to the extent that poetry is both what most resists a psychoanalytical interpretation and what most depends on psychoanalytical effects.[33]

REFERENCES

Bonaparte, M. *Life and Works of Edgar Allan Poe.* Translated by J. Rodker. London: Imago, 1949.

Carlson, E. W., ed. *The Recognition of Edgar Allan Poe: Selected Criticism Since 1829.* Ann Arbor: University of Michigan Press, 1966. Essays referred to here:

    Cooke, P. P. "Edgar A. Poe" (1848).

    Eliot, T. S. "From Poe to Valéry" (1949).

    Higginson, T. W. "Poe" (1879).

    Huxley, A. "Vulgarity in Literature" (1931).

    Lowell, J. R. "Edgar Allan Poe" (1845).

    Rourke, C. M. "Edgar Allan Poe" (1931).

    Shaw, G. B. "Edgar Allan Poe" (1909).

    Wilson, E. "Poe at Home and Abroad" (1926).

    Winters, I. "Edgar Allan Poe: A Crisis in American Obscurantism" (1937).

Krutch, J. W. *Edgar Allan Poe: A Study in Genius.* New York: Knopf, 1926.

Lacan, J. "The Seminar on *The Purloined Letter.*" Translated by J. Mehlman. *French Freud, Yale French Studies* 48 (1972).

Poe, E. A. *Edgar Allan Poe: Selected Writings.* Edited by D. Galloway. New York: Penguin, 1967.

Stovall, F. *Edgar Poe the Poet. Essays New and Old on the Man and His Work.* Charlottesville: University Press of Virginia, 1969.

33. The present essay constitutes the introduction to a more extensive study entitled: *Poetry and Psychoanalysis: The Future of Repetition* (to be published).

6

Border Territories of Defense:
Freud and Defenses of Poetry

MARGARET W. FERGUSON

Having now repelled the objections that have been raised
against us, or having at least indicated where our defensive
weapons lie, we must no longer postpone the task of setting about the psychological investigations for which we
have so long been arming ourselves.
                                    —Freud, *Interpretation of Dreams*

Alas, Love, I would thou couldst as well defend thyself as
thou canst offend others.
                                    —Sidney, *A Defence of Poetry*

This essay asks two questions: how can Freud's writing, as a
rhetorical praxis as well as a metapsychological theory of defense, illuminate those curious moments in literary history
which consist of "defenses of poetry"? and how can literary
defenses illuminate Freud's writing? To ask these mirror questions is to attempt to steer a passage between two temptations:
the Scylla of regarding Freud's work as the locus of a theory
which can simply "explain" literary texts; and the Charybdis of
using literature, or techniques of rhetorical analysis, simply to
"expose" problems in Freud's writing.[1] It is particularly necessary to mention these temptations when one proposes, as I do

1. For a discussion of the need to "reinvent" the mutual relation between
psychoanalysis and literature in a way that subverts the opposition "mas-
tery/slavery," see Shoshana Felman's introduction to *Literature and Psychoanalysis, Yale French Studies,* no. 55/56 (1977).

here, to draw connections between texts which are explicitly concerned with master-slave relations between fields of knowledge.

I described defenses of poetry as "moments" in literary history, and before going any further I should explain that choice of term. It was dictated by necessity, for defenses elude classification according to normal critical categories. Indeed, defenses can best be described as "boundary creatures"—which is a metaphor Freud used to characterize the ego.[2] A brief discussion of defenses as boundary creatures can lead us to see how the questions they raise for the field of literary study are related to questions Freud raised about the ego and its defenses.

The first kind of boundary that defenses of poetry call into question is that which defines a textual "unit." Sidney and Shelley wrote well-known defenses of poetry that are published as entire texts; but in their form as well as their content these works exist as parts of a dialogue whose boundaries are hard to trace. As defenses, they necessarily reply to a prosecution which is "inside" as well as "outside" the rhetorical space of defense. Many works of literature and criticism allude to, or even quote, other works in a way that raises questions about the notions of formal and conceptual "self-containment," but defensive essays like Sidney's and Shelley's point to such questions in a particularly insistent way both in their dialogic rhetoric and in their thematic concern with the relation between parts and wholes.

Many defenses of poetry are in fact parts of texts, often marginal parts like prefaces or postscripts. The preface and final two books of Boccaccio's *Genealogia Deorum Gentilium,* for instance, constitute a defense which has been translated and published as *Boccaccio on Poetry.*[3] Since Boccaccio meditates ob-

2. The metaphor of the *Grenzwesen,* the "frontier" or "boundary" creature, appears in *The Ego and the Id* (1923), p. 56. All citations of Freud's works are to the *Standard Edition;* for the original German I have consulted the *Gesammelte Werke* (London: Imago, 1940–52).

3. The entire *Genealogia,* which Boccaccio worked on from roughly 1340 until his death in 1375, has never been translated into English. Charles Osgood's *Boccaccio on Poetry,* an annotated translation of the Preface and Books 14 and 15, is the text cited throughout this essay.

sessively on the problem of textual disunity (his fears that his readers will seize his book "with their impious jaws and tear it to pieces" are clearly related to his anxiety about his general project, which is to gather the "fragments" of ancient pagan myths), the critic who excerpts a theoretical defense from Boccaccio's work should at least be aware that he or she is performing an act Boccaccio views as "impious."[4]

If defenses raise questions about the boundary between textual wholes and parts, they also tend to erase the boundary between imaginative and critical discourse. Sidney's and Shelley's texts may be included in anthologies of literary criticism (in the special category of "poets' theories" about which professional critics are so often ambivalent), but both authors define poetry as a realm that would include not only their own prose essays, but also many works of philosophy and history—two traditional "enemies" of poetry. "Poetry," Sidney writes, "is an act of imitation, for so Aristotle termeth it in his word mimesis, that is to say, a representing, counterfeiting, or figuring forth."[5] And for Shelley "poetry, in a general sense, may be defined to be 'an expression of the imagination.' "[6] Such inclusive definitions, as we shall see, are related to the *tu quoque* argument that defenders of poetry frequently, use against poetry's rivals; the argument consists of calling attention to the rhetorical nature of all writing, when rhetoric is understood both as a use of tropes and as a will to persuade. For the moment, however, let us explore the implications of this boundary extension for the field of literary study. Such inclusive definitions of poetry blur not only the distinction between imaginative and critical writing, but also a distinction which plays an important role in

4. Boccaccio, p. 17. The metaphor of the torn body, which Boccaccio first employs when he portrays himself as "another Asculpius restoring Hippolytus" (p. 13), appears also in his anxious discussion of his religious integrity; his faith is "implanted" so deeply in his heart, he insists, "that by no influence of pagan antiquity . . . can it be torn out, or cut off, or fall away" (p. 127).

5. *A Defence of Poetry* (written ca. 1580, first published in 1595), *Miscellaneous Prose of Sir Philip Sidney*, ed. Katherine Duncan-Jones and Jan Van Dorsten, pp. 79–80.

6. *A Defense of Poetry* (written 1821, first published in 1839), ed. John E. Jordan, p. 26.

modern critical ideology: that between "aesthetic" and "pragmatic" discourse.

If a defense of poetry is an *example* of the phenomenon it
defends, then the forces of "pragmatic" rhetoric infiltrate the
realms both of literary art and of literary theory. Consider the
case of Ovid. During his banishment in Austria he wrote a book
of elegies, the *Tristia*, whose second poem is a defense of poetry
in general—and also of one poem in particular, the *Ars Amatoria* which had been accused of teaching immorality to the la-
dies of Rome.[7] The defense is addressed to the Emperor
Augustus, who had banished Ovid, and it is clearly an example
of what one modern critic calls "impure persuasion," which
occurs when poetry (not to mention a discourse about poetry) is
used to further egotistical aims.[8]

The astonishing thing is not that poetry should be so used,
but that such uses should offend modern critics. Walter Ong,
for instance, refers to a conflation of poetry and rhetoric as a
"monster" born in certain benighted eras of literary history;
and O. B. Hardison employs similarly charged language when
he discusses the "error" of Renaissance poetic theories which,
like Sidney's, insist on poetry's power to shape a reader's attitudes and actions.[9] "The notion that art must be free of the

7. Ovid, like other classical defenders of poetry (e.g., Plutarch, in the *Moralia*
essay "How the Young Man Should Study Poetry"), compares poetry to a drug
that can be either used or abused. He employs this "double-edged sword"
argument, derived from Aristotle's description of rhetoric (*Rhetoric* 1. 1 [1355
a–b]), to shift the blame for immorality from author to reader. See *Tristia II*, ll.
265 ff. (available in the Loeb Classical Library bilingual edition, tr. A. L.
Wheeler [New York: Putnam, 1924]).

8. See Richard Lanham, "*Astrophil and Stella:* Pure and Impure Persuasion,"
English Literary Renaissance 2, no. 1 (1972) : 100–15.

9. See Ong, "The Province of Rhetoric and Poetic," *The Province of Rhetoric*,
ed. Joseph Schwartz (New York: Ronald Press, 1965), p. 52; and Hardison,
"The Orator and the Poet: The Dilemma of Humanist Literature," *The Journal
of Medieval and Renaissance Studies* 1, no. 1 (1971): 44, 38. The deep suspicion of
rhetoric-as-persuasion in postwar American literary criticism is an ideological
phenomenon that I cannot discuss in detail. It has clearly shaped scholarly as-
sessments of works like Sidney's *Defence* (frequently accused of substituting rhetorical "charm" for "intellectual cogency"); I suspect that some critical responses to the work of Harold Bloom, whom a recent reviewer describes as a

practical functions for which oratory is responsible," Hardison writes, "allows us to recognize that all human activities have their proper spheres and also that the boundaries of those spheres cannot be overstepped without loss" (p. 44). Such critical views, which invoke the Kantian notion of a "disinterested" aesthetic realm, suggest that the desire to mark off a space for innocent art is related to the desire for an innocent criticism— one that would approach the ideal of an objective, scientific field of inquiry. Northrop Frye's "Polemical Introduction" to the *Anatomy of Criticism* neatly illustrates the connection between these desires. His call for a "scientific" criticism (for which adjective, he says, we may substitute "systematic" or "progressive"), goes hand in hand with, in fact depends on, his belief that literature is a "disinterested use of words" which can be distinguished "from the descriptive or assertive writing which derives from the active will and the conscious mind, and which is primarily concerned to 'say' something."[10]

By virtue of their very existence as textual moments that can be classified neither as disinterested art nor as disinterested critical theory, defenses of poetry put a position like Frye's on trial. But defenses like Boccaccio's, Sidney's, and Shelley's, which reflect on the aims and means of their own rhetoric, become active rather than passive advocates for what we might call the claims of the ego. "Self-love," Sidney writes at the beginning of his treatise, "is better than any gilding to make that seem gorgeous wherein our selves be parties" (p. 73). When defenses not only inhabit a border territory of "interested rhetoric" but explore it and attempt to extend its boundaries (by versions of the *tu quoque* argument, for instance), then they can be fruitfully compared to Freud's efforts to explore a similar (and at some places identical) territory. Freud's views on the possibility of a "disinterested" literature are well known: "The writer softens the character of his egoistic day-dreams by altering and disguising it" (*S.E.* 9 : 153). More interesting for

belated defender of poetry, are influenced by the same suspicion of rhetorical discourse. For Bloom as a "defender," see Joseph Riddel's review essay in *The Georgia Review* 30 (1976) : 989–1006.

  10. Frye, *Anatomy of Criticism* (New York: Atheneum, 1967), pp. 7–8, 4–5.

our purposes is the fact that Freud, both in his theory and in his rhetorical practice, acknowledges that the psychoanalyst is also an artist who "softens and disguises" the workings of his ego (which includes, of course, an unconscious portion). Freud's theoretical elaboration of the kinship between the observing and the observed subject (whether that subject is oneself or another) counters the notion that a "human science" can exist in the form envisioned by a critic like Frye, who asserts: "Literature is not a subject of study but an object of study: the fact that it consists of words makes us confuse it with the talking verbal disciplines" (pp. 11–12). Contrast this with Freud's description of the relation between observer and observed in *his* science:

> Every science is based on observations and experiences arrived at through the medium of our psychical apparatus. But since *our* science has as its subject that apparatus itself, the analogy ends here. We make our observations through the medium of the same perceptual apparatus, precisely with the help of the breaks in the sequence of 'psychical' events: we fill in what is omitted by making plausible inferences and translating it into conscious material. [*S.E.* 23 : 159]

There is, of course, more than a mere analogy between the analyst's observation of a "psychical apparatus" and the critic's observation of a text: both acts of observation are also productions, translations which substitute one verbal sequence for another. Freud, who developed his theory of interpretation by analyzing his own dreams as well as others'—indeed, by viewing his dreams as the products of that "other" within, the unconscious—points throughout his work to the possibility of error in interpretations made through the medium of our "perceptual apparatus" (*Wahrnehmungsapparat*). "The reproduction of a perception as a presentation is not always a faithful one; it may be modified by omissions, or changed by the merging of various elements." This sentence, from the paper on "Negation" (*S.E.* 19 : 238), provides a useful gloss on the notion of interpretation as a "filling in" of "what is omitted." Although

Freud insists on the "relative certainty" of psychoanalytic interpretation, it is worth remarking that his defenses of that relative certainty often presuppose a situation where the analyst
can "test" his conjectures against a patient's responses.[11] It may
be true, as Freud insists in his late paper on "Constructions in
Analysis," that an interpretive error "can do no harm" to a patient (*S.E.* 23 : 261); but the problem becomes more severe
when the analyst applies his constructions to a written text
which cannot talk back. I shall return to this problem with reference to Freud's interpretive labor in *Moses and Monotheism;*
here I want to suggest that Freud's theoretical acknowledgment
of the possibility of perceptual error points to a way of locating
the writer's activity in a general field of defense.

   This field is, I think, metaphorically mapped in a chapter of
Beyond the Pleasure Principle which contains a discussion of the
"perceptual apparatus." Because Freud describes that apparatus in terms of a "protective" function, and because he specifically relates the notion of protection against external threats to
the ego's task of defending itself against internal threats, the
chapter provides a useful way of thinking about textual defenses—including Freud's own—as "productions of the ego."
Defenses generally occur as responses to threats which may be
seen as coming from an "external world," and they also characteristically employ a "rhetoric of motives" to express wishes and
fears that may be said to come from within the authorial psyche. The distinction between "internal" and "external" in the
realm of textual defense is, however, no less complex than
Freud suggests it to be in the realm of psychic survival.

   Freud begins the "far-fetched speculations" of chapter 4 by
assigning to the conscious ego (the system *"Pcpt.-Cs."*) a "position in space": "It must lie on the borderline (*Grenze*) between
outside and inside; it must be turned towards the external
world and must envelop the other psychical systems" (*S.E.*

   11. See, for example, the descriptions of the analyst's ability to "confirm" his
interpretation in the essays on "Negation" (1925) and "Constructions in Analysis" (1937). The latter essay is especially interesting in its acknowledgment that
confirmation depends on "future developments" in the relation between analyst and analysand (*S.E.* 23 : 265).

18 : 24). He goes on to "picture" the psyche as a "living vesicle" with a "receptive cortical layer"; the outermost surface of this receptive layer consists of a "membrane" (*Rinde*) which has been "baked through" so that it becomes a "protective shield against stimuli" (*Reizschutz*) (pp. 26–27). Freud powerfully indicates the need for this shield by comparing the psyche to "a little fragment of living substance . . . suspended in the middle of an external world charged with the most powerful energies." Without its shield, the organism would perish, and Freud portrays the shield as a sacrificial victim:

> By its death, the outer layer has saved all the deeper ones from a similar fate—unless, that is to say, stimuli reach it which are so strong that they break through the protective shield. *Protection against* stimuli (*Reizschutz*) is an almost more important function for the living organism than *reception of* stimuli (*Reizaufnahme*). [p. 27]

Freud distinguishes between the ego's relation to the external world and its relation to its own "deeper layers" on the grounds that there can be no "protective shield" against internal stimuli: "The excitations in the deeper layers extend into the system directly and in undiminished amount, in so far as certain of their characteristics give rise to feelings in the pleasure-unpleasure series" (p. 29). But this distinction, drawn to support the point that "feelings of pleasure and unpleasure . . . predominate over all external stimuli," is immediately qualified. The ego which lacks a shield against internal threats may, Freud suggests, create one by a substitutive operation:

> [A] particular way is adopted of dealing with any internal excitations which produce too great an increase of unpleasure: there is a tendency to treat them as though they were acting, not from the inside, but from the outside, so that it may be possible to bring the shield against stimuli into operation as a means of defence (*Abwehrmittel*) against them. This is the origin of *projection*, which is destined to play such a large part in the causation of pathological processes. [p. 29]

This passage could be studied as a metapsychological *prise de position* no less complex than that of *Inhibitions, Symptoms and Anxiety*, where Freud tortuously reflects on the problem of whether anxiety is to be regarded as "transformed libido" or as a reaction to situations of external danger.[12] For our purposes, the chapter's interest lies in the way it sketches a field of defense which has two "frontiers" but which is occupied by a creature capable of treating one frontier "as though" it were the other. We should note, moreover, that the metaphorical operation Freud ascribes to the psyche is very like the one he performs throughout his work when he uses the term *defense* to treat an internal world "as though" it were an external one.

Armed with Freud's metaphorical map of a defensive territory on the border between an internal and an external realm, let us turn to some case studies. I shall focus on the relations between Freud and the defenses by Boccaccio, Sidney, and Shelley, since these texts attempt to justify literature as a general field of knowledge. They do, to be sure, employ rhetorical devices and lines of argument that are similar to those employed by writers—and lawyers and judges—who defend particular literary works against actual political attacks.[13] The "general" defenses are, however, most interesting for our purposes because they respond to attacks which come chiefly from the realm of social judgment; this is an ideological realm whose most prominent citizens are authoritative texts, like Plato's *Republic*. Although Boccaccio, Sidney, and Shelley know that a hostile climate of opinion affects writers materially (one need not be banished, or subject to the censoring power of an Inquisition, to feel that attacks on poetry are "real"), the primary aim of their defenses is to change negative opinions rather than to argue against specific political charges. These defenses there-

12. For a summary of Freud's shifting views on this question, see the editor's introduction to *Inhibitions, Symptoms and Anxiety* (S.E. 20 : 77–86).

13. The lawyer Sénard's defense of Flaubert's *Madame Bovary* in the 1857 civil trial, for example, or Judge John Woolsey's decision in the 1933 *Ulysses* case, could be usefully compared to defensive texts such as Ovid's *Tristia II* or Cicero's speech *Pro Archia Poeta*.

fore occur in a cultural court whose nature is well described by the Jewish founder of a socially offensive science.

In the *New Introductory Lectures,* Freud defines "prejudice" as an "after-effect" of official judgment (*S.E.* 22 : 137); he is referring specifically to the judgment "that was formed upon the young psycho-analysis by the representatives of official science." That judgment continues to have material effects: "You must not expect to hear . . . that the struggle about analysis is over and has ended in its recognition as a science and its admission as a subject for instruction at universities" (p. 138). But Freud is also concerned with immaterial effects, the "polite forms" of prejudice as they appear in conversation and—significantly—in novels, texts which presume to show mastery over Freud's field. If you take up "a German, English or American novel," Freud says, you will often come across "facetious" remarks about psychoanalysis, remarks "intended by the author to display his wide reading and intellectual superiority." Freud compares such remarks to those made in social gatherings: "You will hear the greatest variety of people passing their judgement on [psychoanalysis], mostly in voices of unwavering certainty. It is quite usual for the judgement to be contemptuous or often slanderous or at the least, once again, facetious" (p. 136). Freud goes on to describe the situation of one who is being tried in such a court of opinion to that which occurred during the Middle Ages, "when an evil-doer, or even a mere political opponent, was put in the pillory and given over to maltreatment by the mob" (p. 137). The historical analogy is then extended to include a not-so-distant past, that time when Freud himself was "more or less alone" as the founder of psychoanalysis; and he now considers the tactics a victim of prejudice should *not* employ. "There was no future in polemics," he asserts; and "it was equally senseless to lament and to invoke the help of kindlier spirits, for there were not courts to which such appeals could be made" (pp. 137–38).

Freud dismisses polemics and appeals for aid as *ineffective* means of defense, but we shall see that he uses subtle versions of both tactics. In so doing, he practices a mode of rhetorical defense that we can observe also in Boccaccio's, Sidney's, and

Shelley's texts. This defense involves a complex double movement of attack and courtship, and its aim is not so much to win
a verdict of "innocent" as to lead the prosecution to see that in
some sense it shares the defendant's situation. The aim, in
other words, is to promote *recognition*. The prosecution addressed by such defensive rhetoric includes not only rival cultural authorities (particularly prior texts) but the author's general image of his audience—all those whom he wants to
persuade. This image is created, I think, by a complex process
of introjection and projection. In literary defenses, the audience often seems to be a product of the author's own "court of
conscience"; some of the attacks to which Boccaccio replies, for
instance, sound very like the voices of an "over-noisy" superego.[14] The longest chapter of his work, entitled "That it is not a
deadly sin to read the poets," is a dramatic (and to modern
eyes, nearly comic) example of defensive rhetoric addressed
to a judge who speaks from within as well as from without:
"I grant for the moment what is in reality untrue, that poets
describe all manners of crime. What of it? They were Gentiles
who knew not Christ. . . . Yet I grant freely that it would be
far better to study the sacred books than even the best of these
poets" (p. 81). This passage is, in Donne's phrase, a "dialogue
of one," and it is only a more extreme version of a kind of
dialogue we find in other defensive texts, where the prosecution includes the author in his role of audience·to, and judge
of, his own verbal productions.

With this notion of a composite prosecution in mind, let us
return to Freud and the passage in which he describes his situation in a "court of no appeal." Deciding that polemics were
useless, he tells us that he "took another road." "I made a first
application of psycho-analysis by explaining to myself that this
behaviour of the crowd was a manifestation of the same resistance which I had to struggle against in individual patients"
(*S.E.* 22 : 138). Freud here universalizes the phenomenon of

14. I borrow the phrase "court of conscience" from Kenneth Burke's discussion of the "inferiority complex" in *A Rhetoric of Motives* (New York:
Prentice-Hall, 1950), pp. 281–82. Freud discusses the workings of the "over-
noisy" super-ego in *The Ego and the Id* (*S.E.* 19 : 51).

offensive prejudice by viewing it as a *defense* employed by all psyches. His own move is at once an offense and a defense: it masters the opposition's views not by refuting them but by explaining their origin; and that act of "explaining *to myself*" defends Freud by suggesting that nothing specific in his character, or in his science, has *merited* censure. The "cause" of attack is not in the defendant but in the offenders' psyches.

Freud's own phrasing suggests that psychoanalytic theory here serves a defensive function. In his book *The Ordeal of Civility*, J. M. Cuddihy has argued, indeed, that Freud's entire metapsychology should be seen as an elaborate defense against the problems that Jews faced in bourgeois Christian society. "Freud transformed various social offenses against the *goyim* into various psychological defenses against the id," Cuddihy writes.[15] His argument is interesting but crude, not only because it assumes that a theory which can be used defensively is *merely* a defense, with no conceptual validity independent of its immediate sociological context, but also because it is reductive even as an account of what Freud does in a passage like the one discussed above. There Freud views his *opponents'* social offenses as psychological defenses, doing for the Christians the same thing Cuddihy sees him as doing for the Jews. He does, to be sure, ascribe to the enemies of psychoanalysis precisely the qualities often ascribed to psychoanalysis in particular and to Jews in general: earlier in the passage, he remarks that "there was no violation of . . . propriety and good taste, to which the scientific opponents of psycho-analysis did not give way" (*S.E.* 22 : 137). But this is a tactic defenders of poetry also employ, and in their texts, too, it often appears in conjunction with "universalizing" theories—theories which, while they lack the systematic scope of Freud's, serve as his does to shift attention from the alleged sins of the defendant to the character and motives of the prosecution. These are the *tu quoque* arguments mentioned at the beginning of this essay, and I shall illustrate them after looking at a passage by Boccaccio that offers a

15. Cuddihy, *The Ordeal of Civility: Freud, Marx, Levi Strauss, and the Jewish Struggle with Modernity* (New York: Basic Books, 1974), p. 7.

broader perspective than Cuddihy does on the problem of "social offense." The passage is particularly relevant to Freud because it defines the prosecution as a "mob" which bolsters its attack with appeals to culturally prestigious authority:

> They say poetry is absolutely of no account, and the making of poetry a useless and absurd craft; that poets are tale mongers, or in lower terms, liars; that they live in the country among the woods and mountains because they lack manners and polish. . . . Again and again they cry out that poets are seducers of the mind, prompters of crime . . . and then, without making any distinction, they prop themselves up, as they say, with Plato's authority to the effect that poets ought to be turned out of doors—nay, out of town. . . . [pp. 35–36]

This passage presents the poet's relation to society as a vicious circle: the poet offends social values (and Boccaccio interestingly associates a "lack of manners" with a threat to morals); society defends itself against the poet by threatening to expel him; and this defense paradoxically undermines the social standards which it purportedly protects. As Boccaccio implies, there is an illogical resemblance between the poet's offense of "living in the country" and "lacking manners," and society's unmannerly decision to turn the poet "out of doors—nay, out of town." The poet's dilemma resembles that which Cuddihy describes for late nineteenth-century Jews, the " 'pariah people' closed out from . . . respectable society" because they were "deemed wanting in respectability in the first place." [16]

The very resemblance between the poet's dilemma and the Jew's suggests that Cuddihy overlooks something important when he explains Freud's theory simply as a response to a particular historical situation. If Freud's science offended the "manners and morals" of his society, it constituted a threat similar to the one that many kinds of literature have constituted for various social orders; there seems to be something in both literature and psychoanalysis which *causes*, as well as reflects,

16. Ibid., p. 37.

social tensions.[17] Boccaccio shows that the poet's marginal position is produced not only by the social group's hostility toward one of its members but by the poet's own activity, which requires detachment from the group and, implicitly, from its norms of behavior and value. Poets, as Boccaccio explains, "seek their habitation in solitudes because contemplation . . . is utterly impossible in places like the greedy and mercenary market" (p. 55). The psychoanalyst also practices an art of contemplation that requires detachment from the social group and therefore may be perceived as threatening by those who feel themselves to be (critically) observed. Freud and defenders of poetry acknowledge, moreover, that their practices involve an unmasking or exposure of things that both ordinary and powerful members of society may wish to keep hidden. "Your own eyes cannot see yourself," Sidney wrote to Queen Elizabeth; his defense of poetry testifies to his awareness that the poet courts danger when he attempts to open a person's eyes to the "sack of his own faults . . . hidden behind his back" (p. 96).[18] Defenders of poetry and Freud admit that their arts constitute a threat; at the same time, they protest against society's hostile perception of them. The rhetoric of defense characteristically manifests the author's ambivalent desire to be both outside and inside the social group.

If you believe yourself to be in some sense guilty, the best strategy of defense is to make others see that they share your

17. On Freud's interest in deliberately subverting "the reticent manners and morals of the cultivated classes of the nineteenth century," see Philip Rieff, *Freud: The Mind of the Moralist* (New York: Viking, 1959), pp. 315–17. Cuddihy quotes Rieff and also Freud's remark to Joseph Wortis, "An analysis is not a place for polite exchanges" (pp. 32, 35), but refuses to consider the possibility that Freud's attack on "politeness" has philosophical as well as sociological significance. Cuddihy's approach to a "sociology of knowledge" might be contrasted with that of Leo Strauss in *Persecution and the Art of Writing* (Glencoe, Ill.: Free Press, 1952). Although Strauss does not mention Freud, his discussion of the "self censorship" writers employ against social censorship is relevant to any study of Freud's practice of defense.

18. Sidney's "Letter to the Queen" (a plea that she not endanger the "body politic" by marrying the French Catholic d'Alençon) was written about the same time as the *Defence of Poetry;* it is printed with the *Defence* in *Miscellaneous Prose,* pp. 46–57.

guilt. Defenders of poetry, as I have said, frequently resort to *tu quoque* arguments; "judge not, lest ye be judged," is the ambiguous plea and command which underlies these arguments. Boccaccio offers a relatively simple version of the "judge not" motif when he insists that poetry's opponents should "look to their own speciousness before they try to dim the splendor of others. . . . When they have made themselves clean, let them purify the tales of others, mindful of Christ's commandment to the accusers of the woman taken in adultery, that he who was without sin should cast the first stone" (p. 51). Boccaccio directs this argument explicitly to the philosophers ("If these disparagers still insist in spite of everything that poets are liars, I accuse the philosophers, Aristotle, Plato, and Socrates, of sharing their guilt" [p. 67]); he is more subtle when he addresses poets' most powerful enemies, the theologians. Those who condemn fiction, he writes, should realize that they thereby condemn "the form [of parable] which our Saviour Jesus Christ . . . often used when He was in the flesh" (p. 49). In such arguments Boccaccio does precisely what he says poetry's enemies do when they are threatened by one who differs from them: "It is a trait of abandoned characters to wish above all that others should be like them . . . in self defense" (p. 57).

It is hard to know whether Boccaccio consciously meant such a comment to apply to his own practice of self-defense. Sidney, however, bases his *tu quoque* arguments on a sophisticated analysis of the resemblance between his own practice—as an exercise of "self-love" aimed at gaining power over others—and the practices of the poet's opponents, notably the philosopher and the historian. Sidney presents the former as an amalgam of Puritan moralist and scholastic logician, and attacks him as a hypocrite whose claims to authority are based on vanity: the philosophers are "rudely clothed for to witness outwardly their contempt of outward things, with books in their hands against glory, whereto they set their names" (p. 83). The philosopher is a *writer*, Sidney reminds us, one whose desire for glory makes him resemble the poet. Sidney also accuses the historian of lacking self-knowledge, "better knowing how this world goeth than how his own wit runneth," (p. 83); and he emphasizes the way in which the historian's verbal art resembles the poet's. Far from being a reporter of facts, the historian is an "author" whose "greatest authorities are built upon the notable foundation of hearsay"; he has "much ado to accord differing writers and to pick truth out of their partiality" (p. 83).

These quotations illustrate a strategy Sidney employs throughout his treatise, a strategy of encircling the enemy to show him that he is also, like the poet, a rhetorician and a maker of fictions. Sidney's famous refutation of the charge that poets lie shows the degree to which he is interested less in proving the poet's innocence than in making others recognize their guilt. He argues that the poet is "of all writers under the sun . . . the least liar" because he, unlike his fellows, does not attempt to pass fictions off as the truth.

> The astronomer, with his cousin the geometrician, can hardly escape [lies] when they take upon them to measure the height of the stars. How often, think you, do the physicians lie, when they aver things good for sicknesses, which afterwards send Charon a great number of souls drowned in a potion before they come to his ferry? And no less of the rest, which take upon them to affirm. [p. 102]

The "rest" includes the philosopher and the historian, accused of lying to themselves as well as to others; thus Sidney stretches his net of *tu quoque* over all prestigious cultural discourses. By means of a universalizing theory about the nature of rhetoric, Sidney in effect tells poetry's opponents that they, like Molière's *bourgeois gentilhomme*, have been speaking prose fiction all their lives.

Sidney's arguments define a terrritory which the poet shares not only with his cultural rivals (those who compete, in Sidney's political metaphor, for the "title of princes" in the field of learning) but also with his audience in general, perceived as a social "body" that is hostile toward one of its members.[19] Be-

19. Sidney uses political metaphors throughout his text to dramatize the poet's struggle with his cultural rivals. See, for instance, his description of the historians who "either stole or usurped of poetry their passionate describing of the passions" (p. 75); later Sidney compares the philosophers (particularly

cause the defense aims to make others like the poet (in both senses of the verb) it employs a strategy of courtship as well as of attack. We can observe this double strategy at work in the story Sidney uses to illustrate "the strange effects of this poetical invention." The story, adapted from Plutarch's *Life of Coriolanus*, tells of the time Menenius Agrippa prevented civil war in Rome by calming the rebellious mob with a fable. The plebians, incensed against the patricians who controlled the city's food supplies, "divided themselves from the Senate with apparent show of utter ruin" (p. 93). Menenius Agrippa, chosen by his fellow senators to make peace, came to the people in the guise of "a homely and familiar poet," Sidney says, and offered them an admonitory fable about a body whose parts "made a mutinous conspiracy against the belly, which they thought devoured the fruits of each other's labour; they concluded they would let so unprofitable a spender starve" (p. 93). Menenius "applied" this fable so well that his listeners recognized the similarity between their mutiny against the Senate and the parts of the body's attack on the belly; by means of the fable and its interpretation, Menenius effected a "perfect reconcilement" between the warring parties. Menenius Agrippa is clearly an idealized figure of the poet, but critics have not noted that he is also a figure for Sidney himself, in his role of defender of poetry. Menenius defends the belly, the part of the body accused of being "an unprofitable spender." This phrase, which does not appear in Plutarch, suggests the similarity between the belly and poetry, which Puritans accused of being morally and materially "unprofitable."[20]

Like the orator-poet Menenius Agrippa, Sidney defends his

Plato) to "ungrateful prentices" who try to "overthrow" their "masters" (p. 107). Shelley's *Defense* also presents the poet as the rightful possessor of the "civic crown," and his text is also concerned with the theme of usurpation.

20. See, for example, Stephen Gosson's *Schoole of Abuse* (1579; reprinted London: Shakespeare Society, 1841): "No merveyle though Plato shut them [the poets] out of his schoole, and banished them quite from his commonwealth, as effeminate writers, unprofitable members, and utter enemies to virtue" (pp. 10–11). Sidney's adaptation of Plutarch's allegory to his own purposes is further suggested by his text's repeated descriptions of poetry as a "food for the tenderest stomachs" (p. 87; see also pp. 92–93).

class (an earlier passage refers to the "Senate of poets") against an audience's hostile perception. He, too, wants the members of a social "body" to perceive their mutual dependence, and his allegory implies that the audience will serve its own self-interest by recognizing the poet-belly's contribution to social health. Unlike Menenius Agrippa, of course, Sidney has no way of knowing whether his audience will interpret the parable and its plea for recognition correctly; it is therefore particularly interesting that he demonstrates the poet's power to master an audience by means of a dialogue in which both parties are present to each other's view. Boccaccio and Freud offer similar recognition stories in which a speaker transforms or "converts" his audience; by examining these figurative models of successful persuasion, we can approach the territory of defense that exists between the writer and his own medium of communication.

In Book 14, chapter 22 of the *Genealogia*, Boccaccio "addresses the enemies of poetry in hope of their reform" (p. 97). His exemplary enemy is King Robert of Naples (1278–1343), who until his sixty-sixth year "retained a contempt for Vergil, and . . . called him and the rest mere storytellers, and of no value at all" (p. 98). King Robert is an overdetermined symbol, for he represents not only a contemptuous reader but also the poet's chief cultural rivals: he was, Boccaccio notes, "a distinguished philosopher, an eminent teacher of medicine, and an exceptional theologian." The story Boccaccio tells is this: Petrarch, whom Boccaccio has earlier praised as "a perfect model of honorable and saintly living," went to Naples and offered an allegorical explanation of Virgil's poetry to Robert, who, when he heard the "hidden meaning," was "struck with amazement, and saw and rejected his own error; and I actually heard him say that he had never supposed such great and lofty meaning could lie hidden under so flimsy a cover of poetic fiction as he now saw revealed through the demonstration of this expert critic. With wonderfully keen regret he began upbraiding his own judgment and his misfortune in recognizing so late the true art of poetry" (p. 98). The editor notes that Boccaccio could not really have been present at this "conversion by conversation"; why, then, does he insist on having "actually heard"

King Robert's recantation? He is, I think, constructing a miniature miracle play, and he gives himself the role of "true witness." If he must bend the facts to do so, that is appropriate in
a defense of fiction which uses a fable as its weapon. The fable,
indeed, is modeled on those which Christian preachers traditionally employed to lead audiences to a truth "which eye cannot hear and ear cannot see" (as Bottom, parodying Saint Paul,
puts it in Shakespeare's *A Midsummer Night's Dream*).

Freud resorts to a similar fable of conversion in the *New Introductory Lectures;* the story is a kind of coda to the discussion
of the "court of no appeal" cited earlier in this essay, and it is, I
think, a subtle version of the defensive tactic Freud claimed was
useless to him: the "invocation" of "kindlier spirits." The story
(which, like Boccaccio's, is a "true" one) tells of the time when
Freud "succeeded in effecting a rapid conversion" in a "world-
famous critic's" opinion of psychoanalysis. The prologue, however, must come before the tale. Freud's convert belongs to a
group of "half- or quarter-adherents," people who form "a sort
of buffer-layer" (*Pufferschicht*) between psychoanalysis and its
crude enemies. The buffer-layer, Freud explains, consists of
those who

> allow the validity of some portions of analysis and admit as
> much, subject to the most entertaining qualifications, but
> who on the other hand reject other portions of it, a fact
> which they cannot proclaim too loudly. It is not easy to
> divine what determines their choice in this. It seems to
> depend on personal sympathies. One person will take ob-
> jection to sexuality, another to the unconscious; what
> seems particularly unpopular is the fact of symbolism. [p.
> 138]

This description of a "buffer-layer" recalls the metaphor of the
"protective shield" in *Beyond the Pleasure Principle;* the parallel is
striking because the people who form the buffer layer admit
only portions of psychoanalysis, just as the psyche's perceptual
apparatus admits only selected "stimuli" from the external
world. When Freud goes on to tell how he transformed one of
these "partial" opponents into an admirer of psychoanalysis, his

strategy can also be seen in light of the "protective shield" metaphor: he draws an outsider into the circle of psychoanalysis,
but only on the condition that the outsider relinquish a threatening part of himself—his claim to mastery, his stance of superiority. Freud's story, introduced to illustrate the point that
even those who have admirably "mastered" their own fields
should "suspend their judgment" when they confront psychoanalysis, not only converts an enemy to a friend, but also par-
tially divests him of his power of judgment.

The "rapid conversion" occurred, Freud says, when the
famous critic was past his eightieth year but "still enchanting in
his talk":

> You will easily guess whom I mean. Nor was it I who in-
> troduced the subject of psycho-analysis. It was he who did
> so, by comparing himself with me in the most modest fash-
> ion. 'I am only a literary man,' he said, 'but you are a natu-
> ral scientist and discoverer. However, there is one thing I
> must say to you: I have never had sexual feelings towards
> my mother.' 'But there is no need at all for you to have
> known them,' was my reply; 'to grown-up people those are
> unconscious feelings.' 'Oh! so *that's* what you think!' he said
> with relief, and pressed my hand. We went on talking
> together on the best of terms for another few hours. I
> heard later that in the few remaining years of his life he
> often spoke of analysis in a friendly way and was pleased at
> being able to use a word that was new to him—'repression.'
> [p. 139]

The center of this story is surely the moment of affective unity,
the pressing of hands. The moment occurs when (because?) the
critic accepts the role of pupil and is rewarded by having his
fears allayed. It is not clear why the critic should feel so re-
lieved to learn that he has unconscious desires, but it is clear
that his grateful response is symbolically significant. Psychoanalysis is a "unity from which elements cannot be broken off,"
Freud wrote; and his lecture is concerned not only with the people from other disciplines who accept only "portions" of psy-

choanalysis, but also with those from within Freud's circle who
have "branched off" (p. 143). "You have only to think of the
strong emotional factors that make it hard for many people to
fit themselves in with others or to subordinate themselves," he
writes a few pages later, explaining why the "secessions" of
pupils like Adler "cannot be used either for or against the validity of psycho-analytic theories" (p. 143).

Like Sidney and Boccaccio, Freud uses his conversion story
as a symbolic counter to reality. All three stories represent what
Sidney calls a "golden world": "the poet, disdaining to be tied
to any . . . subjection, lifted up with the vigor of his own invention, doth grow in effect another nature" (p. 78). Symbolism, which Freud termed the most "unpopular" (*unbeliebte*) part
of psychoanalysis, serves to transform the relation between defendant and prosecution into one between master and willing
pupil; hostility is replaced with admiration, disunity with what
Sidney calls "a perfect reconcilement." Rhetoric as persuasion
seems, for a moment, amiably married to rhetoric as a use of
tropes, since these portraits of successful persuasion are mo-
saics of figurative substitutions. But the master trope of these
stories—that which substitutes speaker for writer and audience
for reader—is what makes them only moments of truce in an
ongoing war. Unlike the speaker, the writer cannot have the
narcissistic gratification of being "recognized" by those whom
he addresses. Even if the recognition accorded to a speaker is
partial in an intellectual sense ("Oh, so *that's* what you think,"
says the interlocutor, and Freud's tone implies that the critic
may have learned a "new word," but not its meaning), the affective event of a contact is the important thing. This moment
of contact is absent in the relation between writer and reader;
and it is also absent in the relation between the writer and his
text. The conversion stories can be seen as defenses against this
double absence, but they exist in texts which meditate on the
ways in which "the fact of symbolism" is a double-edged sword.

Freud's *New Introductory Lectures* were never delivered orally.
In the preface Freud explains that "My age had . . . absolved
me from the obligation of giving expression to my membership
of the University (which was in any case a peripheral one) . . .

and a surgical operation had made speaking in public impossible for me. If, therefore, I once more take my place in the lecture room during the remarks that follow, it is only by an artifice of the imagination; it may help me not to forget to bear the reader in mind as I enter more deeply into my subject" (p. 5). This "artifice of the imagination (*Vorspiegelung der Phantasie*) is, one might say, doubly at work in the passage where Freud offers his metaphorical listeners a model dialogue between himself and a "literary man." "You will easily guess whom I mean," he begins, and he creates, with this sentence, an illusion of intimacy, inviting the listener-reader into the charmed circle of his conversation. But the reader, unless he is truly one of Freud's intimates, will not be able to guess the secret. A note in *The Standard Edition* (though not in the *Gesammelte Werke*), provides the omitted name and refers the curious reader to other texts—a letter to Fliess, a letter to Freud's niece Margit, and Ernest Jones's biography.

"It was Georg Brandes, the celebrated Danish scholar (1842–1927), for whom Freud had always had an admiration," the editor tells us, and when we trace the clues we learn, among other things, that in March of 1900 Freud heard Brandes give a lecture "on reading." "The subject," Freud tells Fliess, "was nothing out of the way, the lecture difficult, the voice harsh . . . but the man was refreshing" and spoke "raw home-truths" which "must have seemed pretty outlandish to the worthy Viennese."[21] Impressed by the lecturer, Freud sent a copy of the dream book to him. "So far there has been no response—perhaps he actually took it home to read." Twenty-five years later, during the meeting described in the *New Introductory Lectures,* Brandes did respond—to Freud's conversation and person, not to his book. In a letter to his niece, written after Brandes' death in 1927, Freud gives a slightly different account of the meeting; addressing an intimate audience, he emphasizes his humility toward a man who was not only a literary critic but an eminent Jew:

21. The quotation is from a letter of March 23, 1900, printed in *The Origins of Psychoanalysis,* trans. Eric Mosbacher and James Strachey (New York: Basic Books, 1954), p. 315.

> Probably it wasn't even a question of changing his mind, rather that psychology [psychoanalysis] had always been very alien to him and that . . . disarmed by my guileless- ness, he was ready to relinquish a prejudice where he was unable to form an opinion. He could not fail to realize how highly I respected him. When he modestly tried to take second place behind the 'scientist,' I pointed out to him his position among the descendants of our prophets.[22]

My purpose in quoting these supplementary texts is not to analyze Freud's story in light of them, but to reflect on their implications for the interpretation of defensive writing. Freud's story clearly does not give its readers the "whole" truth; we must approach that truth asymptotically, by going to other texts, and to other places in the lecture itself. This is the pro- cess a reader of Sidney's story must also undertake. I have argued elsewhere that to understand the meaning of the Men- enius Agrippa tale, we must look not only at a network of images in Sidney's treatise, but also at Plutarch's text and at other works by Sidney himself, including his letter to Queen Elizabeth and his poems about his fears of being an "unprofita- ble spender" of his "talents."[23] The nature of writing, as a tem- poral series of signs, prevents us from "recognizing" the au- thor's intention except in the mode of synecdoche: the part for the whole. Insofar as the author is also a reader, of others' signs as well as his own, he too is unable to recognize himself as a "whole" subject.

To explore this problem, I turn at last to Shelley, who offers a dialogue scene in which the interlocutors are pronoun "shifters" and in which the defendant's relation to his audience, to prior texts, and to his own tropes is one of always "partial" recognition:

> Let us for a moment stoop to the arbitration of popular breath, and usurping and uniting in our own persons the

22. *The Letters of Sigmund Freud,* ed. Ernst Freud, trans. Tania and James Stein (New York: Basic Books, 1960), p. 376.

23. See M. Ferguson, "Sidney's *A Defense of Poetry:* A Retrial," *Boundary* 7 (Winter 1979) : 61–95.

incompatible characters of accuser, witness, judge, and ex-
ecutioner, let us decide without trial, testimony, or form,
that certain motives of those who are "there sitting where
we dare not soar," are reprehensible. Let us assume that
Homer was a drunkard, that Virgil was a flatterer, that
Horace was a coward, that Tasso was a madman, that Lord
Bacon was a peculator, that Raphael was a libertine, that
Spenser was a poet laureate. It is inconsistent with this
division of our subject to cite living poets, but Posterity has
done ample justice to the great names now referred to.
Their errors have been weighed and found to have been
dust in the balance; if their sins were as scarlet, they are
now white as snow: they have been washed in the blood of
the mediator and the redeemer, Time. Observe in what
ludicrous chaos the imputations of real or fictitious crimes
have been confused in the contemporary calumnies against
poetry and poets; consider how little is, as it appears—or
appears, as it is; look to your own motives, and judge not,
lest ye be judged [pp. 75–76]

   With the phrase, "Let us . . . stoop"—a subjunctive locution
which creates a fiction of unity between author and reader—
the passage begins its protest against judgment. The metaphor
of stooping implicitly defines one party as higher than the
other; the fictional person initially represented by the pronoun
us belongs, evidently, to the same place in a spatial hierarchy as
the poets who are "there sitting where we dare not soar." By
the time the passage arrives at this quoted fragment, however,
"we" have been incorporated into the body of "incompatible
characters" which prosecutes the poets, so that the perspective
represented by the pronoun we changes from one that looks
down on the "popular breath" to one that looks up at the poets.
   The oscillation of perspectives figured in this passage can be
seen, first, as a response to a text that used imagery of height
and depth to define a hierarchy of cultural value. Thomas Love
Peacock's little pamphlet entitled The Four Ages of Poetry (1820)
argued that in an age of scientific progress,

the poetical audience will not only continually diminish in proportion of its number to that of the rest of the reading public, but will sink lower and lower in the comparison of intellectual achievement. . . . [T]he poet must still please his audience, and must therefore sink to their level, while the rest of the community is rising above it: we may easily conceive that the degraded state of every species of poetry will be as generally recognized as that of dramatic poetry has long been. . . .[24]

Peacock goes on to picture "mathematicians, astronomers, chemists, moralists, metaphysicians, historians, politicians and political economists," as occupying a "pyramid" in the "upper air of intelligence" from which they look down at the "modern Parnassus" and smile "at the little ambition and the circumscribed perceptions with which the little drivellers and mountebanks upon it are contending for the poetical palm and the critical chair."[25]

Although Peacock attacked poetry as a "mental rattle" with his tongue in cheek, facetiousness, for Shelley as for Freud, was offensive. "Your anathemas against poetry itself," Shelley wrote Peacock, "excited me to a sacred rage . . . of vindicating the insulted Muses."[26] Shelley promises to "break a lance" with Peacock, and he does so when he reverses Peacock's spatial hierarchy by portraying poets as "stooping" to popular judgment. This is clearly a stooping to conquer, but it paradoxically confirms Peacock's point that the poet is bound to his audience, to whose level he must "sink." Shelley insists, however, that if his text adopts, for a moment, his opponents' perspective, the gesture is not one of simple subservience; the "uniting" is also a "usurping."

Usurpation, indeed, is both a technique and a theme of Shelley's passage, which literally takes over the opposition's voice by

24. Peacock's *Four Ages of Poetry* is published with Shelley's *Defense* in the edition by John E. Jordan cited earlier; the quotation is from p. 20.

25. Ibid., p. 21.

26. The quotation is from a letter of February 15, 1821, cited by Jordan, p. ix.

quoting a fragment of poetry, "there sitting where we dare not
soar." This extraordinary ventriloquistic moment forces on poetry's enemies a quotation—or rather, a misquotation—of
words spoken by Milton's Satan to the "good angels" who have
found him trying to corrupt Eve in Eden. Elsewhere in the
Defense Shelley praises Milton's Devil as a "moral being . . . far
superior to his God" (p. 60). Shelley's effort to subvert both
Peacock and poetry's general enemies should be seen in light of
his "misprision" of Milton, which is clearly at work in the passage's irony toward "moral" attacks on poets. Shelley's well-
known view of Satan as a figure of imaginative liberty is, however, complicated in this passage, which alludes to a moment
when Satan is epistemologically as well as dramatically trapped
by others' view of him:

> "Know ye not then," said Satan, filled with scorn,
> "Know ye not me? Ye knew me once no mate
> For you, there sitting where ye durst not soar;
> Not to know me argues yourselves unknown,
> The lowest of your throng. . . ."
>
> [*Paradise Lost*, 4. 827–31]

"Know ye not me?" is the question which links Shelley's passage to the parables of recognition by Boccaccio, Sidney, and
Freud. But Shelley shows why the question cannot be affirma-
tively answered. In the very act of asking for recognition the
author hides himself in the tropes of language. Those readers
who already know poetry can, of course, decode the allusion
and see the analogy between the poet's situation and Satan's:
both experience crises of identity when confronted with an audience which knows them not. Shelley's and Milton's passages
present a subject whose self-knowledge, which lies in a sense of
superiority, is radically threatened in the moment when he sees
himself through others' eyes. But Shelley's passage deepens the
crisis by making the poet now "speaking" a part of the very audience that is looking at, but not recognizing, those "there sitting where *we* dare not soar." By substituting *we* for Milton's
pronoun *ye*, Shelley's text dramatizes the loss of identity that
occurs not only when the defendant identifies with the perspec-

tive of a hostile audience, but also when he identifies with another textual persona in a linguistic process which "'unites,'" and makes likenesses, only by "usurping" and making differences.

A couplet spoken by the German Satan, Goethe's Mephistopheles, can link Shelley's analysis of the defendant's dilemma with a passage in which Freud reflects on textual defense.

> Das Beste, was du wissen kannst
> Darfst du den Buben doch nicht sagen.

[The best of what you know may not, after all, be told to boys.]

These lines appear in the chapter "Distortion in Dreams" in *The Interpretation of Dreams*.[27] The couplet, which was one of Freud's favorites, seems a neat formula for expressing an author's sense of superiority toward his readers. Taken in context, however, the quotation suggests that Freud's superiority is ambiguously related to an actual or perceived inferiority—in the realm of power, if not of knowledge. Freud quotes Goethe during the course of explaining the phenomenon of "unrecognizable" wish-fulfillment in dreams:

> [I]n cases where the wish-fulfillment is unrecognizable, where it has been disguised, there must have existed some inclination to put up a defence against the wish; and owing to this defence, the wish was unable to express itself except in a distorted shape. I will try to seek a social parallel to this internal event in the mind. Where can we find a similar distortion of a psychical act in social life? Only where two persons are concerned, one of whom possesses a certain degree of power which the second is obliged to take into account. In such a case the second person will distort his psychical acts or, as we might put it, will dissimulate [*sie verstellt sich*]. The politeness which I practice every day is to a large extent dissimulation of this kind; and when I interpret my dreams for my readers I am obliged [*genötigt*] to

27. See the editor's note, *S.E.* 4 : 142 n. 1, for references to the other places where Freud quotes these lines from *Faust*, part 1, scene 4.

adopt similar distortions. The poet complains of the need
for these distortions in the words:

> Das Beste, was du wissen kannst,
> Darfst du den Buben doch nicht sagen.

[S.E. 4 : 141–42]

It is not hard to see in Freud's "social analogy" the traces of
the Jew's experience in bourgeois Christian culture. But
Freud's extension of the analogy ought to give us pause: "And
when I interpret my dreams for my readers I am obliged to
adopt similar distortions." This sentence and the quotation
which follows it define the relation between author and reader
in a paradoxical way. The reader is first likened to a socially
powerful person who "obliges" a weaker one to dissimulate; but
then the analogy is apparently turned upside down, as the
reader is likened to "boys" who are denied access to secret
knowledge. Who is the master here, who the servant? The passage works like an elaborate Jewish joke, whose turns of wit
flatter the reader, insult him, and then flatter him again. After
all, Freud *is* telling us a secret when he advises us that the text
we are presently reading is not the "whole" truth, only a part of
it.

This moment of metacommentary, with its shifty revelation
of the fact of concealment, works, I think, to undermine both
of the static "superiority-inferiority" models implied by the passage. According to the first model, the reader would be Freud's
superior in power, capable of "obliging" Freud to dissimulate
politeness. According to the second model, the reader would be
Freud's inferior in knowledge, incapable of hearing the master's secrets. Neither of these models can account for the moment when Freud tells the reader that his text dissimulates.

This moment is, I think, emblematic of a mode of defense
that occurs in a realm on the border between the psychic and
the social—a realm in which interpersonal relations are mediated by writing. The kind of dissimulation Freud obliquely
defines when he reflects on his textual practice can be compared to the dissimulation Sidney points to when he warns his

reader that "self-love is better than any gilding to make that seem gorgeous wherein ourselves are parties." This kind of dissimulation is different from the other two kinds mentioned in Freud's passage. The first, the dream distortion, is an unconscious process that occurs in an individual's psyche; the second is a conscious process that occurs when a socially weak person successfuly hides his feelings in an actual encounter with another person. The third kind of dissimulation, if one tries to define it in terms of the distinctions between unconscious and conscious or intrapsychic and interpersonal, would fall somewhere in the middle of the spectrum.

It is, I suggest, a "middle" or "boundary" mode of defense which is characteristic of acts of writing that are also readings or interpretations. Freud is, after all, describing a dissimulation that comes into being when he communicates to his readers what he himself has read from those prior texts that are his dreams. And his chapter indicates that the analyst's "sense organ" of consciousness is engaged in a theoretically interminable struggle against the "power" of the censoring agency, a power which prevents the self-interpreter from perceiving the whole meaning of the "data that arise elsewhere."[28]

I want to conclude by suggesting that the defenses examined in this essay at once perform and reflect on the crime of interpretive distortion. In addition to responding to cultural threats and manifesting desires for power and love, defensive writing defends against the guilt engendered by the tropological nature of writing itself. The "middle" mode of defense is, from this perspective, a defense against defense, when the latter is seen as distortion of meaning. Let me illustrate this hypothesis with examples from Boccaccio and Freud. At the beginning of this essay I mentioned that Boccaccio expresses his fear of his hostile readers by comparing his text to a body

28. See *S.E.* 4 : 144 for the discussion of the censoring agency's effect on the "sense organ" of consciousness; the censor's function as described here is, of course, similar to the function of the "protective shield" as described in *Beyond the Pleasure Principle,* except for the fact that the former filters internal data whereas the latter filters external stimuli.

that will be torn apart by "impious jaws." He also, however, shows that his own text performs a similar act of "tearing" on other texts. "I would warn you now," he tells his readers,

> not to expect that a work of this sort will have a body of perfect proportions. It will, alas, be maimed—not, I hope, in too many members—and . . . shrunken and warped. Furthermore . . . to arrange the members in any order, I must proceed to tear the hidden significations from their rough sheathing, and I promise to do so, though not to the last detail of the authors' original intentions. [p. 11]

These authors are the ancients who wrote the pagan myths Boccaccio is collecting. The "body" of his text, which is an effort to remember the past, is also, necessarily, a dismembering, for the effort to give ancient texts a "rebirth" is also a kind of killing. Boccaccio defends against this impiety by pointing to the "maimed" nature of his own text.

Boccaccio's enterprise invites comparison with the work in which Freud undertook a genealogy of *his* ancient gods, the sacred texts of Judaism. In *Moses and Monotheism,* Freud's remembering is also a dismembering; like Boccaccio, he must "tear the hidden significations from their tough sheathing," and he points to the guilt of such tearing in a description that applies not only to the biblical text but to his own:

> In its implications the distortion of a text resembles a murder: the difficulty is not in perpetrating the deed, but in getting rid of the traces. We might well lend the word '*Entstellung* [distortion]' the double meaning to which it has a claim but of which to-day it makes no use. It should mean not only 'to change the appearance of something' but also 'to put something in another place, to displace.' Accordingly, in many instances of textual distortion, we may nevertheless count on finding what has been suppressed and disavowed hidden away somewhere else, though changed and torn from its context. Only it will not always be easy to recognize it. [*S.E.* 23 : 43]

Freud's interpretation of the Bible does commit a kind of murder, but it defends against the murderer's guilt by *not* hiding the traces. Apologizing to his readers in the preface to part 2 (one of the three strange "prefaces" to this text), Freud writes that his method of exposition "is no less inexpedient than it is inartistic. I myself deplore it unreservedly. Why have I not avoided it? The answer to that is not hard for me to find, but it is not easy to confess. I found myself unable to wipe out the traces of the history of the work's origin" (p. 103). By not wiping out the traces of his textual repetition of the primal murder, Freud's exposition (*Darstellung*) names itself as a distortion (*Entstellung*) whose claim to truth is no less paradoxical than that offered by Touchstone in Shakespeare's *As You Like It*. In a miniature defense of poetry, Touchstone puns on the link between "feigning," as the making of fictions, and "faining," as desire. His speech, like Sidney's "paradoxical but true" argument that the poet is the "least liar" because he at least acknowledges his lies, does not establish the writer's innocence, but rather asks readers to see that they too are guilty of feigning:

> *Audrey:* I do not know what "poetical" is. Is it honest in deed and word? Is it a true thing?

> *Touchstone:* No, truly, for the truest poetry is the most feigning, and lovers are given to poetry; and what they swear in poetry may be said as lovers they do feign.

> [*As You Like It,* III. iii. 17–22]

REFERENCES

Boccaccio, G. *Boccaccio on Poetry.* Preface and Books 14 and 15 of the *Genealogia Deorum Gentilium.* Translated by C. Osgood. Princeton, N.J.: Princeton University Press, 1930. Reprinted, New York: Bobbs-Merrill, 1956.
Freud, S. *Standard Edition of the Complete Psychological Works.* London: Hogarth, 1953–74.
    The Interpretation of Dreams (1900–01), vols. 4, 5.

"Creative Writers and Day-dreaming" (1908), vol. 9.

Beyond the Pleasure Principle (1920), vol. 18.

The Ego and the Id (1923), vol. 19.

"Negation" (1925), vol. 19.

Inhibitions, Symptoms and Anxiety (1926), vol. 20.

New Introductory Lectures in Psycho-Analysis (1933), vol. 22.

Moses and Monotheism (1939), vol. 23.

"Constructions in Analysis" (1937), vol. 23.

An Outline of Psycho-Analysis (1940), vol. 23.

Shelley, P. B. *A Defense of Poetry.* Edited by J. E. Jordan. New York: Bobbs-Merrill, 1965.

Sidney, P. *A Defence of Poetry.* In *Miscellaneous Prose of Sir Philip Sidney.* Edited by K. Duncan-Jones and J. Van Dorsten. Oxford: Clarendon, 1973.

7

Literature and Repression: The Case of Shavian Drama

DAVID J. GORDON

I

Harold Bloom begins his *Poetry and Repression* by inverting the form of a question posed by Jacques Derrida: for Bloom, a literary critic rather than a philosopher, it is more fruitful to ask how a text can be represented by a psyche than to ask how a psyche can be represented by a text.[1] This change suggests why his theory of textuality, unlike Derrida's, is psychologically interesting. Derrida seeks to remove from the consideration of a text the hypothesis of a mind governing its meaning and accounting for its coherence. For him the text belongs not to literature, much less to its author, but to language: and language is not a unified field. Repression, in his view, signifies an absence in relation to a presence—the absence, for example, of the writer in relation to the presence of the written text. It is a dialectical conception but not, at least in a Freudian sense, a dynamic one.[2] Bloom's theory, on the other hand, is emphatically dynamic, indeed agonistic. It asks us to confront texts as collisions of psyches, and to find artistic meaning in these collisions.

1. H. Bloom, *Poetry and Repression: Revisionism from Blake to Stevens* (New Haven: Yale University Press, 1976), p. 1. J. Derrida, "Freud and the Scene of Writing," trans. J. Mehlman, *French Freud: Structural Studies in Psychoanalysis, Yale French Studies* no. 48 (1972), p. 76.
2. J. Derrida, *Of Grammatology,* trans. with introduction by G. C. Spivak (Baltimore: Johns Hopkins University Press, 1976).

A text perceived in relation to a parent text will seem to have distorted that text, and this distortion is understood as a repression of the knowledge of its indebtedness.

What Bloom as theorist illuminates above all is the paradox of originality. He is able to demonstrate, repeatedly and convincingly, that the ambitious poet can only discover his own voice by a twisting and turning struggle with the voices of the predecessors who have most deeply influenced him. Whether this struggle entails a process of repression (in the Freudian sense) I am inclined to doubt. Derrida's theory leads us away from both psychology and criticism into the reaches of epistemology and metaphysics; it can scarcely be said to bear on the questions of explication and evaluation, and indeed, Derrida frankly calls these activities empirical and rejects them precisely because, in his view, empiricism and philosophy are mutually exclusive. Bloom's theory much more closely engages the traditional questions of criticism, but its psychological premise is drawn not from Freud but from the Romantic poets and critics who have influenced him so profoundly: it is the premise of a collective rather than an individual mind, a collective mind identified with the universe of discourse.

Thus Bloom's quarrel with Derrida is to some extent a family affair. For both theorists, psyches may be said to exist wholly within an intertextual or rhetorical universe. Bloom strictly enforces an un-Freudian separation between the man as poet and the man as man. Along with Derrida, he adheres to Jacques Lacan's revisionary doctrine that Freud's unconscious must be thought of as linguistic in structure: "It is neither primordial nor instinctual; what is knows about the elementary is no more than the elements of the signifier."[3] There is no reality more fundamental than verbal representation, and so no importance in Freud's acknowledgment that unconscious reality can only be known through representation. Accordingly, Bloom uses psychoanalytic terms in a revisionary sense, particularly the term *repression*, which signifies in his work a rhetorical rather

3. J. Lacan, "The Insistence of the Letter in the Unconscious," in *Structuralism*, ed. J. Ehrmann (Garden City, N.Y.: Doubleday, 1970), p. 130.

than a psychological process, discoverable not in minds but in texts.

The intertextual approach to literature fostered by his theory certainly helps us gauge the originality of a particular text and thus contributes very usefully toward our understanding of its meaning. But when Bloom applies his theory to interpretation in the stricter sense and presents the collisions of psyches as the center of a text's meaning, he tends either to leave out too much (*how much* of Whitman can be understood as a reaction to Emerson, of *Moby Dick* as a reaction to Shakespeare and the Bible, of Yeats as a reaction to Blake and Shelley, of Shaw as a reaction to Ibsen?) or to strain for his evidence, as when he asserts that the image of "a blind man's eye" in *Tintern Abbey*— which is quite self-explanatory and appropriate in its context— is a definite and anxious allusion to Wordsworth's chief predecessor, the blind Milton.[4] Considering texts in themselves (or as expressions of their authors' minds) rather than in relation to other texts, we would surely wish to say that it is weaker poems that contain evidence, in their derivativeness, of an anxiety of influence, but that stronger poems (the only ones of interest to Bloom) transcend the circumstances of their creation, including their authors' battles with the styles of their predecessors.

For Bloom, repression not only is an inevitable feature of a strong poem but enriches rather than flaws the coherence of a text. This raises an important and perplexing question for critical theory. In what sense is an unconscious process evident within a highly integrated verbal field? The psychoanalytic rule that a patient should relax logical control over his speech is based on the assumption that highly integrated speech does not yield insight into the unconscious. Similarly, it seems to me, a text can only lead us to an intuition of a repressed idea when its coherence is flawed in a certain way—when, that is, its incoherence can be traced to inappropriately charged effects rather than to mere ineptness. We may then attempt to make sense of its "unintended" implications by linking them with an idea not expressed in the text and presumably repressed in the mind of

4. Bloom, *Poetry and Repression*, pp. 68–73.

the author. We have not thereby restored the text's coherence.
Rather, we have gone beyond the text, beyond the job of criticism proper, to explain what is not explicable by literary analysis alone.

Bloom was aware of this argument (presented at length in
my *Literary Art and the Unconscious*)[5] when he wrote *Poetry and
Repression* and in his first chapter offered this rebuttal:

> To say that a poem's true subject is its repression of the
> precursor poem is not to say that the later poem reduces to
> the process of that repression. On a strict Freudian view, a
> good poem is a sublimation, and not a repression. Like any
> work of substitution that replaces the gratification of pro-
> hibited instincts, the poem, as viewed by the Freudians,
> may contain antithetical effects but not unintended or
> counterintended effects. In the Freudian valorization of
> sublimation, the survival of those effects would be flaws in
> the poem. But poems are actually stronger when their
> counterintended effects battle most incessantly against
> their overt intentions. [p. 25]

I cannot here address all aspects of this compact statement, but
I must clarify the obscured term *counterintended*.

Opposing counterintention to "overt intention," Bloom puts
me in the unwelcome position of seeming to equate the coherence of a work with its overt intention, as if I would challenge
the truism that, in profound works of art, the artist creates a
richer network of implications than he is consciously or reflec-
tively aware of. The word *intention,* in reference to the meaning
of a work of art, cannot of course be understood so narrowly,
and no doubt the word itself—a source of much vexation in
modern criticism—connotes a more deliberate purposefulness
than we feel to be characteristic of an imaginative text. If, however, it be accepted as a way of suggesting a nonaccidental coherence, then we can use the word *counterintended* to describe
implications that are not congruous with any coherent interpre-

5. D. J. Gordon, *Literary Art and the Unconscious* (Baton Rouge: Louisiana
State University Press, 1976).

tation we produce. I used the word because I wanted to indicate that the implications leading us to the inference of a repressed idea are not simply the kind we might perceive at the
fringes of a loose artistic structure but the kind that jar against
or subvert what we supposed the work to be saying—just as the
repressed idea discovered in a psychoanalysis will appear alien
to the ego of the analysand. Thus, covert or antithetical implications may well be present in complexly coherent art—it is, in
fact, hard to imagine them absent—but unintended or counterintended implications necessarily flaw its coherence.

I therefore demur from the current critical practice of com-
mending a work of art's contradictoriness. Contradiction is a
logical error and should not be used to describe contrary attitudes within an artistic structure. In these cases we are dealing
not with logical contradiction but with psychological conflict
capable of generating those antithetical effects that are very
common in good art and entirely compatible with the idea of its
overall coherence or intention.

I propose in the following pages to illustrate these two kinds
of cross-implications (antithetical and counterintended) by discussing a particular imaginative oeuvre as successive representations of inner conflict. When the conflicting attitudes energized in Shaw's plays are contained in their structures, we
need not invoke the concept of repression, except as a potential
danger which the artist has successfully offset. When they are
unbalanced, when there are inappropriately charged effects,
we may suggest that a certain idea, as it moved toward expression in the artist's mind, proved frightening and underwent
repression, causing the emotional charge upon it to become attached to another, often an opposite, idea.[6] The mode of analy-

6. As Freud carefully explained, we cannot accurately speak of a repressed
emotion, only of a repressed idea: "It is surely of the essence of an emotion
that we should be aware of it, i.e., that it should become known to consciousness. Thus the possibility of the attribute of unconsciousness would be completely excluded as far as emotions, feelings and affects are concerned. But in
psycho-analytic practice we are accustomed to speak of unconscious love, hate,
anger, etc., and find it impossible to avoid even the strange conjunction, 'unconscious consciousness of guilt', or a paradoxical 'unconscious anxiety'. Is

sis to be pursued is not really unconventional but is focused
more than is customary on the affective danger points in work
that has risked a certain depth of feeling. Such a procedure
ought to sharpen our appreciation for the psychological
achievement of strong art. Lapses testify to the great difficulty
we all have in adequately understanding our own affections;
coherence, combined with force, is a triumph against odds.

II

The typical conflict in Shavian drama has often been described as a conflict between realists and idealists. The terms
are taken from *The Quintessence of Ibsenism* but prove confusing
when applied. For one thing, the realist is clearly an idealist in
the more familiar sense of that word. For another, the heroic
realist must confront not only the deceived idealist but also the
self-possessed commonsensical figure that *The Quintessence* recognizes only with the harsh term *Philistine.* Furthermore, in the
middle and later plays, both forces are often present in the
same figure. The typical conflict, then, is better described as an
opposition between heroic realism, always vulnerable because
of its isolation and rejection of common pleasures, and pragmatic realism, itself always vulnerable because of its compromise with social hypocrisy. The one, epitomized by Don Juan,
seeks its ethical goal in greatness; the other, like the Devil, in
happiness.

The movement of a play by Shaw is usually generated by a
desire to transcend sensuality and marriage, to sublimate eros
so that the mind can embrace a higher idea of unity, imagined

there more meaning in the use of these terms than there is in speaking of 'unconscious instincts'?

"The two cases are in fact not on all fours. In the first place, it may happen
that an affective or emotional impulse is perceived but misconstrued. Owing to
the repression of its proper representative it has been forced to become connected with another idea, and is now regarded by consciousness as the manifestation of that idea. If we restore the true connection, we call the original affective impulse an 'unconscious' one. Yet its affect was never unconscious; all that
had happened was that its *idea* had undergone repression." S. Freud, "The Unconscious," *Standard Edition of the Complete Psychological Works* (London:
Hogarth, 1957), 14 : 177–78.

as a socialist community or as political mastery or as a supreme creative force. The plays repeatedly gather energy from their scorn of "romance," a Victorian code word for sensuality. But what immediately becomes interesting here—and points to an abiding psychological conflict—is that the energy of repudiation is itself romantic and strongly marked by sensual striving.

The word *romance* is peculiarly unstable throughout Shaw's work: it keeps slipping away from his scorn of it to become associated with opposite, heroic attitudes. Shaw could not simply deny sensuality or victory would be hollow, but he could not simply indulge it without arousing anxiety. On the one hand, he did not want (like his degraded Puritan, Mrs. Dudgeon) to make a vice of pleasure and a virtue of self-denial. But on the other hand, he could not imaginatively accommodate sex and marriage to the heroic vision. How to separate the sensual from the heroic without losing pleasure—that was the problem, a problem at once dramaturgical and psychological. We may go one step further and suggest that the source of this problem was Shaw's idealization of his incestuous attachment to his mother, an inference based not only on the biographical record but also on the fact that the plays keep throwing up and trying to integrate the crucial image of a powerful, all-incorporating woman.

A selection of the fifty-odd plays that Shaw wrote between 1892 and 1950 may be freshly though briefly discussed as attempts to find original expression for this basic conflict. Given the emotional and artistic difficulty of the effort, it is not surprising that the period of his highest achievement required some stumbling preparation and that the plays weakened toward the end. We can usefully group as early plays (*Widowers' Houses* through *The Devil's Disciple*) those that show an uncertain but increasingly authoritative command of this conflict; the plays of the middle period (*Man and Superman* through *Back to Methuselah*) are the richest imaginings of conflict and resolution; and in the late plays we shall notice not so much a loss of vivacity as a slackening of tension, a certain complacency and facility that indicate shallow rather than actively repressed emotion.

III

The protagonist of Shaw's first play, *Widowers' Houses,* is offended by the discovery that his fiancée's father is a slum landlord and asks the lady (Blanche), without benefit of explanation, to live on his income alone. But soon Harry Trench is robbed of the moral luxury of his quixotic gesture by learning that this money derives from precisely the same source. The father explains that he serves Trench just as he is served by his unsavory rent collector. "Do you mean to say that I am just as bad as you are?" asks the discouraged young man. To which Blanche's father coolly replies: "You mean that you are just as powerless to alter the state of society." Trench is not ready to accept the higher moral position implied by the idea of a reformed society and hinted at by the titular allusion to Christ's condemnation of men who "devour widows' houses" while clothed in respectability. When his hand is forced, he accepts the hypocrisy, is reunited with Blanche, and exits with her and the others, conspiratorially, to dinner.

What is particularly interesting in this play from our point of view is the sexual energy Shaw assigns to Blanche (the first of a line of heroines who are vital rather than refined) and his difficulty in containing it dramatically. Even in act 1 he had trouble keeping her in check and toned down an earlier version of her initial lovemaking with Trench, but when she is finally enlightened, she becomes a veritable *femme feroce,* raging at her maid and at her lover himself for not telling her at once about his unwillingness to take her tainted money. Then "she crushes him in an ecstatic embrace." Shaw gives her greater strength than the scene requires, and she seems to leap beyond the frame that contains the other characters. The lover is quite paralyzed by her ferocity, and we are puzzled by it. There is surely some idea kept out of the play to which this excessive emotion would have been fittingly attached. But the playwright will soon learn to contain his vital woman more successfully both by modifying her strength and by boosting the strength of those she confronts.

Mrs. Warren's Profession is the first of Shaw's plays in which a heroic position is clearly defined—not merely as the unmasking of illusion but as the taking up of higher ground. In the first of two major confrontations between Vivie and Mrs. Warren, the daughter succumbs to her mother's cogent argument justifying her dubious profession. Mrs. Warren is one of those conscious hypocrites whom her creator respects for getting what she wants from a corrupt society by learning how to play its game. But there are several indications of superior strength in Vivie which suggest the tentativeness of Mrs. Warren's victory; and, in the climatic confrontation, daughter rejects mother, not for having become a prostitute or even for having continued as a procuress after gaining sufficient means, but because the mother has remained at heart a conventional moralist.

This is not a facile victory. Mrs. Warren makes a strong point in saying, "God help us if everyone took to living without hypocrisy." It is dangerous to defy social morality with an individual code. As John Tanner will wittily put it, "It is dangerous to be sincere unless you are also stupid," and Vivie is not stupid. She risks the danger and repudiates the morality of her mother's society (the holiness of property, the absolute rights of parents over children, and so forth), rising to the rhetorical height of God instructing Job: "My ways are not your ways." The allusion has been earned and is dramatically strong.

The chief problematic aspect of this admirable play is most evident at the end, when Vivie's moving and effective rejection of her mother somehow entails her far less convincing rejection of Frank. And not merely of Frank as a particular suitor—for his idleness has been made clear—but of what he represents: love's young dream, romance, sexual love, marriage. The fudging of the incest question earlier in the play is part of this problem. Shaw tries to suggest, as a Shelleyan moralist, that consanguinity is merely an artificial barrier to sexual love, and that, even if it could be definitely established in this case, it would not matter to these independent-minded young people. But it does matter to them. After the revelation, Vivie says earnestly what she would not have said before, that "the brother-sister relationship is the only one I care for," and at the final curtain, when she sits as if forever with her actuarial tables,

there is a distinct impression of overkill, of heroic stature purchased at the price of a more thorough renunciation than Shaw
meant to suggest.

I pass over the charming *Arms and the Man,* the first of the
plays to give full expression to Shaw's comic genius, and turn
next to *Candida* because it is centrally concerned with conflicting attitudes toward love and marriage. The directness of its
address to this charged subject marks it as a notable advance in
Shaw's development, yet—and probably for the same reason—
it is the most thoroughly problematic of the early plays, the one
most flawed (with the possible exception of the weaker *Philan-
derer*) by inconsistent effects.

There is a discrepancy between Shaw's judgment of each of
his three major characters and what he shows them to be.
Marchbanks is the poetical character incarnate, modeled on
Shelley (whom Shaw much admired), but he is not convincing
either as poet or lover. Although he does show force and acute-
ness in his perception of the hidden weakness of his rival's marriage, and perhaps a touch of authentic Shelleyan yearning
("Love is like a ghost: it cannot speak unless it is first spoken
to"), his pseudo-Romantic language and excessive fastidi-
ousness become embarrassing. The much discussed secret in
the poet's heart is a problem indeed, but not because it is ambiguous. There can be little doubt that it signifies, as Shaw
often said it did, the higher experience of creative joy enabling
the poet to do without, though he may yearn for, the common
satisfaction of bourgeois marriage. What makes the secret a
problem is simply that the play does not sufficiently support
such a heroic view of Marchbanks.

Nor does the characterization of Morrell do justice to Shaw's
sincere commitment either to socialism or to the spirit of Protestant Christianity. The description of him—"vigorous, genial,
popular, goodlooking . . . with pleasant hearty manners and a
sound, unaffected voice"—implies more charm and less pom-
posity than we find in the actual role. His sermons and orations
turn out to be effective only in inspiring the adoration of
women like his secretary and of men like his curate. The play
does occasionally (for example, at the first- and second-act cur-

tain) demonstrate his basic honesty and dignity, but for the
most part he is as vulnerable to his wife's deflation as is Marchbanks. Candida calls him a "silly boy" and belittles his sermons
("mere phrases you cheat yourself with"), just as she calls
Marchbanks "a bad boy," and scorns both his poetry, which
bores her, and his amorous pretension: "Do you call that a
man?"

Candida herself is the most serious inconsistency in the play.
Shaw associates her with Titian's Virgin Mother—an image, he
wrote Ellen Terry, one never tires of adoring.[7] "An amused
maternal indulgence" is supposed to be her "characteristic expression," and her "serene brow, courageous eyes, well set
mouth and chin" are said to indicate a largeness of mind and
dignity of character that ennoble her manipulation of the rivals. But all this is hardly consistent with her contempt and
condescension. Shaw admired her both too much and too little,
not fully understanding either feeling. In short, neither the
charm of bourgeois marriage nor the critique of it is dramatically convincing. It took Shaw time to realize that, unlike
Ibsen and Tolstoi, he could not present married love except in
a comic spirit. More energy had to be given to those who tried
to transcend it, like Tanner, or evade it, like Henry Higgins.

The Devil's Disciple reestablishes the triangular situation of
Candida with much clearer definition. Shaw has come to understand that his man of action and man of thought, his soldier
and his saint, are sublimities in his imagination and to understand that they attain their stature by a springing resistance to
the woman's claim for comfort, security, and happiness.

Giving full scope to the two heroes, Dick Dudgeon and Rev-
erend Anderson, who recognize, each in his own way, the
charm of marriage but are not to be turned aside by it from
fulfilling their highest destinies, Shaw is able to present the
claims of a sane, lower realism with much more candor. Although Judith Anderson begins rather like Raina (in *Arms and*

7. "One does not get tired of adoring the Virgin Mother. . . . And Candida,
between you and me, is the Virgin Mother and nobody else." *Bernard Shaw:
Collected Letters,* 1874–97, ed. D. H. Laurence (New York: Dodd, Mead, 1965),
p. 623.

the Man) as "a sentimental character formed by dreams," and although she remains a romantic idealist to some extent whereas Raina undergoes a more constructive disillusionment, she nevertheless scores some telling points, as Morrell and Candida really did not, for the doctrine of happiness as opposed to greatness. And what she says from the position of a victim of the heroic ideal is notably enforced by the firmly drawn picture of General Burgoyne, spokesman for the gentleman's code.

With Burgoyne, Shaw began to make sustained dramatic use of the insight that the self-possession attained by the conviction of a special destiny or by devotion to a communal vision could also be acquired within the bounds of social convention. It only required someone able to recognize and accept the compromises those conventions entailed. Passionate as Shaw was about ideas, he was not an ideologue: it was the poise and inner strength which the possession of ideas could give that he chiefly valued. And so he lent his sympathy to the self-assured temporizers of this world as well as to the moral geniuses. There are thus rich possibilities for interaction among the four principal characters of *The Devil's Disciple:* two contrasting moral geniuses, the protesting victim of their exalted egotism, and the witty gentleman who assesses idealism from a comfortably conventional point of view—not to mention the ironies provided by a variety of deftly turned farcical figures. Formally, if not intellectually, this is Shaw's first fully mature play, and may be said to bring to a close the first phase of his dramatic career.

The achievement of *Man and Superman* that especially merits our attention is that it gives full scope both to the sensually powerful woman and to an equal and opposite force represented here by an intellectually powerful man. Shaw charges the figures of Ann and Tanner with heroic, transpersonal aspiration, and balances them by making the creative vitality of the one biological and instinctive and of the other conscious and articulate. Tanner, the artist-philosopher, is deceived, to be sure, in imagining that the goal for which he is spokesman cannot be reconciled with the woman's goal of marriage and parenthood, yet the play endorses him, too, by moving the two figures toward a sort of mystic marriage that synthesizes both aspirations.

Ann is another of the conscious hypocrites whom Shaw admires: she gets what she wants (as does Violet, in a different way) within a society frightened by direct and aggressive women. But unlike Mrs. Warren, she needn't lose out finally, because her goal coincides with the cultural and racial need for marriage and children; as with Shaw's Caesar, what she wants to do and what she ought to do are identical. Her cunning, along with Violet's, propels the comic action and sets up the ironic humor of its situations. Tanner is vulnerable to deflation by the weakness inherent in his very strength. Ablaze with intellect, he brilliantly exposes the unconscious hypocrisy of Ramsden and Octavius—and even Ann's hypocrisy to some extent—but lacks the common shrewdness to discern the practical purposes of the two women: in the first act, he gets carried away by the idea of an unmarried mother and is humiliated by Violet's severe conventionalism; in the second, he gets carried away by the idea of a daughter's freedom from her mother and falls promptly into the trap set by Ann. The other foils to Tanner's idealism (Ann's mother, Tanner's chauffeur, Violet's husband, the brigand Mendoza) are self-assuredly conventional in quite distinct ways. Shaw maximizes the ironic comedy without undermining the heroic aspect of his modern Don Juan.

The dream sequence is a bold and successful invention. Written first, it fits the overall design by interpreting and enlarging the significance of a story whose actors must remain naïve to some degree if their comic possibilities are to be realized. It is necessary that Ann be instinctively rather than intellectually aware, but Dona Ana can be enlightened, can perceive that the Superman is not yet created and that her role is to find His father and be His mother. Through the Devil, the argument that Shaw's adherents to conventional morality (and immorality) could make for themselves, if they were able, is expressed with consummate poise and plausibility. And Don Juan himself, liberated from the role of Tanner in the comic plot, articulates to the full extent of his creator's powers a Blakean-Nietzschean argument for a transvaluation of values. The dramatic tension of the sequence arises from dialectic rather than from a clash of temperaments. The cynicism latent in the position of Shaw's pragmatic realists is brought to the surface, while his heroic realist exposes by his very intensity the underlying inhumanity of his position—so much so that Shaw sends Don Juan off toward Heaven before letting the Devil deliver his most telling riposte: "Beware of the pursuit of the Superhuman: it leads to an indiscriminate contempt for the human."

Man and Superman is the first of half a dozen plays to present a hero as millionaire. Shaw was quick in this case to seize on the ironic possibilities inherent in the idea of a revolutionary socialist who admits to being a member of the idle rich class. But however brilliantly managed here (and again in *Major Barbara*), the idea of a millionaire-hero tends to weaken or at least genialize the moral force of certain speeches. Shaw had married his "Irish millionairess" shortly before writing *Man and Superman,* after many years of genteel poverty and strict frugality, and he clearly felt ambivalent about her wealth. As Daniel Dervin perceptively observed, he once used his vegetarianism as a disclaimer of interest in his wife's fortune, which "is something of a *non sequitur* unless he attributed a forbidden emotional significance" to it.[8] Doubtless that significance was sexual, and, from a psychological point of view, we may regard the writing of *Man and Superman* and *Major Barbara* as attempts on Shaw's part to ease his guilt by making the millionaire a Shavian moralist.

The uneasiness behind the attempt perplexes the third act of *Major Barbara.* In the quite wonderful first two acts, as fine as anything in Shaw, the role of the millionaire-diabolist is perfectly contrived. In a nice series of confrontations, Undershaft brings his morally acute daughter and her intellectually acute fiancé to an awareness of the truth that the will to good is futile without the possession of worldly power. But this lesson is really learned by the end of act 2, and, as a result, his role in act 3 becomes dubious. When he can no longer serve as an exposer

8. D. Dervin, *Bernard Shaw: A Psychological Study* (Lewisburg, Pa.: Bucknell University Press, 1975), p. 44.

of unconscious hypocrisy, he must appear as a sort of human god whose model government still depends on the wealth gained from exploiting the unregenerate greed and competitiveness of the outside world. And this undermines our willingness to accept the change in him from a diabolist who manufactures lethal weapons without moral scruple to a moralist who challenges Barbara and Cusins "to make war on war."

The other side of Shaw's conflict in regard to the possession of wealth is most fully expressed in *John Bull's Other Island* and *Heartbreak House*. There was an undercurrent of despair in the Shavian vision right from the start because of the resistance of the heroic temperament to the vulgar world of happiness. But this despair is quite muted in *Man and Superman* and *Major Barbara*, which are suffused with a sense of instinctual gratification by virtue of the pervasive imagery of wealth and privilege. Although images of sensuality and money seem to have derived from a common emotional base in Shaw's mind, the image of money apparently generated less anxiety and could be genially displayed. But in the Irish play, written after a trip the Shaws made to their abandoned homeland, the pervasive images are poverty and helplessness, sensual and spiritual as well as economic. The hapless Nora and her ineffectual Irish lover—these two along with the defrocked priest who describes his eloquent vision of a true human community as "the dream of a madman"—are presented with remarkable sympathetic insight, and the whole play is, expressively if not formally, Shaw's nearest attempt at tragedy. But *Heartbreak House* particularly solicits our attention here because it so energetically contemns both money and sensuality, though it does not, I think, quite integrate the two ideas.

The play anatomizes the sterility of a society governed by plutocrats and fallen into sexual enslavement. The vigor of its repudiations is such as to make one wish Shaw had more often sacrificed charm to force and unleashed his imagination of disaster. But the repudiative emotion is in excess of the images to which it is attached. The only representation in the play of what Captain Shotover calls the "hogs" that keep us "forever in the mud" is Boss Mangan, who is too weak to bear convincingly

the obloquy heaped upon him by the others and whose final
destruction by a falling bomb seems a kind of spite on Shaw's
part rather than poetic justice. Ellie's heartbreak, too, is over
the mark; her recoil from the temptation of "accursed happiness" into fierce self-sufficiency is too sudden; her girlish adoration of Hector is not well enough imagined to justify the ferocity of her renunciation.

The theme of sexual enslavement is clear enough—the refined seductiveness of Hesione Hushabye, in particular, is
finely drawn—but it is difficult to perceive its relation to the political theme. The preface adverts us to a play about "cultured,
leisured Europe before the War" that "shrank from politics," as
if a failure of will explains the fall of Shaw's characters into a
charming boredom so oppressive that they finally welcome the
violence of unidentified bombs. But in the play itself the
charming boredom is simply a given, neither cause nor consequence of political inaction—somewhat in the Chekhovian
manner. The subtitle acknowledges the influence of Chekhov,
which is most apparent formally in the casual and swirling progression of encounters and thematically in the considerable
sympathy Shaw manages to bestow upon his "pretty and amia-
ble voluptuaries." The sympathy is offset, of course, by the prophetic Shotover, who denounces sensuality and money, now
one, now the other. Out of hatred of the political power of
money, he madly seeks (in a symbolic darkness: "money is not
made in the light") to invent something that will make a fortune and destroy the idle rich:

> Shotover. We must win power of life and death over them. I
> refuse to die until I have invented the means.
>
> Hector. Who are we that we should judge them?
>
> Shotover. Who are they that they should judge us? Yet they
> do, unhesitatingly. There is enmity between our seed
> and their seed. They know it and act on it, strangling
> our souls. They believe in themselves. When we believe
> in ourselves, we shall kill them.
>
> Hector. It is the same seed. We are members of one an-
> other.

The passage is strongest out of context, balancing Shaw's rage and tolerance, his radical heart and liberal head. In context, we are aware not only of his failure to imagine Shotover's enemy fully enough but also of the deflection of Shotover's hatred onto another target, for the passage is preceded and followed by rather incongruous attacks on the damnable fascination of women.

The connection between dalliance and greed in Shaw's mind seems to be the idea of luxury or self-indulgence: both imply loss of self-control, waste, inefficiency, all of which Shaw feared and loathed with an intensity that invites psychological speculation. It is enough to say here that because the connection is not sufficiently objectified in the play, one is tempted to look beyond, to seek an explanation in, for example, the temporal contiguity of Shaw's disappointment in his last bid for romance with Mrs. Pat Campbell and the disappointment of his political hopes in the Great War. In any case, and despite its imbalances, *Heartbreak House* comes closer than any other play by Shaw (with the possible exception of the last parts of *Back to Methuselah*) to reaching out beyond a social frame toward a more abstract and essentially poetic idea.

Taking up the idea of the Life Force introduced in *Man and Superman*, *Back to Methuselah*, though a much less stageworthy play, extends the Shavian thought-adventure to its farthest point, and is the proper terminus of his middle and major phase.

The Medusa allusions afford the readiest entry into what, in the context of this essay, is most interesting about *Methuselah*. Freud and Ferenczi, we recall, interpreted the mythic Medusa, whose gaze from beneath her serpentine hair turned men to stone, as a symbolic representation of the mother's genitalia, the sight of which arouses in the male child a fear of castration. One of Shaw's memories of childhood suggests his susceptibility to such an image and his preconscious interpretation of it along these lines:

> I well remember, when I was a small boy, receiving perhaps a greater shock than I have ever received since. I had

been brought up in a world in which woman, the angel, presented to me the appearance of a spreading mountain, a sort of Primrose Hill. On the peak there was perched a small, pinched upper part, and on top of that a human head. That, to me, at the period of life when one is young and receiving indelible impressions, was a woman. One day, when I was perhaps five years of age, a lady paid us a visit, a very handsome lady who was always in advance of the fashion. Crinolines were going out; and she had discarded hers. I, an innocent unprepared child, walked bang into the room and suddenly saw, for the first time, a woman not shaped like Primrose Hill, but with a narrow skirt which evidently wrapped a pair of human legs. I have never recovered from the shock, and never shall.[9]

The shock is displaced upward in *Methuselah,* as in the myth, and is to some extent denied as well, for the lethal countenance of the powerful woman overtly symbolizes a severe transcendence of sexuality, but in a quasi-sexual manner it horrifies the all-too-human figures who meet its gaze. When in part 3 the first of the long livers is revealed ("She is a handsome woman . . . with the walk of a goddess. Her expression and deportment are grave, swift, decisive, awful, and unanswerable."), one of the short livers is "glad to escape from her gaze," and another, trying feebly to flirt with her, "suddenly covers his eyes with his hands." In part 4 The Man of Destiny, seeking escape from his specific talent of stirring men to the love of glory and slaughter, consults an oracular Veiled Woman who tells him that, though his mesmeric pull is strong for a short-lived person, he could not endure her presence if she were not veiled and robed: at his command she throws back her veil and disrobes, whereupon he shrieks, staggers, covers his eyes, and says he is dying. A similar fate befalls the Elderly Gentleman, who, like Gulliver in Houyhnhnm land, begs to be allowed to stay:

> *The Oracle.* Be it so, then. You may stay. *She offers him her hands. He grasps them and raises himself a little by clinging to*

9. B. Shaw, *Platform and Pulpit,* ed. with introduction by D. H. Laurence (New York: Hill and Wang, 1961), p. 173.

her. She looks steadily into his face. He stiffens; a little convul-
sion shakes him; his grasp relaxes; and he falls dead.

The Oracle [*looking down at the body*]. Poor shortlived thing!
What else could I do for you?

Shaw had always been inclined to heroicize the transcendence of sexual desire, but in earlier plays this was dramatized
by confrontations among characters in recognizable social situations. In *Methuselah,* dramatic tension is achieved by more abstract means. The claim of spirit against flesh is presented with
a ferocity that contains its own negation rather than being opposed by a plausible counterclaim. The Handsome Woman
scorns the "children" around her, yet is lonely: "You are all
such children. And I never was very fond of children, except
that one girl who woke up the mother passion in me. I have
been very lonely sometimes."—almost the very words Shaw was
to use in an autobiographical passage to describe his mother.[10]

The contempt of the long livers for those still enslaved by
images and metaphors, their contempt for childhood and indeed for the human situation itself, is so uncompromising that
it allows us to be repelled as well as fascinated. Shaw lets his
Ancients energetically scorn every grace and solace—youth,
beauty, love, nature, speech, art—that tempers the ideal of
pure thought, pure self-contemplation. Archangel Michael (Mi-
chelangelo) appears and says that he has gone beyond the depiction of youth and beauty and seeks now to render only the
majesty of mind at its intensest. Pygmalion appears, not in the
form of an engaging martinet who converts a flower-girl into a
lady, but as a transcendent artist who strives by vitalist science
to create an improved human being: he is bitten to death by his
Eve-like creature, who herself, with her mate, collapses in dis-
couragement under the severely judging gaze of the Ancients.

The last words are given to Lilith, prophetess of the Life
Force, who has witnessed the development of human consciousness from the beginning to A.D. 31,920. Her speech combines a threat of punishment for a race not fully redeemed
from the flesh with a tolerance born of the thought that Life, as

10. B. Shaw, *Sixteen Self Sketches* (New York: Dodd, Mead, 1949), p. 29.

distinct from Matter, is beyond any conceivable embodiment and thus beyond her own comprehension. Her severity and even her tolerance indicate how unwilling Shaw was, always, to compromise with a powerful primitive fantasy. He prefers despair and rage to resignation, though, unfortunately for the strength of the late plays, he also came to defend himself against despair and rage with attenuated farce.

The less interesting third phase of Shaw's dramatic career can be discussed here rather briefly. To be sure, it begins with one of Shaw's strongest plays, but the strengths of *Saint Joan* are of a less personal kind and there is, moreover, a certain problem in the conception of the heroine that is characteristic of the later plays. Joan's superiority is too readily assumed, somewhat facile and complacent, particularly in the first three scenes, which build effective but rather cheap climaxes on the basis of successive miracles.

In the Shavian oeuvre, the effect of insufficiently earned elevation first appears in *Caesar and Cleopatra,* where the conception of Caesar, though beguiling in its novelty and variously illustrated, keeps him at a too comfortable distance from the human struggle. Caesar's attitude toward revenge is presented more as a lesson than a true enactment, and his relation to Cleopatra (avuncular rather than, as the historical record indicates, sexual) is coy, lacking the firm irony of Higgins' similar relation to Eliza. (It is perhaps noteworthy that Higgins' sexual inhibitedness is clearly related to his feeling for his mother.) The plays of Shaw's major phase are not untouched by this effect—for example, the aviatrix in *Misalliance* and Mrs. George in *Getting Married*—but it does not become a typical problem until the later ones.

In *The Apple Cart,* the ability of the hereditary monarch to defeat the elected prime minister at his own democratic game, though witty, is too easily demonstrated. The king runs for office with unfair advantages, not only more experience (which seems to be Shaw's point) but also the charisma of his title and the exceptional acumen that Shaw attributes to him. In *Too True To Be Good* (subtitled, like *The Apple Cart* and other late plays, an extravaganza), the reversals are so frequent and rapid, the conventionality so thin and the unconventionality so loose and freewheeling, that the energy of the work lacks definition and direction. Private Meek, a tribute to T. E. Lawrence, is the factotum of popular fantasy, rather like the role played by Clifton Webb in the Mr. Belvedere films. The Patient's Shavian defense of the higher centers against the lower and the Elder's warning that in a crumbling universe, "let women be silent and men rise to something nobler than kissing them," both lack the force of similar earlier attacks because the source of disillusionment is so diffuse, not only sex but also science, war, and in fact every aspect of the social order. Shaw makes a point of this diffusion by having all his characters feel that they are falling into a bottomless abyss, but it is the playwright as well who appears to be floundering. His despair in this play, like his confidence in authoritarian leadership in *The Apple Cart, On the Rocks,* and *Geneva,* is facile. Approximating the stance of "nothing matters," Shaw's late despair lacks the intensity and direction it had in *Heartbreak House* and *Back to Methuselah.*

Giving himself the last words of *Too True To Be Good,* Shaw endorses not Aubrey, who delivers a summary sermon, but the woman of action (The Patient), whose will to clean up the world was presumably not given enough scope in the play he had written. As if to compensate, he conceives in *The Millionairess* a supremely forceful woman who simply overrides everyone in her will to efficiency. But there is nothing for Epifania to attach her extraordinary energy to, nothing that matters, and all Shaw can do is suggest, feebly, in an alternate ending, that she might find a proper outlet for her talents in the society of Soviet Russia.

We can round out our picture of the oeuvre by commenting on a counterpart to *The Millionairess,* a sketch entitled *Why She Would Not,* written in the very last months of its author's long life. A young upstart named Bossborn rescues a lady named Serafina from a burglar and claims as his reward a humble position in the business of her wealthy grandfather. Soon he has replaced his superiors, expanded the business, torn down the family estate, and rebuilt a modern efficient home for Serafina. But she is not pleased with his way of doing things, his idea of progress and efficiency, and refuses to marry him. In a long preface to *The Millionairess,* Shaw attacked bosses, though that play itself can hardly be said to attack the bossy Epifania. In *Why She Would Not,* on the other hand, the born boss is put down but the result is similar. The young man seems to come out of fantasy rather than any deep imaginative impulse, and seems to be rebuffed at last simply because his creator hasn't enough belief in his purpose to let it be engaged by the real world. Bossborn cannot wrestle with his angel any more than Epifania can find a man to resist her force; the despair in both plays is thin because the desire of the hero is superficially imagined. In Shaw's most satisfying artistic structures, there is a springboard effect: renunciation sublimates the energy of the body into the fire of intellect.[11] Without that dynamic relation, his heroic comedy tends to become a mere shell.

IV

To say that in Shaw's late plays the imaginative impulse is attenuated is to imply that imagination is a faculty which engages the reality of feelings to a certain depth and expresses those feelings with a certain concentration gained from the pressure of intellect upon them. Strong art does, therefore, bear a relation to the repressed, for the artist who does not dig below the surface can hardly produce more than fantasy. But to become part of a coherent design, the repressed must be subjected to a process of understanding, and in doing so, ceases to be quite hidden from consciousness.

If our focus were biography or the creative process, we would allow a larger importance to the role of repression. I believe, in fact, that one reason why Bloom's studies in the anxiety of influence contain so much psychological insight is that they are at the margin of criticism, as much concerned with the creative process as with the interpretation of texts. In those of his books that focus closely on individual poems (*Yeats, The*

11. In this connection, Norman N. Holland remarks suggestively of Shaw in a recent essay: "he fears being incorporated into some larger, needing, hungry being; he defends by a sense of purpose that guarantees one's own mental existence." "Human Identity," *Critical Inquiry* 4, no. 3 (1978) : p. 457.

Visionary Company, and so forth), there is frequent casual recognition of just the sort of obtrusive unconscious influence that has concerned me in these remarks on the plays of Shaw. It cannot be said that Bloom's understanding of repression quite coincides with mine, and it is apparently true that his present interest in a theory of intertextuality makes him less interested in explication as such, but I do not think he would altogether disagree that the dual challenge to the conscious artist is to release a portion of his affective life from repression and yet keep out of his art those counterintended effects that can only be explained with reference to an idea that has remained repressed. In any case, the plays of Shaw provide many examples of this challenge, more or less successfully met, and a mode of interpretation that emphasizes affective danger-points can lend reasoned support to our usually unexamined conviction that strong art is no ordinary triumph.

8

Diction and Defense in Wordsworth

Geoffrey Hartman

Hamlet. Let her not walk i' the' Sun; conception is a blessing, but not as your daughter may conceive.

I wish to discuss a poem Wordsworth wrote in 1816, when he
was forty-six and his daughter Dora, twelve. We perceive only
dimly the personal circumstances: the Continent had opened
up again to English travelers after Napoleon's fall; Wordsworth
was thinking of going back for the first time since the Peace of
Amiens of 1803, when he had visited his illegitimate daughter
Caroline (from a liaison with Annette Valon contracted during
his 1792 stay in revolutionary France); Dora is approaching
puberty; and his eyesight is troubling him. As he is enjoying
the idea of walking with Dora in the English countryside one
sunny morning, his mind is usurped by a voice: more precisely,
by the opening lines of Milton's *Samson Agonistes.* They depict
Samson at Gaza, blind, humiliated, and having to be led; and
the quotation (words within words) echoes the opening of
Sophocles' *Oedipus at Colonus,* where the blind Oedipus is
guided by Antigone. Wordsworth cannot understand the intrusion of this voice, for what it describes is a situation exactly
the reverse of his: instead of a father leading his child into the
sunny Lake District, and perhaps into the Alps, the quotation
depicts a blind man led by his daughter, a man who is guilt-rid-
den and burdened by his role in divine history. I quote the first
thirty-two (out of fifty-seven) lines of the poem:

> *"A LITTLE onward lend thy guiding hand*
> *To these dark steps, a little further on!"*

    —What trick of memory to *my* voice hath brought
    This mournful iteration? For though Time,
5   The Conqueror, crowns the Conquered, on his brow
    Planting his favourite silver diadem,
    Nor he, nor minister of his—intent
    To run before him, hath enrolled me yet,
    Though not unmenaced, among those who lean
10 Upon a living staff, with borrowed sight.
    —O my own Dora, my beloved child!
    Should that day come—but hark! the birds salute
    The cheerful dawn, brightening for me the east;
    For me, thy natural leader, once again
15 Impatient to conduct thee, not as erst
    A tottering infant, with compliant stoop
    From flower to flower supported; but to curb
    Thy nymph-like step swift-bounding o'er the lawn,
    Along the loose rocks, or the slippery verge
20 Of foaming torrents.—From thy orisons
    Come forth: and, while the morning air is yet
    Transparent as the soul of innocent youth,
    Let me, thy happy guide, now point thy way,
    And now precede thee, winding to and fro,
25 Till we by perseverance gain the top
    Of some smooth ridge, whose brink precipitous
    Kindles intense desire for powers withheld
    From this corporeal frame; whereon who stands
    Is seized with strong incitement to push forth
30 His arms, as swimmers use, and plunge—dread thought,
    For pastime plunge—into the "abrupt abyss,"
    Where ravens spread their plumy vans, at ease![1]

It is hard to know what is most peculiar here. First, why the image of the blind man? Then, is there an emphasis on the very idea of beginning, of taking that step, since it is unusual to have a poem open with a quotation, and even more so to have the reaction to that quotation be part of the subject? Finally,

1. For the entire poem, see E. de Selincourt and H. Darbishire, eds., *The Poetical Works of William Wordsworth* (Oxford: Clarendon, 1947), 4 : 92–94.

should we explore the similarity of the quotation to an inner voice?

I will offer some thoughts about all these matters, starting with the last. The question of "inner voices" is a large one, and well known to psychoanalytic literature. Poetry, I will surmise, is the working-through of such "voices," which are often projected as coming from the outside, or attributed to supernatural agency. They summon or entice the hearer, they urge him to some fatal step. They come from the "abrupt abyss" (l. 31) or bring him close to it. So in the case of the strange and glorious death of Oedipus at Colonus:

> Suddenly a voice
> Call'd him aloud: awestruck we stood aghast:
> Again, and oft it call'd him, "Oedipus,
> Why Oedipus, delay we to depart?
> Thine this delay . . . ."
> . . . we backwards turn'd
> Our eyes; the man was no where to be found;
> He was not; but we saw the king [Theseus] alone;
> He stood, and o'er his face his hands he spread
> Shading his eyes, as if with terror struck
> At something horribe to human sight.[2]

The entire speech (by one of the citizens of Colonus) is suggestive, for it shows Oedipus becoming a guide once more, leading his daughters to "the rent rock's craggy verge" and taking his station near "the gulf's yawning mouth" (cf. ll. 26 ff.). What happens next remains mysterious, but the voice must have done its work, for Oedipus disappears, divine victim or suicide, "haply by the gods / Borne thence, or sinking through the friendly earth, / Which in her deeply-rifted bosom oped / A painless passage to the realms below."

That "passage," in Wordsworth, often leads from eye to ear. Voice, by a strange law of exchange, seems to imply a darkened eye. Sometimes merely an "eye made quiet" (*Tintern Abbey*); at other times, as in a visionary episode of *The Prelude*, nature ex-

2. *The Tragedies of Sophocles,* trans. R. Potter (London: 1788), pp. 177–78.

hibits the emblem of a mind "that broods / Over the dark abyss, intent to hear / Its voices. . . ." It is as if the eye entered the ear to recover a lost conjunction, or to shelter in its darker recess. "Why was the sight," Samson laments in Milton's poem, which provided Wordsworth's opening verses, "To such a tender ball as the eye confined?" The sense of vulnerability, psychic as well as physical, is extreme. Voice exposes that vulnerability yet also evokes a deeper faculty, which is, as it were, an eye without the eyes. Wordsworth's ode *On the Power of Sound* describes it as "The cell of Hearing dark and blind, / . . . more dread for thought / To enter than oracular cave."

"More dread for thought to enter"? Compare "and plunge—dread thought, / For pastime plunge—into the 'abrupt abyss' " (ll. 30–31). A katabasis with traumatic implications is suggested. The inner or "abrupt" voice points at one and the same time to an ideal blindness (voice beyond sight), and a terrible blinding (voice purchased by the loss of sight). The dependence on voice has always been symptomatic of an intimate relation to inspiration or divine guidance (the oracular cave). That presumption is also the danger, call it enthusiasm or ecstasy, delusion of grandeur or omnipotence fantasy, bardic or visionary power. "Visionary power," Wordsworth writes in the fifth book of *The Prelude*, "attends the motion of the viewless winds / Embodied in the mystery of words." The contrast of "visionary" and "viewless" also moves us beyond sight. No wonder Wordsworth is "blinded" by the passage from *Samson Agonistes*.

Not till the very end does the poet foresee a "passage clear" (l. 52); for even after he finds his way again (ll. 23 ff.) he comes to a "brink precipitous" that halts him once more, like the opening verses. At this point allusions to Milton return: "abrupt abyss" is a conflation of *Paradise Lost* 2. 405 and 409; more significantly, the sequence from "whereon who stands" to "plumy vans" recalls *Paradise Regained* 4. 541–83, in which Christ resists the Tempter's voice. Satan asks Christ to show his godhead by casting himself from a pinnacle, and Christ resists that presumption of divinity. It is as if Wordsworth quoted Milton to resist in himself a similar presumption.

Usurpation by a voice, then, is itself a mixed traumatic event.

It is both defensive and inspirational. It at once blocks and originates the poem. It breaks into thought in a way that breaks thought, yet it has something of the divinity of oracle or fiat. On the one hand, the carefree wish (restated in l. 20 as "From thy orisons / Come forth . . .") becomes a burden through the intervention of an ominous quotation. Time is apocalyptically speeded up, the roles of father and daughter reversed, and Wordsworth approaches the position of Samson and Oedipus just before their exalted deaths. On the other hand, the poem is launched, and works against that perspective, and establishes a development of sorts. The poet becomes active from passive and voices the voice he hears.[3]

Though we cannot locate the trauma with precision, because diction and interdiction, or the ideal and terrible in this "diction," blend so intricately, the traumatic effect can be described further. What is wounded here? The answer must be *human time* itself, or *growth* considered from a psychic and developmental perspective. Wordsworth finds himself in the situation of a man who, because of the shock he has suffered, moves as if the ground before him were not reliable. He takes "dark steps," and so does his language, which seeks to recover its previous state related to the innocence of wishing and walking. Yet it remains "diction" rather than "language." Now this is still very abstract, but it becomes telling when we recall that Wordsworth had been thinking about his daughter and that the blocking quotation links his thoughts involuntarily to the story of Oedipus as well as Samson.

In both these stories there is guilt, and a guilt partly linked to sexual transgression. In the case of Oedipus there is unconscious incest. Incest is itself a collapse of human and developmental time: it merges lifelines that should be kept separate. Wordsworth was, in fact, too separated from one child, Caroline; he has also passed through an extraordinary union, through what can only be called a symbiotic relation, with his sister Dorothy ("She gave me ears, she gave me eyes"). Is he

3. For a full consideration of the poem's development, see my "Words, Wish, Worth: Wordsworth," in *Deconstruction and Criticism,* essays by H. Bloom and others (New York: Seabury Press, forthcoming).

uncertain and anxious about his future relations with Dora? The proleptic image of blindness that comes to him in the form of Milton's voice (the blind Milton, whose daughters became his amanuenses) may indicate a guilt of the eyes, a fear for their punishment or "castration," or the wish to avoid such a trial by an imaginary exclusion of the guilty organ, by its ideal "sheltering" or "immunization." The fear may not be directly connected with sexual thoughts; rather with the wish to be so closely in touch (the poet guiding the thoughts or hands of Dora) that the eyes are actually wished away.

In this overdetermined situation there can be no single resolving hypothesis. The situation is further entangled by the fact that Wordsworth had real eye trouble, whether or not it was psychogenic; and that the association of blindness and prophetic power was a literary commonplace. Are we confined, then, to impotent speculation?

I think not. The maze has to be respected; yet the very act of limning it, of making it visible, leads out as well as in. We have not yet taken up the peculiar emphasis on beginnings in this poem: the Miltonic verses are so strong that all the rest appear to be commentary, or revision. Whatever the private psychic reason for the usurping lines, they make Milton's beginning Wordsworth's beginning. What is the connection between this emphasis on beginnings, the theme of blindness, and the father-daughter relation?

It is important to observe that though "In the beginning was the Word" is true of this poem, an absolute beginning in terms of literary sources is hard to locate. Milton's lines reiterate those of Sophocles; and this leading back is not the end of the matter. For the words of Oedipus or Samson form a highly allusive quotation which evokes something just beyond: a dangerous and sacred space, a fatal threshold or *templum* of some kind. ("A little onward" is an ambiguous phrase, moreover, when referred back to *Oedipus at Colonus,* for there a similar plea occurs twice, when Oedipus asks Antigone to lead him *into* the sacred grove at Colonus, and then when he is led, at the insistence of the Colonians, *out of* that sacred plot.) In short, there is so remarkable an abbreviation or condensation of several contexts that no one literary source can be cited as the

original, even though all the contexts together drive us back
(like the Oedipus myth itself) to beginnings, and project the
image of a potent place where something "original"—
theophanic—is to happen.

This structure, however paradoxical, establishes words—or
their potential of condensed, literary expression—as a boundary beyond which the empirical search for origins—as when
psychoanalysis locates the cause of a trauma—becomes mythi-
cizing in its drift. "Each most obvious and particular thought,"
Wordsworth writes in The Prelude," . . . hath no beginning."
The quotation that begins the poem of 1816 acts as a boundary
that limits and even admonishes our desire for self-inauguration: for being present in or at the origin. The intertextual condensation, moreover, displayed by literature, is an opacity akin
to blindness. It reinforces the ceremonious "diction" by means
of which liminal anxieties are raised and the threshold becomes
a dwelling place. We cannot step beyond it into unmediated
vision.

In the Romantic period, and still today, the faculty that
moves us toward original or unmediated vision—vision more
intimate and direct than even the eyes afford—is given the
name of *imagination*. Wordsworth once called it an "unfathered
vapor." It tends to block as well as facilitate; to take away fa-
therhood (authority) as well as be a fathering power. To think
of it in these terms, in metaphors derived from the family
nexus, is bound to produce a contradiction, because imagination, like Freud's Eros, drives beyond the natural family and
toward more ultimate or exalted forms of union.

The first step in "A little onward" goes backward, toward
beginnings. It is a quotation, an unfathered (psychically abrupt)
yet unoriginal fragment, that reveals a verbal abyss (words
within words). The poem's second step is equally dark and
backward. Wordsworth's querulous reflection,

> What trick of memory to *my* voice hath brought
> This mournful iteration?

embodies a further quotation, more covert than the first, yet
raising with equal force the issue of beginnings.

These lines contain not only a significant pun but also a far-reaching echo of Shakespeare's *King Lear*.[4] They dislocate the words of another blinded man, Gloucester, when he meets a Lear now driven mad by the cruelty of his elder daughters as well as by the memory of his own cruelty to his youngest daughter. Gloucester says:

> The trick of that voice I do well remember.
>
> [IV.vi.105]

In the context of the outrageous wordplay that characterizes this scene and focuses through the puns on what eyes see or cannot see—

> *Edgar.* O thou side-piercing sight!
>
> . . . .
>
> *Lear.* Read.
>
> *Gloucester.* What, with the case of eyes?
>
> *Lear.* Oh ho, are you there with me? No eyes in your head, no money in your purse? Your eyes are in a heavy case, your purse in a light; yet you see how this world goes.
>
> *Gloucester.* I see it feelingly.
>
> [IV.vi. 85, 141–47]

—in this context, "trick" meaning habit or characteristic trait, moves toward "trick" meaning trickiness or deceiving quality. "Give the word" says Lear (IV. vi. 92),[5] recalling the play's first

4. "Iteration" means journeying as well as repetition, on the basis of the Latin *iter*. "Mournful iteration" has, in any case, a double referent, in that it alludes both to the internal, structural phrasing, "A little onward . . . a little further on," and to the temporal or historical echo of Oedipus' words by Milton's Samson. In what follows I do not mention all the Shakespearean echoes: the "brink precipitous," for example, can recall the imaginary cliff near Dover which in *King Lear*, act 4, plays a central role in the survival of Gloucester. He comes on stage "poorly led" (scene 1, line 9) and asks an Edgar, who is disguised and speaks with "altered voice" (scene 6, line 7), to lead him up a cliff "from whence / I shall no leading need" (scene 1, line 78). Edgar pretends to do his bidding and persuades his father, by a fanciful description of the supposed precipice, that he has jumped down and survived. Cf. also *Hamlet* I. iv. 69.

5. Lear's pathetic mimicry of the sentinel's role (Edgar replies "Sweet Marjoram," Lear says "Pass," then comes Gloucester's "I know that voice") also links words to defenses via the notion of password.

scene, in which everything had been made to depend by him on a *trick of speech.*

That first scene opposed Cordelia's "Nothing" to Lear's "Speak." Lear's command is a kind of fiat; and from this beginning everything devolves, as from the "dark and vicious place" where Gloucester begot Edmund. Sexual force is, in fact, more potent than the fiat in human relations. Lear cannot force Cordelia.[6] Lear wants love and speech, Eros and Logos, to coincide; but there can be no fiat in the sphere of the emotions. The defeat of the "omnific word" (Milton's phrase for the fiat), especially in the bosom of the family, means that Logos has brought death, not love. Cordelia fails to be the daughter of Lear's word.

With this defeat of the fiat the problematic of self-inauguration comes into view again and explains Wordsworth's borrowing of Milton's and Shakespeare's hand. Both allusions, one too explicit, one too implicit, not only reinforce the theme of blindness but associate it with the pressure of imagination: its drive toward originality or self-inauguration. The repressed and repressive fiat shows *its* hand as a "trick of memory," allied to what today is called unconscious process. The fiat is, of course, a word in the beginning, one that creates what it inaugurates; and its conflation with the theme of blindness expresses the poet's anxiety about the "awful power" of imagination. The father's wish to guide his daughter—no more dangerous, surely, than Lear asking for words of love—betrays a fantasy about the fathering power of words. Even, perhaps, an omnipotence fantasy, a desire for "powers withheld / From this corporeal frame" (ll. 27–28), which would allow the poet to transcend natural limits or social taboos. The end of the poem (ll. 52 ff.) seems to consecrate the union of daughter and father, as they advance "hand in hand" into a beyond.

It is well known that Wordsworth, who rebelled in the name of Nature against the artificiality of eighteenth-century "poetic diction," returned to a comparable style in such poems as "A

6. Ophelia, too, when she becomes mad, knows "There's tricks i' th' world," and her "speech is nothing" (IV. v. 5 ff.) even if "This nothing's more than matter" (IV. v. 177).

little onward." My analysis suggests that his language here is indeed a diction, yet not a relapse into conventionality. The new diction, in its allusive and condensed character, creates time for the poet: it slows down something precipitous, it allows him a response. In the poem of 1816 the compelling element is a voice or a blind thought; it may also be, as in other poems, a "glimpse of glory" that comes unbidden, or a "spirit" that leaps out from the past, recalling and even radically modifying his memory of an event.

Also modified is his understanding of the poetic diction previously rejected: the attenuated and conspicuously secondary style imitating the great poets of the English Renaissance. Wordsworth revalues the relation of diction and defense. Poetic diction, as it develops after Spenser, Shakespeare, and Milton, is a compromise with them, which incorporates in an urbane and distanced, rather than open and creative way, many of their "tricks." Originally creative, the fiat can also be a decreating word—as in *Lear,* and perhaps in the pressure of poet on poet. Harold Bloom insists that what is defended against is always the overwhelming solicitation of a precursor poet: the voice of Milton, for instance, which initiates this very poem.

Yet in this area more care is needed. The inner voice has a traumatic resonance that evokes the exchange of eyes for ears, as if a blinding of that kind could restore Voice to its most powerful mode, that of Logos or fiat. Hearing voices implies a backward journeying, through mourning or mania (the "plunge" of ll. 30–31, where "pastime" is also "past time"). For what comes back with those voices is the dream of divinity, of our unmediated or self-inaugurated power. "By our own spirits are we deified," Wordsworth writes in *Resolution and Independence,* a poem about the fate of poets.

It is, however, the defeat or impotence of the fiatlike voice— its deadly rather than loving effect in the context of family life—which causes grief and puts the vocation of the poet in doubt. In his earlier and more famous poetry, Wordsworth is very subtle in terms of passives and actives, and seems to escape from fiat into an atmosphere where everything is reciprocal, at once given and received, or half-perceived and half-created. Surely the Wordsworth who renews poetic diction is on the defensive once more: cornered by the repressed strength of the fiat in him, arrested by an image of Voice he cannot evade. Yet it remains a strong defense, as they say in chess, because his diction is also genuinely neoclassic, not only defensive but mediational. Through Sophocles and others he absorbs a sense of nature like his own, of the earth as having, or having had, a "lustre too intense / To be sustained" so that "Mortals bowed / The front in self-defence" (*Ode to Lycoris,* 1817). As he walks through the Lake District, his steps may suddenly become dark in that knowledge, and the mild English countryside may disclose an oracular cave:

> Long as the heat shall rage, let that dim cave
> Protect us, there decyphering as we may
> Diluvian records; or the sighs of Earth
> Interpreting; or counting for old Time
> His minutes, by reiterated drops,
> Audible tears, from some invisible source
> That deepens upon fancy. . . .
>
> [*Further Ode to Lycoris,* 1817]

A final remark on the "defensive" character of Wordsworth's allusions to Shakespeare and Milton: the allusions to Milton are interesting yet patent. Why, then, a "viewless," or devious and inwrought, diction when it comes to *Lear?* It seems to me that Wordsworth approaches Shakespeare *through* Milton. The overt presence, Milton's, may be the less dangerous one: it is possible that the real block, or the poet defended against, because of the power of his word, or the way he represents its wounding effect—wounded eyes and ears pictured by means of brazen pun and stage spectacle—is Shakespeare. In the poem of 1816, at least, Milton is a screen, or part of the "outwork" (Freud's metaphor) erected by Wordsworth's imagination to keep it from a starker scene. The poet's tribute to the "mystery of words" in the fifth book of *The Prelude,*

> There darkness makes abode, and all the host
> Of shadowy things do work their changes there,

has a Shakespearean rather than a Miltonic ring.

9

Figurations of the Writer's Death: Freud and Hart Crane

JOHN T. IRWIN

Let me begin by juxtaposing two passages—one from Freud, one from Hart Crane—as pretexts for discussing the way in which a writer deals with the inscribed image of his own death—both the certain death of his physical body and the possible death of the body of his work. The Freudian passage is a footnote to his essay "The Uncanny" (1919). After discussing instances of the uncanny "from the realm of fiction" and "imaginative writing," Freud turns, near the end of the essay, to another class of the phenomenon, the uncanny in real life, and offers a marginal example from his own experience:

> Since the uncanny effect of a 'double' also belongs to this same group it is interesting to observe what the effect is of meeting one's own image unbidden and unexpected. Ernst Mach has related two such observations in his *Analyse der Empfindungen* (1900, 3). On the first occasion he was not a little startled when he realized that the face before him was his own. The second time he formed a very unfavourable opinion about the supposed stranger who entered the omnibus, and thought 'What a shabby-looking school-master that man is who is getting in!'—I can report a similar adventure. I was sitting alone in my *wagon-lit* compartment when a more than usually violent jolt of the train swung back the door of the adjoining washing-cabinet, and an elderly gentleman in a dressing-gown and a travelling cap

came in. I assumed that in leaving the washing-cabinet, which lay between the two compartments, he had taken the wrong direction and come into my compartment by mistake. Jumping up with the intention of putting him right, I at once realized to my dismay that the intruder was nothing but my own reflection in the looking-glass on the open door. I can still recollect that I thoroughly disliked his appearance. Instead, therefore, of being *frightened* by our 'doubles', both Mach and I simply failed to recognize them as such. Is it not possible, though, that our dislike of them was a vestigial trace of the archaic reaction which feels the 'double' to be something uncanny? [p. 248 n.]

The Crane passage is taken from the opening section of his long poem *The Bridge*. Having described the bridge at dawn in the first four stanzas of "To Brooklyn Bridge," Crane suddenly shifts the mood in the fifth stanza with the description of a suicide:

> Out of some subway scuttle, cell or loft
> A bedlamite speeds to thy parapets,
> Tilting there momently, shrill shirt ballooning,
> A jest falls from the speechless caravan.

[p. 45]

It is obvious enough how the bedlamite's leap from the Brooklyn Bridge into the East River can be read, retrospectively, as a foreshadowing of Crane's own suicidal leap from the deck of the S.S. *Orizaba* into the Caribbean Sea some two years after *The Bridge*'s publication. The prefiguration becomes even more striking when we recall that in the poem's final section, "Atlantis," the image of the bridge metamorphoses into that of a ship, its cables transformed into "cordage," its girders into "spars," with the seafarer Jason aloft in its rigging. Moreover, if one considers the poet Weldon Kees's presumed suicide from the Golden Gate Bridge in 1955 and John Berryman's 1972 leap from the bridge over the Mississippi River in Minneapolis in light of the reference to the Golden Gate at the beginning of the "Van Winkle" section and the image of the poet's body floating down the Mississippi in "The River," then *The Bridge* seems prefigurative not only of Crane's fate but of the fate of a certain type of lyric poet in twentieth-century America.

Obvious as the foreshadowing of Crane's suicide is in the passage from *The Bridge,* it is much less obvious that the passage from Freud presents an image of the writer's death—indeed, that it presents, in its tale of Freud's not recognizing his mirror-image, any image of death at all. Yet I would argue that the passage can be so interpreted on at least three counts. First of all, Freud characterizes both Mach's experience and his own as an encounter with a double. Earlier in the essay, discussing Otto Rank's study of doubling, Freud had remarked how the figure of the double, which had originally been "an insurance against the destruction of the ego, an 'energetic denial of the power of death' " (1919, p. 235), reversed its significance when primitive man passed the stage of primary narcissism. The double changed from "an assurance of immortality" into "the uncanny harbinger of death" (p. 235). In encountering one's double, then, one meets the prefiguration or foreshadowing of one's own fate, one's own fatality. Secondly, both Mach and Freud report that, on first seeing their doubles, they failed to recognize them as images of themselves. Since it is literally impossible to imagine one's own death, to imagine the end of imagining or think the absence of thought, one always conceives of one's own death as if it were the death of another—one's consciousness still being in existence as onlooker. If we grant, then, that any image of one's own death always implies this continued presence of oneself as observer of the image, then to see one's image in a mirror and not to recognize it is perhaps as close as we can come to depicting the loss of self-consciousness, the absence of the self as observer. Thirdly, what Mach and Freud each saw was a mirror-image—that is, a spatial double—but what Freud also encountered at some point, as the note makes clear, was a temporal doubling, in that his own experience was a repetition of Mach's earlier experience. In reading Mach's account of not recognizing his mirror-image, Freud encountered Mach as a double. Since Freud doesn't comment on *this* double, are we to assume that he didn't recognize the doubling between himself and Mach, just as he and Mach hadn't recognized their mirror-images? It would be a curious lapse, but no more curious than the footnote itself; for to put it bluntly, there is something fishy about the note, something oddly strained about Freud's introducing Mach's experience into the essay, as if Freud needed corroboration of his own somewhat far-fetched story. Mach's account of not recognizing his image occurs in the first chapter of *The Analysis of Sensations,* in a footnote to his remark that "Personally, people know themselves very poorly":

> Once, when a young man, I noticed in the street the profile of a face that was very displeasing and repulsive to me. I was not a little taken aback when a moment afterwards I found that it was my own face which, in passing by a shop where mirrors were sold, I had perceived reflected from two mirrors that were inclined at the proper angle to each other.
>
> Not long ago, after a trying railway journey by night, when I was very tired, I got into an omnibus, just as another man appeared at the other end. "What a shabby pedagogue that is, that has just entered," thought I. It was myself: opposite me hung a large mirror. The physiognomy of my class, accordingly, was better known to me than my own. [p. 4]

The Analysis of Sensations was first published in 1886 (though it contained material that had appeared in print as early as the 1860s), and by 1906 the book was in its fifth edition. Freud cites the second edition (1900). Mach died in 1916, and Freud completed his essay "The Uncanny" in the middle of 1919, publishing it in autumn of the same year. Though there seems to have been no direct personal contact between Mach and Freud, Thomas Szasz has argued, in his introduction to *The Analysis of Sensations,* that Freud was "much influenced by the general *epistemological* outlook inherent in Mach's psychological writings. This, particularly as it involved his views concerning the relationship between physics (medicine) and psychology, Freud borrowed from Mach. Indeed, perhaps Mach's prestige and authority may have even handicapped Freud, and the other founders of the science of psychoanalysis, from fully re-

alizing the physicalistic basis upon which they have placed psychoanalysis" (p. xix). Szasz also contends that in *The Analysis of
Sensations* Mach had anticipated some of the fundamental concepts of psychoanalysis. In a letter dated June 12, 1900, to his
friend Wilhelm Fliess, Freud refers to Mach's book:

> Do you suppose that some day a marble tablet will be
> placed on the house, inscribed with these words:
>
> 'In this house on July 24th, 1895, The Secret of Dreams
> was revealed to Dr. Sigmund Freud.'
>
> At this moment, I see little prospect of it. But when I
> read the latest psychological books (Mach's *Analyse der Emp-
> findungen,* second edition, Kroell's *Aufbau der Seele,* etc.) all
> of which have the same kind of aims as my work, and see
> what they have to say about dreams, I am as delighted as
> the dwarf in the fairy tale because 'the princess doesn't
> know.' [Freud, 1887–1902, p. 322]

Commenting on this passage, Szasz notes that

> Mach, at this time, was a full Professor in the University of
> Vienna, and he had already achieved world-renown as a
> physicist and philosopher. Yet, Freud referred to him as if
> he were a psychologist and an expert on dreams. Surely, it
> is true that *The Analysis of Sensations* does not contain any-
> thing of value concerning dream-psychology. Nor was it
> addressed to this topic. Freud, as we know, had much cov-
> eted the social recognition which a regular professorship at
> the outstanding University of Vienna implied. . . . he se-
> lected—presumably not without reason—Mach's somewhat
> unrelated work with which to compare what he felt was his
> *magnum opus. The Interpretation of Dreams,* it must be re-
> membered, was also his first psychological book written
> alone.* He thus compared his work—in his own mind and
> to his friend—with that of the well-recognized University
> professor, Mach, in order to prove its originality and
> worth.

---

* Freud's first book, *Aphasia,* published in 1891, was a neurological
work. It was dedicated to Breuer. . . . [p. xviii]

As further evidence of Freud's general sensitivity to the question of influence versus originality in his work, consider the following passage from *An Autobiographical Study* (1925):

> Even when I have moved away from observation, I have carefully avoided any contact with philosophy proper. This avoidance has been greatly facilitated by constitutional incapacity. I was always open to the ideas of G. T. Fechner and have followed that thinker upon many important points. The large extent to which psycho-analysis coincides with the philosophy of Schopenhauer—not only did he assert the dominance of the emotions and the supreme importance of sexuality but he was even aware of the mechanism of repression—is not to be traced to my acquaintance with his teaching. I read Schopenhauer very late in my life. Nietzsche, another philosopher whose guesses and intuitions often agree in the most astonishing way with the laborious findings of psycho-analysis, was for a long time avoided by me on that very account; I was less concerned with the question of priority than with keeping my mind unembarrassed. [pp. 59–60]

Yet, twenty-five years earlier, in his letter to Fliess, Freud was clearly concerned with the question of priority, concerned with the fact that on July 24, 1895, he knew "the Secret of Dreams" while, to judge from the 1900 edition of *The Analysis of Sensations,* the famous Ernst Mach still didn't know the secret. And as the reference to the "marble tablet" shows, he was concerned about whether his own originality would ever achieve public recognition. It is significant that in the passage from *An Autobiographical Study* in which Freud denies the influence of Schopenhauer and Nietzsche on his work, he freely acknowledges the influence of Fechner, just as Mach freely acknowledged Fechner's influence in *The Analysis of Sensations.* Mach notes in the preface to the first edition that "My natural bent for the study of these questions received its strongest stimulus twenty-five years ago from Fechner's *Elemente der Psychophysik* (Leipzig, 1860)" (p. xxxvi). And in the book's final chapter he says that "Fechner's psychophysics, which have had so important an influence, did not fail to stimulate me exceedingly at the time" (p. 370), though one of the aims of *The Analysis of Sensations,* as Mach makes clear, is to separate his own work from Fechner's, to distinguish his notion of *"the complete parallelism of the psychical and the physical"* (p. 60) from "Fechner's conception of the physical and psychical as two different aspects of one and the same reality" (p. 61).

Now putting the question of influence aside for a moment, we can say that, just as there is a philosophical line of thought that runs from Schopenhauer to Nietzsche to Freud, a recognizable similarity in their psychological insights that Freud openly acknowledged, so too there is a scientific line of thought that runs from Fechner to Mach to Freud, a recognizable similarity in their questioning of the relationship between the physical and the psychical that Freud openly acknowledged in the case of Fechner and privately acknowledged in the case of Mach (the letter to Fliess). For our purposes, then, it is important to distinguish between the question of influence and the question of priority. Though Freud denies the influence of Schopenhauer and Nietzsche, the very necessity, the very appropriateness, of such a denial is an admission that many of Schopenhauer's and Nietzsche's insights into human motivations and the mechanisms of the psyche are similar to his own and precede his own writings, often by many years. As a rhetorical defense against this feeling of his work's having been anticipated, of its not being original, Freud distinguishes between the "philosophical" nature of Schopenhauer's and Nietzsche's work, which he deprecatingly characterizes with such words as *guesses* and *intuitions,* and the scientific nature of his own work, "the laborious findings of psychoanalysis."

What is uncanny, or perhaps not so uncanny, is that Mach used the same strategy in *The Analysis of Sensations* many years earlier. At the very start of the book, Mach points out that "the physiology of the senses" has gradually abandoned "the method of investigating sensations in themselves followed by men like Goethe, Schopenhauer and . . . Johannes Muller" and has "assumed an almost exclusively physical character" (p. 1). Though Mach acknowledges the helpfulness of insights

drawn from philosophy and deplores any absolute separation
between philosophy and natural science, it is clear that he clas-
sifies himself as a man of science and that, however useful his
scientific findings may be to philosophy, "there is no such thing
as 'the philosophy of Mach' " (p. 368). Just as Freud claimed to
have formed conclusions resembling Schopenhauer's long before he had ever read Schopenhauer's work, so Mach says that
it was "by studying the physiology of the senses, and by reading
Herbart" that he "arrived at views akin to those of Hume,"
though at the time he "was still unacquainted with Hume himself" (p. 368). Moreover, aware that his scientific critique of the
substantial existence of the ego and Nietzsche's philosophical
critique of the ego might be interpreted as having the same
ethical effect, Mach takes pains to point out that the "ethical
ideal" which he believes will follow from a renunciation of the
ego and individual immortality is "far removed" from "the
ideal of an overweening Nietzschean 'superman,' who cannot,
and I hope will not, be tolerated by his fellow-men" (p. 25).

Consequently, though Freud could logically distinguish his
scientific work from the philosophical writings of Schopenhauer and Nietzsche, it would have been impossible for him to
represent his research as being more scientific than Mach's,
particularly when Mach had made use of the same invidious
distinction between science and philosophy years before. What
we are left with is a situation in which Freud, no matter what
the influence of Mach's research on his own, would have been
aware of the similarities in certain areas between his writings
and Mach's prior writings and thus could have easily felt,
granting his sensitivity to the question of priority as evidenced
by his reaction to Schopenhauer and Nietzsche, that Mach's
work called into question the originality of his own work in certain areas and thus threatened its survival. In short, it is a situation in which the temporal doubling between Freud and Mach
would have presented Freud with an image of the possible
death of parts of his own work by reason of their seeming to be
merely psychoanalytic rephrasings of Mach's previous insights,
a situation in which Freud not only would not have had at his
disposal the rhetorical defense-mechanism that he used against

Schopenhauer and Nietzsche but would have found in that very mechanism another example of Mach's priority.

With these considerations in mind, let us examine more closely the circumstances surrounding the composition of "The Uncanny." The essay, which was first published in the autumn of 1919, "is mentioned by Freud in a letter to Ferenczi of May 12 of the same year, in which he says he has dug an old paper out of a drawer and is rewriting it. Nothing is known as to when it was originally written or how much it was changed, though the footnote quoted from *Totem and Taboo* . . . shows that the subject was present in his mind as early as 1913. The passages dealing with the 'compulsion to repeat' . . . must in any case have formed part of the revision" (1919, editors' note, p. 218). In discussing the uncanny effect of coincidences or "similar recurrences" as related to infantile psychology, Freud refers the reader to "another work, already completed, in which this has been gone into in detail, but in a different connection. For it is possible to recognize the dominance in the unconscious mind of a 'compulsion to repeat' proceeding from the instinctual impulses and probably inherent in the very nature of the instincts—a compulsion powerful enough to overrule the pleasure principle, lending to certain aspects of the mind their daemonic character, and still very clearly expressed in the impulses of small children; a compulsion, too, which is responsible for a part of the course taken by the analyses of neurotic patients. All these considerations prepare us for the discovery that whatever reminds us of this inner 'compulsion to repeat' is perceived as uncanny" (p. 238). The work to which Freud refers in this passage is *Beyond the Pleasure Principle,* which he had begun writing in March 1919. In the same letter to Ferenczi in which Freud mentions the essay on the uncanny, he reports that a draft of the longer work has been completed. However, Freud held back publication of *Beyond the Pleasure Principle* and continued to work on the manuscript through the early part of 1920, finally publishing it later that year.

In *Beyond the Pleasure Principle* Freud introduces what is perhaps his most controversial notion, the concept of a death instinct inherent in all living matter. As Freud indicates in the passage from "The Uncanny" quoted above, he was led to this concept by the observation that in the play of small children and in the actions of some neurotics there seems to be a compulsion to repeat that does not depend on the pleasurableness of the repeated action. More often than not, the repeated material is traumatic, and the repetition is an effort to master the trauma by transforming the original affront from something passively suffered by the individual into something which he actively initiates in the form of a repetition, and thus controls. The aim of this mastery is to reduce the level of excitation in the traumatized organism to what it was before the affront. Having identified this compulsion as "instinctual," Freud asks, "But how is the predicate of being 'instinctual' related to the compulsion to repeat? At this point we cannot escape a suspicion that we may have come upon the track of a universal attribute of instincts and perhaps of organic life in general which has not hitherto been clearly recognized or at least not explicitly stressed. *It seems, then, that an instinct is an urge inherent in organic life to restore an earlier state of things* which the living entity has been obliged to abandon under the pressure of external disturbing forces" (1920, p. 36). The instincts are "an expression of the *conservative* nature of living substance" (p. 36), and the ultimate goal of the instincts, the ultimate "earlier state of things" which the compulsion to repeat seeks to restore, is the inorganic state from which life sprang, the state of zero excitation. Freud concludes that "If we are to take it as a truth that knows no exception that everything living dies for *internal* reasons—becomes inorganic once again—then we shall be compelled to say that '*the aim of all life is death*' " (p. 38). The death instinct is, then, not simply one type of instinct among others; it is the archetypal operating principle of all the instincts, of instinctual behavior. Even in the case of something as apparently opposed to death as the pleasure principle, Freud asserts, "The pleasure principle seems actually to serve the death instincts" (p. 63).

Clearly, in *Beyond the Pleasure Principle* Freud is only too aware of the controversial nature of this theory, that is, aware of the largely *theoretical* character of the notion of the death instinct. Thus, for example, the death instinct depends upon the assumption that death is the inevitable fate of living matter, that without exception "everything dies for *internal* reasons." If that is not true, then the death instinct is not the principle of all instinctual behavior. It may simply be one of two major types of instinct, its opposite being the sex instinct, the drive to reproduce life. Or if death is an accidental rather than a necessary feature of life, there may be no death instinct at all.

In section 6 of *Beyond the Pleasure Principle*, Freud surveys recent work in biology to see if any data exists that "would flatly contradict the recognition of death instincts" (p. 49); and after reviewing the work of Weismann, Goette, Hartmann, Woodruff, Maupas, Calkins, and others, and noting "how little agreement there is among biologists on the subject of natural death," he judges that there is no data which would rule out the possibility of a death instinct. What is significant in this procedure is not only Freud's turning to biology "to test the validity of the belief" (p. 45), but the ambivalent way in which he handles this scientific evidence. Freud was aware that the "theoretical grounds" on which his notion of a death instinct was based could just as easily be characterized as "speculative" or "philosophical." By seeking evidence from a natural science like biology, Freud makes his own position seem less philosophical. But there is also a danger in this procedure; for though Freud was ostensibly searching for data that might contradict his theory, he was also looking for any evidence that might support it. Yet biological data that was similar enough to his own theory to be supportive, might also turn out to be preemptive of his discovery, revealing that his notion of a death instinct had been anticipated by the natural sciences. Freud's strategy is to represent the biological data which he cites as being like, but not too like, his own theory. Thus, in dealing with Weismann's work, he notes "the striking similarity between Weismann's distinction of soma and germ-plasm" and his own "separation of the death instincts from the life instincts" (p. 49), but he points out that "the appearance of a significant correspondence is dissipated as soon as we discover Weismann's views on the problem of death" (p. 46). However, in one of his citations of scientific opinion, Freud reveals a significant link between the reading he had been doing for this section of *Beyond the Pleasure Principle* and the essay he was writing on the uncanny. He says,

> According to E. Hering's theory, two kinds of processes are constantly at work in living substance, operating in contrary directions, one constructive or assimilatory and the other destructive or dissimilatory. May we venture to recognize in these two directions taken by the vital processes the activity of our two instinctual impulses, the life instincts and the death instincts? There is something else, at any rate, that we cannot remain blind to. We have unwittingly steered our course into the harbour of Schopenhauer's philosophy. For him death is the 'true result and to that extent the purpose of life,' while the sexual instinct is the embodiment of the will to live. [pp. 49–50]

The passage attracts our interest for a variety of reasons. First, it is a clear example of Freud's effort to chart an "original" course between the Scylla and Charybdis of natural science and philosophy, represented here by the work of Hering and Schopenhauer respectively. Second, it is an equally clear example of his sensitivity to the question of priority and repetition in his writing, his sensitivity to the fact that he has "unwittingly" (does that mean "unconsciously"?) repeated an insight from Schopenhauer's philosophy, a repetition that "we cannot remain blind to" (who had tried to remain blind to it?). Finally, and most important, the reference to Hering recalls the context within which Freud, in the essay on the uncanny, discusses the compulsion to repeat and mentions the existence of a longer work on the subject—*Beyond the Pleasure Principle*. At that point in the essay, Freud has been giving examples of the uncanny effect of coincidences, of "similar recurrences," and the example which immediately precedes his suggestion of the link between the uncanny and the compulsion to repeat is this: "suppose one is engaged in reading the works of the famous physiologist, Hering, and within the space of a few days receives two letters from two different countries, each from a person called Hering, though one has never before had any dealings with anyone of that name" (1919, p. 238). Obviously, the person who was "engaged in reading the works of the famous physiologist, Hering" at that moment was Freud himself. To judge from the reference in *Beyond the Pleasure Principle*, Hering's works were among the texts in natural science which Freud was surveying for data that might contradict or support the notion of a death instinct. And what seems likely is that the reason the physiologist Hering was on Freud's mind at the time he was writing "The Uncanny" is the same reason that Ernst Mach was on his mind: that besides surveying works in biology and physiology, Freud read certain psychophysical works as well, and that among these he reread Mach's *The Analysis of Sensations*, which, according to the letter to Fliess, he had first read almost twenty years earlier. Thus, just as Hering emerged from Freud's survey of scientific data on natural death to become an instance of uncanny recurrence, so Mach emerged from the same survey to become an example of uncanny doubling.

The likelihood that Freud was reading psychophysical texts at the time is confirmed by the fact that the opening section of *Beyond the Pleasure Principle* includes, as part of a discussion of originality in research, a lengthy quote from Fechner. Freud says,

> It is of no concern to us in this connection to enquire how far, with this hypothesis of the pleasure principle, we have approached or adopted any particular, historically established, philosophical system. We have arrived at these speculative assumptions in an attempt to describe and to account for the facts of daily observation in our field of study. Priority and originality are not among the aims that psycho-analytic work sets itself; and the impressions that underlie the hypothesis of the pleasure principle are so obvious that they can scarcely be overlooked. On the other hand we would readily express our gratitude to any philosophical or psychological theory which was able to inform us of the meaning of the feelings of pleasure and unplea-

sure which act so imperatively upon us. But on this point
we are, alas, offered nothing to our purpose. . . .

  We cannot, however, remain indifferent to the discovery
that an investigator of such penetration as G. T. Fechner
held a view on the subject of pleasure and unpleasure
which coincides in all essentials with the one that has been
forced upon us by psycho-analytic work. [1920, pp. 7–8]

  Freud then goes on to quote a passage from Fechner's *Einige
Ideen zur Schöpfungs- und Entwicklungsgeschichte der Organismen*
(1873). What interests us here is that Freud characterizes the
similarity between Fechner's "view on the subject of pleasure
and unpleasure," and his own concept of the pleasure principle,
as a "discovery," as something that he had recently become
aware of, thus suggesting that he had only recently read or
reread Fechner's book. (Perhaps Freud's willingness to acknowledge the similarity between the pleasure principle and
Fechner's view of pleasure and unpleasure is due to the fact
that Freud himself was about to advance beyond the pleasure
principle in the development of his thought.)

  Further evidence suggesting the likelihood that Mach's *The
Analysis of Sensations* was one of the works which Freud
searched for data that might bear on the death instinct is to be
found in the book itself. Mach says in the preface to the first
edition that he is "under especial obligations to those investiga-
tors, such as E. Hering, V. Hensen, W. Preyer and others, who
have directed attention either to the matter of my writings or to
my methodological expositions," and he adds that though his
"natural bent for the study of these questions received its
strongest stimulus twenty-five years ago from Fechner's *Elemente
der Psychophysik*," his "greatest assistance" was derived from
Hering's work (pp. xxxvi–xxxvii). Throughout the book, Mach
frequently refers to the scientific contributions of Hering and
Weismann, and at one point, in discussing Hering's notion of
an unconscious memory inherent in cells and simple organisms
that accounts for the hereditary transmission of information by
cells and thus the repetition of functions by the organisms
which they compose, Mach is led to discuss Weismann's notion

of "death as a phenomenon of heredity" (p. 72). (If death is a phenomenon of heredity, that is, a "memory outside the organ of conciousness" [p. 73], does that mean that death is an instinct?)

Clearly, the connections between Mach's work and the work of most of the scientists whom Freud mentions in section 6 of *Beyond the Pleasure Principle* are so close that it would have been virtually unthinkable for a researcher as meticulous as Freud not to have included *The Analysis of Sensations* in his survey of scientific literature on natural death. What this all means, then, is that at the time when Freud quoted, as a footnote to "The Uncanny," the passage from *The Analysis of Sensations* in which Mach tells the story of not recognizing his double, Freud had in all likelihood been rereading Mach's book in the context of the death instinct and the compulsion to repeat.

Now just as meeting one's double is, as Freud notes, an image of death, so too a "coincidence" or "similar recurrence" like that which Freud points out between Mach's uncanny experience and his own is also an image of death, because it recalls the "inner compulsion to repeat"—that is, the death instinct. Yet the only comment Freud makes on these similar experiences is: "Instead, therefore, of being *frightened* by our 'doubles', both Mach and I simply failed to recognize them as such. Is it not possible, though, that our dislike of them was a vestigial trace of the archaic reaction which feels the 'double' to be something uncanny?" (1919, p. 248 n.). Rather, is it not possible that Freud's footnote on Mach represents an irruption of the uncanny within the essay on the uncanny? Is it not possible that the footnote is "a vestigial trace" of an act of repression? Freud points out in the essay that "the uncanny (*unheimlich*) is something which is secretly familiar (*heimlich-heimisch*), which has undergone repression and then returned from it (p. 245). And concerning the uncanny in real life, he says, "an uncanny experience occurs either when infantile complexes which have been repressed are once more revived by some impression, or when primitive beliefs which have been surmounted seem once more to be confirmed" (p. 249). Is the footnote, then, which remarks an interesting but seemingly insignificant similarity in the experiences of Mach and Freud, the trace left by Freud's repression of a more important, and a more disquieting, sense of the similarity between himself and Mach, a similarity Freud would have confronted in rereading *The Analysis of Sensations?*

If Freud's footnote is such a trace, then it should send us back to *The Analysis of Sensations* to examine the context in which Mach tells the story of meeting his double. It occurs in the opening chapter during Mach's discussion of the ego as a temporary unity, as being "only of relative permanency" (p. 3):

> The apparent permanency of the ego consists chiefly in the single fact of its continuity, in the slowness of its changes. The many thoughts and plans of yesterday that are continued to-day, and of which our environment in waking hours incessantly reminds us (whence in dreams the ego can be very indistinct, doubled, or entirely wanting), and the little habits that are unconsciously and involuntarily kept up for long periods of time, constitute the groundwork of the ego. There can hardly be greater differences in the egos of different people, than occur in the course of years in one person. When I recall to-day my early youth, I should take the boy that I then was, with the exception of a few individual features, for a different person, were it not for the existence of the chain of memories. Many an article that I myself penned twenty years ago impresses me now as something quite foreign to myself. The very gradual character of the changes of the body also contributes to the stability of the ego, but in a much less degree than people imagine. Such things are much less analyzed and noticed than the intellectual and the moral ego. Personally, people know themselves very poorly. When I wrote these lines in 1886, Ribot's admirable little book, *The Diseases of Personality* (second edition, Paris, 1888, Chicago 1895), was unknown to me. Ribot ascribes the principal role in preserving the continuity of the ego to the general sensibility. Generally, I am in perfect accord with his views.

The ego is as little absolutely permanent as are bodies. That which we so much dread in death, the annihilation of our permanency, actually occurs in life in abundant measure. That which is most valued by us, remains preserved in countless copies, or, in cases of exceptional excellence, is even preserved of itself. In the best human being, however, there are individual traits, the loss of which neither he himself nor others need regret. Indeed, at times, death, viewed as a liberation from individuality, may even become a pleasant thought. Such reflections of course do not make physiological death any the easier to bear. [pp. 3–5]

One can imagine Freud rereading this passage—almost twenty years after his remark in the letter to Fliess that *The Analysis of Sensations* was one of "the latest psychological books" having "the same kind of aims as my work"—and experiencing an uncanny sensation similar to that of seeing what one had thought was another person turn out to be one's own image. Mach was a physicist interested in psychology who worked on psychophysical parallelism, Freud a neurologist interested in psychology who worked in psychoanalysis. Each felt that important insights in his own work had been anticipated by philosophers, and each took pains to distinguish his own scientific findings from philosophical intuitions. But in the passage quoted above, the similarity between Mach and Freud must have seemed to Freud, at the precise moment when he was working on "The Uncanny" and *Beyond the Pleasure Principle*, almost overwhelming. As an example of how completely one's ego changes over a period of years, Mach reports the experience of looking at articles he had written twenty years earlier and finding them "quite foreign" (alien? dead?) to himself; and then, three sentences later, as a footnote to the statement that "Personally, people know themselves very poorly," he tells the story of not recognizing his mirror-image on two separate occasions. The association is clear: one's writings are an inscribed image of the self similar to one's mirror-image, and just as Mach has had the experience of looking at essays he had written twenty years earlier and not recognizing himself, so he has also had the experience of seeing his mirror-image and not recognizing himself.

The essay in which Freud refers to Mach's story was an old paper Freud had dug out of a drawer and was rewriting. Further, the Mach text that contains the story was one that Freud had read twenty years earlier. Thus, in rewriting an old paper on the uncanny during the middle of 1919, Freud was confronting an earlier written image of himself at the same time that he was reexperiencing the twenty-year-old written image of Mach in *The Analysis of Sensations*. Add to this the fact that, immediately after the sentence containing the footnote about not recognizing his double, Mach calls attention to his *own* revision of his original text, remarking that "When I wrote these lines in 1886, Ribot's admirable little book, *The Diseases of Personality* . . . was unknown to me." What Freud read in 1900 and quoted in 1919 was the second edition of *The Analysis of Sensations*—that is, Mach's own encounter with an earlier written image of himself. And the result of Mach's retrospective encounter was that an earlier book (Ribot's), which Mach had been unaware of at the time of the first writing, had to be acknowledged, in the second edition, as putting part of Mach's text in question on the grounds of both priority and broader knowledge—a moment that would have rendered transparent Freud's own concerns about originality and priority in rereading Mach. And Freud would not even have had the excuse Mach had in regard to Ribot, for Freud was aware of *The Analysis of Sensations* from the very beginning of his psychoanalytic writing. When Mach then goes on to remark that what "we so much dread in death, the annihilation of our permanency, actually occurs in life in abundant measure," he points out what seems to be a deathlike, unconscious operating principle in the self. And when he proceeds to distinguish between those valuable traits in the self which are "preserved in countless copies" and those traits whose loss is not to be regretted, and then relates this natural process by which traits die out of the self during life to the notion that "at times, death, viewed as a liberation from individuality, may even become a pleasant thought," he seems not only to make a distinction similar to that between the life instincts whose aim is survival and the death instincts whose ultimate aim is annihilation, but also to associate the instinct to survive with the act of writing, with that which "remains preserved in countless copies."

Suffice it to say that if Freud, at the time when he quoted Mach's story of doubling in "The Uncanny," was rereading *The Analysis of Sensations* in light of the death instinct and the compulsion to repeat for the survey of scientific data in *Beyond the Pleasure Principle,* then the context in which Mach tells of not recognizing his mirror-image would have fulfilled in Freud's case all the criteria of an uncanny experience in real life—an experience that would have been much more uncanny than the one involving the coincidental repetition of Hering's name which Freud reports in the essay. More uncanny because more threatening, for the experience could well have aroused Freud's fear that the similarity between Mach's insights and his own (which would have been threatening enough in itself to Freud's sense of his own originality) was *not* coincidental, the fear that Freud had absorbed more of Mach's ideas in his original reading of *The Analysis of Sensations* than he had realized, and that he had been unconsciously influenced by Mach's work in his own subsequent writings, until, in rereading Mach, he confronted that anxiety-ridden similarity and repressed it, the footnote on Mach being the trace of the repression.

Now, based on the hypersensitivity which Freud exhibits, in his published writings and his correspondence, to the question of priority and originality, it is no great insight to suggest that Freud suffered from an originality neurosis, nor much more of an insight to point out the connection between such a neurosis and the castration complex. For the threat in an originality neurosis is that the writings of an older man (Mach was Freud's senior by eighteen years), through their similarity and priority, preempt the possibility of originality for the younger man's writings and thus threaten the survival of the younger man's work—that is, they prefigure the death of the younger man's written corpus, prefigure it in this instance in a doubly uncanny manner through Mach's anticipation of the death instinct. The similarity between Mach's insights and Freud's would, then, fall into that category of experiences which are uncanny because they revive repressed infantile complexes, in this case the threat posed by the father to the son's potency and viability, the son's feeling of being a passive repetition of the original. In such a case, Mach could easily symbolize for Freud all those writers whose prior work Freud felt to be a threat to his own originality.

One such writer, Nietzsche, is a particularly menacing presence in both "The Uncanny" and *Beyond the Pleasure Principle,* and there is evidence to suggest that Freud's intellectual relationship to Nietzsche was tinged with oedipal anxieties. (In the triangle of Nietzsche, Lou Andreas-Salomé, and Freud, the role of intellectual mentor to the beautiful, intelligent Lou had been played first by the older man, Nietzsche, and then by Freud, and to judge from their correspondence one of the things that Lou and Freud discussed was the resemblances between Nietzsche's thought and Freud's.) In the essay on the uncanny, Freud refers to the uncanny effect of "the constant recurrence of the same thing . . . through several consecutive generations" (p. 234), and again, to the uncanny theme of "the unintended recurrence of the same thing" (p. 246). And in *Beyond the Pleasure Principle,* discussing the "daemonic" character which the compulsion to repeat gives to the actions of some neurotics, he remarks,

> This 'perpetual recurrence of the same thing' causes us no astonishment when it relates to *active* behaviour on the part of the person concerned and when we can discern in him an essential character-trait which always remains the same and which is compelled to find expression in a repetition of the same experiences. We are much more impressed by cases where the subject appears to have a *passive* experience, over which he has no influence, but in which he meets with a repetition of the same fatality. [p. 22]

Clearly, the allusion in each of the instances quoted is to Nietzsche's concept of "the eternal recurrence of the same" from *Thus Spoke Zarathustra,* part 3 (1884). The impulse which

Freud evokes by the names "the compulsion to repeat" and "the death instinct" is, broadly speaking, an aspect of the same dynamic principle that Nietzsche named "the eternal recurrence of the same," just as Freud's "life instincts" or "sex instincts" are an aspect of the principle that Nietzsche named "the will to power." It is Zarathustra's role to proclaim two related concepts—the eternal recurrence of the same and the overman—concepts that are related because the overman is that theoretical being who is capable of willing the eternal recurrence of the same, capable of changing the endless recurrences of time and the death which time inevitably brings from something passively suffered to something actively willed, of raising that repetition (which seeks to return to an original state of sameness) from an unconscious compulsion to a conscious desire. Yet something very much like that is what Freud proclaims in *Beyond the Pleasure Principle,* for in identifying the death instinct (that compulsion to repeat whose ultimate goal is a return to the quiescence of the inorganic state), Freud tries to raise it from the instinctual level to the level of thought. In enunciating the principle that *"the aim of all life is death,"* that man's destiny is not personal immortality in an otherworld, Freud, like Nietzsche, aims to do away with the complex network of metaphysical illusions that are based on the belief in personal survival, aims to reconcile man to the reality of the human condition, an aim which Freud pursues in such later works as *The Future of an Illusion* (1927).

Yet in *The Analysis of Sensations,* published two years after *Zarathustra* (part 3), Mach, in denying the permanency of the go and "individual immortality" (p. 25), aims at a similar clearing away of illusions, as indicated by the title of the first chapter, "Introductory Remarks: Antimetaphysical." His assertion that "The ego is just as little absolutely permanent as are bodies" might well have seemed to Freud an echo of the moment when Zarathustra's animals, discussing the eternal recurrence and the overman, tell Zarathustra, "The soul is as mortal as the body" (p. 333). It is precisely because Mach is aware of the apparent similarity, in terms of the effect on human conduct, of Nietzsche's antimetaphysical critique and his own that he goes out of his way to distinguish "the ethical ideal" which will be founded on the impermanency of the ego and the renunciation of individual immortality from "the ideal of an overweening Nietzschean 'superman' ", he who wills the eternal recurrence of the same. Freud would have confronted, then, in *The Analysis of Sensations,* not only Nietzsche's seeming priority in this area of thought, but also what appeared to be Mach's prior attempt to circumvent that priority.

If the footnote on Mach in "The Uncanny" is the "vestigial trace" of an act of repression, if it marks the burial place, the encrypting of the image of the possible death of Freud's written corpus, then there are various ways in which the footnote's cryptic message can be translated. Through its symbolic language the footnote may say: just as Mach didn't recognize his double, so I don't recognize my double (Mach); turnabout is fair play; if Mach is not wrong in doing this, then I am not wrong in doing the same thing to Mach. (The footnote would then imply that though Mach is prior to Freud, he is no more original than Freud, for Mach has his own threatening predecessors whom *he* has tried to repress.) Or the footnote may say: just as Mach was not afraid of his own double, but simply disliked his appearance, so I am not afraid of my double (Mach), I simply don't like his looks. (However, Freud himself hints that this dislike of the double's appearance masks an original fear.) Or the footnote may say: if we let the similarity between Mach's experience of not recognizing his double and my own experience stand for all the recognized and unrecognized similarities between my work and the work of previous writers, then I hereby declare that those similarities are not significant enough to be included in the body of the text, they are of marginal importance. (The threat to the written corpus would thus be expelled from the body of the text and "buried in a footnote.") Yet Mach's own account of not recognizing his double was also given in a footnote to *The Analysis of Sensations.* Is Freud, then, repeating Mach once more in the very attempt to repress the fear of repeating Mach? The structure of Freud's footnote— the spatial doubling involved in each man's encounter with his mirror-image, which is in turn temporally doubled by the way Freud's experience repeats Mach's, which is itself a doubling of Freud's encounter with Mach's written image in *The Analysis of Sensations*—is like a house of mirrors; its doubling of doubles seems to insure that whichever way we translate the note's cryptic message, whichever way Freud tries to repress his fear of repeating Mach, Freud ends up repeating a strategy that Mach himself had previously used. The act of repression reinscribes the feared repetition that it is meant to repress, thus assuring the cycle of re-return and re-repression.

Keeping this structure in mind, let us turn back to the passage from Hart Crane's *The Bridge*. If in Freud's text we found that a quotation about the uncanny effect of doubling seemed to be a trace, a veiled image, of the writer's repressed fear of the death of his work, might we then expect to find that Crane's description of the bedlamite's leap from the Brooklyn Bridge, a form of death that seems to be an uncanny prefiguration of Crane's own suicide by drowning, contains a veiled quotation? Presenting itself as a kind of summation and commentary upon the American symbolist tradition, *The Bridge* abounds with quotations from, and allusions to, the works of Whitman, Poe, Melville, and Emily Dickinson. Moreover, Whitman and Poe appear as characters in "Cape Hatteras" and "The Tunnel" respectively. Yet it is not to any of these major writers that the faint echo in Crane's description of the suicide directs our attention, but rather to a minor nineteenth-century American poet. When Crane characterizes the bedlamite's death with the words, "A jest falls from the speechless caravan," we seem to recall somewhere in American poetry another silent "caravan" associated with death. I refer, of course, to the closing lines of William Cullen Bryant's "Thanatopsis," the most famous passage from Bryant's most famous poem and a standard text for memorization in American schools for decades. At the end of the poem—which seeks to assuage the fear of death through the love of nature, showing that the natural world which nurtures us continues this care by providing us our final resting place—the poet says:

So live, that when thy summons comes to join
The innumerable caravan, which moves
To that mysterious realm, where each shall take
His chamber in the silent halls of death,
Thou go not, like the quarry-slave at night,
Scourged to his dungeon, but, sustained and soothed
By an unfaltering trust, approach thy grave,
Like one who wraps the drapery of his couch
About him, and lies down to pleasant dreams.

Whether Crane's "speechless caravan" is a conscious or unconscious echo of Bryant's "innumerable caravan," at least one critic, R. W. B. Lewis, has suggested that *The Bridge* does indeed owe a conscious debt of influence to another Bryant poem, "The Fountain" (Lewis, p. 235). And I would contend that that debt, which is by no means an inconsiderable one, was of a particularly threatening character to Crane. In "The Fountain," Bryant depicts the historical alteration of the American landscape through the changes which the woodland fountain has witnessed in its natural setting over the years. At least two sections of *The Bridge*—"The River" and "The Dance"—appear to owe part of their general conception and certain descriptive details, as well as their tone of visionary union with the Indian world, to Bryant's account of the Indians being supplanted by the white settlers. The reworking of descriptive details is perhaps the easiest of these to illustrate. Thus, Bryant's depiction of the felling of the woods by the white man's axe—"Then all around was heard the crash of trees / Trembling awhile and rushing to the ground" (Bryant, p. 187)—is echoed in Crane's description of the thunderstorm in the forest—"The oak grove circles in a crash of leaves" (Crane, p. 73). While Bryant's "ranks of spiky maize / Rose like a host embattled" is echoed by Crane's address to the rain-god Maquokeeta, "Lo, through what infinite seasons dost thou gaze— / Across what bivouacs of thine angered slain, / And see'st thy bride immortal in the maize?"

Yet these debts are minor compared to the debt that Crane appears to owe to the conclusion of Bryant's poem, where, in imagining the future of the land, Bryant associates four image patterns whose symbolic interaction becomes a major structural element in *The Bridge*. "The Fountain" ends:

> Here the sage,
> Gazing into thy self-replenished depth,
> Has seen eternal order circumscribe
> And bound the motions of eternal change,
> And from the gushing of thy simple fount
> Has reasoned to the mighty universe.
>
> Is there no other change for thee, that lurks
> Among the future ages? Will not man
> Seek out strange arts to wither and deform
> The pleasant landscape which thou makest green?
> Or shall the veins that feed thy constant stream
> Be choked in middle earth, and flow no more
> For ever, that the water-plants along
> Thy channel perish, and the bird in vain
> Alight to drink? Haply shall these green hills
> Sink, with the lapse of years, into the gulf
> Of ocean waters, and thy source be lost
> Amidst the bitter brine? Or shall they rise,
> Upheaved in broken cliffs and airy peaks,
> Haunts of the eagle and the snake, and thou
> Gush midway from the bare and barren steep?

The four image patterns linked here are: first, the circularization of power ("the motions of eternal change" are "circumscribed and bound" by the concentric circles of the pool which, by turning the power back upon itself, makes it self-replenishing); second, the fountain; third, the sinking/rising of the land; and fourth, the eagle and the snake.

The image of the circle dominates *The Bridge*, its great emblem being the arc of the bridge above the river and the arc of the tunnel below, the two together forming the circle of eternity through which the river of time flows. For Crane the circularization of power is, broadly speaking, a Platonic motif—the notion that energy turned back upon itself controls or orders itself without the loss of energy, like a fountain whose jet fills a circular pool that catches the water and replenishes the source of the fountain. Or like the suspension bridge whose counter-balanced forces Crane evokes as a "motion ever unspent in thy stride, / Implicitly thy freedom staying thee!" (p. 45). But Crane also draws on Henry Adams' image of circular power, the dynamo, in passages that evoke the deadening mechanization of the circle. In "Cape Hatteras" he addresses the dynamo as "O murmurless and shined / In oilrinsed circles of blind ecstasy!" (p. 90), and transferring this mechanistic image of the circle to the universe, Crane writes:

> But that star-glistered salver of infinity,
> The circle, blind crucible of endless space,
> Is sluiced by motion,—subjugated never.
> Adam and Adam's answer in the forest
> Left Hesperus mirrored in the lucid pool.
> Now the eagle dominates our days, is jurist
> Of the ambiguous cloud. We know the strident rule
> Of wings imperious. . . .
>
> [p. 89]

Crane later describes the propellers of the imperious eagle-airplanes as "marauding circles" (p. 91). In the passage quoted above, the circular power that Crane opposes to the blind, mechanical circles lies in the concentric rings of the lucid, mirroring pool of the intellect. Adam's answer to the "blind crucible of endless space" is language—the naming of the evening star, Hesperus, that leaves it mirrored in the pool of the mind. The circular power of language is further embodied in the self-referentiality of the poem; for though the bridge referred to in the poem is ostensibly the Brooklyn Bridge, it is also the poem called *The Bridge*. The poem's subject is the act of symbolization considered as a bridge between mind and world and between mind and mind. The bridging or bridgeship that the poem thematizes is wholly linguistic. Thus it is that the litany of names applied to the bridge in the opening and closing sections of the poem, many of which make no sense if the referent is the real Brooklyn Bridge, are perfectly comprehensible if the referent is the symbolic bridge, the bridge of symbolization.

Crane's use of the second and third image patterns—the fountain and the sinking/rising of the land—can best be illustrated by starting with a passage from "The River" in which Crane depicts the submersion of the Indian world by the white settlers:

> The old gods of the rain lie wrapped in pools
> Where eyeless fish curvet a sunken fountain
> And re-descend with corn from querulous crows.
> Such pilferings make up their timeless eatage,
> Propitiate them for their timber torn
> By iron, iron—always the iron dealt cleavage!
> They doze now, below axe and powder horn.
>
> [p. 66]

Crane's symbol for the ideal land that the original settlers of America dreamed of, the ideal land that has been submerged by greed and materialism but that might some day reemerge, is the island continent of Atlantis, the beautiful, favored land that sank beneath the sea. As Plato tells the story in the *Critias,* the island of Atlantis belonged to the sea-god Poseidon. Enamored of a maiden named Clito who lived on a hill at the center of the island, Poseidon "fortified the hill where she had her abode by a fence of alternate rings of sea and land, smaller and greater, one within another. He fashioned two such round wheels . . . of earth and three of sea from the very center of the island, at uniform distances. . . . The island left at their center he adorned with his own hand . . . causing two fountains to flow from underground springs, one warm, one cold, and the soil to send up abundance of food plants of all kinds" (113d). At first, Poseidon's descendants by Clito were virtuous; they "found the weight of their gold and other possessions a light load. Wealth made them not drunken with wantonness" (121a). But in later generations the people of Atlantis took "the infection of wicked covetousness and pride of power" (121b), and for this they were punished by the gods—their island vanished beneath the waves.

In the "Cutty Sark" section, Crane associates Atlantis, a sunken land of Platonic concentric circles at whose center were fountains, with the sperm whale, whose islandlike body rises

and sinks beneath the sea and bears a fountain in its back. In
Moby-Dick, the chapter describing the whale's spout is called
"The Fountain," and clearly Melville is the proper allusive
background here, for this section of *The Bridge* begins with an
epigraph from one of his poems and the sailor in "Cutty Sark"
is described in terms reminiscent of Ishmael:

> Murmurs of Leviathan he spoke
> and rum was Plato in our heads . . .
>
> [p. 82]

> "—that spiracle!" he shot a finger out the door . . .
> "O life's a geyser. . . ."
>
> [p. 83]

Like Atlantis, the whale with the fountain in its back symbolizes
for Crane that bountifulness of nature which has been submerged and almost destroyed by human greed and by a blind
will-to-power whose goal is the absolute domination of physical
nature. As a counterpoint to the narrative line of "Cutty Sark,"
the song of "Atlantis Rose" weaves into the text its image of
*"teased remnants of the skeletons of cities— / and galleries, galleries of
watergutted lava"* (p. 83)

The fourth image pattern, the eagle and the snake, is an almost universal symbol of the bounding extremes (the highest
and the lowest), while the conjunction of the eagle and the
snake, as in the feathered serpent, is a symbol of the coincidence of opposites. The image, which can be found in contexts
as various as the Mexican flag and *Thus Spoke Zarathustra,* is
used by Crane as a symbol of the spatial and temporal integration of the idealized nature-world of the Indians. In "The
River" the poet senses the presence of the virgin body of the
continent, the maiden Pocahontas, beneath the commercial dis-
figuration of the land and says,

> . . . I knew her body there,
> Time like a serpent down her shoulder, dark,
> And space, an eaglet's wing, laid on her hair.
>
> [p. 66]

This image leads immediately into the passage describing the
Indian rain-gods who "lie wrapped in pools" containing a

"sunken fountain," and it prepares us for the moment in "The
Dance" when the rain-god Maquokeeta, with "eagle feathers"
down his back, arrives as the thunderbird during the rain
dance—that is, the snake dance—to fertilize the virgin land,
feathered serpent and fountain both being symbols of fertiliza-
tion and harmonious union. "The Dance" ends with the image
of "The serpent with the eagle in the boughs" (p. 75). The
modern, mechanical parodies of the eagle of space and the serpent of time are the death-dealing airplanes of "Cape Hatteras"
and the nightmarish serpent-train of "The Tunnel"; yet in the
final section, "Atlantis," Crane reaffirms his belief that the in-
seminating power of the poetic word, the phallic bridging
power of language, can raise the ideal land with its bountiful
fountains and harmonious concentric rings, the land where
"rainbows ring / The serpent with the eagle in the leaves" (p.
117).

I have discussed Crane's use of these related image patterns
at some length not only to show how substantial a debt Crane
owes to Bryant's poem, but also to show how far he has sur-
passed Bryant in his complex interweaving of these images. Indeed, Crane has so completely transformed the minor art of his
source into the major art of his own poem that it is difficult to
see how he could feel threatened enough by his debt to Bryant
to repress it, particularly when he acknowledges in *The Bridge*
his debts to much more talented and, one would presume,
more threatening writers, such as Whitman and Poe. Yet I
would suggest that it is precisely in Crane's strategy of thema-
tizing his literary debts to writers like Whitman and Poe that
the repression of Bryant is rooted; for one of the things that
Crane aims at in portraying himself as Whitman's younger
brother in "Cape Hatteras" and in confronting the image of his
own physical death through the image of Poe's death in "The
Tunnel" is what we might call "achievement by association."
Crane treats these and other major nineteenth-century American writers as if he were their rightful heir and prospective
equal. The possibility that there exists any lesser poetic context
in which his work could be interpreted is never entertained for
a moment in the poem. It would not matter, then, how much
Crane had transcended Bryant's use of these same images; the

strategy of *The Bridge* would simply not admit the appropriateness of any comparison between Crane and Bryant.

Yet I would argue that the echo of Bryant's "Thanatopsis" in
"To Brooklyn Bridge," considered as a vestigial trace of
Crane's repressed debt to Bryant, depends upon an even more
complicated mechanism of repression. In comparing the contexts of Crane's "speechless caravan" and Bryant's "innumerable caravan," one is struck by a curious reversal. Crane's caravan moving across the Brooklyn Bridge clearly represents the
living, while Bryant's caravan journeying to "the silent halls of
death" just as clearly represents the dead, yet Crane attributes
to the living caravan a quality generally associated with the
dead—speechlessness—while he describes the bedlamite's suicidal death as a linguistic act, a jest (in the sense both of a joke
and a heroic deed). Now if we label the various elements in
these two poetic contexts, we come up with a list like this: (1) a
crowd of people moving across a bridge; (2) the vast numbers
of the dead; (3) the living described as if they were dead, that
is, the speechlessness of the living dead; and (4) suicidal death
as a linguistic act of ambiguous significance. Keeping these elements in mind, let us look at the passage in "The Tunnel"
where Crane, during the nightmarish subway ride under the
river, explicitly confronts his own physical death in the image
of Poe's death:

> And why do I often meet your visage here,
> Your eyes like agate lanterns—on and on
> Below the toothpaste and the dandruff ads?
> —And did their riding eyes right through your side,
> And did their eyes like unwashed platters ride?
> And Death, aloft,—gigantically down
> Probing through you—toward me, O evermore!
> And when they dragged your retching flesh,
> Your trembling hands that night through Baltimore—
> That last night on the ballot rounds, did you
> Shaking, did you deny the ticket, Poe?
>
> For Gravesend Manor change at Chambers Street.
> The platform hurries along to a dead stop.

> The intent escalator lifts a serenade
> Stilly
> Of shoes, umbrellas, each eye attending its shoe, then
> Bolting outright somewhere above where streets
> Burst suddenly in rain . . .
>
> [pp. 110–11]

What catches our attention in this passage is the phrase "each eye attending its shoe," an echo of one of the most famous passages in Eliot's *The Waste Land*. Evoking the living dead of the modern metropolis, Eliot writes,

> Unreal City,
> Under the brown fog of a winter dawn,
> A crowd flowed over London Bridge, so many,
> I had not thought death had undone so many.
> Sighs, short and infrequent, were exhaled,
> And each man fixed his eyes before his feet.
>
> [Eliot, p. 39]

The line "I had not thought death had undone so many" is, as Eliot points out in a footnote, an allusion to the moment in canto 3 of *The Inferno* when Dante sees the living dead, those "who lived without blame, and without praise" and thus, refused by both heaven and hell, "have no hope of death" yet lead a "blind life so mean, that they are envious of every other lot" (Dante Alighieri, p. 23). And the next line—"Sighs, short and infrequent, were exhaled"—is an allusion, as Eliot again points out in a note, to the moment in canto 4 of *The Inferno* when Dante, having entered the first circle of hell, first sees the dead and notices that they speak no words, but only sigh. We recall that in between these two moments Dante is refused passage across the dismal river into hell by the steersman, Charon, because Dante is not dead, and that at the end of canto 3 Dante loses consciousness and reawakens at the beginning of canto 4 on the other side of the river, the loss of consciousness apparently being a symbolic death which allows his entrance into the realm of the dead.

Now one can see how Crane's allusion to the passage from

The Waste Land is meant to associate the lifeless swarms in the subway with the living dead of Eliot's "unreal city" and those of Dante's inferno, as well as to associate Crane's subway journey under the East River with Dante's passage across the dismal river into hell, both poets symbolically enacting their own deaths. But what is particularly significant for our purposes is that the passage from *The Waste Land,* with its allusions to Dante, contains all the elements that we had enumerated in the comparison of Crane's "speechless caravan" and Bryant's "innumerable caravan": the crowd flowing over the bridge; the vast numbers of the dead; the speechlessness of the living dead; and an individual death that is both self-willed and linguistic, that is, symbolic. Whereas the death in "To Brooklyn Bridge" was a suicide described as a linguistic act, a "jest," Crane's confronting of his own fate through the image of Poe's death, and Dante's fictive loss of consciousness in order to enter the world of the dead are both symbolic deaths, each poet's self-willed imaging of his own fate. Yet I have suggested that the description of the suicide in "To Brooklyn Bridge" is also an image of the poet's death—a more or less literal image of Crane's suicide by drowning and a veiled image of his feared death as a poet due to the unoriginality of his work—an unoriginality symbolized by quotation, by the repetition of prior work. What this suggests in turn is an analogy between the "self-willed" character of death in an actual suicide on the one hand and in a writer's symbolic representation of his own death on the other. But what we make of this analogy depends in this case on what we make of the similarity between the image pattern evoked by the echo of Bryant's "Thanatopsis" in the description of the suicide and that evoked by the echo of Eliot's *The Waste Land* in Crane's imaging of his own fate. Could it be that the really menacing presence for Crane in *The Bridge* is not Bryant but Eliot?

We do know from Crane's correspondence that from its inception *The Bridge* was meant to be a reply to the pessimism of *The Waste Land,* an "affirmation of experience, and to that extent . . . 'positive' rather than 'negative' in the sense that *The*

Waste Land is negative," as Crane said in a letter to Selden Rodman in May 1930 (*Letters,* p. 351). Crane's myth of the in-
seminating power of the poetic imagination, its power to resur-
rect Atlantis and its fertile fountain, is meant to counterbalance
Eliot's myth of the impotent Fisher King and the drying up of
the land. In the year he began work on *The Bridge,* Crane wrote
to Gorham Munson:

> You already know, I think, that my work for the past two
> years (those meagre drops!) has been more influenced by
> Eliot than any other modern. . . .
>   There is no one writing in English who can command so
> much respect, to my mind, as Eliot. However, I take Eliot
> as a point of departure toward an almost complete reverse
> of direction. His pessimism is amply justified, in his own
> case. But I would apply as much of his erudition and tech-
> nique as I can absorb and assemble toward a more positive,
> or (if [I] must put it so in a sceptical age) ecstatic goal. . . .
> Certainly the man has dug the ground and buried hope as
> deep and direfully as it can ever be done. . . .
>   After this perfection of death—nothing is possible in
> motion but a resurrection of some kind. Or else, as every-
> one persists in announcing in the deep and dirgeful *Dial,*
> the fruits of civilization are entirely harvested. Everyone,
> of course, wants to die as soon and as painlessly as possible!
> Now is the time for humor, and the Dance of Death. All I
> know through very much suffering and dullness . . . is
> that it interests me to still affirm certain things. [*Letters,* pp.
> 114–15]

In another letter to Gorham Munson some three years later
(March 5, 1926), Crane announced the completion of the "Atlantis" section:

> the finale of *The Bridge* is written, the other five or six parts
> are in feverish embryo. They will require at least a year or
> more for completion; however bad this work may be, it
> ought to be hugely and unforgivably, distinguishedly bad.

In a way it's a test of materials as much as a test of one's imagination. *Is* the last statement sentimentally made by Eliot,

> "This is the way the world ends,
> This is the way the world ends,—
> Not with a bang but a whimper."

is this acceptable or not as the poetic determinism of our age?! I, of course, can say no, to myself, and believe it. But in the face of a stern conviction of death on the part of the only group of people whose verbal sophistication is likely to take an interest in a style such as mine—what can I expect? However, I know my way by now, regardless. I shall at least continue to grip with the problem without relaxing into the easy acceptance (in the name of "elegance, nostalgia, wit, splenetic splendor") of death which I see most of my friends doing. [*Letters,* p. 236]

Yet in a letter to Waldo Frank only three months later (June 20, 1926), the doubt that Crane expressed to Munson had turned into a general disillusionment with the project of *The Bridge:*

> Emotionally I should like to write *The Bridge;* intellectually judged the whole theme and project seems more and more absurd. A fear of personal impotence in this matter wouldn't affect me half so much as the convictions that arise from other sources . . . I had what I thought were authentic materials that would have been a pleasurable-agony of wrestling, eventuating or not in perfection—at least being worthy of the most supreme efforts I could muster.
>
> These "materials" were valid to me to the extent that I presumed them to be (articulate or not) at least organic and active factors in the experience and perceptions of our common race, time and belief. The very idea of a bridge, of course, is a form peculiarly dependent on such spiritual convictions. It is an act of faith besides being a communication. . . . however great their subjective signifi-

cance to me is concerned—these forms, materials, dynamics are simply non-existent in the world. I may amuse and delight and flatter myself as much as I please—but I am only evading a recognition and playing Don Quixote in an immorally conscious way.

. . . The bridge as a symbol today has no significance beyond an economical approach to shorter hours, quicker lunches, behaviorism and toothpicks. And inasmuch as the bridge is a symbol of all such poetry as I am interested in writing it is my present fancy that a year from now I'll be more contented working in an office than before. Rimbaud was the last great poet that our civilization will see—he let off all the great cannon crackers in Valhalla's parapets, the sun has set theatrically several times since while Laforgue, Eliot and others of that kidney have whimpered fastidiously. [*Letters,* p. 261]

During the next four years of work on *The Bridge,* Crane's attitude toward the poem swung back and forth between intellectual disillusionment and emotional affirmation, a doubleness toward the work that is, I would suggest, reflected in his description of the suicide's leap from the bridge as a "jest." At times Crane thought that in projecting a modern epic of the American imagination he had involved himself in a quixotic delusion, a delusion that could only end in poetic self-destruction, a suicidal leap from *The Bridge*—either in the sense that he would be unable to finish his much-publicized epic or that the completed poem would turn out to be a ridiculous failure. In either case Crane thought that he would be a laughingstock, "a jest," and that his poetic career would be destroyed. Yet at other times Crane felt that the writing of *The Bridge* was a leap of faith, a leap which might or might not turn out to be suicidal, but which had to be made. He felt that he must run the risk of his death as a poet, the risk of becoming a jest, if he was to achieve the *beau geste* he projected; indeed, as the work progressed, he felt that the very taking of that risk was a *beau geste* in itself, that even if *The Bridge* turned out to be a failure, it would "be hugely and unforgivably, distinguishedly bad," that if the poem did not exhibit the power of imaginative achievement, at least it would indicate the scope of imaginative desire.

What is clear from Crane's correspondence is that the doubleness of his attitude toward the poem is directly related to the doubleness of his attitude toward Eliot. On the one hand, he admired Eliot's poetic artistry, but on the other he deplored his pessimism, that "perfection of death" which he found in *The Waste Land*. In writing *The Bridge*, Crane planned to use the poetic artistry of *The Waste Land* against the content of *The Waste Land*, planned to use Eliot's "erudition and technique" to achieve "an almost complete reverse of direction." Yet as Crane worked on *The Bridge* he seems to have realized that Eliot's artistic technique and the content of Eliot's poetry were not really two different things, that if one adopted the technique, then one got the pessimistic content along with it. Eliot's immediate poetic tradition was that of the French symbolists and the English decadents, a tradition that responded to the loss of belief in God and the ideal otherworld by making art the highest value in life. As Nietzsche says in *The Birth of Tragedy*, "it is only as an *aesthetic phenomenon* that existence and the world are eternally *justified*" (*Birth of Tragedy*, p. 52). Or as Walter Pater says in the conclusion to *The Renaissance*, "we are all under sentence of death but with a sort of indefinite reprieve . . . we have an interval, and then our place knows us no more. Some spend this interval in listlessness, some in high passions, the wisest, at least among 'the children of this world,' in art and song. . . . Of such wisdom the poetic passion, the desire of beauty, the love of art for its own sake, has most" (Pater, pp. 238–39).

Yet the problem with the religion of art is that what starts out to be life-enhancing ends up being life-negating. In his critique of the Christian afterlife, Nietzsche points out that the effect of the absolute valuation of the otherworld is the disvaluation of this world; in comparison to the ideal afterlife, the real life of the present is made to seem worthless. But what occurs in the religion of art is much the same: the aesthetic ideal tends to become located not in a fictive otherworld but in the historical past, a past whose accumulated riches must inevitably make the

present seem worthless in comparison. The technique of frag-
mented cultural allusion employed by Eliot in *The Waste Land*
and by Pound in *Hugh Selwyn Mauberley* and *The Cantos* involves
the amassing of the past's riches against the present, the mar-
shalling of the vast numbers of the great dead to do battle with
the living dead. In a letter to Herbert Weinstock in April 1930,
Crane said that it took him "nearly five years, with innumerable
readings" to convince himself of "the essential unity" of *The
Waste Land:* "And *The Bridge* is at least as complicated in its
structure and inferences as *The Waste Land*—perhaps more so"
(*Letters,* p. 350). Yet it was Crane's use of the technique of frag-
mented cultural allusion in *The Bridge* that probably led him,
after his enthusiastic start in composing "Atlantis," to write to
Waldo Frank that "The form of the poem arises out of a past
that so overwhelms the present with its worth and vision that
I'm at a loss to explain my delusion that there exist any real
links between that past and a future destiny worthy of it. The
'destiny' is long since completed, perhaps the little last section
of my poem is a hangover echo of it—but it hangs suspended
somewhere in ether like an Absalom by his hair" (*Letters,* p.
261).

Setting out to make a positive statement about the unify-
ing/vivifying power of the creative imagination in response to
Eliot's pessimism, Crane located himself in that art-for-art's-
sake tradition which posits the imagination as an absolute
value, a tradition that makes art not just the highest value in
life but a value higher than life, an aesthetic ideal to which the
dedicated artist ends up sacrificing himself. In the hagiography
of the religion of art as formulated by the French symbolists,
Edgar Allan Poe is an early martyr, and it is Poe's martyrdom,
the sacrifice of his life in pursuing his aesthetic ideal in a materialistic society, that Crane makes the image of his own fate in
"The Tunnel."

Now it is one thing to die like Poe if one's works can live like
Poe's, but it is quite another thing to die like Poe when one has
begun to feel that the "past so overwhelms the present with its
worth and vision" that no major artistic achievement is possible,
that no present or future writing will ever be able to survive

like Poe's. If one thinks that a "'destiny' is long since completed," that "Rimbaud was the last great poet that our civilization will see," then the self-sacrifice of the artist's life to the aesthetic ideal, an ideal that can no longer be approached in any realistic sense, begins to seem like deluded self-destruction. Confronting this dilemma in the "Quaker Hill" section of *The Bridge,* Crane begins with an epigraph attributed to Isadora Duncan: "I see only the ideal. But no ideals have ever been fully successful on this earth"; and ends

> So, must we from the hawk's far stemming view,
> Must we descend as worm's eye to construe
> Our love of all we touch, and take it to the Gate
> As humbly as a guest who knows himself too late,
> His news already told? Yes, while the heart is wrung,
> Arise—yes, take this sheaf of dust upon your tongue!
> In one last angelus lift throbbing throat—
> Listen, transmuting silence with that stilly note
>
> Of pain that Emily, that Isadora knew!
> While high from dim elm-chancels hung with dew,
> That triple-noted clause of moonlight—
> Yes, whip-poor-will, unhusks the heart of fright
> Breaks us and saves, yes, breaks the heart, yet yields
> That patience that is armour and that shields
> Love from despair—when love forsees the end—
> Leaf after autumnal leaf
>   break off,
>   descend—
>   descend—

In trying to write a modern epic of the creative imagination, Crane had begun to feel like "a guest who knows himself too late, / His news already told." Though he could reconcile himself to the fact of physical death, the possible death of his work—that his poetry might be a "sheaf of dust"—was another matter. What defense, what armor or shield, was possible against the image of the death of his written corpus, an image that threatened to become a self-fulfilling prefiguration by des-

troying the affirming energy of his imagination through despair? Whatever that defense might be, it was clear that it
would have to be a defense against Eliot, for Crane realized
that in adopting Eliot's "erudition and technique" in order to
make a positive statement whose antithetical starting point was
the pessimism of *The Waste Land,* he had outwitted himself. Setting out to confute Eliot's pessimistic rule, Crane found himself
in danger of becoming an example of that rule. Crane simply
had to free himself and his poem from Eliot, but the problem
was, that in terms of both technique and antithetical content,
The Waste Land was so much a part of *The Bridge* that to repress
Eliot directly, to psychically kill him, would destroy *The Bridge*
and finish Crane as a poet. Furthermore, Eliot was one of the
leaders of that "group of people whose verbal sophistication"
Crane looked to for an appreciation of his complex style, that
group whose influence he counted on to introduce his poem
favorably to a wider audience. Crane sent "The Tunnel," with
its image of Poe's death and its echo of *The Waste Land,* to Eliot
at *The Criterion,* and Eliot published it. And in a letter (September 12, 1927) to his benefactor Otto Kahn, Crane bragged
about this acceptance: "I have been especially gratified by the
reception accorded me by *The Criterion,* whose director Mr.
T. S. Eliot, is representative of the most exacting literary standards of our times" (*Letters,* p. 308).

Faced, then, with both the need to free himself from Eliot's
influence and the virtual impossibility of any direct repression
or overt repudiation of Eliot, Crane, by one of those elliptical
associations that characterize his poetic style, linked Eliot,
whose *Waste Land* represented the "perfection of death," with
Bryant, the poet of "Thanatopsis" and the "Hymn to Death,"
thereby superimposing upon one poet of death the repression
of another poet of death. In this case, the echo of Bryant's
"Thanatopsis" in the description of the suicide would be less a
vestigial trace of the repression of Bryant than a trace of the
mechanism by which Bryant and Eliot were associated so that
the repression of Bryant could serve as the symbolic repression
of Eliot. Considered from one point of view, the repression of
Bryant would be overdetermined by the association with Eliot;

while from another point of view, Bryant would serve as a screen-figure for Eliot, thus allowing the attempt to satisfy the wished-for repression of the modern poet of death but not allowing that direct negation or psychic killing of the antithetical double which would turn out to be the self-destruction of *The Bridge.* However, it would not, I think, be accurate to say that Bryant is simply a substitute for Eliot if by "substitute" one meant a figure whose *sole purpose* was to represent another figure. Bryant is present in *The Bridge* for other reasons than to serve as Eliot's scapegoat, and given the psychological mechanism of *The Bridge,* Bryant's repression would occur, Eliot or no. I would argue, then, that because of the associative link between Bryant and Eliot as poets of death, the image of Eliot is simply allowed to ride double on the preexisting repression of Bryant, so that the symbolic repression of Eliot occurs *as if* by coincidence, thus keeping uncompromised Crane's ambivalent attitude toward Eliot.

Granting all this, we are left, then, with the problem of how to translate the cryptic message of the suicide's leap from the bridge. If the echo of Bryant's "innumerable caravan" of the dead by Crane's "speechless caravan" is meant to characterize the people on the bridge as the living dead and thus equate them with the lifeless masses crossing London Bridge in *The Waste Land,* then the bedlamite's leap would be a rejection of the Eliotic bridge of sighs and its condemned masses. But what is the significance of that rejection? Does it represent an act of despair, a decision that it is better to be one of the dead than one of the living dead? Or does it represent an act of affirmation, an attempt to maintain the possibility of an aesthetic ideal to which the artist can sacrifice his life, an attempt to make one's own death the ultimate aesthetic (symbolic) act simply by demonstrating that death is not a meaningless event that we passively (impotently) suffer but an action to which meaning can be given by willing the form that one's death takes. In this case, the jest/*geste* would signify, through the self-destruction of the artist's power in his failed quest for an aesthetic absolute, the scope of the artist's desire; it would affirm the artist's belief that death is not a means to escape the condition of the living

dead, but a means to join the great dead who, because they sacrificed their lives to their art, have survived in their works.

The same ambiguous significance that attaches to the suicide
in the poem—an act of despair or an act of affirmation—informs Crane's own death as well, and it is in this context that a
final comparison of Crane's and Freud's figurations of death
may be made. Faced with death's loss of meaning because of
the loss of belief in God and an afterlife, Freud and Crane attempt to preserve the meaningfulness of death without falling
back into metaphysical illusions—attempt on the one hand to
confront death realistically as the annihilation of the personal
self, and on the other to keep death's obliteration of the individual bearer of meaning from putting death itself beyond the
control of meaning.

Through his notion of an unconscious death instinct (which
the notion itself raises to the level of consciousness in a dictum
like *"the aim of all life is death"*), Freud tries to remove death
from an area beyond human control (that is, the unconscious)
by giving it a teleological significance within the myth of a natural return to origins (the living organism's instinctive compulsion to return to the inorganic state from which it originally
derived), tries to change man's helpless passivity before the
meaningless through/into the active control of naming. Yet the
danger of this approach is that Freud's notion of death as the
aim of life can easily be interpreted as a justification for suicide.
Freud seems to address this possibility when he notes that the
self-preservative instincts "are component instincts whose function it is to assure that the organism shall follow its own path to
death, and to ward off any possible ways of returning to inorganic existence other than those which are immanent in the
organism. . . . What we are left with is the fact that the organism wishes to die only in its own fashion. Thus these guardians of life, too, were originally myrmidons of death. Hence
arises the paradoxical situation that the living organism struggles most energetically against events (dangers, in fact) which
might help it to attain its life's aim rapidly—by a kind of short-
circuit. Such behaviour is, however, precisely what characterizes purely instinctual as contrasted with intelligent efforts"

(1920, p. 39). Freud himself describes this as an "extreme view of the self-preservative instincts" (p. 39 n.), one that needs to be balanced by other insights; but it is a view that reveals Freud's intention to preserve death's meaning by making death part of a natural design "immanent in the organism." In section 6 of *Beyond the Pleasure Principle* he is even more explicit. Discussing our "belief in the internal necessity of dying," Freud says, "Perhaps we have adopted the belief because there is some comfort in it. If we are to die ourselves, and first to lose in death those who are dearest to us, it is easier to submit to a remorseless law of nature, to the sublime' Ἀνάγχη [Necessity], than to a chance which might perhaps have been escaped" (p. 45).

In place of the Judeo-Christian notion of death's meaning, Freud proposes a scientific version of the Greek concept of willing (submitting to, concurring in) the sublime Necessity. Freud's project of raising to the level of will that "remorseless law of nature" whose biological expression is the death instinct clearly shows itself in his characterization of instinctual behavior as if it were volitional ("the organism *wishes* to die only in its own fashion"), as if the design inherent in this "law of nature" resulted from something like the Schopenhauerian "world will." Yet if the avoidance of those very dangers which would shorten the organism's natural path to death is precisely what distinguishes instinctual *as opposed* to intelligent behavior, then Freud's project of raising the death instinct to the level of intelligent action would seem to do away with this instinctual avoidance of an immediate achievement of the goal, would seem to make that shortening of the path to death "natural" for—immanent within—a self-conscious organism, one that knew its ultimate goal and could achieve it immediately by suicide. Freud realized that the correlative of the Greek notion of willing the beautiful Necessity was the equally Greek notion that what is best for man is never to be born and what is next best is to die soon. And the problem of suicide, implicit in raising the death instinct to the level of consciousness, remains unresolved in *Beyond the Pleasure Principle*.

One senses in Freud's project the influence of Nietzsche's

The Birth of Tragedy and its ideal of Dionysian wisdom, of tragic joy in the annihilation of the personal self. Freud would have man will the sublime Necessity on the grounds of the reality principle; while Nietzsche would have man will the beautiful Ananke on aesthetic (nonmoral) grounds; yet for Nietzsche these aesthetic grounds *are* the reality principle, because in this world coming-to-be and passing-away result solely from the innocent play of opposites: "play as artists and children engage in it, exhibits coming-to-be and passing away, structuring and destroying, without any moral additive, in forever equal innocence. And as children and artists play, so plays the ever-living fire. It constructs and destroys, all in innocence" (*Philosophy in Tragic Age*, p. 62).

Crane's attempt to preserve the meaningfulness of death by maintaining the possibility of the artist's self-sacrifice to an aesthetic ideal relies heavily on Nietzsche's thought (Nietzsche was one of Crane's favorite writers, and the adjective *Nietzschean* was one of Crane's highest terms of praise) and in particular on the notion found in *The Birth of Tragedy* that in song and dance the artist himself becomes his own work of art. Indeed, there is a sense in which Crane's most moving poem is the aesthetic figure of his own life; and that poem's most moving moment is its almost sacramental closure. Unlike the sacrifice of one's life to a religious ideal whose compensation is the survival of the self in a glorified afterlife, the sacrifice of the artist's life to an aesthetic ideal can have, as an annihilation of the self, only a prefigurative compensation, that is, a compensatory prefiguration. For both Freud and Crane, the ability to come to terms with the fact of their physical deaths involves the confrontation with the written figuration of that death; but the figuration of one's own death depends on an illusion (as a figure it implies the continued presence, as an observer of the figure, of the very self whose annihilation it depicts), an illusion that encrypts the sense of the self's survival in the image of its nonsurvival. But this compensatory prefiguration must itself, then, be protected from the image of its own possible death due to unoriginality. Thus, for the analyst as for the artist, the willing of the sublime

Necessity, the acceptance of death as the annihilation of the personal self, depends precisely on the repression of the possible annihilation of the figure of that death, the written self.

REFERENCES

Alighieri, Dante. *The Divine Comedy.* Carlyle-Wicksteed translation. New York: Random House, 1950.

Bryant, W. C. *The Poetical Works of William Cullen Bryant.* New York: Appleton, 1908.

Crane, H. *The Letters of Hart Crane, 1916–1932.* Edited by B. Weber. Berkeley: University of California Press, 1965.

————. *The Complete Poems and Selected Letters and Prose of Hart Crane.* Edited by B. Weber. Garden City, N.Y.: Doubleday, 1966.

Eliot, T. S. *The Complete Poems and Plays 1909–1950.* New York: Harcourt, Brace & World, 1962.

Freud, S. *The Origins of Psycho-Analysis, Letters to Wilhelm Fliess, Drafts and Notes: 1887–1902.* Edited by M. Bonaparte et al. New York: Basic Books, 1954.

————. *Standard Edition of the Complete Psychological Works.* London: Hogarth, 1953–74.

    "The 'Uncanny' " (1919), vol. 17.

    Beyond the Pleasure Principle (1920), vol. 18.

    An Autobiographical Study (1925), vol. 20.

    The Future of an Illusion (1927), vol. 21.

Lewis, R. W. B. *The Poetry of Hart Crane.* Princeton, N.J.: Princeton University Press, 1967.

Mach, E. *The Analysis of Sensations.* Introduction by T. Szasz. Translated, from first German edition, by C. M. Williams; revised and supplemented from fifth German edition by S. Waterlow. New York: Dover, 1959. All passages quoted from the revised English translation are in the second German edition (Jena; Fischer, 1900), which Freud used.

Nietzsche, F. *Thus Spoke Zarathustra.* In *The Portable Nietzsche.* Translated by W. Kaufmann. New York: Viking Press, 1954.

————. *Philosophy in the Tragic Age of the Greeks.* Translated by M. Cowan. Chicago: Henry Regnery, 1962.

————. *The Birth of Tragedy and the Case of Wagner.* Translated by W. Kaufmann. New York: Vintage Books, 1967.

Pater, W. *The Works of Walter Pater.* Vol. 1. London: Macmillan, 1910.

10

The Articulation of the Ego
in the English Renaissance

WILLIAM KERRIGAN

The day he was to lecture at Johns Hopkins University, Jacques Lacan rose early and gazed from his hotel room at the waking city. There he saw evidence of thought in the absence of a thinker:

> I could see Baltimore through the window and it was a very interesting moment because it was not quite daylight and a neon sign indicated to me every minute the change of time, and naturally there was heavy traffic, and I remarked to myself that exactly all that I could see, except for some trees in the distance, was the result of thoughts, actively thinking thoughts, where the function played by the subjects was not completely obvious. . . . The best image to sum up the unconscious is Baltimore in the early morning. [Lacan, 1970, p. 189]

The Freudian unconscious is *It*—activity within a structure that bears no clear relationship to a controlling subject. The commonsense model of ideation, where we suppose an *I* directing the resources of the mind, becomes immediately problematic when imposed upon unconscious ideation. Our ready assumption that "something always thinks" confronts, in the city of dreams, "actively thinking thoughts." Psychoanalytic inquiries into the creative acts of artists or scientists have tried to locate a transition between It and I, reconstructing the dynamics by which unconscious thoughts come to be deployed by a conscious object. "Regression in the service of the ego" (Kris, 1952) is the best-known formula: the neurotic subject is possessed by the forces of the unconscious, and where ego was, id comes to be, but the creative subject extends his domain into an otherwise unsubjected territory. Such theories, which tend to oppose the rigidities of the unconscious to the freely, swiftly analogical modes of the preconscious (Kubie, 1958), have great value for the study of creativity so long as we realize their essential limitations. It is crucial to understand that we can only see, in Lacan's phrase, "the result of thoughts." Except in highly derivative form, Id is always and forever It, a mystery of the a priori beyond our knowing.

Chomsky (1972) has maintained that the operations of intelligence manifest in ordinary linguistic competence remain hidden from introspection. We have every reason to expect, in view of this fundamental concealment, that the advent of significant novelty among extraordinary members of our symbol-using species cannot be explored directly. Imagine the ideally informative manuscript of a poem, one finer than any the author himself, with the lag between brain and pen, could have provided. Our manuscript reproduces every language event that transpired between the moment of conception and the moment of completion. Though necessarily serial, it indicates through some systematic notation the precise rhythm of unfolding: we can position every thought in time. Before us is an iconic transcript of a creative consciousness, with its stops and starts, attentions and reveries, associations and fantasies and memories, its visions ahead and revisions behind. But do we have a record of the creative act? I would say that we do not. The act is by its nature mute. It resides in the blank spaces between the verbal events of consciousness, for such events signal not the act of creation, but the completion of this act. While an ideal manuscript would increase the bulk of our data, this plenitude would allow us no more favorable a vantage point for theorizing about the creative act than a fair copy of the finished poem. We must always deal with product, not process; what we loosely term "process" in this case can never be revealed as other than a sequence of products. No matter how exact a ren-

dering of the events in a creating mind we achieve, the inter-
stices between these events will continue to veil the creative act:
our problem simply dissolves into the larger mystery of cognition. It begins to appear, in fact, as if Baltimore in the early
morning is an image for consciousness itself.

The act being in principle inaccessible, work on creativity
(rather like cosmology in physics) has been ruled almost solely
by hypothesis. Psychologists confirm their beliefs by reference
to what is, apparently, a generous spectrum of examples drawn
from various disciplines and historical periods. But a fuller acquaintance with the literature of creativity reveals that the examples have become fixed counters to be construed this way or
that way in a game for theoreticians. Literary examples usually
come from the Romantic period or later, times when reason
has been depreciated as an attribute of art or artists, while
writers on scientific creativity pick over the classic cases of the
rational anticipated by the irrational, examples with a curious
resemblance to precognition—Poincaré and his epiphany about
Fuchsian functions; Kekulé and his reverie of the serpent
coiled into the benzene ring; Einstein and his adolescent dream
of staring, at the speed of light, into an empty mirror. Rarely
have these innovations been studied in their full historical contexts. Because of the emphasis on abstracting a universal tax-
onomy of creative acts, creativity has yet to find an adequate
historian. Among psychoanalysts, Ernst Kris—especially in his
work with Gombrich (Kris, 1952, pp. 189–203; also Gombrich,
1971, pp. 30–44)—made serious efforts in this direction. But
here, too, a timeless schema absorbs the unique historical moment. In his papers on inspiration (1952, pp. 291–318), Kris
began to approach this subject from a fresh perspective, writing not about the creative process itself but about the history of
conceptions of the creative process; by the end, however, Plato,
Newton, and contemporary patients have been grouped
together on the same synchronic plane, all of them examples of
the universal tendency of creative people to project the
emergence of ideas from the inside as the intrusion of ideas
from the outside.

Creativity must be submitted to time. If the beast itself recedes before us, forever elusive, we may nonetheless track its path through the evolution of culture. It would be fruitful, I think, to construct along psychoanalytic lines a history exploring the interrelationships among three variables—conceptions of the creative process dominant in a given period, features that mark the actual creations of this period, and cultural assumptions (always somewhat diffuse, but tending toward unity at some level of generalization) that were the context for both. The idea of novelty having a history is but a superficial paradox. Because there is a history of ideas, there is surely a history of emotions. It is therefore difficult to believe that there is not, as well, a history of originality. In what follows I will attempt to begin this undertaking, or at least to suggest its dimensions, for the period of the English Renaissance—defined here, arbitrarily no doubt, as the century and a half between the humanist revolution of the early sixteenth century and the death of Milton in 1674.

It was a culture of image-makers. In the Renaissance *homo ludens* devoted immense imaginative energy to the symbolizing and resymbolizing of his own coherence. Beyond the voice of Montaigne, we hear little in the way of cultural relativism (but see Bainton, 1962): these were the people of God, favored with revealed knowledge, and the purpose of history was their salvation. One modern anthropologist has noted in some surprise that Christianity, unlike most religions, displays openly the meaning of its sacred symbols (Sperber, 1975, p. 20). The significance of the cross, for example, is not limited to a priestly class, but exoteric, available to all; exegesis was the constant companion of symbolic expression during the Middle Ages, and the majority of Renaissance books, continuing this tradition, were designed to publicize the meaning of symbols in the sacred Scriptures. Translators of symbols, men fashioned them for all occasions. Allegorical pageantry organized the public life, and the social life of aristocrats became, through the genre of the masque, a living art dramatizing their ideal roles and virtues. Many of them designed their own *impresa* or personal emblem to supplement inherited seals and coats-of-arms. The guilds, too, cultivated their own inheritance of iconography—freemasonry, which may date back to the sixteenth century (Yates, 1972, pp. 89–127), being a particularly vivid instance of this tendency. Like the gardens and buildings of the time—which, indeed, they often represent—the title pages of Renaissance books are resplendent with symbolic designs. Bacon feared that a deep affinity with symbol might prevent man from apprehending the world. But he loved masques and designed one himself. When he presented his vision of scientific progress in the utopian genre, he subordinated fiction to ideology and gave a bare, sketchy representation of the society of his New Atlanteans; it is especially suggestive, then, that he did bother to invent an elaborate iconography for these perfect citizens. The possession of symbols was itself symbolic of power, dignity, and participation in the life of knowledge. To create them was a sign of intellectual substance.

Language reigned in this kingdom of symbols. Never, perhaps, have words been held in more esteem. Christ was the Word. A logophilic God gave language to Adam before he gave him woman. Devotional life centered on sermon, hymn, and prayer. Medieval monks had illuminated letters in gold, treating the word itself as an object of art. But the Renaissance invented the book and looked in wonder at the Gutenberg Galaxy. Texts were not inanimate. "For books," Milton wrote in his *Areopagitica,* "are not absolutely dead things, but do contain a potency of life in them to be as active as that soul was whose progeny they are"—a premise that led him to find censorship tantamount to murder, an obliteration of the image (writing) of the image (thinking) of God. By passing on the spirit of one mind to another mind, the circuit of author-text-reader performed a miraculous telepathy. Descartes, among others, testified to the power that lay in authorship:

> On the same paper, with the same pen and ink, by merely moving the point of the pen over the paper in a particular way, we can trace letters that will raise in the minds of our readers the thoughts of combats, tempests, or the furies, and the passions of indignation and sorrow; in place of

which, if the pen be moved in another way hardly different from the former, this slight change will cause
thoughts widely different from the above, such as those of
repose, peace, pleasantness, and the quite opposite passions of love and joy. [Quoted in Riese, 1972, p. 163]

Authors really did *impress* themselves on readers in this transmission of intellectual force. In order to empathize with Renaissance writers, we must reclaim books from the commonplace
things they have become.

Another primary assumption of Christianity about symbols,
one corollary to their openness, made the quasi-magical domain of words coextensive with all symbolic expression. Symbols in myth and ritual do not have a "meaning" in the linguistic sense, nor do they, contra Lévi-Strauss, have the structure of
language (Sperber, 1975, pp. 1–84). In the definitive moment
of Christianity, however, the Logos was nailed to the cross.
More than the companion of symbolic expression, exegesis was
its fulfillment. The speech of the interpreter, like the body of
Christ, manifested the linguistic potential waiting in the symbol
itself. This correspondence between symbolism and exegesis
should be understood as one instance of a universal design,
since the entire world beckoned to hermeneutics. Signs pointed
to things, and things, being hieroglyphic, pointed back to signs:
nature was the first book of God. Created by the Word, unified
by a linguistic conception of meaning, all aspects of the universe were mutually translatable. The emblem book, where
poems and pictures illustrated each other, was one popular
consequence of universal translatability; the mystical tradition,
drenched in Cabalistic and Lullist notions of language as the
master key to all reality (Yates, 1964, pp. 92–94, 270–71), was
another. Breaking subtly with the medieval practice, Renaissance mystics did not, on the whole, focus their efforts upon
the overcoming or transcending of language. Robert Fludd
composed in his alchemical manuscripts lengthy accounts of his
experiments and conclusions, interrupting his expository task
now and again to instruct the engraver about symbolic designs

for "illuminating" his ideas (Josten, 1963; see also French, 1972, pp. 62–88). Emblematic meaning was simultaneous, while the discursive appeared in time. But, granted this important difference, the two modes were interchangeable with respect to the deep model of significance.

Broadly speaking, the result of the primacy of language was to make the apparently nonlinguistic arts—painting, architecture, dance, music—articulate. They emerged from linguistic suppositions and endeavored to express meanings intelligible in language. Artists worked for exegetes. A history of Renaissance creativity begins appropriately, then, with the teaching of the word.

Imitation

Everywhere in Renaissance culture we discover the equation of the prior with the best, an ethical imperative to shoulder the yoke of authority. The closer we inspect the "revolutionary" movements of the period, the more we realize how profoundly they were anchored in a venerable past. Protestantism was a "re-formation," a return to the purity of the Apostolic Church uncorrupted by Romish elaborations. In literature, Ben Jonson adapted Latin comedy and epigram to contemporary English life; Spenser wrote of medieval chivalry in the archaic diction of Chaucer; Milton reconceived the major classical genres. Even Bacon, who believed himself to have refuted all previous philosophies and who tried to generate a psychology of innovation for Renaissance man, suggested in *The Wisdom of the Ancients* that Greek myths contained, as in a dark glass, the truths of modern empiricism (Rossi, 1968, pp. 73–134; Jardine, 1974, pp. 179–93). His utopia was a *New* Atlantis in which man assumed the dominion over nature granted him in Hebraic thought but lost through the philosophical hubris of Greek thought.

Progress understood itself as return. Finding the new concealed in the old was a long-standing habit of Christian culture, its prime sanction being the typological conception of the Bible; there also, in the famous formulation of Augustine, one found

"the New veiled in the Old, and the Old revealed in the New."
Reading 1 Kings 4 : 32–33,[1] botanists, zoologists, physicians,
and alchemists encountered a divine precedent for their contemporary labors. Jean de Lorin published a commentary on
Ecclesiastes in which he noted its allegorical representation of
modern discoveries (Bozanich, 1976); in 1660 a physician
named John Smith insisted that in Ecclesiastes 12 : 1–6, "as
plainly as his Figurative Method would give leave, Solomon described the Circular Motion of the Blood." It was no accident
that the scientists of the *New Atlantis* belonged to "Salomon's
House." There was indeed nothing new under the sun, and
William Harvey, who had published the *De Motu Cordis* in 1627,
was only a rediscoverer.

One important embodiment of this large impulse toward
veneration was the humanist movement which, in its "Northern" or Erasmian form, had tremendous influence on the
grammar schools and universities of England. Rejecting the
scholastic efforts to purify Latin into a philosophical language
(Heath, 1971), these men exalted a rhetoric based on literary
models from the classical past. Elegant speech was the corner-
stone of a stable civilization, and "barbarous Latin" was precisely that—a language corrupted by the barbarian invasion of
Rome. Frozen into the rotundities of Cicero and the obliquities
of Seneca, Latin was never again to be a living language.

"Imitation" was the key principle of humanist education.
This concept had descended through the Middle Ages from
the tradition of the *Rhetoric* rather than the *Poetics* of Aristotle
(McKeon, 1952). Generally, in humanist discussions of language and literature (the major exception being in Italy) the
word *imitation* has only a weak bond with the issue of representation, the aesthetics of verisimilitude, but is instead a pedagogical concept, a theory of learning. It denotes the imitation of
model authors from the classical past, summarizing the humanist concern with a stable language capable of sustaining a con-

1. "And he spoke of trees, from the cedar that is in Lebanon even unto the
hyssop that springeth out of the wall; he spoke also of beasts, and of fowl, and
of creeping things, and of fishes" (1 Kings 5 : 13 in some editions).

tinuous culture (McKeon, p. 138). Northern humanists would have agreed with Aristotle that man is a mimetic animal who learns by imitating those who have already learned. The figure of Art in Renaissance iconography often appears in the guise of an ape. *Ars simia naturae* was the classical maxim (Panofsky, 1968, pp. 202–04), but in a humanist grammar school, nature meant previous art.

In sixteenth-century England, where More, Colet, and Erasmus had established a humanist program, boys—and only boys, with few exceptions—entered a grammar school at the age of seven or eight and stayed for about as many years. There was no appreciation for childhood as a distinct and lovely phase of life. Since Adam had been created upright, his erect posture symbolizing his superiority to the beasts, Renaissance infants were placed in elaborate contraptions, similar to those used by Schreber's father, to restrain the phylogenetic regression of crawling. Renaissance children peer at us from their portraits with the dour faces of adults, wearing the same clothes as adults: they seem invaded by their future maturity. At St. Paul's in London, endowed by Colet and designed by Erasmus, lessons began at six in the summer and seven in the winter, paused from eleven to one, and resumed again till five. Children brought their own candles. There were no long vacations, but many short ones in accord with the liturgical year. Should attention wander, corporal punishment was swift; we possess a substantial body of poetic doggerel concerning the "whipping fits" of Renaissance schoolmasters. What boys learned in this rigid, masculine world was Latin—perhaps, later on, a little Greek and Hebrew. As the boy was separated from women, so he was divorced from the mother tongue.

Training in the advanced forms continued the medieval practice of *disputatio*. Students were assigned one side or the other of a philosophical or ethical question ("Who was wiser, Crates who threw away his gold or Midas for whom nothing was more important than gold?") and then engaged in formal Latin debate. This mode of instruction became still more prominent in the universities. It has been suggested that such practices functioned as a male puberty rite, containing aggression even as they gave voice to aggression, in a masculine ritual in a masculine tongue (Ong, 1959; 1962, pp. 206–19).

First truly and then figuratively, the schoolroom (like the church and the court) was a scene often at the margins of Renaissance literature. To honor the poet, or to defend his fiction-making, Englishmen called him "teacher." *Paradise Lost* was the creation of a man who hired himself out as a tutor, wrote about education, compiled a Latin thesaurus, produced textbooks in grammar and logic, and hoped to be doctrinal to a nation; he structured the drama of his epic in pedagogical relationships between poet and muse, God and Christ, Raphael and Adam, Adam and Eve, Satan and Eve, Michael and Adam. The schoolroom was to Renaissance poetry approximately what the mead-hall was to Anglo-Saxon poetry, and even when the place of pedagogy was not directly represented, the verse often seems to come forth in the spectral presence of its memory. The traces of disputation in Renaissance literature, in the style of all Renaissance discourse—habitually contentious, constantly in need of generating an opponent—have been well documented. I would like to examine the actual assimilation of the second tongue during the early years of the grammar school. Humanists grounded this process in the virtue of "copiousness," which Erasmus believed to echo the variety of both nature and culture: "What clothing is to our body, diction is to the expression of our thoughts. . . . And the reason for changing clothes and for varying speech is one and the same" (Erasmus, p. 18).

Copiousness was the ability to say the same thing, clothe the same body, in a multitude of fashions. "We should of set purpose," he contends, "select certain expressions and make as many variations of them as possible in the way Quintilian advises, 'just as several different figures are commonly formed from the same piece of wax'" (p. 17). Living in a universe created by the Word and reading their salvation in a sacred book, Renaissance educators aimed above all at the defeat of speechlessness. Copiousness, like the intricate mnemonic systems that fascinated Renaissance men (Yates, 1966), was intended to guarantee a fulsome, ready plenitude of speech. Erasmus provided examples of this virtue, writing 200 variations on the sentence "Tuae literae me magnopere delectarunt," and 150 on "Semper vivam tui meminero."

Johann Sturm, in his *Nobilitas Literata* (1549), was one of many to adapt this principle for grammar-school training. Students began with Latin sentences in anthologies called "vulgaria" or "colloquies." They made an English translation, then proceeded to ring copious changes on the Latin statement. Two rules governed these exercises: the rule of deep repetition—all the variations must have the same meaning; and the rule of superficial novelty—no two variations can be identical (in which case they would cease to be variations). Marion Trousdale has argued that the theory of "copy" behind the game of *copia* was Platonic, and an essential idea, immune to vicissitude, was thought to survive through all the manipulations of the student. Sturm went so far as to construct geometrical "figures" to represent the immutable structure of the Latin text. Ultimately, then, a mystical interchange between the Latin past and the Renaissance present occurred in those dim classrooms. Students acquired "like shape of eloquence," assimilating in their particular ways the generative archetype inherent in the exemplar. Certainly the development of *copia* in the work of Roger Ascham, tutor to Queen Elizabeth, would suggest a process of internalization based on Platonic principles, since his technique of "double translation" directed students to vary their English translation and then, without reference back to the original, recast the sentence in Latin.

But the idea of source was surely primary. Sturm's own definition of imitation shows how "likeness" was controlled by "nearness": "Imitation is not in things that be all one, but in things that be like, and that which is like, must be, not the same, but another thing, and yet near unto it, which nearness is measured by the end and form of speech" (Trousdale, p. 168). Originality consisted of "nearness" to origins. The speech community of the Renaissance grammar school was more a speech family, characterized by adherence to fixed laws of grammar, diction, and idiom, where children assimilated the language of the fathers. The Italian Cinthio noted that a good imitation should appear to be "the son of the father, the brother of the other, come into life from the same sources as the other" (Trousdale, p. 178). When Sturm's *Nobilitas Literata* was translated into English, it was given the title *A Ritch Storehouse or Treasurie for Nobilitye and Gentlemen* (1570): students inherited language as a wealth accumulated by noble predecessors.

For several years the boys read complete works but did not compose them. After long praxis with atomistic fragments, moving out from and returning to a single statement, they were allowed to compose an entire oration or epistle. This delay in allowing them to compose a whole work strikes me as particularly important for the history of Renaissance innovation.

In his studies on aphasia (1956, 1963), Jakobson extended Sausurre's distinction between the syntagmatic and paradigmatic operations of language into his famous dichotomy of metonymy and metaphor. The terms represent the minimum structural requirements of a language: metonymy is the principle of continuity or combination, the linear axis of syntax; metaphor is the principle of likeness or selection, the synchronic axis of semantics. Jakobson indicated that these terms might retain their descriptive power when brought to the problem of organizing aesthetic categories in both the verbal and the visual arts. Applying his polarity to the macrolinguistic event of language learning, we may say that metaphor in humanist pedagogy was the prisoner of metonymy.

Ascham wrote: "Imitation is a faculty to express lively and perfectly that example which you go about to follow" (1865, vol. 3, p. 210). If "express" implies creation from within, "follow" absorbs this interior act to assert the value of contiguity with the prior and external; "to express . . . perfectly that example": a secondary perfection, one would imagine, since Ascham goes on to argue that God has favored Latin with the "perfect examples of eloquence." How could practice make perfect, when practice by definition wandered from an established perfection? ". . . you go about to follow": humanist imitation is a kind of grammar for the restraint of the creative act, a way of generating the novel from the prior with maximum stability. Through the exercises of *copia*, resemblance itself has been positioned in a temporal order; the whole heft of the concept of imitation is toward veneration and precedence, forming the new *from*, and not *alongside*, the fixed ideal of the classical original. In keeping with the metonymic definition of metaphor professed by their teachers, the earliest praxis of Renaissance pupils unfolded contiguously from Latin models, back into which, ultimately, the mother tongue disappeared. Original composition, which might bear a primarily metaphorical rather than metonymic relationship to its "source," was undertaken only after a year or more of "following" through the worshipful variations of copiousness.

This subordination may be felt throughout Renaissance literature. When Ascham spoke of literary history, he imagined that all important creation had proceeded along the lines of *imitatio;* Virgil quite literally had his Homer open before him while composing the *Aeneid* and "followed" his great predecessor with elegant variety. Now imitation is a form of influence, and influence, Ascham aside, is a psychological event that may not be measured or even understood in the form of quantified tabulations of borrowings and shared usages. Among the humanists we find a theory of literary history based on a concept of influence yet developed in the absence of a psychology of influence: the crystallization of this theory in their own labors was the annotated edition, the humanist genre par excellence, wherein sufficient commentary on a text involves little more than the identification of the passages imitated and the authors followed. The lessons were learned. Paths of contiguity crisscross the literature of their students. In the Renaissance, poems have lineages, plays have definite sources, metaphors have histories. It is no accident that scholars of this period find more use for the concept of tradition than scholars working in subsequent centuries, for artistic originality had yet to distance itself from influence, and influence had yet to be divided into adaptation and plagiarism. With the relative scarcity of invented plots, the relative profusion of repetition—with the clear, because externally observable, tracks of authors following authors—Renaissance literature comes to us having already organized itself in a historical dimension. Inspired creation, whose defenders were mostly outside the academies, operated as an alternative to imitation, especially in Italy. But inspiration itself took place within a network of precedents. Attempting inspired composition with more vigor than any other major poet of the era, Milton incorporated the achievements of an entire culture into his "unpremeditated" epic (Kerrigan, 1974a).

During the seventeenth century, the reforming spirit of Protestantism, empiricism, and other movements combined to affect the decline of Latinity and thereby to loosen the hold of precedent on the educational system (Debus, 1970; Webster, 1976). Classical literature retained its stature in the poetics of the eighteenth century. But during the Romantic period, when for the first time contiguity was widely attacked in a literary context, influential poets and critics offered in its place a new aesthetics of inspiration, natural diction, and self-expression, severing originality from its root connection with origins. As inspiration became spontaneity, the Romantic elevation of the unique self settled into our morality. Metaphor and metonymy have switched places in the modern classroom. "Write a poem," the young are told, "find your own voice." We assume that the poem (or picture, or dance) will sufficiently resemble existing works in order to be recognized as a poem: the old servant is the new master; contiguity is the captive of resemblance.

As the relatively coherent body of Renaissance literature reflects the doctrine of imitation, so the disparities of contemporary literature mirror the triumph of uniqueness. Instability and discontinuity characterize the history of the arts in the modern period. Aesthetic movements appear and disappear in bewildering profusion, rather like the planned obsolescences of our industrial economies. It is difficult to organize modern writers or, more precisely, all too easy to organize them, since the various schools and groups seem isolated from each other: there is not, as in the Renaissance, a sense of communal elaboration in the arts. The growth of literary study in the academies has taken place coincidentally with these developments. Perhaps the slow evolution of this discipline from a primarily historical to a primarily aesthetic orientation responds to a modern necessity—a need to systematize diversity in a manner that is, like the diversity itself, synchronic in emphasis. When the metonymies of history weaken, atemporal structures must supply our order.

Given the ascendance of priority in education and in culture generally, one would expect Renaissance creators to be uncertainly deferential and rebellious toward their forebears, anxiously clearing a space for their own ambitions. One would expect to find, that is, all the ambivalent dynamics of the oppressed son. Protestant theologians and occult philosophers, figures such as Bacon and Descartes, did indeed express their scorn for the authorities enshrined in the educational system. Reformers such as Jan Comenius devalued the literary basis of the humanist tradition, calling for a return to "things"; the technological revolution brought a new mistrust of verbal skills and a conviction, stated in Sprat's *History of the Royal Society* but preceded by a century of polemics, that linguistic elegance distorts our capacity to think accurately about the material world (Rossi, 1970). During the seventeenth century an entire genre, the debate between "ancients" and "moderns," addressed itself to the problem of veneration in conflict with aspiration (R. F. Jones, 1961). Yet, despite these signs of unrest, the Renaissance was not for the most part uncomfortable with its burden of antecedents. Veneration existed fairly peacefully alongside a cult of fame. Unlike the large share of medieval creators, who left their works anonymous and rarely dramatized their own creativity, the Renaissance followed Dante and Petrarch in their concern with reputation, self-dramatization, and praise that might endure as long as time itself (Quinones, 1972).

Imitation was not usually in conflict with narcissism. The Renaissance sonneteer who followed Petrarch, often line by line, confidently promised (in that transference of narcissism familiar to theorists of object relations) to make *his* lady immortal. Ambition was, if anything, overreaching. Bacon committed himself to an intellectual life-plan that included a survey of all knowledge, a complete encyclopaedia of physical events, a new logic, a resolution of several scientific controversies by means of

THE EGO IN THE ENGLISH RENAISSANCE

new axioms, and a history of "Forerunners, or Anticipations of the New Philosophy" (Mazzeo, 1967, pp. 198–99). Like the *New Atlantis,* this mammoth design was "not perfected," and one is hardly surprised that Bacon wrote, in his *Historie of Life and Death,* the first treatise devoted solely to macrobiotics.

Imprisoned in the Tower of London, Walter Ralegh began the history of the world, a massive fragment that leaves off somewhere in the Pentateuch. Spenser outlined a structure for an unimaginably complex poem in twelve books, each of them concerned with a particular virtue. He finished only six, and perhaps the fragment of another—one of his major themes is the danger of weariness, that vulnerable moment when an exhausted knight removes his armor. Donne vowed to write a lengthy eulogy, a kind of metaphysical progress report on the decay of the world, every year of his life to mark the anniversary of Elizabeth Drury's death; his resolve faded after he had completed two of these bizarre exercises in grieving. Comenius hoped to produce "Pansophia," a master textbook containing all knowledge; we possess only the fragments of his scheme.

Shakespeare, on the other hand, managed to explore all the genres of drama; the time-haunted Milton, torn as a young man between the fear of premature exposure and the fear of belatedness, left a major work in each of the major literary forms, including a pangeneric epic whose subject is everything. Precedents are not lacking, of course—Chaucer could not complete the intricate design for his tales, nor could Boccaccio—but the scholastic philosophers both conceived enormous projects and often completed them. Beyond the Renaissance, extraordinary, all-encompassing ambition is familiar enough in the eighteenth-century encyclopaedists, the idealist philosophers, the great cycle-novels of the nineteenth and twentieth centuries. But peculiar to the Renaissance, I think, is the happy poise between worship for the past and ambition for the future, the awareness of having been preceded balancing, rather than straining against, the determination to excel.

Why should Renaissance creators have suffered so little of the "anxiety of influence" (Bloom, 1973), so few symptoms of the "need-fear dilemma" (Burnham, 1969, 1976), characteristic of later periods? How can we account for the relative compatibility of imitation and self-assertion? One answer might rest on the fact that the activity of imaginative writing (with the exception of the drama) had yet to become a vocation. The flattering dedications that preface so many Renaissance works reveal, behind the energies of art, a system of pensions and preferments administered by the patronizing hands of the court aristocracy. For those in search of a living, poetry was a means to other ends. For those enjoying a secure livelihood, literature was a form of recreation. So we might argue that because the primary channels for the ego-drives were elsewhere, literary creation did not involve the urgencies of identity so thoroughly as it has with the collapse of patronage. But few poets of the last three centuries have depended solely on the word for their support. Nor should the historian of motive ignore the striking prevalence of the theme of immortality in Renaissance literature: toward the end of the Middle Ages this theme emerged from a long hiatus, and when the printed book, with its solidity and its potential for endless uniform reproduction, replaced the fragile manuscript, immortality through art must have beckoned the Renaissance creator with a newly realistic lure. Language was, moreover, the treasury of Christian man. Our discussion of Renaissance pedagogy has laid the groundwork for a deeper exploration of the (relatively) happy psychodynamics implicit in this literature. First, however, we must make a detour into the theory of the ego.

Linguistic Ego

French psychoanalysis borrows Jakobson's metaphor and metonymy to restate Freudian metapsychology, especially the problem of the genesis of the ego, in a structuralist framework. These analysts have, in fact, used the two terms with such ontological dignity that it is desirable, before examining their reformulation, to consider the problems stemming from this grant of stature. Within the history of philosophy, the concepts of resemblance and contiguity have been invoked by empiricists from the seventeenth century on as a way of giving law to the association of ideas. Scholars interested in the underlying pat-

terns of culture have often tapped the explanatory power of
these terms in psychological matters; Sir James Frazer, for example, distinguished between two kinds of magic, one operating on an object contiguous with the object to be affected (a
lock of hair, the weapon that caused the wound, the Christian
relic), another operating on a likeness of the object to be affected (a rain dance, the phallic ritual that assures the growth
of crops, the Christian icon). The terms have a still longer history in the tradition of rhetoric. Jakobson (1956) has argued
that the profusion of tropes defined by classical, medieval, and
Renaissance rhetoricians can be reduced to metaphor (the
transference of names on the basis of similarity) and metonymy
(the substitution of part for whole, result for process, and so
forth). Recently Michel Foucault, appealing to the explanatory
power of these concepts in rhetorical matters, has suggested
that language developed through a gradual dissociation of
word from thing, first by slippage along the axis of contiguity
and then by leaps of analogy along the axis of resemblance
(1973, pp. 110–15).

When Freud considered the interpretation of dreams, he was
exploring a subject at once psychological and rhetorical: the
dream was both a mental event and a text requiring explication. Part of his genius lay in extracting from the traditions of
psychology and rhetoric the overlap in their explanatory mechanisms. For condensation and displacement, which together
comprise both the semantics of the dream text and the associative laws of the unconscious mind, are surely versions of metaphor and metonymy. Displacement proceeds by the hidden association of contiguous ideas, while condensation unites ideas
on the basis of resemblance. In their barest structural form, the
old doctrines used to organize the mechanistic association of
ideas and the linguistic association of terms have sunk down
into the dream-work and, from this manifestation, have been
posited in the unconscious itself. So Lacan concludes that the
unconscious is structured "as a language."

He gives priority, that is, to the version of metaphor and metonymy stemming from the rhetorical tradition. Uneasy with
this imbalance, Jean Laplanche has reaffirmed the empirical

strand of Freudian thought. Whereas for Lacan the mind is bound into the universe of discourse, psychic determinism for Laplanche presupposes the derivation of real psychic entities. He notes that, even in Lacan's formulation, the phrase "as a language" indicates that metaphor and metonymy are being invoked metaphorically (Laplanche, 1976, pp. 132–33; also Lacan, 1970, p. 198). On the other hand, the use of these terms to unravel the problems of psychogenesis has dangers peculiar to itself. Although "psychoanalytic investigation demonstrates that the emergence of a 'psychic reality' and its consolidation occur electively at . . . metaphorico-metonymical intersections" (1976, p. 77), we must remember that in this direction lies the biological mysticism of Freud's *Beyond the Pleasure Principle* and Ferenczi's *Thalassa:*

> It would . . . be an undue limitation of our conclusions to restrict them to the formula: the human being is through and through structured by the phenomena of language. Would not that be tantamount to forgetting, for example, that at the very level of biology, a phenomenon such as generation may properly be related to these two axes: continuity with parental organism, resemblance to it. Is not the moment of separation, of birth, the one that introduces the break, making of a simple appendix of the mother a being in her image?
>
> More fundamentally still, at the very level of cellular or chromosomal life, are we not now progressing toward an understanding of processes capable of recreating the "same" out of what was initially in continuity, of moving from unity, within a single molecular structure, to the creation—outside of that structure and through an obscure phenomenon of induction—of a second structure identical to the first? Should the reproduction, the multiplication of the pattern of a "viral" molecule, such as biologists are now beginning to discover, incite us to expand into elementary biology the domains of metaphorico-metonymic derivation?
>
> Yet we in turn should pause, lest we be unduly seduced

by the biological metaphor—or fantasy—even if illustrious
predecessors, like Freud or Ferenczi, have already shown
the way. [Laplanche, 1976, pp. 138–39]

A signed photograph is metonymic by virtue of the signature
and metaphoric by virtue of the likeness. But only a reckless
semiologist would claim that this object bears the structure of a
language. Everything one may fix on these axes is not, in any
important sense, language or languagelike. Metonymy has been
connected with linearity and causation, metaphor with simul-
taneity and structure: pushed too far, these terms simply fade
into the ancient contrasts between time and eternity or becoming and being.

Sometimes, though, and sometimes in science, it is necessary
to exhaust analogies in order to show the reason for positing
them at all. Freud tried to restrain the anthropomorphic drift
of his formulations with the vocabulary of energies and hy-
draulics. While his physics and physiology have been discred-
ited, the terms remain fruitful (Loewald), if not crucial: instinctively, these mechanistic metaphors were as brilliant as the
anthropomorphic conceptions of the ego as a censor or as the
beleaguered servant of three masters, for somewhere in its
linguistic resources psychoanalysis needs, as Ricoeur has
argued (1970, pp. 69–158), a "semantics of force," a vocabulary
that acknowledges the pressure of desire. I think we may allow
a metaphorical use of metaphor and metonymy in grappling
with the problems of psychic genesis and psychic structure so
long as we pause, like Laplanche, to mark those places where
metaphor shades off into cosmic fantasy. Above all, our metaphors must not break loose from the strategy that released
them initially. To organize metapsychology about the poles of
metaphor and metonymy is, given the double role of these concepts in intellectual history, to accent the conjunction of mind
and language—precisely the region where one would hope to
locate the act of creation.

We turn now to the creation presupposed by all creativity.
Freud spoke of the ego as a "precipitate" on the perceptual in-

terface between the organism and the environment. As the primitive registering of sensual experience gradually stratified and "thickened," the earliest ego function—protecting against overstimulation—extended to the internal world of the drives. The ego in this scenario is contiguous with the organism whose access to motor behavior it slowly comes to govern (Laplanche, 1976, pp. 134–35; Laplanche and Pontalis, 1973, pp. 130–43). But Freud also defined the ego as "a mental projection of the surface of the body" (1923, p. 26 n.). Here, as in "On Narcissism," the ego appears to be derived, not only from a linear process, but from a moment of identification. Lacan has attempted to conceptualize this drama of incarnation, of metaphor come alive, in his *stade du miroir* (1949, 1953). Since the early phenomena of projection and introjection observed in the Kleinian tradition imply some sense of boundary, Lacan posits a recognition of the wholeness of "the Other"—one indistinct enough to justify this philosophical abstraction—that is both objectifying and identifying. Perceiving wholeness externally, the infant accedes to a first wholeness within. The ego indeed takes shape as "a mental projection of the surface of the body," but this first structure of the internal world is a reflection of the perceived structure of the body of the mother. Metaphoric structure from the outside circumscribes metonymic accretion from the inside.

We must be dealing here with a minimal and therefore, to an adult mind, abstract differentiation. Theorists in the visual arts have shown some interest in the question of minimal representation—of when, for a child, the sawhorse will become a hobby-horse or the simple lines a stick figure (Gombrich, 1971, pp. 1–12). In accordance with such notions, Lacan imagines little more than a perception of outline and contour, the sack of skin. Modeled on the body of the Other, the ego is almost literally "constituted" and "incorporated." This fluid circumscription is, so to speak, our first posture toward the world. Out of *bios* comes *logos*. At first an envelope in which to be, the destined articulation of the psychic body is thought. But recalling how often, in paranoid states and in other phenomena related to transitivism (Lacan, 1953), the ego will feel possessed by the Other, it is important to emphasize that its founding differentiation results from an identification. *I* is a back-formation from *Thou*. Given the helplessness of the child and given the ascendancy of part-objects during the prior autoerotic phase, the infant identifies with the autonomy, mobility, and coordination of the Other. From the very moment of its founding identification, the ego is already an ideal ego.

The dynamics of narcissism proceed immediately from the state of the mirror. If we follow Lacan, "narcissism—and even 'primary narcissism'—is no longer seen as a state independent of any inter-subjective relationship, but rather as the internalization of a relationship" (Laplanche and Pontalis, p. 256). It seems obvious, for example, that the impressively coordinated body of the Other eventually achieves organization as Kohut's "idealized parental imago," while the continued reflection of this body in the structure of the ego, subject to the redesignings of wish, evolves into Kohut's "grandiose self" (1971, pp. 1–34). Lacan believes that one can infer the joints and sinews of an imaginary anatomy from various pathological symptoms, such as the somatic conversions of hysteria:

> If the hysterical symptom is a symbolic way of expressing a conflict between various forces, what strikes us is the extraordinary effect that this "symbolic expression" has when it produces segmental anaesthesia or muscular paralysis unaccountable for by any known grouping of sensory nerves or muscles. To call these symptoms functional is but to confess our ignorance, for they follow the pattern of a certain imaginary anatomy which has typical forms of its own. In other words, the astonishing somatic compliance which is the outward sign of this imaginary anatomy is only shown within certain definite limits. I would emphasize that the imaginary anatomy referred to here varies with the ideas (clear or confused) about bodily functions which are prevalent in a given culture. . . .
>
> Furthermore, this image is selectively vulnerable along its lines of cleavage. The fantasies which reveal this cleav-

age to us seem to deserve to be grouped under some such term as the 'image of the body in bits and pieces' (*imago du corps morcelé*). . . . [Lacan, 1953, p. 13]

Redesigned by wish and contorted by defense, the imaginary body remains as the primal organization of the ego—arguably the most telling percept in the history of self-consciousness.

Lacan would insist that the ego, formed in the image of the Other, forfeits the subject primordially. There is, in other words, an initial subordination of self to object, and what the enamored libido cathects in the first embrace of narcissism is not so much the ego as the reflection of the Other. Later, installing itself as the mediator between wish and action, the ego will attempt to "pass itself off" as the subject of desire when in fact it is the object of desire and, indeed, the object of desire only in the guise of the imagined Other. Within the uncompromising world of French psychoanalysis, the ego leads a fugitive existence far more precarious than the one enjoyed by its hearty counterpart in American ego psychology, who sallies forth from Heideggerian shadows into the sunny world of object relations.

But insofar as the ego, in whatever kind of Freudianism, does assert a subjectivity uniquely its own, language must constitute its major sphere of autonomy. Language is a godsend for an ego struggling to establish itself as the master of—and source of—desire. It brings the gift of *I, me, mine*. It opens negotiations with the Other. Words solve, as best they can, the problem of the absent object (Smith, 1976). If the recalcitrant world will not budge, names will. And although language is a playground for magical thinking (Ferenczi, 1911; Abraham, 1923; Hartmann, 1956, pp. 255–56), wishes cast in words must, such is the nature of the medium, submit to the restraints of secondary process. With the activation of the universal grammar (Chomsky, 1972, 1975), the psychic body comes into its precious inheritance of coordination.

As a science of interpretation, psychoanalysis decodes the translation made in human development from the somatic to the psychic. If early experience of the body stresses what enters, remains, and departs, the rhythm of nourishment, then the mechanisms of introjection and projection beat out a comparable rhythm for the psyche. The names of orifices and organs have complex meanings in the Freudian vocabulary—which is not to say that psychoanalysis is unscientifically anthropomorphic, for the psyche is itself anthropomorphic. Even language, the least physical of the possessions of the ego, continues the translation of body into mind. Etymologists from Plato onward have noted that nearly every word, if traced to its earliest significance, will disclose a physical reference. The history of language as a gradual process of abstraction appears contracted in the maturing of every speaker. Werner and Kaplan (1963, pp. 207–39) emphasize the "shift from strongly physiognomized vocal forms to the conventional forms of everyday speech" (p. 207). Abse contends that, in the psychogenesis of metaphor, "the displacement originally occurs from the body image to images of others, including animistic projection to inanimate external objects" (1971, p. 43). Because the *soma* is the fulcrum of semantic equation, the slow fading of metaphor in linguistic development cannot be separated from the whole process of repression (Abse, pp. 23–27). Language retains, in the concrete locutions we treat as abstract, the forgotten physicality of an earlier connection with the world. Although words enable the ego to construct an orderly reality, uncluttered by internal fantasies, they also preserve and elaborate the architecture of the psychic body in whose image the ego was founded.

We babble before we speak. Might not the acquisition of language, the sense of an *I* commanding words and expressing through them the ongoing record of its own centrality, repeat after a fashion the original formation of the ego? Might not the genesis of expression, like the genesis of the ego, involve in the early stages a wishful identification with the linguistic coordination of the Other? Psycholinguists acknowledge the teleological character of language learning (Werner and Kaplan, p. 5). Could the unfolding of this *telos* entail an early identification that really does, in a sense, insert the end into the beginning?

Certainly the learning of a second language in the Renaissance grammar school resembles a staged redramatization of the birth of the ego. The long period of metonymic imitation dealt with single maxims and adages, the part-objects of discourse. The exercises designed to instill copiousness seem, despite the rigidity of the game, playfully ritualistic, a kind of verbal autoerotism that would sometimes explore, between Latin and Latin, the flexibility of the mother tongue. If we suppose that languages may be acquired under the power of an initial identification with the accomplished grace of fluid speakers (or, in the case of second languages, fluid texts), then the delayed moment of original composition realized this founding metaphor. Now the body of speech was whole—and, in the image of another, completely one's own. I should like to speak of the *linguistic ego* of these students, modeled like the ego itself on the coordination of a prior entity and internalized at last after years of "exercises." But the linguistic ego of the Renaissance grammar school was a superego as well.

This second linguistic birth, the absorption of the vernacular *I* into the Latin *ego,* was a wholly male achievement. Coming to a male teacher of the male tongue at seven or eight, most boys had already completed the identification with their fathers that normally resolves the Oedipus complex. Because he fears castration, an injury to that part of the anatomy, real and imaginary, capable of joining the ego with the mother, the male child once again constructs an internal agency on the model of a superior body—a lawgiver whose authority, like its threat, derives from the phallic narcissism of the ego. Ideally the child makes this identification on the basis of "to be like," postponing his wish to usurp the father (Freud, 1923). For this is, of course, the most arduous test of the reality principle. By placing his psychic body in subjection to the omnipotent image of that body, the child relinquishes his grandiosity only to keep himself intact for a future fulfillment; an incorrigible desire to possess, in time, the fantastic anatomy of the paternal image, and thus to repossess the mother, motivates his obedience. I think the experience of the Renaissance grammar school must have reconfirmed, to a degree, the correctness of the ideal solution. Latin was the gift of a severe, if ultimately forthcoming, father. It was an initiation into the mysteries of his ways, and the ardors of metonymic imitation, following the rules in the slow assimilations of "to be like," finally yielded to possession—the freedom, in original composition, of having for oneself. Veneration was rewarded by a new and male articulation of the ego. Henry David Thoreau understood the distinction I am about to press when he compared English as a spoken tongue ("the one") with Latin as a written tongue ("the other"):

> for there is a memorable interval between the spoken and the written language, the language heard and the language read. The one is commonly transitory, a sound, a tongue, a dialect merely, almost brutish, and we learn it unconsciously, like the brutes, of our mothers. The other is the maturity and experience of that; if that is our mother tongue, this is our father tongue, a reserved and select expression, too significant to be heard by the ear, which we must be born again in order to speak. [1961, p. 133]

Psychoanalysts have noted that when Latin appears in the contemporary dreamlife it often expresses the imperatives of conscience: to this day, the superego speaks Latin (Altman, pp. 14–15). Since all legal affairs in the ecclesiastical courts of England were conducted in the ancient tongue, Renaissance Latin was, in point of fact, the language of law.

We are especially concerned with those students who returned in their maturity to the vernacular. The itinerary of such men, the authors of the English Renaissance, as they journeyed through the life of discourse, reflects a familiar sequence—*the* familiar sequence. A natural acquisition of the mother tongue, a formal and superego-dominated imitation of the male tongue, a mature return to the matrix of mother English: the lifetime course of the Renaissance linguistic ego, circling back to its first object, mirrors in broad outline the course of the ego itself. The stages of linguistic selfhood coincide with the major phases of psychic life. Returning to their unruly vernacular, many students brought with them the standards of humanist Latin. There were constant attempts to classicize the English language, to fix its grammar, purify its idiom, quantify its accentual meter. England could have its Helicon and its Parnassus. The old genres could flourish again, dignifying what Spenser called, in a tradition as old as Lydgate, his "dull tong." Elizabeth presided over a revival of the *imperium,* joining the native cult of chivalry with a political mysticism eager to appropriate the symbols of Rome, including the adornment of Roman literature (Yates, 1975). But these movements, which generated many of the works we value from this period, do not suggest the anxiety of influence so much as the anxiety of being uninfluenced—of handling the first language without the guidance of paternal authority. While their shadow fell across the vernacular, the laws and monuments of the linguistic superego were codified in a separate medium. Renaissance authors had the task of integrating two languages corresponding roughly to the two formative moments of the ego and the two parental figures. I think that the finest achievements of Renaissance literature display such an untroubled balance between veneration and ambition because, put simply, the psychic discomforts of veneration could be left in the male tongue, the language of priority, while the masculine ambitions of imperial Roman literature could be transferred to the mother tongue and pursued in relative freedom from the inhibitions of the law.

The linguistic ego of the Renaissance doubled back to a first object whom no man, after all, had mastered definitively. By the sixteenth century, Chaucer was an archaic writer. Spenser, great as he was, chose to recreate this obsolete idiom; although few readers would have agreed with Jonson's dictum that "Spenser writ no language," the "English Virgil" had, to some extent, distanced his achievement from the life of the speech community. So veneration in Latin had room to become ambition in English. Students inspired by that moment in the grammar school when metonymic yielded to metaphoric imitation could find, in their native English, a language waiting to be populated with resemblances of the past. Their linguistic egos in tune with the rhythms of psychic life, these men internalized a masculine language and then, mature in words, fathered a great literature in its image.

They chose to build in their native English memorials that might verify, for all time, the authenticity of their being. We owe the determination of these authors a brief tribute; for during the Renaissance, to entrust one's ambitions to the vernacular required an act of faith. At least the romantic creator knew, with the fading of Latinity, that English had classic writers; among his anxieties was not the fear of the extinction of his medium. As late as the mid-seventeenth century, Edmund Waller instructed all English poets desirous of immortality to return to the stony languages of the schoolroom:

> Poets that lasting marble seek,
> Must carve in Latin, or in Greek.
> We write in sand, our language grows,
> And like the tide, our work o'erflows.
>   [R. F. Jones, 1966, pp. 263–64]

Certain authors, like Bacon, tooks no chances with their survival, leaving us a body of work inscribed in two languages. Even Sir Thomas Browne, whose persistent theme is the folly of immortality beneath the sun, made a double wager with the comprehension of the future, twinning English and Latin words in the same phrase as if he would combine in one the two texts of Bacon. But however he equivocated, Browne, like the others we remember best, remained faithful to his first tongue. In this fidelity, offered despite the attitudes born at their introduction into culture, I discern the precultural faith that mothers alone make possible—basic trust, the fundamental optimism. The turn from Latin to English that gave us the English literature of the Renaissance was more than a gesture of linguistic nationalism or a flight from paternal priority: it was also a trust in the mother as the true progenitrix of time, the mistress of futurity. Latin, said an admiring Hobbes, "hath put off flesh and blood" (R. F. Jones, 1966, p. 264). But humanist Latin boasted a barren immutability—all but completed, intolerant of novelty—while English was forever coming into being. English had never smarted beneath the rod of the schoolmaster. It was shifting, like sand in a tide, with the mortal dross of time. It was the language children were learning, brutishly. Permanence came indeed to those who transcended the prejudicial equation, buried deep in their training, between immutability and genuine being.

If the formation of the linguistic ego does recapitulate the formation of the psychic ego, one should be able to perceive in the creations of these, or any, writers the articulation of the imaginary anatomy. The Latin (also English) word for the works of an author is *corpus* and we often equate rhetoric with anatomy, speaking of the "members" of a sentence or the "body" of a poem. Writing is an activity charged with the configurations of narcissism—a revealing of ideal forms of the ego. Noting how novelists present an intense scrutiny of the lives of their characters for public consumption, Bergler remarked that "in the process of writing, voyeurism is changed into exhibitionism" (1949, p. 189). Allen (1974) has related the proportions of clarity to obscurity in art to conflicts of this sort. It is hardly unusual to find, in the history of literary creation (or in the nervous members of a writing class), an implied equation between the body of the author and the body of his text. Certain writers shun publication out of exaggerated contempt for the audience or a concern for achieving an impossible perfectionism, while others seem extraordinarily interested in their books as physical objects and, beyond that, with the reception of these precious pages once they have been released to the alien (and potentially injurious) gaze of readers. The prefaces of Nabokov, for example, whose vitriolic assaults intend to purge away undesirable readers, attempt to extend his lordly mastery over the detail of the text into the actual reception of the text; the allegorists of the Middle Ages and the Renaissance also endeavored to create simultaneously a fiction and the single interpretation of this fiction, controlling both characters and readers. If the text is covertly a psychic body, and if the fate of a text is to be incorporated by others, then it must not be delivered into their hands unarmed against judgment.

I propose that there is a form of narcissism, as well as a form of the imaginary anatomy, peculiar to Renaissance literature. Because, as Lacan maintains, the shapes of the psychic body vary "with the ideas (clear or confused) about bodily functions which are prevalent in a given culture," our anatomy of Renaissance creativity must next explore the shared symbolic context within which the ego spoke.

Anthropocosmos

The famous "Hymn of Man" in the *Rig-Veda,* our oldest collection of poems, tells how the universe originated from a "divided Man" (Le Mée, 1975, pp. 57–63). The dispersal of a body produced the structural unity of the cosmos, including its reliability and self-sameness through time: "Thus the worlds were regulated," the poem closes. Although in Genesis the creation of the universe antedated the molding of the human form, the isomorphism between the two was no less exact for a Christian culture. "Let the world's riches, which dispersed lie," proclaims the God of George Herbert's "The Pulley" as he fashions mankind, "Contract into a span" (1941, p. 157): from the dispersal of the cosmos came the unity of the body, precisely as in the differentiation of the ego. Metonymic with the earth, the dust of Adam had been shaped into a radiant metaphor of all Creation. The elaboration of the lawfulness of Creation in Renaissance science, and the celebration of its harmony in Renaissance art, can be viewed as brotherly articulations of this metaphor.

The ancient theme of the mirror relationship between microcosm and macrocosm—man as a universe, the universe as a man—found expression in nearly every aspect of the culture. In the plants of the natural world and the buildings of the cultural world, in the body politic, the earth, and the heavens, men perceived the human structure, dilating traditional metaphors with remarkable new elaborations. Old as myth itself, this primary cosmological assumption still flourished. We witness, in the Renaissance, the energetic last days of mythical thinking on such a scale, at such a pitch of confidence. The very prose of the world was poetry.

All fiction takes place in the theater of the body. But in Renaissance literature the body served, not only to localize character, but often to contain the entire action. The great allegorical poems of this era tend to reach outward, via analogical metaphors, to the meaning of everything. We can catch meaning in its flight, as it were, and behold one of the essential presuppositions of its dynamic, at those moments when analogy itself coalesces into the human form. Spenser's House of Alma in Book 2 of the *Faerie Queene* is the most overt of many episodes in that huge poem projecting the human anatomy as an architectural structure—one of the monotonous equations Freud discovered in the dream-work. Although the castle of the body was popular in medieval literature, Spenser was probably imitating a similar physiological allegory in *The Divine Weekes* of Du Bartas. Following both Spenser and Du Bartas, Phineas Fletcher wrote a long pastoral romance, *The Purple Island,* in which the topography of an island represented both England and, in minute detail, the human anatomy (Langdale, p. 117). This work should not be considered as the fantasia of a literary mind on the prosaic materials of physiology, since physicians themselves expressed their knowledge in allegorical modes equating the body with topography and architecture. Girolamo Fracastoro, for example, was the first to describe accurately (and to name) a famous disease, and he did so in the form of a Latin eclogue about the shepherd boy Syphilus. Robert Fludd illustrated his exogenous theory of disease with a diagram showing the "castle of health" invaded by malign substances (Debus, 1966, plate 5). We can see immediately, I think, that the psychic body of a Renaissance ego was destined to encounter multiple images of its own yearnings, defenses, illnesses, and triumphs in the symbolism of mature thought.

A generation ago intellectual historians were still imposing the modern antagonism between science and the uncritical coherences of superstition, religion, and mysticism on the Renaissance, understanding the new scientists as courageous opponents of stubborn myths. Such "medieval" notions as the correspondence between microcosm and macrocosm, when they surfaced in the work of heroic empiricists, were dismissed as examples of concession or regression. Now, however, much of the excitement in Renaissance studies radiates from a new history of science proclaiming that this movement, if reconstructed from the logic of its own premises, was not encumbered by the vestiges of mythical thinking: science in the years between Copernicus and Newton was actually nurtured by occultism, displaying at every important turn the fertile interaction of observed reality and projected fantasy. Bacon, to be sure, did attack the blinding narcissism of the microcosm-macrocosm relationship, but he also held little appreciation for mathematics. Numbers, the language of the "new philosophy," bore an intractably mystical lineage for the Renaissance.

Whitehead noted that science could only develop in a rational, continuous, and predictable universe that sequestered from view, through the force of its deepest assumptions, the fallacy of induction exposed by David Hume (Whitehead, 1925, pp. 3–5); science was therefore a Western triumph, in part because Judeo-Christian monotheism, granting *logos* to the Lord of Time, provided this expectation of stability. But it was the Greek traditions of occult mathesis and philosophical numerology that furnished the actual schema for a world created "in number, weight, and measure." Moving from material things to abstract ratios, the scientific magicians of the Renaissance realized the old mystical urge to find an invisible world by reference to which, and only by reference to which, the visible one became comprehensible (Popper, 1963, pp. 73–89; Boas, 1967). Since numbering is the readiest sanction of all for analogical thought, the very language of the new science could appear to strengthen the old anatomical cosmology, anchoring the structures of the body (four limbs, five senses, seven major organs, nine orifices) in the cosmos at large (four elements, the five points of a biaxial system or a cross, the seven planets, the nine spheres or nine orders of angels).

Within the broad outline of the Freudian (and Comtean) theory of human history, progressing from magic to religion to science, we might say that the origins of modern science involved a reversion, lasting well over a century, of the religious back into the magical. Copernicus announced in his famous encomium that the sun was exactly where Hermes Trismegistus had indicated—at the center, sovereign and majestic (Kuhn, 1957, p. 130). Treasured by Renaissance neoplatonists, Hermes was believed to have been an Egyptian priest, earlier than

Moses in some accounts, who had composed a group of mystical dialogues hinting at a solar magic to be performed by godlike operators (Yates, 1964).

The medical historian Walter Pagel has shown that the stature of the circle as an ordering symbol—one within which both the celestial motions and the human body could be inscribed, thus linking astronomy with medicine—encouraged William Harvey to search for this pattern in the orbits of the human body (Pagel, 1967, pp. 89–126; 1976, pp. 20–21). When Harvey published his new theory of the circulation of the blood, he insisted that the heart is "the sun of the microcosm, even as the sun in turn might well be designated the heart of the world" (Harvey, p. 47). A recognized classic of inductive argument, this discovery could also be viewed as a late Renaissance adjustment of the little world of the body to accord with the Copernican revolution in the large body of the universe. Even as the knowledge of the scientists advanced, the old correspondence held true. Myth and insight, symbol and fact, superstition and observation: the history of Renaissance science was not the gradual decrease of the one and growth of the other, but a fruitful reciprocity between the two, as mythical thinking preconditioned genuine discovery, and genuine discovery, in turn, reenergized mythical thinking. William Gilbert learned by empirical reasoning that the earth generated a magnetic field, but he believed that he had located in magnetism the vital soul of this sentient world.

Time and again, at such conjunctions of the empirical and the occult during the Renaissance, we find medicine. This was the master discipline. Because a revitalized analogy between microcosm and macrocosm continued to order and inspire the intellectual projects of the Renaissance, many of the physical sciences clustered about the compact world of the human body. Botany, as we observe in Pliny and still observe in Conrad Gesner, addressed itself to the medicinal properties of herbs and flowers. Since the body of man was sympathetic with the body of the earth, Paracelsus substituted mineral for herbal pharmacology, annexing the fields of alchemy and geology for the realm of medicine; it was through the halfway house of iatrochemistry that alchemy slowly arrived at its modern form (Debus, 1966, pp. 28–29; Webster, pp. 330–31). Astronomy, too, was in part a medical subspecialty. Physicians designed their remedies in harmony with the horoscopes of their patients; the influence of the natal sky comprised a major element in any medical history, and horoscopes were brought to Renaissance physicians much as we bring our blood types and family histories to contemporary physicians. I have already suggested how the "pure" science of mathematics had profound connections, through the Pythagorean-Platonic tradition, with the nature and health of the body. Plants, minerals, planets, numbers, and the arts (especially music) were all conscripted to defend the castle of health: a Renaissance physician doctored the world.

The development of the modern sciences proceeds from an indistinct set of disciplines touching at the human body. Each of them, by discovering its own particular field of work, eventually established an integrity apart from medicine. The unitary nature of Renaissance medicine has been obscured by historians of science who divide their books according to the modern classification of scientific fields. Given the analogical relationship between body and world, Renaissance medicine was necessarily the magnetic center of investigation, the place where knowledge of one kind might confront knowledge of another kind. It could be argued, on the contrary, that the current array of the sciences resulted from a fragmentation of the macrocosmic body that once clothed the soul of our civilization.

It is essential to remember that Renaissance physicians, even the most sophisticated of them, were not describing the body of modern anatomical textbooks. Teeming with metaphors and configurations that we are disposed to think of solely in relation to the unconscious mind, the best academic medicine of the Renaissance invested the real anatomy with features that modern dreamers attribute to their imaginary anatomies. Galen, for example, had organized all physiology on the model of digestion (Siegel, 1968). The separation of nourishment, with the consequent assimilation of "like" substance and evacuation of "unlike" substance, recurred in every part of the body. The operation of the brain itself followed this digestive scenario, and late in the Renaissance, neuroanatomists were still presupposing the doctrine of the three ventricles developed in medieval Galenism. Soft and moist, the anterior cell housed the *sensus communis* where the sensorium was formed from the input of the sensory organs and re-formed by the imagination; the middle cell, warmest of the three, housed reason, which organized information from the anterior cell into categories based on likeness and unlikeness, performing its act of judgment; the third chamber, cool and dry, was the warehouse of information, the place of mnemonic storage—adventitiously, the third ventricle was encased by the firm cerebellum and therefore suitable for retention. So imagination gathered, reason cooked, memory assimilated: the human mind ate, digested, and incorporated the external world; unwanted information escaping in highly spiritous form from the cranial sutures was actually called, in medical Latin, *flatus*. The word *digest* in Renaissance English meant primarily "to order" or "to organize," as it sometimes does today. But during this period, the abstract and literal senses of this (and related) terms had yet to be clearly differentiated.

The body was also understood to produce a trinity of corporeal "spirits" to execute the commands of mind. Originating in the liver, the heart, and the brain, these spirits represented a physiological incarnation of the Platonic soul. Their motions explained various emotional reflexes, but their role in vision was particularly crucial. According to the most common theory, they escaped from the pupils to "propagate" with light and multiply the visual image in the continuum between the object and the eye. Since the semen ("seminal spirits") was derived from the same substance, it would be no idle analogy to remark that seeing was making love to the world.

Fenichel (1953, pp. 373–97) has demonstrated that vision can represent the intrusive aspirations or oral aggressions of the psychic body. Such connections, we know, stem from the unconscious residues of early fantasizing. But in the fantastic anatomy constructed by Renaissance physicians, vision really was both phallic and incorporative; the structures typical of unconscious fantasy were duplicated by the commonplace, literal truths of Renaissance medicine. To learn about one's body during this period was to receive public knowledge from an inherited past that echoed, with extraordinary precision, repressed knowledge from an experienced past. Literature responded to this invitation. A glance at Renaissance sonnet sequences, with their intense dramas of visual coitus, would reveal a widespread enthusiasm for the displacement of sexuality onto seeing (Kerrigan, 1974b, p. 357).

Psychoanalysis is a psychology formulated in and for a scientific age. It tends to posit a radical disjunction between the external reality and the unconscious fantasy mediated by the ego. As we apply its theories to earlier periods, they must be imaginatively recast in order to account for entirely different relationships between the inner recesses of the mind and the shared conceptions of a culture. Insofar as artistic creation involves the public elaboration of unconscious fantasy, the assumptions about man and the universe sanctioned by Renaissance science must have facilitated this process. The fantastic was reputable: the world itself was an inducement to the imagination, an encounter, in the guise of perception, with the earliest, deeply affective articulations of the mind. Given the prestige of scientific endorsement, the foundations of subjectivity could emerge into a congenial intersubjective reality.

Dreamers often journey through the body of a parent symbolized by a landscape whose weather represents bodily processes. Among the most typical of the images of the oneiric world, this dreamscape hints that the logic of the microcosm-macrocosm analogy rules at the source of our symbolizing. Psychosomatic conversions, where the whole of the imaginary anatomy may attach itself to any part of the real anatomy, spring from the same logic; Freud (1915, p. 198; 1941, pp. 82–85) considered hypochondria to be the "organ-speech" of "genital" wishes. The ego is prone to construct homunculi of itself within the framework of the body, imprinting the seal of the whole upon the part. Because the Renaissance body contained the universe and was contained within the universe, the mirror worlds of its allegorists frequently remind us of these psychoanalytic structures, as do the anatomical catalogues of the popular "blazon."

Synecdoche becoming similitude, the embodied characters of Fletcher wander across an island-as-body to encounter a castle-as-body. The spatial design of his poem suggests an etiology of the ego, with the largest container, the "isle of man," representing in its unstable coincidence with the ocean the earliest body ego of the mirror phase; the castle representing a later, defensive structuring of the self; and the characters themselves representing the various ideals and identifications of the mature ego who must survey this psychic terrain in order to establish their community there. When Adam eats the forbidden fruit in Book 9 of *Paradise Lost,* "Earth trembled from her entrails" (9. 1000). Here again is the primary law of symbolism that seems to make inside-out the equivalent of outside-in. As poison enters the container of the human body, the containing universe homologous with that body has a bellyache. Who is within whom? This is the question implicit in the differentiation of ego from Other, the problem posed in the dynamics of the mirror phase. The symbolic cosmos of Renaissance culture permitted its authors to resume, in whatever tone they chose, that first and urgent problematic of identity.

As the images of interior fantasy converge upon the truths of external reality, the need for censorship—the fear of exposure and embarrassment—lessens proportionately. Milton went blind, as he understood his condition in the terms of Renaissance ophthalmology, because vapors from ill-digested food had risen to his head and congealed in the optic nerves; among his unconscious interpretations of this affliction one would expect to find some condensation of the poisoned nourishment of his mother, who also had poor eyesight, and the treachery of Mary Powell, the bitter wife who was feeding him as his vision deteriorated. Writing *Paradise Lost* about the great myth of the evil meal, Milton could *organize* his cosmology about the digestive process (see Book 5) and, with this open pathway between the two sides of his ego, create a symbolic drama that gathered into a shared cosmic frame his unconscious version of his own wounding. He was not compelled to deal with mere metaphors.

All three of the masters of the ego—libido, superego, and reality—could approve for their own reasons the same representational act.

Freud established as a basic rule of dream interpretation that
the presence of more than one phallic symbol always signifies
the castration theme. It might be suggested, in this context,
that the presence of more than one body points always to the
dynamics of narcissism. I have argued that the metaphorical
structures of Renaissance thought coaxed the imagination into
the purview of rational knowing; fantasies of all kinds, vital to
art, could find a home in this symbolic cosmos. Surely there
were other advantages for the creative act. Klein (1937) related
the artistic urge to reparation, the attempt to bestow new life
upon internal objects and imagos damaged by aggressive
wishes. And indeed, Renaissance creators were forever restoring, repairing, and remaking the various bodies that comprised
the unity of the world. But I suspect that their rage for order
served other purposes as well, for the cosmic expansions of the
ego must have had their fearful aspect.

An eclipse of the narcissistic ego may be glimpsed even in its
apotheosis. Elevating the faculty of imagination, Renaissance
neoplatonists paralleled the genesis of mental images with the
genesis of the cosmos; as Hermes had written, "Intellect
renders itself visible in the act of creating, God in the act of
thinking" (Walker, 1958; Michel, 1973, p. 117; Nohrnberg,
1976, pp. 519–68). The creating ego of the Renaissance beheld,
in this tradition, a trememdous analogon of its own ideal coordination. Stretching outward in the act of knowing, the course
of the ego was to coincide with this indescribably magnificent
reflection of itself. Ultimately, the Other became the All, and
that initial envelope, no more than an outline of being, was
adored yet again in the fulsome designs of Creation. The ego
was grand, but having expanded into the province of God, it
was impersonal as well. There is a peculiar emptiness, a lacuna,
in neoplatonic thought and the art it inspired. Contemplation is
contemplated, knowing known: the act itself remains at a distance of reflexivity, and emphasis falls upon the internal modi-

fication of the ego during this rapturous ascent, not upon the object of its knowing.

Perhaps we should discern, in this characteristic gesture, a desire to reverse the contract between self and cosmos, ego and God—to replace the Other in the mirror with an internal "object-self," thereby forestalling the absorption of the ego in the Otherness of its creator. It is suggestive that the triumph of the Renaissance fascination with reflexivity should be the *cogito ergo sum* of Descartes, for here the ego confers birth and being upon itself. Then, reshaping the ontological argument for God, this self-generated and ubiquitous ego proceeds to make the existence of its creator dependent upon *its own idea* of that creator. Man creates God in order to know that God creates man. If, as Lacan would imply, the supreme desire of the ego is to occupy for the Other the same position that the Other once occupied for the ego, then the metaphysics of Descartes, for all his agony of doubting, can be understood as a consummation.

Neoplatonism gave to Renaissance literature a cosmic space and a motive, a force of transcendent love, for exploring its inexhaustible correspondences. From Nicholas of Cusa to Ralph Cudworth, these philosophers addressed themselves to questions of unity—the cosmogony of emanation, the metaphysics of part-whole relationships, the synonymity of symbols drawn from diverse religions, the resolution of the conflict between diverse philosophies. This pool of ideas guarded the poets in their expansions toward universality. It is both the glory and, at times, the tedium of Renaissance art consistently to project a wholeness, a determined articulation of the anthropocosmos that must trace and retrace the lines of its integrity. Authors aspired to the illusion of completeness, often using the word *anatomy* in their titles (Beaurline, 1969). Plays, sonnet sequences, and allegories leave us with the sense that all combinations and permutations in the interaction of characters or the turning of ideas have been exhausted, rather like sentences varied in every possible way for the sake of copiousness. Even tiny works evoke a universal perspective. Whatever his subject—the disheveled dress of a lady, the praise of a book, a bottle of good sack—a Renaissance poet will tend to view it in a universal context, cross-indexing the trivial with the cosmic. Here is Richard Lovelace on the subject of a snail:

> Compendious Snayl! Thou seem'st to me
> Large Euclid's strict Epitome.
>
> [Howarth, p. 321]

This was intellectual seeing; the price of cosmic harmony was often a loss of particularity. Poets schematized their creations with numerology, astrology, salvation history, liturgical cycles, and the many lists of corresponding structures—the three mental faculties and the Trinity, the four seasons and the four humors, the seven virtues and the seven ages and the seven planets and so on, world without end. . . . The stuff of art was bound into an encyclopaedia whose entries invariably contained the following commentary: "See every other entry." This willful projection of unity bears some resemblance to a compelled exhibitionism that must confirm, again and again, the boundaries of the object on display.

Renaissance literature records a prolonged tension between containment, putting the world into the human, and expansion, putting the human into the world. The imperative to stay at home, to explore the densities of tiny worlds, is one of the familiar morals of late Renaissance literature. Donne himself constantly opposed the miniature world of lovers to the world at large, expressing an agoraphobic wish for self-sufficient microcosms contracted densely against the macrocosm. But the Donne of the *Anniversaries,* the Spenser of the *Fowre Hymnes* or the *Mutabilitie Cantos,* the Shakespeare of the storm scene in *King Lear,* and the Milton of *Paradise Lost* dilated the snug human world outward into the potential diffusions of the cosmos. With the increasing popularization of the infinite universe, containment and expansion froze into a sharper polarity. Giordano Bruno, like a prisoner before whom the walls of the jail had crumbled (Koyré, 1957), declared to Elizabethan England that, as we cannot imagine infinity, so we cannot imagine finitude either: we always conceive a beyond. All boundaries dissolved, infinity freed him to pursue the receding horizon of thought and imagination, expanding ever outward from a center which was, in an infinite cosmos, everywhere.

Others felt profoundly disoriented in the new and shapeless universe. Nicolson (1960) distinguished the "aesthetics of content" from the "aesthetics of aspiration" in seventeenth-century poetry, relating these tendencies to the "breaking of the circle" by conceptions such as infinity. We may reapprehend the power of this crisis from the vantage point of depth psychology. Once the image of the Other, bound and circumscribed, the cosmic body had regressed into the undifferentiated state of earliest infancy. With this new cosmology, the ego confronted the danger of merger with the pre-ego mother that Freud (1924) understood as the intersection between Eros and Thanatos. Beyond the real figure in the real mirror opened a distance no metaphor could close; anthropomorphism was exposed as a solely interior phenomenon. In a sense, the creation myth of Genesis had been rewritten backwards and the unity of the body redispersed into the vastness of a cosmos which, given the conditions of our thinking, we could never again fix in one stable image.

When science at last divested itself of magic, delineating a mechanistic world, the correspondence between internal and external reality was redefined appropriately. In the associationist psychology of Locke and Hume, the mind conceded vitality by mirroring the colorless, quantified physics of Newton. Nature was still a work of art, but one whose structural configurations of body, mass, and energy frustrated the anthropomorphic insistence of the creative instinct. As Christianity faded toward deism, satire became the dominant form of literature. This genre required for its coherence the traditional moral teachings of Christianity—precisely the aspect of religious faith that did not depend for its validity or appeal upon the nexus of cosmological assumptions so prominent in Renaissance literature. Although order was celebrated and disorder condemned, the cosmic body was already a relic.

More and more the arbiter of the mind, science conferred belief. As the ego accepted this new version of its external master, the passage between unconscious fantasy and sanctioned reality suffered an obstruction. Art was declining into "mere art," metaphor into "mere metaphor." We cannot underestimate the consequences of this injury to the imagination. By the time of the Romantic period, the naïve narcissism of Renaissance literature had given way to a more anxious grandiosity. The truths of imaginative creation were miraculous, the confidence of German idealism was inspiring, but we must judge these Romantic assertions against a science that had drained substance from the mythical impulse that had guided art from the beginning. Is there a shrillness in these voices? They praise the imagination in terms reminiscent of Renaissance neoplatonism, but the language has drifted into opposition with the language of science: there are two sorts of conviction, an imagination and a reality, in a way there never was for the Renaissance. Now the bounty of the primary process had to be defended, in its external projection, against an alien world. Now the artist had become an exile, his labor a solitary agony. Now the culture of Greece and Rome had diminished in the school and now English boasted classic, immortal writers. In this situation, then, the anxiety of influence appears with unprecedented regularity—the jealousy of prior creators, the fear that the imagination has been preceded and its energies co-opted.

The literary phenomenon that Harold Bloom has called to our attention may be viewed as the unwillingness of the artist to adjust for a new realism his narcissistic self-esteem. Romantic poets recognized, quite accurately, the confident and commanding quality of the Miltonic or Shakespearean achievement. But they were in no position to claim this authority—not simply because they were later, but because of the actual history that made them later. The inability to maintain inspiration, to free the way between unconscious and conscious, emerged as a familiar theme of both the lives and the works of these poets, imagination finding new life, as with the "Dejection Ode" of Coleridge or *The Prelude* of Wordsworth, in the subject of its own impotence. Behind the melancholy of Romantic literature is an elegy for the lost myth of anthropocosmos. Victor Frankenstein, the artist as scientist, assembled a fantastic body from the *imago du corps morcelé*. Innocent as the monster was, his imaginary anatomy found no place in this world.

Conclusion

Art is the phenomenology of the imagination, a record and description of exactly what has been imagined (Ingarden, 1973). Giving us so much, art cannot give us direct access to the process of its own creation: the first question of aesthetics (where does art come from?) remains, unlike the similar riddle about babies, unanswerable. In the order of history, however, it is possible to reconstruct the contexts of creativity and, granting ourselves the explanatory power of psychoanalysis, to examine the relationship between what has been imagined, theories or presuppositions about the imagination, and the matrix of culture. The Renaissance imagination was subjected to two languages, permitting a rough split between a space of veneration and a space of ambition. The lawgivers of literary creation spoke dead tongues. Having modeled itself on these immortal fathers in the humanist schools, the linguistic ego could repossess mother English in pursuit of its own deathless memorial. The progress of speech corresponded to the sequence of identifications that constitute the ego in psychic development. Ultimately the anatomy of the ego might coincide, through language, with the structures and textures of the cosmos—a (relatively) benevolent narcissism that helps to explain the pronounced integrity of Renaissance literature, its disaffinity with fragmentation. Language *reached*. A highly integrated and essentially anthropomorphic symbolism encouraged the expansive poet to feel that his *parole* might encompass the *langue* of world-order, just as the contractive poet might hope to retain, enfolded within his firmer boundaries, an epitome of the whole design. In stressing the themes of this narcissistic dimension, where ideals of coordination and compendiousness form an unbroken line of purpose between the creation of the ego and the ego of creation, I have not, of course, exhausted the fantasmatic regions of Renaissance culture.

It was a time for creation. Soon a Newton would step forth from the astral robes of a John Dee, and soon thereafter Kant would effect his own Copernican revolution by interrogating the apparent conquest of nature with an idealist philosophy. Become a crisis more than a problem, the seeming antagonism between objective knowledge and subjective consciousness would also occupy the mind of Husserl. The truths of the new science, presented as independent of the knower, appeared to demand the tribute of an absolutely self-effacing assent. Such truths, with their resemblance to the inert thingness of brute matter, recalled the ancient enemy of philosophical thought, and to escape their tyranny, Husserl descended into the radical subjectivity of the *epoché*. But during the transition toward this modern dilemma, science appeared to identify the subject, not to obscure him. What Husserl would call the noetic and the noematic sides of consciousness metamorphosed into each other with a liberty advantageous to the imagination, whereas his own phenomenology can only oscillate from one fixed pole to the other. Perhaps the phenomenological tradition, whether through the egology of Husserl or the ontology of Heidegger, promises a new union between knowledge and imagination. Yet this remating, if it occurs, will occur within horizons restricted by a critical awareness far more acute than the one that permitted the consummation of the Renaissance. A psychic body coextensive with the universe whose articulation is the truth of itself and the truth of the universe: this is the deep wish of the imaginative life that, in light of a realistic critique, subsequent creators have done without. I suspect its fragments lie strewn about the landscape of our dreams.

REFERENCES

Abraham, K. "Psychoanalytical Views on Some Characteristics of Early Infantile Thinking" (1923). In *Clinical Papers and Essays on Psychoanalysis,* vol. 2. Translated by H. Abraham et al. New York: Basic Books, 1955.

Abse, W. *Speech and Reason.* Charlottesville: University Press of Virginia, 1971.

Allen, D. *The Fear of Looking or Scopophilic-Exhibitionistic Conflicts.* Charlottesville: University Press of Virginia, 1974.

Altman, L. *The Dream in Psychoanalysis*. New York: International Universities Press, 1975.

Ascham, R. *The Whole Works of Roger Ascham*. 3 vols. London: John Russell Smith, 1865.

Bainton, R. "Man, God, and the Church in the Age of the Renaissance" (1962). In *The Renaissance: Six Essays*. New York: Harper & Row, 1962.

Beaurline, L. A. "Ben Jonson and the Illusion of Completeness." *Publications of the Modern Language Association* 84 (1969) : 51–59.

Bergler, E. *The Basic Neurosis: Oral Regression and Psychic Masochism*. New York: Grune & Stratton, 1949.

Bloom, H. *The Anxiety of Influence: A Theory of Poetry*. New York: Oxford University Press, 1973.

Boas, G. "Philosophies of Science in Florentine Platonism." In C. Singleton, ed., *Art, Science, and History in the Renaissance*. Baltimore: Johns Hopkins University Press, 1967.

Bozanich, R. "Donne and Ecclesiastes." *Publications of the Modern Language Association* 90 (1976) : 270–76.

Burnham, D. L.; Gladstone, A. L.; and Gibson, R. W. *Schizophrenia and the Need-Fear Dilemma*. New York: International Universities Press, 1969.

Burnham, D. L., and Bergmann, S. A. "August Strindberg's Need-Fear Dilemma." In J. H. Smith, ed., *Psychiatry and the Humanities*, vol. 1. New Haven: Yale University Press, 1976.

Chomsky, N. *Language and Mind*, enlarged ed. New York: Harcourt, Brace, Jovanovich, 1972.

———. *Reflections on Language*. New York: Pantheon Books, 1975.

Debus, A. *The English Paracelsians*. New York: Franklin Watts, 1966.

———. *Science and Education in the Seventeenth Century: The Webster-Ward Debate*. London: Macdonald, 1970.

Erasmus. *On Copia of Words and Ideas*. Translated by D. King and H. D. Rix. Milwaukee: Marquette University Press, 1963.

Fenichel, O. *The Collected Papers of Otto Fenichel: First Series*. New York: Norton, 1953.

Ferenczi, S. "On Obscene Words" (1911). In *Sex and Psychoanalysis*. Translated by E. Jones. New York: Dover, 1956.

Foucault, M. *The Order of Things: An Archaeology of the Human Sciences*. New York: Vintage Books, 1973.

French, P. *John Dee: The World of an Elizabethan Magus*. London: Routledge & Kegan Paul, 1972.

Freud, S. *Standard Edition of the Complete Psychological Works*. London: Hogarth, 1953–74:

"On Narcissism: An Introduction" (1914), vol. 14

"The Unconscious" (1915), vol. 14.

The Ego and the Id (1923), vol. 19.

"The Economic Problem of Masochism" (1924), vol. 19.

Gombrich, Sir Ernst. *Meditations on a Hobby Horse.* London: Phaidon Press, 1971.

Hartmann, H. "Notes on the Reality Principle" (1956). In *Essays on Ego Psychology.* New York: International Universities Press, 1964.

Harvey, W. *The Works of William Harvey.* Translated by R. Willis. London: Sydenham Society, 1847.

Heath, T. "Logical Grammar, Grammatical Logic, and Humanism in Three German Universities." *Studies in the Renaissance* 18 (1971): 9–64.

Herbert, G. *The Works of George Herbert.* Edited by F. E. Hutchinson. Oxford: Oxford University Press, 1941.

Howarth, R. G., ed. *Minor Poets of the Seventeenth Century.* London: J. M. Dent, 1931.

Ingarden, R. *The Literary Work of Art: An Investigation on the Borderlines of Ontology, Logic, and Theory of Literature.* Translated by G. Grabowicz. Evanston, Ill.: Northwestern University Press, 1973.

Jakobson, R. "Two Aspects of Language and Two Types of Aphasic Disturbances" (1956); "Toward a Linguistic Classification of Aphasic Impairments" (1963). In *Selected Writings,* vol. 2. The Hague: Mouton, 1971.

Jardine, L. *Francis Bacon: Discovery and the Art of Discourse.* Cambridge, England: Cambridge University Press, 1974.

Jones, R. F. *Ancients and Moderns.* Berkeley: University of California Press, 1961.

———. *The Triumph of the English Language.* Stanford, Calif.: Stanford University Press, 1966.

Josten, C. H. "Robert Fludd's 'Philosophical Key' and His Alchemical Experiment on Wheat." *Ambix* 11 (1963) : 1–23.

Kerrigan, W. *The Prophetic Milton.* Charlottesville: University Press of Virginia, 1974a.

———. "The Fearful Accommodations of John Donne." *English Literary Renaissance* 4 (1974b) : 337–63.

Klein, M. "Love, Guilt, and Reparation." In M. Klein and J. Riviere, *Love, Hate, Reparation.* London: Hogarth, 1937.

Kohut, H. *The Analysis of the Self.* New York: International Universities Press, 1971.

Koyré, A. *From the Closed World to the Infinite Universe.* Baltimore: Johns Hopkins University Press, 1957.

Kris, E. *Psychoanalytic Explorations in Art.* New York: International Universities Press, 1952.

Kubie, L. *Neurotic Distortion of the Creative Process.* Topeka: University of Kansas Press, 1958.

Kuhn, T. *The Copernican Revolution.* Cambridge, Mass.: Harvard University Press, 1957.

Lacan, J. "Le Stade du miroir comme dormateur de la fontion du Je." *Revue Française de Psychanalyse* 13 (1949) : 449–55.

———. "Some Reflections on the Ego." *International Journal of Psycho-Analysis* 34 (1953) : 11–17.

———. "Of Structure as an Inmixing of an Otherness Prerequisite to Any Subject Whatever." In R. Macksey and E. Donato, eds., *The Structuralist Controversy.* Baltimore: Johns Hopkins University Press, 1970.

Langdale, A. *Phineas Fletcher: Man of Letters, Science and Divinity* (1937). New York: Octagon Books, 1968.

Laplanche, J. *Life and Death in Psychoanalysis.* Translated by J. Mehlman. Baltimore: Johns Hopkins University Press, 1976.

Laplanche, J., and Pontalis, J. B. *The Language of Psychoanalysis.* Translated by D. Nicholson-Smith. New York: Norton, 1973.

Le Mée, J. *Hymns from the Rig-Veda.* New York: Knopf, 1975.

Loewald, H. "Primary Process, Secondary Process, and Language." In J. H. Smith, ed., *Psychiatry and the Humanities*, vol. 3. New Haven: Yale University Press, 1978.

McKeon, R. "Literary Criticism and the Concept of Imitation in Antiquity." In R. Crane, ed., *Critics and Criticism.* Chicago: University of Chicago Press, 1952.

Mazzeo, J. *Renaissance and Revolution: Backgrounds to Seventeenth-Century English Literature.* New York: Pantheon Books, 1967.

Michel, P.-H. *The Cosmology of Giordano Bruno.* Translated by R. E. W. Maddison. Ithaca, N.Y.: Cornell University Press, 1973.

Nicolson, M. *The Breaking of the Circle.* New York: Columbia University Press, 1960.

Nohrnberg, J. *The Analogy of the Faerie Queene.* Princeton, N.J.: Princeton University Press, 1976.

Ong, W. "Latin Language Study as a Renaissance Puberty Rite." *Studies in Philology* 56 (1959) : 103–24.

———. *The Barbarian Within.* New York: Macmillan, 1962.

Pagel, W. *William Harvey's Biological Ideas.* Basel: S. Karger, 1967.

———. *New Light on William Harvey.* Basel: S. Karger, 1976.

Panofsky, E. *Idea: A Concept in Art Theory.* Translated by J. Peake. New York: Harper & Row, 1968.

Popper, K. *Conjectures and Refutations: The Growth of Scientific Knowledge.* New York: Basic Books, 1963.

Quinones, R. *The Renaissance Discovery of Time.* Cambridge, Mass.: Harvard University Press, 1972.

Ricoeur, P. *Freud and Philosophy: An Essay on Interpretation.* Translated by D. Savage. New Haven: Yale University Press, 1970

Riese, W. "On Symbolic Thought in Cartesianism." In A. Debus, ed., *Science, Medicine, and Society in the Renaissance.* New York: Science History Publications, 1972.

Rossi, P. *Francis Bacon: From Magic to Science.* Translated by S. Rabinovitch. Chicago: University of Chicago Press, 1968.

―――. *Philosophy, Technology, and the Arts in the Early Modern Era.* Translated by S. Attanasio. New York: Harper & Row, 1970.

Siegel, R. *Galen's System of Physiology and Medicine.* Basel: S. Karger, 1968.

Smith, J. H. "Language and the Genealogy of the Absent Object." In J. H. Smith, ed., *Psychiatry and the Humanities,* vol. 1. New Haven: Yale University Press, 1976.

Sperber, D. *Rethinking Symbolism.* Translated by A. Morton. New York: Cambridge University Press, 1975.

Thoreau, H. D. *Walden.* New York: Norton, 1961.

Trousdale, M. "Recurrence and Renaissance: Rhetorical Imitation in Ascham and Sturm." *English Literary Renaissance* 6 (1976) : 156–79.

Walker, D. P. *Spiritual and Demonic Magic from Ficino to Campanella.* London: Warburg Institute, 1958.

Webster, C. *The Great Instauration: Science, Medicine, and Reform 1626–1660.* New York: Holmes and Meier, 1976.

Werner, H., and Kaplan, B. *Symbol Formation.* New York: Wiley, 1963.

Whitehead, A. N. *Science and the Modern World.* New York: Macmillan, 1925.

Yates, F. *Giordano Bruno and the Hermetic Tradition* (1964). New York: Vintage Books Edition, 1969.

―――. *The Art of Memory.* London: Routledge & Kegan Paul, 1966.

―――. *The Rosicrucian Enlightenment.* London: Routledge & Kegan Paul, 1972.

―――. *Astraea: The Imperial Theme in the Sixteenth Century.* London: Routledge & Kegan Paul, 1975.

11

The Need to Connect:
Representations of Freud's
Psychical Apparatus

HUMPHREY MORRIS

Reification of psychoanalytic concepts in the post-Freudian era
was a foreseeable vicissitude of a theory cut off from its author,
as was, perhaps, the current radical rereading of the original
text, initiated by Jacques Lacan. In any case, the two treatments
seem to be actings-out according to principles elaborated by
Freud himself, principles bearing on approaches to, and re-
proaches toward, the lost object. Freud never ceased to emphasize to what extent these movements took place within language, and his own text often brought attention to its tendency
in one or the other of these directions: "When we think in abstractions there is a danger that we may neglect the relations of
words to unconscious thing-presentations, and it must be con-
fessed that the expression and content of our philosophizing
then begins to acquire an unwelcome resemblance to the mode
of operation of schizophrenics."[1] Schizophrenics, according to
Freud, cathect preconscious word-presentations in an attempt
to recover unconscious thing-presentations: "These endeavours
are directed towards regaining the lost object, and it may well
be that to achieve this purpose they set off on a path that leads
to the object *via* the verbal part of it, but then find themselves
obliged to be content with words instead of things" (*S.E.*

---

1. Sigmund Freud, *The Standard Edition of the Complete Psychological Works of
Sigmund Freud*, 14 : 204. From here on, all references to the Standard Edition,
abbreviated "*S.E.*," will be placed in parentheses after the quotation.

14 : 204). Might not the psychoanalytic theorist face similar difficulties as he pursues his object, which is the psychical apparatus itself? I aim here to trace paths of lost objects by considering how several Freudian concepts, such as transference and
the primary and secondary processes, inscribe themselves in
this problematic of recovery. My referent is Freud's text; the
data of clinical psychiatry are not invoked.

False Connections

In the beginning, before psychoanalysis had a name, Freud
was stopping twice a day at a local nursing home to hear the accounts of Frau Emmy von N. "She was a hysteric," he writes,
"and could be put into a state of somnambulism with the greatest ease; when I became aware of this I decided that I would
make use of Breuer's technique of investigation under hypnosis" (*Studies on Hysteria*, S.E. 2 : 48). One day, about two
weeks into the case, Freud found his patient in a restless state.
"In reply to a question she told me that the Pension in which
her children were staying was on the fourth floor of a building
and reached by a lift. She had insisted yesterday that the children should make use of the lift for coming down as well as
going up, and now was reproaching herself about this, because
the lift was not entirely to be trusted" (*S.E.* 2 : 66). Under hypnosis, the woman accounted differently for her restlessness: "In
place of her doubts about the lift, she informed me that she
had been afraid that her period was going to start again and
would again interfere with the massage" (*S.E.* 2 : 67). (A part of
the therapeutic routine was that Freud massaged her whole
body twice a day.) In a footnote to the text Freud comments on
the relation between Frau Emmy's two explanations: "When
she woke up in the morning she found herself in an anxious
mood, and to account for it she grasped at the first anxious
idea that came to mind. . . . Her consciousness did not present
her with the *real* cause of her anxiety; *that* only emerged—but
now it did so without any hesitation—when I questioned her
about it in hypnosis. . . . There seems to be a necessity [*Bedürfnis*] for bringing psychical phenomena of which one becomes
conscious into causal connection [*kausale Verknüpfung*] with

other conscious material. In cases in which the true causation evades conscious perception one does not hesitate to attempt to make another connection, which one believes, although it is false [*obwohl sie falsch ist*]. . . . It is quite a regular thing for the mood attaching to an experience and the subject-matter of that experience to come into different relations [*Beziehung*] to the primary consciousness" (*S.E.* 2 : 67–69 n.). The false connection depends upon a substitution: ideas about her children and the lift take the place, in the subject's consciousness, of ideas about her period and the massage, and feelings originally connected to one set of ideas find a false connection, in conscious narrative, to the other.

The patient, it seems, is suffering from the disease of false connections. Freud, trained as a doctor, assumes his own immunity, and takes the vigorous approach: "I shall massage her whole body twice a day" (*S.E.* 2 : 50). And before he knows it, the physician is caught in the spread of the disease. What he first notices, to his annoyance, is that the patient has ceased to cooperate with the treatment. The explanation is discerned with advantage of hindsight in the theoretical discussion at the end of *Studies on Hysteria:*

> The patient is frightened at finding that she is transferring on to the figure of the physician the distressing ideas which arise from the content of the analysis. This is a frequent, and indeed in some analyses a regular, occurrence. Transference [*Übertragung*] on to the physician takes place through a *false connection* [*falsche Verknüpfung*]. I must give an example of this. In one of my patients the origin of a particular hysterical symptom lay in a wish, which she had had many years earlier and had at once relegated to the unconscious, that the man she was talking to at the time might boldly take the initiative and give her a kiss. On one occasion, at the end of a session, a similar wish came up in her about me. . . . What had happened therefore was this. The content of the wish had appeared first of all in the patient's consciousness without any memories of the surrounding circumstances which would have assigned it to a

past time. The wish which was present then, owing to the
compulsion to associate [*Assoziationzwang*] which was dominant in her consciousness, linked [*verknüpft*] to my person,
with which the patient was legitimately concerned; and as
the result of this *mésalliance*—which I describe as a 'false
connection'—the same affect was provoked which had
forced the patient long before to repudiate this forbidden
wish. [*S.E.* 2 : 302–03]

Things have proceeded from massage to *mésalliance,* and
Freud marks his point with a touch of wit by using the foreign
word in a deliberately ambiguous manner: it may be taken either in its proper, or primary sense of an inappropriate marriage, or in its metaphorical acceptance as a misalliance of some
other sort. The choice is left to the reader, and the steps he
must go through—albeit almost instantaneously and almost unconsciously—to decide which meaning of *mésalliance* pertains
here, mirror the process described by the paragraph. For on
first association, before he has taken the context into account,
the reader will understand *mésalliance* in its sexual acceptance,
and will allow himself a small bonus of pleasure as he sees the
humor of Freud's awkward situation. Only then does the
reader, responsibly, catch himself and, looking to the context,
see that this instructs him to understand *mésalliance* in a metaphorical acceptance, here as a false connection of the mental
variety. In an analogical way, the patient, when she first "reads"
her wish, takes it to mean that she would like Freud to give her
a kiss, and only later looks to the "surrounding circumstances"
of the wish and sees that they instruct her to assign it to another man and another time.
    It seems there is a similarity between the way transference or
Übertragung functions in a treatment and the way metaphor
functions in a text. *Übertragen* and *metapherein* are synonyms,
both meaning to transfer, to carry over or beyond, and I. A.
Richards pointed out a long time ago in *The Philosophy of Rhetoric* that what psychoanalysts call transference is another name
for metaphor. Freud himself writes: "a dream never tells us
whether its elements are to be interpreted literally or in a figu-

rative sense [*wörtlich oder im übertragenden Sinne*]" (*S.E.* 5 : 341). Freud's discussion of false connections in the mechanics of the psyche raises questions that bear on the mechanics of texts which represent the psyche. For Frau Emmy, it is the necessity of bringing psychical material of which she becomes conscious into causal connection (*kausale Verknüpfung*) with other conscious material that results, at times when the "true causation evades conscious perception," in the formation of "false connections" (*falsche Verknüpfungen*). But if false connections are preferable to no connections at all, under pressure of the compulsion to associate, then causal discourse, and text, cannot be kept free from processes of falsification, and what Freud means by the "true causation" is no longer obvious. When one undoes a false connection and substitutes another connection, as in the reading of *mésalliance,* what assures that the second is more true than the first? Might not this kind of undecidability, as the French call it—that is, this impossibility of choosing between two different meanings—might not this undecidability jeopardize the security of any original or primary meaning arrived at by psychoanalytic restoration?

Freud's original representation of the psyche in a systematic theoretical exposition is chapter 7 of *The Interpretation of Dreams.* To be exact, chapter 7 is the manifest original, for under it lies a suppressed earlier version, the 1895 *Project for a Scientific Psychology,* which was not published during Freud's lifetime; Freud's original presentation of his theory is a *re*-presentation of an earlier text. The aim of this presentation, he states at the outset, is "to arrive at an understanding [*Verständnis*]" of the "most notable" characteristic of dreams: their "transformations of ideas into sensory images [*Verwandlung von Vorstellungen in Sinnesbilder*]" (*S.E.* 5 : 535). A remark of Fechner's serves as the "starting-point for our enquiry": *"the scene of action of dreams is different from that of waking ideational life [der Schauplatz der Träume ein anderer sei als der des wachen Vorstellungslebens*]" (*S.E.* 5 : 536; Freud's emphasis):

> What is presented to us in these words is the idea of *psychical locality.* I shall entirely disregard the fact that the mental

apparatus with which we are here concerned is also known
to us in the form of an anatomical preparation, and I shall
carefully avoid the temptation to determine psychical local-
ity in any anatomical fashion. I shall remain upon psychological ground, and I propose simply to follow the suggestion that we should picture [*wir uns . . . vorstellen*] the
instrument which carries out our mental functions as resembling a compound microscope or a photographic apparatus, or something of the kind. On that basis, psychical lo-
cality will correspond to a point inside the apparatus at
which one of the preliminary stages of an image [*Bild*]
comes into being. In the microscope and telescope, as we
know, these occur in part at ideal points, regions in which
no tangible component of the apparatus is situated. I see
no necessity to apologize for the imperfections of this or of
any similar imagery [*Bilder*]. Analogies [*Gleichnisse*] of this
kind are only intended to assist us in our attempt to make
the complications of mental functioning intelligible by dissecting the function and assigning its different constituents
to different component parts of the apparatus. So far as I
know, the experiment has not hitherto been made of using
this method of dissection in order to investigate the way in
which the mental instrument is put together, and I can see
no harm in it [*Er scheint mir harmlos*]. We are justified, in
my view, in giving free rein to our speculations so long as
we retain the coolness of our judgement and do not mistake the scaffolding for the building. And since at our first
approach to something unknown all that we need is the assistance of provisional ideas [*Hilfsvorstellungen*], I shall give
preference in the first instance to hypotheses of the cru-
dest and most concrete description. [*S.E.* 5 : 536]

The question is how a psychical image comes into being. The
dream's transformation of an idea—*Vorstellung*—into a sensory
image—*Sinnesbild*—is a move to a different stage—*ein anderer
Schauplatz*. This displacement of *Vorstellung*, which means not
only "idea," but "presentation," "representation," or "theatrical
performance," is the representational task Freud's text ap-

proaches with such polemical vigor. Representation of the mental apparatus will be displaced from its conventional form. The referent we should "picture" (*vorstellen*) is not an anatomical preparation, not even any one model of the mental apparatus, but rather certain forms of language: "imagery" (*Bilder*), "analogies" (*Gleichnisse*), "provisional ideas" (*Hilfsvorstellungen*), which will be given "free rein." From start to finish, Freud will find it necessary to use such vehicles of expression. *Studies on Hysteria*, 1895: "it still strikes me myself as strange that the case histories I write should read like short stories and that, as one might say, they lack the serious stamp of science. I must console myself with the reflection that the nature of the subject is evidently responsible for this, rather than any preference of my own" (*S.E.* 2 : 160). *New Introductory Lectures on Psycho-Analysis*, 1933: "We approach the id with analogies" (*S.E.* 22 : 73). In *The Interpretation of Dreams*, where it is a question of the transformation of a *Vorstellung* into a *Bild*, the *Hilfsvorstellung* the text invokes is the imagery (*Bilder*) of an optical apparatus in which one of the preliminary stages of an image (*Bild*) comes into being, and Freud defends this metaphorical displacement by arguing, implausibly in the context, that accessory representations may be kept extrinsic to that which they "dissect." The reflexive process of representing the mental apparatus in the mental apparatus—*wir uns vorstellen*—is represented by a text in which layers of language are hard to keep apart: the *Hilfsvorstellungen* of figurative language merge with the mental *Vorstellungen* to which they are supposed accessories, and the *Bilder* of textual imagery overlap the *Bild* of an intrapsychic image. We might have been warned of these displacements by the counterphobic clang of Freud's own remark about his "method of dissection": "I see no harm in it [*Er scheint mir harmlos*]." What, if not the method itself, so jeopardizes "the coolness of our judgement"?

With this introduction, Freud moves on to a description of the psychical apparatus. Like a reflex apparatus, it has a sensory and a motor end. A perception impinging upon the sensory end leaves a trace (*Spur*): "This we may describe as a 'memory-trace' [*Erinnerungsspur*]; and to the function relating

to it we give the name of 'memory' [*Gedächtnis*]" (*S.E.* 5 : 538).
What happens in dreams is that "the excitation moves in a
backward direction. Instead of being transmitted towards the
motor end of the apparatus it moves towards the *sensory* end and
finally reaches the perceptual system. . . . This regression,
then, is undoubtedly one of the psychological characteristics of
the process of dreaming; but we must remember that it does
not occur only in dreams. Intentional recollection and other
constituent processes of our normal thinking involve a retrogressive movement in the psychical apparatus from a complex ideational act back to the raw material of the memory-
traces underlying it [*von irgendwelchem komplexen Vorstellungsakt
auf das Rohmaterial der Erinnerungsspuren, die ihm zugrunde
liegen*]" (*S.E.* 5 : 542–43). The vehicle of this movement, in
dreams, is a transference onto the day's residues:

> It must be that they [the day's residues] are essential ingre-
> dients in the formation of dreams, since experience has
> revealed the surprising fact that in the content of every
> dream some link [*Anknüpfung*] with a recent daytime im-
> pression—often of the most insignificant sort—is to be de-
> tected. . . . an unconscious idea [*die unbewusste Vorstellung*]
> is as such quite incapable of entering the preconscious . . .
> it can only exercise any effect there by establishing a con-
> nection with an idea which already belongs to the precon-
> scious [*mit einer harmlosen . . . Vorstellung in Verbindung setzt*],
> by transferring [*überträgt*] its intensity on to it and by get-
> ting itself 'covered' [*decken*] by it. Here we have the fact of
> transference' [*Übertragung*], which provides an explanation
> of so many striking phenomena in the mental life of neu-
> rotics. [*S.E.* 5 : 562]

Transference, which revealed itself in interpersonal relations, is an intrapsychic mechanism, a transfer of intensity from
one *Vorstellung* to another. The manifest dream, an intrapsychic representation, is produced by transferences onto the metaphorical covers of the day's residues. We note that Freud uses
the adjective *harmlos* (which the English translation has overlooked) to describe the preconscious *Vorstellung* picked by the

transference; this was the word he chose to designate his own devices of exposition. What is it that the text, like the text of the dream, seeks to cover with "harmless" figuration?

The Theoretical Fiction of a Psychical Apparatus

The transference has brought Freud to what we might call representations of the psychical apparatus, in both the subjective and the objective senses of this undecidable genitive construction, that is, both in the sense of representations that depict the psychical apparatus, and in the sense of representations produced within the psychical apparatus. In a well-known passage of chapter 7 that he will refer to as his "theoretical fiction" Freud represents the psychical apparatus representing. This theoretical fiction depends for its very origin upon a connection—*Verknüpfung*—of the sort we have been considering. Freud has proposed to show "why it is that the unconscious has nothing else to offer during sleep but the motive force for the fulfilment of a *wish*" (*S.E.* 5 : 565), and he proceeds by constructing a genetic argument which states that the psychical apparatus has "only reached its present perfection after a long period of development," and that "at first the apparatus's efforts were directed towards keeping itself as far as possible free from stimuli." Here again is the primary model: a reflex apparatus functioning according to the Principle of Constancy. "But the exigencies of life interfere with this simple function"—that is, with the function of keeping free from stimuli—"and it is to them, too, that the apparatus owes the impetus to further development." Pushed ahead by stimuli it cannot simply discharge along a reflex path, the apparatus must develop other ways of defending itself, and the first defense will be a first scheme of representation:

> The exigencies of life confront it first in the form of the major somatic needs [*Körperbedürfnisse*]. The excitations produced by internal needs [*Bedürfnis*] seek discharge in movement, which may be described as an 'internal change' or an 'expression of emotion'. A hungry baby screams or kicks helplessly. But the situation remains unaltered, for

the excitation arising from an internal need is not due to a force producing a *momentary* impact but to one which is in continuous operation. A change can only come about if in some way or other (in the case of the baby, through outside help) an 'experience of satisfaction' can be achieved which puts an end to the internal stimulus. An essential component of this experience of satisfaction is a particular perception [*Wahrnehmung*] (that of nourishment, in our example) the mnemic image [*Erinnerungsbild*] of which remains associated [*assoziiert*] thenceforward with the memory-trace [*Gedächtnisspur*] of the excitation produced by the need. As a result of the link [*Verknüpfung*] that has thus been established, next time this need arises a psychical impulse will at once emerge which will seek to re-cathect the mnemic image of the perception itself, that is to say, to reestablish the situation of the original satisfaction. [*S.E.* 5 : 565–66]

The hungry baby, like Frau Emmy, has a compulsion to associate. In this fiction of pure primary process, the apparatus, driven by an internal need (*Bedürfnis*), establishes a link (*Verknüpfung*) between a mnemic image (*Erinnerungsbild*) of a perception and a memory-trace (*Gedächtnisspur*) of a need. Freud proposed, at the start of his theoretical development, to investigate transformations of ideas (*Vorstellungen*) into sensory images (*Sinnesbilder*). He argued that in dreams excitation proceeds in a backward direction, toward the sensory end of the apparatus, and now he invents a fiction which suggests that the sensory *Bild* dreams seek to recover is maintained within the apparatus not alone, but in connection—*Verknüpfung*—with a form of memory-registration he calls a trace—*Spur*. The need—*Bedürfnis*—which drives the apparatus to form this link sends us back to Frau Emmy, of whom Freud had written: "There seems to be a necessity [*Bedürfnis*] for bringing psychical phenomena of which one becomes conscious into causal connection [*kausale Verknüpfung*] with other conscious material." But in this theoretical fiction, *Bedürfnis* refers to the major somatic needs, like hunger, and these would seem to differ

from the need to make connections. Perhaps not. For the argument is that a need establishes a connection, and that thenceforward that need is in the psychical apparatus to the extent
that it is in that connection, or rather, to the extent that it *is*
that connection. The need to make connections and the connections made to needs cannot be kept apart in this apparatus,
in this text. This ambiguity settles in around the question of origin which Freud's theoretical fiction of pure primary process
seeks to address. It is with the formation of the doubled structure of *Bild* and *Spur* that the reflex apparatus becomes, for the
first time, "psychical." But this doubled structure, which the
theoretical fiction invokes as its starting-point, provides no
punctate origin for psychical processes. For it is a structure of
transference, a metaphor, in which a *Bild* conveys a *Spur* by
covering it. Already, at the origin, there is a transformation, a
repetition with a difference. Always already[2] intrapsychic representation is re-presentation, and the starting-point of a theoretical fiction which set out to explain the transformation of
one form of representation into another is another such transformation. It is worth noting that earlier in the chapter a memory-trace was termed *Erinnerungsspur,* and the function relating to it *Gedächtnis,* while here *Bild* attaches to *Erinnerung,* and
Spur has been displaced to *Gedächtnis.* Representation depends
upon difference, but it seems that the poles of this difference
are hard to keep apart.

The originary[3] metaphor of the psychical apparatus, this
doubled structure of mnemic image and memory-trace is an attempted defense against the need for outside help. The next
time a need arises, Freud has specified, an impulse will emerge
in the apparatus that will seek to short-circuit the need for outside help and directly reestablish, through the internal connection, the situation of the original satisfaction: "An impulse of

---

2. I borrow Jacques Derrida's phrase, "toujours déjà." A basic source-text
for the discussion of Freud's deconstruction of the concept of primariness is
Derrida's essay, "Freud and the Scene of Writing," trans. Jeffrey Mehlman,
Yale French Studies, vol. 48 (1972).

3. I use this word to emphasize the meaning "derived *from,*" as opposed to
"underived," which "original" tends to convey.

this kind is what we call a wish; the reappearance of the perception is the fulfilment of the wish, and the shortest path [*kürzeste Weg*] to the fulfilment of the wish is a path leading direct from the excitation produced by the need to a complete cathexis of the perception. Nothing prevents us from assuming that there was a primitive state of the psychical apparatus in which this path [*Weg*] was actually traversed, that is, in which wishing ended in hallucinating. Thus the aim of this first psychical activity was to produce a 'perceptual identity'—a repetition of the perception which was linked [*verknüpft*] with the satisfaction of the need" (*S.E.* 5 : 566). Here, hallucination turns away from reality and generates a metaphor by re-presenting what is outside the apparatus inside it. This hallucinatory representation of absent nourishment, which Freud calls the "shortest path" back to "original satisfaction," is made possible by the originary link—*Verknüpfung*. But the hallucination leaves something out, and the shortest path is a circumvention. The originary structure of representations, by bringing the outside inside, re-presents an absence as a presence, and the first connection is a false connection.

Such is the primitive state of the psychical apparatus, the state of first psychical activity which Freud will designate the "primary process." This primary process is the starting-point from which the next paragraph sets out to develop metaphors of a secondary psychical process. For the purposes of clear exposition—that is, of causal connection—Freud has chosen to present as a genetic fiction the relationship between two systems of intrapsychic representation. Designating one system "primary" and the other "secondary," he implies not only that they can be ordered in developmental time, but that one is the source of the other. Throughout his work, Freud will comment on the necessity of such genetic fictions. Here in chapter 7, he writes: "In venturing on an attempt to penetrate more deeply into the psychology of dream-processes, I have set myself a hard task, and one to which my powers of exposition [*meine Darstellungskunst;* literally, "art of representation"] are scarcely equal. Elements in this complicated whole which are in fact simultaneous can only be represented successively in my description of them" (*S.E.* 5 : 588). Genetic fictions propose themselves as an expository necessity and in that gesture attempt both to justify and to remain conscious of the false connections which generate them. But Freud himself has shown that false connections tend to escape consciousness, and there are times when, with advantage of hindsight, he finds that the fictions control him, not he them. The 1905 first edition of *Three Essays on Sexuality*, for example, describes separate developmental stages of autoerotism and object-love. But in a 1910 footnote to that text, Freud comments that he has become "aware of a defect in the account I have given in the text [*Darstellung*], which, in the interests of lucidity, describes the conceptual distinction between the two phases of auto-erotism and object-love as though it were also a separation in time" (*S.E.* 7 : 194 n.). A genetic false connection was unconsciously introduced into the text, or *Darstellung*, by an author whose *Darstellungskunst*, which he had pleaded was insufficient and "*harmlos*," in fact had him in its sway.

Darstellung, a basic Freudian term used here to mean "text," can also be translated "representation." Freud uses *Darstellung* repeatedly in *The Interpretation of Dreams* to refer to intrapsychic representations, and a glance at the table of contents reveals that the word occurs in three of the section headings of chapter 6: "Die Darstellungsmittel des Traums" ("The Means of Representation in Dreams"), "Die Rücksicht auf Darstellbarkeit" ("Considerations of Representability"), and "Die Darstellung durch Symbole im Traume" ("Representation by Symbols in Dreams"). That Freud should use the same word to denote representation in text and representation in the psychical apparatus suggests, again, that representation in text of the psychical apparatus is determined by the very processes and structures upon which it proposes to abstract, and that Freud's text is no less enigmatic than that which it describes.

The theoretical fiction which posits an original, pure, primary process admits its status as a fiction: "It is true that, so far as we know, no psychical apparatus exists which possesses a primary process only and that such an apparatus is to that extent a theoretical fiction" (*S.E.* 5 : 603). Yet even as a fiction it does not manage to maintain control over the connections upon which it depends; the shortest path to satisfaction of a need was always already a circumvention, and the originary psychical connection was a false connection. The first psychical structure was a metaphorical turning-away, a defensive trope which rendered enigmatic the notions of a shortest, original connection, of a pure primary process, of an origin that was not always already a metaphor. We should not be surprised to find that a text which has already deconstructed its own fiction of orderly succession has anticipated its own next move:

> The bitter experience of life must have changed this primitive thought-activity into a more expedient secondary one. The establishment of a perceptual identity along the short path of regression [*auf dem kurzen regredienten Wege*] within the apparatus does not have the same result elsewhere in the mind as does the cathexis of the same perception from without. Satisfaction does not follow; the need persists. An internal cathexis could only have the same value as an external one if it were maintained unceasingly, as in fact occurs in hallucinatory psychoses and hunger phantasies, which exhaust their whole psychical activity in clinging to the object of their wish. In order to arrive at a more efficient expenditure of psychical force, it is necessary to bring the regression to a halt before it becomes complete, so that it does not proceed beyond the mnemic image, and is able to seek out other paths [*andere Wege*] which lead eventually to the desired perceptual identity being established from the direction of the external world. This inhibition [*Hemmung*] of the regression and the subsequent diversion of the excitation become the business of a second system, which is in control of voluntary movement—which for the first time, that is, makes use of movement for purposes remembered in advance. But all the complicated thought-activity which is spun out from the mnemic image to the moment at which the perceptual identity is established by the external world—all this activity of thought merely constitutes a roundabout path [*Um-*

weg] to wish-fulfilment which has been made necessary by experience. [*S.E.* 5 : 566–67]

The exposition hinges on the word "inhibition" (*Hemmung*). Secondary-process inhibition brings regression to a halt at the *Bild*, before it can traverse the *Verknüpfung* and reach the *Spur*. The apparatus may then follow the roundabout path of thought, circumventing the link to the memory-trace and securing in the external world, by motor activity, the object that corresponds to the *Bild*. Freud will designate the inhibitory function, in later papers, by the words *Aufschub*, or postponement, which is related to *Aufschubsperiode*, or latency period, and *Verspätung*, or delay. What secondary process introduces into the organism, through inhibition, postponement, and delay, is time. Along this secondary-process line, psychical representations settle into the orderly succession of genetic fictions. It seems that the origin of genetic fictions lies in the genetic fiction of origins.

Freud's figuration of the line of thought as a "roundabout path to wish-fulfilment [*Umweg zur Wunscherfüllung*]" will become one of his primal metaphors. In *Beyond the Pleasure Principle, Umweg* designates the movement of life itself, which, according to the unsettling apothegm, "*the aim of all life is death*," is "striving to return by the circuitous paths [*Umwege*] along which its development leads" (*S.E.* 18 : 38). And in the 1935 postscript to his *An Autobiographical Study (Selbstdarstellung)*, Freud applies *Umweg* to himself: "My interest, after making a lifelong *détour* [*Umweg*] through the natural sciences, medicine and psychotherapy, returned to the cultural problems which had fascinated me long before, when I was a youth scarcely old enough for thinking" (*S.E.* 20 : 72). In the passage from *The Interpretation of Dreams*, the aim of *Umweg* is to establish a perceptual identity "by the external world." Later in the chapter, Freud will name this secondary-process linkage of image and trace a "thought identity," to distinguish it from the primary perceptual identity for which it substitutes.

Secondary process is metaphorically represented as a roundabout path that bypasses primary process. But primary process could not be isolated pure. The short path it followed was always already a circumvention, which is to say that secondary process was always already there, and that secondary thought identity was always already substituted for primary perceptual identity. The genetic fiction cannot maintain the dualism upon which it depends. Freud, to the extent that he formulates this problem, does so from within the fiction: in chapter 7, as in the case of Frau Emmy, he would have it that falsification of the secondary process is caused by the primary process: "Thinking must concern itself with the connecting paths between ideas [*die Verbindungswege zwischen Vorstellungen*], without being led astray by the *intensities* of those ideas. But is is obvious that condensations of ideas [*die Verdichtungen von Vorstellungen*], as well as intermediate and compromise structures [*Mittel- und Kompromissbildungen*] must obstruct the attainment of the identity aimed at [a thought identity]" (*S.E.* 5 : 602). Unconscious *Vorstellungen*, through transference, come to bear on the preconscious material with which thought concerns itself; and "The preconscious idea [*Vorstellung*], which thus acquires an undeserved degree of intensity, may either be left unaltered by the transference, or may have a modification forced upon it" (*S.E.* 5 : 562–63). These compromise structures pose a challenge to linear thinking: "A dream never tells us whether its elements are to be interpreted literally or in a figurative sense [*wörtlich oder im übertragenden Sinne*]" (*S.E.* 5 : 341). The secondary process cannot know to what extent the representations from which it starts out are already metaphors, to be taken *im übertragenden Sinne*.

Just as, in the fiction, primary process comes into being through the link between a *Spur* and a *Bild*, secondary process, in the fiction, has its origin in the link between representations of two orders. In the metapsychological paper "The Unconscious," Freud describes this origin in a way that makes the dualism *wörtlich: übertragenden* undecidable: "The system *Ucs.* contains the thing-cathexes of the objects [*Sachbesetzungen der Objekte*], the first and true object-cathexes; the system *Pcs.* comes about by this thing-presentation being hypercathected through being linked with the word-presentations corresponding to it [*durch die Verknüpfung mit den ihr entsprechenden*

Wortvorstellungen]. It is these hypercathexes, we may suppose, that bring about a higher psychical organization and make it possible for the primary process to be succeeded by the secondary process which is dominant in the *Pcs*" (*S.E.* 14 : 201–02). Verbal residues are to thought what the day's residues are to dreams: points of attachment, covers, for transferential representation. But the connections of transference are false, and thought, like the dream, will be distorted by the very links that produce it. "Our thinking always remains exposed to falsification by interference from the unpleasure principle" (*S.E.* 5 : 603), that is, from the unconscious. Following Freud, we ask: Does a text ever tell us whether its elements are to be taken *wörtlich oder im übertragenden Sinne?* Just as transference works the text of the dream, so does metaphor work the text in which it represents the apparatus that produces the dream.

Frau Emmy's false connections posed the question: What are the mechanisms of psychical transformation? Freud traces them out by retracing the way; with the dream as guide, he moves in "a backward direction," and follows "transformations of ideas into sensory images." He warns, at the outset, that "in order to arrive at an understanding of it [this transformation] we must embark on a discussion that will take us far afield" (*S.E.* 5 : 535). Indeed, the metaphor of *Umweg*, the roundabout path, determines the text. Freud's argument is that secondary process is an *Umweg* to recovery of a primary state of things, and this argument depends upon a genetic fiction that secondary process has its origin in primary process. This fiction "explains" false connections: secondary process can never free itself from its origin in primary process, and the compromise structures which effect the transformation from one to the other lead to "falsification" of thought. But falsification as intrusion of the primary order into the secondary can only occur if the basic dualism is secure, that is, if the two orders are separable. This necessity dictates the fiction's opening move, which is to posit an apparatus "which possesses a primary process only," an Eden of representation that would pre-date falsification. The genetic fiction may then derive the second pole of the dualism from the first, and from the dualism may derive schemes of intrapsychic representation, which explain, or rather are inextricable from, falsification.

What of the text that invokes the genetic fiction as *Hilfsvorstellung* through which "to arrive at an understanding" of psychical falsification? This text falsifies its own genetic argument, for it is unable to establish a first representation that is not always already a compromise structure between two orders of representation (*Spur–Bild, Bild–Vorstellung*), and the re-presentation of one in terms of the other forges a constitutive first *Verknüpfung* which is always *falsch*. Even in the terms of the fiction, there never was a time when the "shortest path" to satisfaction was not already an *Umweg,* or when thought identity was not already substituted for perceptual identity. Pure primary process, even within the fiction, is no more a possibility than pure secondary process: there are only compromise structures.

A text about false connections exemplifies the kind of falsification it set out to deconstruct. Its opening moves suggest why this is so. Freud introduced his theoretical fiction by invoking *Hilfsvorstellungen,* or metaphors, and through them, a kind of writing not ordinarily applied to the subject at hand. Using this "imagery," he suggested an explanation of the compromise structures of the psyche, structures that arise from the transformation of one order of representation into another. The explanation, moving "backward," posited a state of things before there were any compromise structures. But to represent this state, the explanation invoked imagery which was itself a compromise structure, and this gesture displaced the text from the representational space it sought to *ein anderer Schauplatz.* The attempted "explanation" of transformations and compromise structures, following the traces backward, is instead a mirroring: we are back to Freud's metaphor of an optical apparatus, to a mutual reflection of *Bilder* (images) in the psychical apparatus and *Bilder* (imagery) in the text. A genetic argument that would explain the substitution of thought identity for perceptual identity, a repetition with a difference, deconstructs its own representational structures, exposing them as just such repetitions. It follows that the poles of Freud's representational scheme are hard to keep apart, for each is structured by the difference their relationship was intended to explain. The theoretical fiction is caught in an impasse between its argument, or attempt to persuade, and its *Hilfsvorstellungen*, or metaphors, upon which the argument depends but which it deconstructs.[4] The text arrives at "an understanding" only of this deconstruction of itself; psychoanalytic metalanguage is implicated in that upon which it purports to abstract.

Repeating and Remembering

Frau Emmy's compulsion to associate led to the question of false connections, which led to the fiction of the primary and secondary processes, and that raised questions of representation and re-presentation, of repetition and its relation to that which it attempts to repeat. One compulsion leads to another; starting, in 1894, from the compulsion to associate, Freud arrives, in 1914, at the compulsion to repeat. "As long as the patient is in the treatment," he writes in "Remembering, Repeating and Working-Through," "he cannot escape from this compulsion to repeat [*Zwang zur Wiederholung*]; and in the end we understand that this is his way of remembering. What interests us most of all is naturally the relation of this compulsion to repeat to the transference and to resistance. We soon perceive that the transference is itself only a piece of repetition [*die Übertragung ist selbst nur ein Stück Wiederholung*], and that the repetition is a transference of the forgotten past not only on to the doctor but also on to all the other aspects of the current situation" (*S.E.* 12 : 150–51). That transference is a repetition, or an attempted repetition, seems obvious; but that the repetition is a transference seems less obvious. In the context, here, the statement could be taken to mean that it is *as* transference that the compulsion to repeat manifests itself in treatment. But

4. On the *aporia* between rhetoric as persuasion and rhetoric as a system of tropes, see Paul de Man, *Blindness and Insight* (1971). On the impact of metaphor in the Freudian text, and of the Freudian text on current theories of metaphor, and of the consequent implications for the possibility of metalanguage, see Jean-Michel Rey's exhaustive study, *Parcours de Freud* (1974).

then we are not taking Freud at his word, for he writes that the repetition *is* a transference. Repetition in the psychical apparatus *is* the transferential process, whether onto the day's residues in a dream or onto all aspects of the current situation in a treatment. Transference is a piece of repetition, repetition is transference; it seems that transference is an intrapsychic synecdoche for repetition, a substitution on the basis of a part–whole relation.

The scheme of representation is refining itself. Transference is a metaphor, in the sense of substitution on the basis of resemblance, but it is also a synecdoche, or substitution on the basis of a part–whole relation. Here we seem to be courting a problem of logical types by suggesting both that intrapsychic metaphors and synecdoches are members of the class "transference" and that the class "transference" is itself a metaphor or a synecdoche. Bertrand Russell resolved this problem by deciding that a class cannot be a member of itself. But such a decree would achieve closure on questions we should like to keep open. For what is at issue in Freud's text is precisely the relation between one layer of discourse and another. We have seen already that psychoanalytic metalanguage cannot keep itself free of the processes upon which it purports to abstract; this introduces into it an undecidability that jeopardizes its authority as metalanguage. It seems impossible to determine, in psychical text, what is *in* what and what *is* what, whether a need is in a connection or a need is a connection, whether the psyche is in a text or the psyche is a text. Let us keep these questions open, and examine more closely the scheme of representation by asking how metaphorical and synecdochical transferences, and their relation, participate in the generation of Freud's text, in the construction or deconstruction of its fiction of origins.

An approach to this question might be to consider the ways in which material from the past enters into the psychoanalytic situation. Freud defines clearly the two extremes: conscious remembering, and unconscious repeating in the transference. The analyst advocates the first in the form of free association; the patient tends toward the second, in the form of associative compulsion. The ongoing discourse of a psychoanalysis is the interaction of these two modes of re-presentation. "For our experience has shown us," Freud writes in the 1912 paper "The Dynamics of Transference," "that if a patient's free associations fail the stoppage can invariably be removed by an assurance that he is being dominated at the moment by an association which is concerned with the doctor himself or with something connected with him" (S.E. 12 : 101). The false connections of transference interfere with conscious remembering by free association, yet they are, Freud reminds us, necessary to the analysis: "But it should not be forgotten that it is precisely they that do us the inestimable service of making the patient's hidden and forgotten erotic impulses immediate and manifest" (S.E. 12 : 108). Intrapsychic representation, first elaborated by the circumventions of *Umweg*, is now, on the threshold of metapsychology, located in the interplay of the differently structured discourses of conscious free association, or remembering, and unconscious false connection, or repeating.

Freud's argument, in "The Dynamics of Transference," is that "each individual, through the combined operation of his innate disposition and the influences brought to bear on him during his early years, has acquired a specific method of his own in his conduct of his erotic life. . . . This produces what might be described as a stereotype plate (or several such), which is constantly repeated [*wiederholt*]—constantly reprinted afresh [*neu abgedruckt*]—in the course of a person's life" (S.E. 12:99–100). The transferential repetitions of the psychical apparatus have become the reimpressions of a printing apparatus.[5] When a patient's libidinal cathexis is directed, in the treatment, onto the figure of the doctor, "this cathexis will have recourse to prototypes, will attach itself [*wird sich anknüpfen*] to one of the stereotype plates which are present in the subject; or, to put the position another way, the cathexis will introduce the doctor into one of the psychical 'series' [*Reihen*] which the patient has already formed" (S.E. 12 : 100). The patient is connected to his past, in the repetition model of representation, by

5. Jacques Derrida has admirably commented upon the various editions of this metaphorical scheme in "Freud and the Scene of Writing."

a series, each member of which is related to, but different from, the one preceding it. This metaphor is set in apposition to the metaphor of printing, in which repetition with difference is made possible by alterations of the stereotype plates. Here, one cannot help but think of Freud's own method of periodically, and repeatedly, revising several of his texts—notably *The Interpretation of Dreams* and *Three Essays*—and not, in the German editions, indicating the additions or deletions, so that, without James Strachey's analytic reconstructions, we are faced with a text that contains, but suppresses, its own earlier versions.

The series that bears particularly on re-presentation as repetition in the transference, and its relation to some original version, is the series of surrogates. In "A Special Type of Choice of Object Made by Men" (1910), Freud writes that in the lives of certain men, "the love-objects may replace one another so frequently that a *long series of them* [*einer langen Reihe*] *is formed*" (*S.E.* 11 : 168):

> If we are to understand the love-objects chosen by our type as being above all mother-surrogates, then the formation of a series of them, which seems so flatly to contradict the condition of being faithful to one, can now also be understood. We have learnt from psycho-analysis in other examples that the notion of something irreplaceable, when it is active in the unconscious, frequently appears as broken up into an endless series [*eine unendliche Reihe*]: endless for the reason that every surrogate nevertheless fails to provide the desired satisfaction. This is the explanation of the insatiable urge to ask questions shown by children at a certain age: they have one single question to ask, but it never crosses their lips. It explains, too, the garrulity of some people affected by neurosis; they are under the pressure of a secret which is burning to be disclosed but which, despite all temptation, they never reveal. [*S.E.* 11 : 169–70]

Endless series, like *Umweg*, is a drive back to original satisfaction; but what is original, as always, is enigmatic, for the so-called original satisfaction can occur only with a surrogate: the average man never did possess his mother sexually. What Freud calls "the notion of something irreplaceable" is given a radical twist, for it is a question of that which cannot be replaced because it was never possessed. As for Freud's striking connection—all in one breath, as it were—between the notion of irreplaceability and certain kinds of talking, like insatiable questioning and unstoppable garrulity, I shall get back to it.

Surrogates, the actors in the *Schauplatz* of transferential drama, pose a problem for the analyst. In "Observations on Transference-Love" (1915), Freud warns: "I shall state it as a fundamental principle that the patient's need and longing must be allowed to persist in her, in order that they may serve as forces impelling her to do work and to make changes, and that we must beware of appeasing those forces by means of surrogates" (*S.E.* 12 : 165). But on the next page he makes it clear that surrogates are necessary to the analysis, for the one class of women who become unanalyzable when their transference-love flourishes are "women of elemental passionateness who tolerate no surrogates. They are children of nature who refuse to accept the psychical in place of the material, who, in the poet's words, are accessible only to 'the logic of soup, with dumplings for arguments' " (*S.E.* 12 : 166–67). The analyst must offer himself as a psychical surrogate, a transferential point of attachment, if the pathogenic wish for an original, irreplaceable object is to become manifest. But the analyst must not offer himself as a material surrogate, for this leads to stoppage.

The question is how to treat the disease of irreplaceable originals. It seems that analytic discourse in large, or long, doses is the only cure, and that a capacity for metaphor is the only safeguard against the stoppage of the analytic discourse. Freud discovered early that hypnosis, which led to remembering rather than repeating, could not cure the disease, since symptoms would endlessly substitute one for another. The new method of free association worked, apparently, but only by consigning the analyst to an intermediate position between remembering and repeating: "For him, remembering in the old manner—reproduction in the psychical field—is the aim to which he adheres, even though he knows that such an aim cannot be achieved in the new technique. He is prepared for a perpetual struggle . . . to keep in the psychical sphere all the impulses which the patient would like to direct into the motor sphere" (S.E. 12 : 153). The task of the analyst is to force *Umweg* on himself and on the patient; only by this path of abstinence can they together attempt to deconstruct the myth of irreplaceable originals which nourishes the disease. It is another attempt to persuade that deconstructs the representations upon which it depends.

We have examined representation by unconscious repeating in an attempt better to understand the relation of psychoanalytic metalanguage to its object. Repetitive re-presentation is a series of surrogates, generated by metaphorical transformations, or a series of stereotype plates, or an unstoppable series of questions. We are back to problems of undecidability: how, for instance, can one determine in what proportions the extremes of a series—be they metaphor and synecdoche, repeating and remembering, hysteria and obsessionality, or, to mention Freud's favorite, feminine and masculine—in what proportions they occur in any given member of the series? Between the stoppage of literalized transference and the unstoppability of neurotic garrulity lies the question: What, or where, or when is the original edition of the psychical printing-press? And what keeps the press going? Freud, in a footnote to "The Dynamics of Transference," points a way. He has been discussing what he calls the "complemental series" (*Ergänzungsreihe*) of constitution and accident, which bear in varying proportions on the causation of any given neurosis. He concludes with the remark: "Incidentally, one might venture to regard constitution itself as a precipitate from the accidental effects produced on the endlessly long chain of our ancestors [*die unendlich grosse Reihe der Ahnen*]" (S.E. 12 : 99 n.). It is a paradigmatic psychoanalytic gesture. The inside is projected outside, and constitution is shown to be determined by its apparent antithesis, accident. The two extremes of the series lose their security as reference points and themselves enter into an endless series of inside–outside exchanges. Imprinting, or constitution, is ultimately just printing, and the series of stereotype plates stretches out infinitely as our intrapsychic surrogates, projected outward, become the endlessly long series of our ancestors. Any original object of psychoanalytic metalanguage is lost in the mirror-play regress, for nothing, it seems, is irreducible. Should we wonder that at the end of his life Freud would arrive at the question of "Die Endliche und die Unendliche Analyse"—"Analysis Terminable and Interminable"?

If the theoretical model of representation by unconscious metaphorical repetition turns out to build upon the very false connections it deconstructs, this is not to say that the other model of representation by conscious remembering builds upon any kind of simple re-presentation. To begin with, it is clearly a device of exposition to discuss the two separately. But even allowing that, and assuming that remembering can be isolated pure, we know that if there is one thing of which Freud has managed to convince the world at large, it is that memory is no simple business. Yet the theoretical description of memory in *The Interpretation of Dreams* seems uncomplicated: "Intentional recollection and other constituent processes of our normal thinking involve a retrogressive movement in the psychical apparatus from a complex ideational act [*Vorstellungsakt*] back to the raw material of the memory-traces underlying it [*an das Rohmaterial der Erinnerungsspuren*]" (*S.E.* 5 : 542–43). This vision of a neurological mechanism of recovery from the storage-place of psychical inscription is the conceptual basis of the theoretical fiction of pure primary process and *Umweg*, which itself has every intention of being uncomplicated. It is in a contemporary, relatively minor, text, the 1899 paper "Screen Memories" ("Über Deckerinnerungen"), that Freud does complicate his major theoretical statement: "The falsified memory is the first that we become aware of: the raw material of memory-traces out of which it was forged remains unknown to us in its original form" (*S.E.* 3 : 322). The simultaneous composition of these two texts is a typical Freudian gesture, repeated, for instance, with "The Uncanny" and *Beyond The Pleasure Principle*. There would be much to say about the relationship of the minor text, which is, to a first approximation, more "literary," to the contemporary, more "scientific," major text, and of the relation between literary and scientific figurations in any of Freud's texts, and of the way this relation bears on the question of undecidability. The paper "Screen Memories," especially, should be considered from this angle, for this coy, elegant text, which builds on a disguised autobiographical anecdote, is the quintessence of literary–scientific undecidability. The central dialogue, the literary object, is framed in a scientific exposition that interprets it; or at least this is the fiction the reader is asked to accept. In fact the anecdote, which is about disguises put on in the service of repression, disguises its own authorship, and the unwitting reader who accepts the fiction of scientific interpretation is fooled. Truly a psychoanalytic parable.

But the question at hand is the relation of a memory to the raw material of memory-traces out of which is was forged. The metaphorical apparatus in "Screen Memories" has taken the form of an industrial machine, and the metaphor of production, in which a memory product is "forged" from "raw material," punctuates the entire text. At one point the analyst character tells the analysand character: "Yes. You projected the two phantasies on to one another and made a childhood memory of them. The element about the alpine flowers is as it were a stamp [*Marke*] giving the date of manufacture [*die Zeit dieser Fabrikation*]. I can assure you that people often construct such things unconsciously—almost like works of fiction [*dass man solche Dinge sehr häufig unbewusst macht, gleichsam dichtet*]" (*S.E.* 3 : 315). In the German, the simile of the last sentence connects two verbs: *machen,* "to make," and *dichten,* "to write poetry or fiction." Intrapsychic manufacture, in an almost offhand gesture, becomes writing, and Freud invites us to compare the various steps in the production of a memory and the production of a text.

The problem the essay sets out to address is by now familiar: "In the course of my psycho-analytic treatment of cases of hysteria, obsessional neurosis, etc., I have often had to deal with fragmentary recollections which have remained in the patient's memory from the earliest years of his childhood. . . . It is only from the sixth or seventh year onwards—in many cases only after the tenth year—that our lives can be reproduced in memory as a connected chain of events" (*S.E.* 3 : 303). This is *the* synecdochic Freudian problem: how can we know a thing from its fragments, how restore a chain made up mostly of gaps? The argument is that screen memories center on apparently insignificant details, or, as Freud calls them, residues, onto which has been transferred the intensity originally belonging to other, now repressed, ideas. The paradigm, of course, is the dream. "It is a case of displacement on to something associated by continuity [*Kontiguitätsassoziation*]; or, looking at the process as a whole, a case of repression accompanied by the substitution of something in the neighborhood (whether in space or time)" (*S.E.* 3 : 307–08). The psychic defense at issue in screen memories is a metonymy.[6]

Toward the end of the essay Freud speculates not only upon screen memories but "upon the origin of conscious memories in general": "It looks as though a memory-trace from childhood had here been translated back into a plastic and visual form at a later date—the date of the memory's arousal. But no reproduction of the original impression [*Eindruck*] has ever entered the subject's consciousness. . . . the falsified memory is the first that we become aware of: the raw material of memory-traces out of which it was forged remains unknown to us in its original form" (*S.E.* 3 : 321–22). *Eindruck,* which means not only psychical impression but the impression of a printing press, sends us back to the stereotype plates of the transferential series, which are constantly reprinted afresh—*neu abgedruckt.* The synecdoches of conscious memory and the metaphors of unconscious repetition were points of reference, for the purposes of both Freud's exposition and ours. But it appears that the representational scheme traced between these two poles of re-presentation is plagued by undecidability. For this representational scheme builds upon a raw material known only as its falsified products, depends upon a fiction of an undis-coverable original impression, and arrives at understanding only as self-deconstruction.

6. See Harold Bloom's discussion of psychic defenses and rhetorical tropes in *A Map of Misreading* (1975), chap. 5.

Paternal Fictions

Freud introduces his theoretical speculation as a search for "understanding" (*Verständnis*); let us conclude by asking how this connects to schemes of representation. Freud's search for understanding led him early on to that moment of the life cycle when every human is a researcher: "At about the same time as the sexual life of children reaches its first peak," he writes in the 1915 edition of *Three Essays on Sexuality*, "between the ages of three and five, they also begin to show signs of the activity which may be ascribed to the instinct for knowledge or research. . . . the first problem with which it deals is not the question of the distinction between the sexes but the riddle of where babies come from" (*S.E.* 7 : 194–95). Freud's young investigator starts out on the right path. "I now know that the change which takes place in the mother during pregnancy does not escape the child's sharp eyes and that he is very well able before long to establish the true connection [*den richtigen Zusammenhang*] between the increase in his mother's stoutness and the appearance of the baby" ("On the Sexual Theories of Children," *S.E.* 9 : 214). But having correctly interpreted his mother's stoutness, the child can make a next step in the development of his theory only through a false connection, for he does not know that impregnation results from sexual intercourse: "But his further progress is inhibited by a piece of ignorance which cannot be made good and by false theories [*falsche Theorien*] which the state of his own sexuality imposes on him. These false sexual theories . . . all have one very curious characteristic. Although they go astray in a grotesque fashion, yet each one of them contains a fragment of real truth [*ein Stück echter Wahrheit*]; and in this they are analogous to the attempts of adults, which are looked at as strokes of genius, at solving the problems of the universe which are too hard for human comprehension" (*S.E.* 9 : 215). Freudian researchers young and old must settle for an understanding that is synecdochically elusive, a fragment—*Stück*—lost in the heap of misunderstanding. The power of the false theories to bias the interpretations of the researcher is such that even if the child witnesses parental intercourse, he misunderstands it: "I have not been able to ascertain that children recognize this behaviour which they have witnessed between their parents as the missing link [*erforderliche Stück*] needed for solving the problem of babies; it appears more often that the connection [*Beziehung*] is overlooked by them for the very reason that they have interpreted the act of love as an act of violence" (*S.E.* 9 : 220–21).

The missing connection of sexual intercourse is filled in by false connections, false theories. One of these starts out from the functional undecidability of the organ that makes the connection. "The sexual organ of the male has two functions; and there are those to whom this association is an annoyance. It serves for the evacuation of the bladder, and it carries out the act of love which sets the craving of the genital libido at rest. The child still believes he can unite the two functions. According to a theory of his, babies are made by the man urinating into the woman's body" ("The Acquisition and Control of Fire," *S.E.* 22 : 192). This undecidability sets up false connections not just in the minds of children. Freud, who did say that sometimes a cigar is just a cigar, also saw, late in life, the pen in penis: in certain cases of neurotic inhibition, "writing, which entails making a liquid flow out of a tube onto a white piece of paper, assumes the significance of copulation" (*Inhibitions, Symptoms and Anxiety*, 1926, *S.E.* 20 : 90).

The child substitutes false theories for the true connection of intercourse, which he overlooks; the act of writing is another substitute for copulation. Writing and theory-building never free themselves from the problematic of false connections, and perhaps we should attend to the connection between problems of metalanguage and the mysteries of the originary sexual link. Freud shows the way. In the 1909 paper "Family Romances" he considers children's fantasies about their parentage. At first, "at a time at which the child is still in ignorance of the sexual determinants of procreation," he develops "a phantasy in which both his parents are replaced by others of better birth" (*S.E.* 9 : 239). This is yet another false sexual theory, generated under pressure of ignorance. What becomes of the theory when ignorance is dissipated? "When presently the child comes to know the difference in the parts played by fathers and mothers in their sexual relations, and realizes that '*pater semper incertus est*' (paternity is always uncertain), while the mother is '*certissima*' (most certain), the family romance undergoes a curious curtailment: it contents itself with exalting the child's father, but no longer casts any doubts on his maternal origin, which is regarded as something unalterable" (*S.E.* 9 : 239). Ignorance, it seems, is never quite dissipated; even after one knows the facts of life, Freud would have it that *pater semper incertus est*, and the copulatory connection, no longer overlooked, is still uncertain. In response to this perpetual uncertainty of the father, the child continues to exalt him in fantasies, or, as Freud also terms them in this paper, "works of fiction [*Dichtungen*]" (*S.E.* 9 : 240).

The major Freudian text on family romances, which originally admitted itself to be a work of fiction but later called itself history, is the family romance of Sigmund Freud himself. *The Man Moses, a Historical Novel*, or, as we know it now, *Moses and Monotheism*, preoccupied and haunted Freud through the last years of his life; it is a forceful indication that the question of paternity retains its power to generate fictions long, long beyond childhood. This late myth of origins hovers almost obsessionally around the question of originary undecidability. After the Jews had left Egypt, Freud recounts, they wanted both to preserve the figure of their ex-leader, Moses, and to repress the memory that they had murdered him. "So it was that the first compromise came about, and it was probably soon recorded in writing [*eine schriftliche Fixierung fand*]. The people who had come from Egypt had brought writing and the desire to write history along with them; but it was to be a long time before historical writing realized that it was pledged to unswerving truthfulness. To begin with it had no scruples about shaping its narratives according to the needs and purposes of the moment, as though it had not yet recognized the concept of falsification" (*S.E.* 23 : 68). All that Freud has to work from, as he writes his family romance, is this other written account. Forty years before, at the time of the death of his own father, psychoanalytic writing had come into being as Freud inter-

rogated the text of the dream. Now, at the time when Freud
faces his own death, psychoanalytic writing drives toward an
end-point—or is it a starting-point?—as it interrogates the text
of the Bible:

> The text, however, as we possess it to-day, will tell us
> enough about its own vicissitudes. Two mutually opposed
> treatments have left their traces [*Spuren*] on it. On the one
> hand it has been subjected to revisions which have falsified
> it in the sense of their secret aims, have mutilated and
> amplified it and have even changed it into its reverse; on
> the other hand a solicitous piety has presided over it and
> has sought to preserve everything as it was, no matter
> whether it was consistent or contradicted itself. Thus al-
> most everywhere noticeable gaps, disturbing repetitions
> and obvious contradictions have come about—indications
> which reveal things to us which it was not intended to com-
> municate. In its implications the distortion of a text resem-
> bles a murder: the difficulty is not in perpetrating the
> deed, but in getting rid of its traces [*Spuren*]. [*S.E.* 23 : 43]

Textual false connections resemble a murder, or rather, *the*
murder: parricide. And it seems to have been this murder
which set the text in motion; or was it the text which set this
murder in motion? We remember the child, who, in his fiction
of origins, substituted a scene of violence for sexual intercourse. *Moses and Monotheism* hovers at the scene of this textual
crime, obsessed with a murder that is covered, and so revealed.
We remember the preface to the second edition of *The Interpretation of Dreams,* in which Freud relates problems of revision to
what that text had set in motion: "An equal durability and
power to withstand any far-reaching alterations during the process of revision has been shown by the *material* [*Material*] of the
book. . . . For this book has a further subjective significance
for me personally—a significance which I only grasped after I
had completed it. It was, I found, a portion [*Stück*] of my own
self-analysis, my reaction to my father's death—that is to say, to
the most important event, the most poignant loss, of a man's
life. Having discovered that this was so, I felt unable to obli-

340 THE NEED TO CONNECT

terate the traces of the experience [*die Spuren dieser Einwirkung zu verwischen*]" (*S.E.* 4 : xxvi). That which showed such durability, that which returned unaltered at the time of the father's death, was Freud's infantile parricidal wish. Its psychical traces, he lets us know, are inextricable from the traces of the text. *Moses and Monotheism,* too, confesses by its very form to being implicated in the cover-up it describes. The introduction to the final section of the text is explicit: "The part of this study which follows. . . . is nothing other than a faithful (and often word-for-word) repetition of the first part. . . . I am aware that a method of exposition [*Darstellung*] such as this is no less inexpedient than it is inartistic. I myself deplore it unreservedly. Why have I not avoided it? The answer to that is not hard for me to find, but it is not easy to confess. I found myself unable to wipe out the traces [*die Spuren . . . zu verwischen*] of the work's origin, which was in any case unusual" (*S.E.* 23 : 103). Freud's text, like the text it interprets, cannot eliminate "indications which reveal things to us which it was not intended to communicate." Texts displace themselves beyond the limits of intentional exposition. As Freud writes in the passage on textual distortion and murder: "We might well lend the word '*Entstellung* [distortion]' the double meaning to which it has a claim, but of which to-day it makes no use. It should mean not only 'to change the appearance of something' but also 'to put something in another place, to displace' " (*S.E.* 23 : 43).

Memory-traces lie, in both senses, at the limits of representation. They cannot be re-presented in their original form ("Screen Memories"), but they cannot be obliterated. In *Moses and Monotheism,* they support a central argument of the text, "that men have always known (in this special way) that they once possessed a primal father and killed him" (*S.E.* 23 : 101). The special way is the way of "archaic heritage": "The archaic heritage of human beings comprises not only dispositions but also subject-matter—memory-traces of the experience of earlier generations. . . . Granted that at the time we have no stronger evidence for the presence of memory-traces in the archaic heritage than the residual phenomena [*Resterscheinungen*] of the work of analysis which call for a phylogenetic derivation, yet this evidence seems to us strong enough to postulate that such is the fact" (*S.E.* 23 : 99–100). As always, analysis must work synecdochically, building on fragments; here one bit of evidence Freud marshals for the phylogenetic transmission of memory-traces is the "universality of symbolism in language," which is apparent in "the very common figures of speech in which this symbolism is recorded [*Redensarten . . . in denen sich diese Symbolik fixiert findet*]" (*S.E.* 23 : 98). *Fixieren* is the verb Freud has always used to refer to instinctual fixation; *Moses and Monotheism*, in a move that sends us back to the hungry baby, displaces that meaning to include the fixation of first metaphors: "The symbolic representation [*Vertretung*] of one object by another—the same thing applies to actions—is familiar to all our children and comes to them, as it were, as a matter of course. . . . It is a question of an original knowledge which adults afterwards forget" (*S.E.* 23 : 98). An original knowledge, but also an original re-presentational false connection. Original fixation is displaced into language, and we are not to be surprised to find that this is simply a return to Freud's primal figuration of memory: the "first compromise," the first distortion of the story of Moses, "was probably soon recorded in writing [*eine schriftliche Fixierung fand*]." Original fixation, in memory-traces and in writing, sets up an endless series of compromises, substitutions by false connection of one object for another.

"An event such as the elimination of the primal father by the company of his sons must inevitably have left ineradicable traces [*Spuren*] in the history of humanity; and the less it itself was recollected, the more numerous must have been the substitutes [*Ersatzbildungen*] to which it gave rise [*zum Ausdruck bringen*]" (*Totem and Taboo, S.E.* 13 : 155). The murder inscribes a trace, the trace finds expression (*Ausdruck*) in a substitute; the repressed murder is re-presented by "harmless" figurations. The Freudian model of symptom and dream formation extends itself to thoughts and texts, and starting from the pair *Spur–Bild*, gives rise to a series of dualisms in which the second member re-presents the first: primary process–secondary process; repeating–remembering; writing-as-tracing–writing-as-figuration; dead father–god. The theory of representation traced out by these dualisms depends upon a seeming paradox: in each case, the secondary representation is connected to the first by an *Umweg* or false connection, which is so designated in relation to a hypothetical direct, or true, connection. But "harmless" secondary imagery displaces the text that invoked it, and the secondary scheme of transferential substitutions traced by *Umweg* deconstructs the original connection it posited. Even parricide, as true origin of representation, is dis-coverable only as the displacement of textual (self-) falsification.

In Freud's text, understanding and representation fall into undecidability as they take up the question of the father. We are back to the relation of metalanguage and that upon which it purports to abstract. The murdered primal father, abstracted through the false connections of a counterphobic fiction of de-ification, requires us to restate this relation. We may do this by turning to Freud's account, in *Moses and Monotheism*, of the nec-essary prerequisites to the founding of monotheistic religion. His argument is that before the Jews could accept one God, they had to have made the revolutionary change from a ma-triarchal social order to a patriarchal one. This change, in turn, had to have been prepared for by another revolution, this one a revolution in the mind and body, "the development of speech, which resulted in such an extraordinary advancement of intellectual activities." As a result of this change, "The new realm of intellectuality was opened up, in which ideas, memo-ries and inferences became decisive in contrast to the lower psychical activity which had direct perceptions by the sense-organs as its content" (*S.E.* 23 : 113). We are reminded of the passage in *The Interpretation of Dreams* in which a secondary thought identity is substituted for primary perceptual identity. But why should the development of speech, with its attendant ideas, memories, and inferences, be a necessary precondition of patriarchal social order? "Maternity is proved by the evidence of the senses while paternity is a hypothesis, based on an infer-ence and a premise" (*S.E.* 23 : 114). Paternity is established in a hypothesis, a secondary-process thought identity, an *Umweg*. But paternity is established *only* in an *Umweg*, only in the false connections of a psychotextual apparatus in which it is the originary substitute for an originary missing connection. The problem of establishing authoritative metalanguage *is* the problem of establishing paternity. Authoritative metalanguage, which could keep itself free of the false connections it purported to interpret, would be paternal language, language with *auctoritas*. But as Freud the author—*auctor*—could not forget, *pater semper incertus est.*

REFERENCES

Bloom, H. *A Map of Misreading.* New York: Oxford University Press, 1975.

de Man, P. *Blindness and Insight.* New York: Oxford University Press, 1971.

Derrida, J. "Freud and the Scene of Writing." Translated by J. Mehlman. *French Freud, Yale French Studies* 48 (1972) : 73–117.

Freud, S. *Gesammelte Werke.* London: Imago, 1940.

———. *The Standard Edition of the Complete Psychological Works.* London: Hogarth, 1953–74.

Studies on Hysteria (1893–95), vol. 2 [with J. Breuer].

"Screen Memories" (1899), vol. 3.

The Interpretation of Dreams (1900–01), vols. 4, 5.

Three Essays on Sexuality (1905), vol. 7.

"On the Sexual Theories of Children" (1908), vol. 9.

"Family Romances" (1909), vol. 9.

"A Special Type of Choice of Object Made by Men" (1910), vol. 11.

"The Dynamics of Transference" (1912), vol. 12.

"Remembering, Repeating and Working-Through" (1914), vol. 12.

"Observations on Transference-Love" (1915), vol. 12.

Totem and Taboo (1913), vol. 13.

"The Unconscious" (1915), vol. 14.

"The 'Uncanny' " (1919), vol. 17.

Beyond the Pleasure Principle (1920), vol. 18.

An Autobiographical Study (1925), vol. 20.

Inhibitions, Symptoms and Anxiety (1926), vol. 20.

"The Acquisition and Control of Fire" (1932), vol. 22.

New Introductory Lectures on Psycho-Analysis (1933), vol. 22.

"Analysis Terminable and Interminable" (1937), vol. 23.
    Moses and Monotheism (1939), vol. 23.
Lacan, J. *Écrits*. Paris: Éditions du Seuil, 1966. (Also: *Écrits: A Selection*.
    Translated by A. Sheridan. New York: Norton, 1977.)
Rey, J.-M. *Parcours de Freud*. Paris: Éditions Galilée, 1974.
Richards, I. A. *The Philosophy of Rhetoric*. New York: Oxford University
    Press, 1936.

12

Revisions and Rereadings in Dreams and Allegories

MEREDITH ANNE SKURA

What it will be Questioned When the Sun rises do you not
see a round Disk of fire somewhat like a Guinea O no no I
see an Innumerable company of the Heavenly host crying
Holy Holy Holy is the Lord God Almighty.

William Blake

Methinks I see these things with parted eye, When everything looks double.

Lovers in *Midsummer Night's Dream*

When Freud announced that he had found "the secret of
dreams," he introduced a formula for interpretation which has
continued to tantalize—and to disappoint—not only dream interpreters but literary critics ever since. What Freud did was to
divert attention from the dream's overt content and to look instead at its function: the puzzling dream images could now be
explained—no longer dismissed as gibberish or worshipped as
divine revelation, they could now be seen as the traces of a
struggle between forces we hadn't known about before. Every
dreamer was like Browning's Childe Roland wandering
through his nightmare landscape wondering what "savage
battle" had left this rough plash behind.

Freud's formula for interpreting dreams in terms of motive
was as simple as Pavlov's: every dream fulfills a wish. The perception of a need becomes associated with the "mnemic image"
of past satisfaction (Freud, 1900–01, p. 565), so that when I am

345

thirsty, I dream that I drink. That's all. Or, in the more complicated general case where the censor is at work, "*a dream is
a (disguised) fulfilment of a . . . (repressed) wish*" (ibid., p. 160).
Even though it was simple, however, the formula promised an
entirely new way of seeing how meaning and motive were related. Freud's was not an attempt to reduce mental life to sexual forces (an "erotics of the mind," as Kenneth Burke has
since called it), although both analysts and their critics have
sometimes seen it this way. On the contrary, Freud was trying
to sketch a "semantics of desire," a way of seeing "how the vicissitudes of motive are worked out only in the vicissitudes of
meaning," as Paul Ricoeur has said. In suggesting the intimate
connection between *the way we say something* in our dreams and
what we expect to achieve by saying it, Freud's work promises one
answer, too, for the more recent critical question[1] about the
relation between rhetoric as figure and rhetoric as persuasion.

    And at first, the idea of conflict—wish battling repression—
did seem to open a fresh approach to texts, by showing that
they, like dreams, were dynamic products of tension, the results of a process and not simply given. In one way or another
most of the applications of Freud's dream theory to literature
have been nothing more than an increasingly sophisticated use
of what analysts have learned about that psychic tension. Literary critics learned how to look not only for raw wishes in literature, or for crude battles between wishes and defenses, but also
for the ways in which authors and readers can work out adap-
tive transformations of primitive wishes within the safely
marked-off bounds of the literary text. But finally, Freud's
focus on the single dimension of instinctual conflict ignored so
much of the dream, let alone the literary texts that people have
tried to treat like dreams, that its use is limited. What I want to
suggest here is that what Freud really discovered was not a tension between wishes, but between two wholly different ways of
seeing and representing experience, both of which are embodied in the dream—ways that depend not only on the dreamer's

1. Many have discussed this question since Paul de Man posed it in his
Blindness and Insight, though he rejects a reductively Freudian analysis of the
relation between figure and persuasion.

motives but also on his modes of representation, and even on his relation to his implied audience.

Though Freud would not have put it this way, much of what he says—and certainly much of what he *does* in the course of actual dream interpretations—implies that it is this larger conflict which defines the dream's special nature and which must be dealt with in interpreting it. Implications of a larger conflict are especially noticeable in Freud's self-contradictory descriptions of the single quality which most distinguishes dreams from waking experience, and which Freud was the first to emphasize: their regressive quality. The dreamer, Freud says, takes off his civilized extensions one by one—like the man taking out his false teeth and removing his eyeglasses before going to bed—and regresses both to his infantile wishes and to his infantile form of expression, visual hallucinations. The contrast between waking and dreaming, Freud implies, is explained by the contrast between our mature, civilized selves and our infantile selves. It is explained first of all by the difference between our daytime obedience to the reality principle and our nighttime regression to the pleasure principle; and second, by the difference between our sophisticated use of verbal thinking by day and our recourse to visual thinking at night.

So far this makes sense and presents no trouble. But once Freud goes on to describe exactly how the regression works, he makes two contradictory claims. In the case of regression to an infantile wish, Freud reductively assumes that the *literal* wish (for example, for the breast, or for some infantile masturbation fantasy-object) is the "ultimate" meaning of and source for the dream. But when he talks about the dreamer's regression to infantile forms of representation, Freud makes it clear that these are not to be assumed as literally final in themselves. The "regression" to a visual scene does not mean that the ultimate meaning of a dream is an infantile visual experience. Visual or pictorial representation, Freud says, is only an old tool being somewhat crampedly used—in the absence of a better and more modern one—for new adult purposes. The dreamer is like the political cartoonist, forced to condense and distort and simplify his ideas so that they fit into cartoon form. (Rather than being like a person who has lost all use of language and logic, and has regressed to a state where indeed *all* he knows are pictorial and sensual experiences.)

In the one case the regression is absolute and ultimate; in the other it is only a means for expressing something else. In the one case—infantile wish—we get closer to the "truth"; in the other—infantile modes of representation—we are distracted from the truth by its having been translated into an alien and inappropriate language. Despite Freud's smooth generalization about regression in the dream, there is finally no way to reconcile its two different roles. What I shall argue, however, is that the contradictory functions of regression permeate every aspect of the dream—both its motive and its mode of representation. The dream's unique quality, in fact, derives from the conflict between these roles as it forces an interpreter to switch from one mode of reading the dream to another. The conflict is less like the tug-of-war Freud describes than like the perceptual conflict about ambiguous "duck-rabbit" figures, or like the intellectual conflict in a debate, or like the conflict between biblical interpretations; it involves simultaneous conflict between readings like the sequential misreading Harold Bloom has described in one poet's reading of another.

Freud came closer to describing this ambivalent struggle in dreams, *not* when he talked about the struggle between wish and censor on the borders of consciousness, but when he talked about a second "factor" at work "after the dream has been presented before consciousness as an object of perception" (Freud, 1933, p. 21). This was the "secondary revision" which reworked the dream-stuff into logically presentable form. Actually, Freud recognized just such an ambivalent struggle in every realm of mental life; and he came back, again and again—not only in describing dream formation—to the idea that there is always a kind of secondary revision, or a "secondary gain" in symptom, or a "secondary repression" in the many-layered process of symptom formation, or a secondary "restitution" after the psychotic has disavowed reality. He of course was interested in the nugget of original stuff "revised," "repressed," or whatever; I will be interested here in the nature of the play between the two processes, and the way in which they work on and interpret one another.

In the first of the following sections I will reexamine Freud's original version of the conflict—wish and censorship—to show how the concepts of wish and censorship quickly loosened in his actual practice to imply a much wider conflict in dreams. The second section demonstrates the widened conflict in a reexamination of one of Freud's most important sample dream analyses. Finally, in the third section, I want to suggest how conflict in dreams can be a useful starting point for understanding the way certain literary texts work.

Beyond Instinctual Conflicts

In Freud's description, one part of the dreamer's mind sleepily regresses to hallucinatory fulfillment of an infantile wish, while a still-alert censor in another part of the mind merely makes use of regressive dream-work mechanisms as a way of serving its adult purposes in thwarting the wish-fulfillment. But in neither case are things that simple.

Take the wish. For Freud, the wish is the thing itself, the original source and meaning behind the manifest dream's false façade. Without the censor interfering, every dream would be as simple as Freud's paradigm "dream of convenience," in which, for example, the thirsty sleeper dreams that he is drinking so he won't have to wake up and get himself a drink. "There is a dream I can produce in myself as often as I like— experimentally as it were," Freud says, "If I eat anchovies or olives . . . in the evening [before bed]" (1900–01, p. 123). In practice, however, it is not as easy as Freud suggests to separate the wish from everything else in the dream. Nor is any wish, even a physiological one like thirst, so easily separable from its later associations outside the dream—indeed, its own meaning and power for the adult, far from being literally obvious, may actually derive from its own supposed derivatives.

Even Freud's example of the "experimental" convenience dream quietly demonstrates these complications. After eating anchovies one night Freud did dream about drinking—but that wasn't all he dreamt. His wife was giving him a drink from a valuable urn which he had in reality just given away as a present. The difference between this and the simple glass of water which would have done just as well to fulfill the physiological need is no accident, and it is not easy to isolate the original wish from its supposedly "accidental" content. As W. R. D. Fairbairn has said in arguing against a purely wish-based metapsychology, an impulse is not "a kick in the pants administered out of the blue to a surprised ego, but *somebody's* impulse to do something to somebody else" (1946, p. 36). Freud wants the water, but his merely physiological need is inseparable from his more complex esthetic desires for the urn, and from his wish to be served by his wife. Who is to say which of these wishes is ultimate? The physical act of drinking is a common denominator for several different wishes and the occasion for several different *kinds* of "wishing" in the dream.

Perhaps with Freud's anchovies in mind, Jean Laplanche and Serge Leclaire have even reported a dream "which fulfills the need to drink but without *any* reference to drinking" (1966, pp. 138–39). Here the original wish disappears altogether from the dream of convenience, but not because of any simple censorship—rather because of a complexity of what "wish" means. The dreamer is Philippe, who woke thirsty from a dream about walking through the woods with a girlfriend. The fulfillment of "drinking" came in only in Philippe's associations to the walk, which included several memories about drinks and people who gave him drinks, and the time he learned to cup his hands and scoop water up for himself. The wish to drink was here inseparable from its later derivatives (wishes to seduce people into serving him, to be independent and get drinks for himself, and so forth). The "fulfillment" in the manifest dream is not so much disguised as simply elaborated to correspond to the elaboration of the wish.

Not only is the "wish" sometimes inseparable from its derivatives, but it may even turn out to be a symbolic disguise for one of its derivatives. In a dream about a related convenience, for example, Freud reports waking with a "pressing need to micturate" and remembers that he was just dreaming about bringing his father a urinal. This time, however, he suggests that his painful thoughts about his father's weakness came first and only then called up his own physiological need as a distraction—or disguise—for those thoughts.

Clearly, the physiological model will not work to represent complex psychological motives. And in fact, though he ostensibly keeps the model throughout *The Interpretation of Dreams,* Freud unobtrusively complicates it until it becomes almost a reverse of itself. The first wishes he points to are simple, recognizable adult wishes: to be famous, to pursue forbidden hobbies. But soon he has to talk about the "wishes" that lie behind frightening and unpleasant dreams—wishes, he explains, "from another part of the mind" (1900–01, pp. 145 ff., 157 ff.). While perfectly plausible, this claim modifies "wish" to include the very "censorship" which was supposed to be fighting "wishes." In addition, Freud reveals that even the first sort of wishes are regressive infantile wishes, which, if taken literally, are not recognizable as wishes any more. They are, in other words, inseparable from the childhood context and way of seeing things in which they arose.[2] When Freud, finally, talks about the *ego*'s wish to sleep (1900–01, p. 570), he moves entirely out of the realm of specific wishes into talking about general conditions of experience and ways of coping with wishes in general.

By this point it is quite clear that Freud's "wish" is very different from a simple physiological sensation that can be satisfied by a simple physical act. "Wish-fulfilling" no longer means "gratifying" but simply psychologically meaningful and determined. Freud has moved from the supposedly single wish to the larger network of "dream-thoughts" that mutually determine the manifest dream. When he called the dream "wish-ful-

2. Although the dream formula thus refers to repressed infantile wishes, Freud's sample analyses seldom go further than uncovering the more recognizable adult wish associated with and covering for the infantile wish. Freud reveals the formula itself only in stages. First he says dreams fulfill wishes (chaps. 2, 3), then that they do so only in a distorted way (chap. 4); and only at the end of chapter 4 does the full formula, indicating that the wishes are repressed wishes, emerge (p. 160). Not until well into chapter 5 does he suggest that these repressed wishes may go back to childhood in every case (p. 219), and not until chapter 7 does he make the full claim.

filling" he was finally contrasting it not to "painful" but to "accidental" experiences and representations of them. The wish pleasure principle no longer means pleasure-seeking (Smith, 1976), and Freud's goal is not to find the infantile pleasures of the text but the reasons for it—which, as we shall see, include adult play with infantile "wishes."

Just as there are problems in trying to see the dream's source and meaning in a single "wish," there are similar problems in trying to see its strange surface as the product of the single motive of "disguise" or censorship. The conflict in dreams is not between wish and censor, but between two—or more—entire ways of seeing and communicating experience. Just as the wish is inseparable from an entire context of thoughts and experiences, "censorship" is also inseparable from a more general mode of seeing and communicating. The dream's distortions are attributable not to censorship alone but to something more like a general psychological determination. The "distortions" do not simply destroy an otherwise realistic presentation of wish-fulfillment, but actually help present one more version of the dreamer's thoughts.

Freud's paradigm for censorship is as simple as his convenience-dream paradigm for wishes: the censor is a destructive force only, mindlessly breaking down the real wish-fulfilling dream-thoughts to produce a meaningless manifest surface. It breaks the dream down and repacks the pieces randomly "like pack ice," making use of accidental and trivial connections between the thoughts to condense and displace them. Even if the manifest dream

has an apparently sensible exterior, we know this has only come about through dream-distortion and can have as little organic relation to the internal content of the dream as the façade of an Italian church has to its structure and plan. . . .

In general one must avoid seeking to explain one part of the manifest dream by another, as though the dream had been coherently conceived and was a logically arranged narrative. On the contrary, it is as a rule like a piece of breccia, composed of various fragments of rock held together by a binding medium, so that the designs that appear on it do not belong to the original rocks imbedded in it.[3]

The resulting bricolage—or Viennese *geshnas* trick picture, as Freud calls it—cannot be taken as a whole but only decoded piece by piece. At best the façade may be related to the dream-thoughts like a rebus, punningly revealing a message once the elements are turned into words: the young man who dreams that the radiator overflowed when he turned the spigot is really saying, "every time I let off steam I get into hot water." But more often the elements lead outward in several different ways, and one of the difficulties in interpreting dreams is in knowing just how to read each one. The one rule, for Freud, is to distrust a literal or even a symbolic reading. A lion in a dream is probably not a lion; nor is it a symbol for Hercules or even for "courage," as it might be in a respectable poem. And once we ignore these obvious meanings, the lion may mean anything. It may be a rebuslike reference to the dreamer's desire to "lie on" certain couches; it may be an allusion to the dreamer's cousin Daniel, or to his recent trip to the zoo. Or its dark mane—in contrast to the almost white mane of the lion the dreamer had actually seen—may even signal that "everything in this dream is a reversal of the truth."

As Freud said, "the kernel of my theory of dreams lies in my derivation of dream-distortion from the censorship," and I have been suggesting that he emphasized the strictly censorial aspects of the dream-work (1900–01, p. 308 n.). But we can say nonetheless that the dream-work generally has wider compass with purposes of its own. The radiator dream is more than a rebus. Its imagery does more than disguise; it actually calls up infantile urination fantasies associated with the more adult

3. *Introductory Lectures* (1915–16), pp. 181–82. See also *Interpretation of Dreams*, pp. 104, 449, 500. Of course, Freud here, as in so many of his central proposals, often contradicts himself (see, e.g., David Carroll, "Freud and the Myth of Origin," *New Literary History* 7 [1975] : 513–28; and Marshall Edelson, "Language and Dreams: *The Interpretation of Dreams* Revisited," *Psychoanalytic Study of the Child* 27 [1972] : 203–82).

thoughts about "letting off steam," conveying them in the only possible symbolic terms for the infantile, exaggerated intensity of such early fantasies. If two ideas have been—from an adult point of view—"condensed," this is because the infantile memory being expressed comes from a time when the two were not separated: the stream of urine *was* a burning jet of steam. The image expresses the thought rather than destroying it.

In other words, there are always at least two ways of reading a dream. Freud continually argued that we must ignore the ordinary way of reading and assume that the manifest dream has no connection with mature, commonsense thinking and communication. He was calling attention to the second way of reading the manifest dream, which he had just discovered. In fact, both kinds of reading are necessary, and it is their interplay which is important. The special quality of dreams lies in our confusion about how to read them: they tempt us into one easy reading but then demand another as well. What Freud's work established was not a simple battle between wish and censor, but the fact that the dream is multiply determined. He showed that its meaning becomes clear only if we read flexibly enough to suspend an initial impression of meaninglessness—or of a too easy meaning—and then reintegrate that impression again.

This larger conflict between whole ways of seeing the dream is indicated by Freud indirectly, and we can see it best if we notice the ambivalence with which he treated the "censor" and its supposed product, the manifest dream. Just as Freud ultimately invoked many different wishing agencies and kinds of wishes, so he invokes several different kinds of disguise and constraint in the dream and attributes them all to the censor. As a result, he paradoxically uses the censor to explain *both* the infantile dream-work mechanisms of condensation and displacement, *and* an all-but-conscious "secondary revision" or "elaboration" (*Bearbeitung*) which joins pieces together and tries to make sense of them and shape the *geshnas* into a picture that makes sense on its own. Though Freud sees both processes as censorship, even he waffles at times and wonders whether some of the dream's distortions are not attributable to other constraints on representation besides censorship and independent of its operation (1915–16, p. 173). Clearly, what happens is that there are two different ways of representing experience at work, both vying for the same dream space, pulling it into different patterns, and making different use of it.

In other words, it is not enough to invoke simple regression to explain the dream's special quality. Neither an infantile motive nor an infantile means of representation is enough to explain the dream. What matters is not the fact that the dreamer regresses to a more primitive mode of experience, but rather *how* he uses the regression and whether it takes him closer to the truth of his experience or only serves as a distancing mediation representing truth. What matters is the inevitable confusion in understanding the dream as we switch between the various possibilities. The true nature of dreams is not that they discard mature meaning and motives but that they suddenly make us uncertain about both, and play them both against other, more primitive ones.

And there always *is* a confusion. Dreams always seem to mean more than the wakened dreamer can tell. In part this is because he never has the original dream directly before him. Dreams if told are always *re*-told; we know them only after we have lost them—and lost our original "reading" of the hallucinatory experience, which we didn't even know we had to "read" at all. So now we look back, puzzled: what seemed so horrifying last night now seems only puzzling—why was I terrified by the way the sunlight fell across my mother's hands? And what we took for granted last night now seems absurd. Sometimes the gap between dream experience and the attempt at retelling it seems so great as to be unbridgeable ("I can't put it into words, Doctor"). And, oddly enough, it's not always clear which is prior in this strange relationship where the play *between* two versions of the dream is more important than either one. In the radiator dream about turning on the spigot, which I cited above, at first the dreamer's nighttime experience seems obviously prior, but as soon as he translates it into the derivative narrative and overhears his own words—"let off steam" and "into hot water"—suddenly the verbal statement seems to be the prior meaning and the original dream only a code for it. The play between these two possibilities is the dream's defining quality and a main source of its unsettling power.

The gap between dreaming and telling is only partly responsible for the confusion, however. Even if he seems to describe it exactly, the wakened dreamer always misreads his own dream at first if he takes it literally. There is always another gap—this time between the commonsense interpretation of the dream and some other interpretation which hovers behind it. Freud tried to invoke regressive mechanisms as the determinants of this other meaning, but the invocation will not always work. It is true that the dreamer has access to a primitive and nonmimetic mode of representation—this is what makes even the most mundane dream surface so different from life. But the primitive surface may work in different ways. In the first case it may indicate that the dreamer has actually gone back to a primitive way of seeing and representing the world, a time when feelings *were* in the landscape, parents *were* kings and queens, penises *were* telephone poles, and a stream of urine *was* an explosive jet of steam. This is not a wrenching away from a reality but a return to a mode of thinking in which we had not yet sorted out wish from reality—or fear from reality, or any other subjective, emotionally tinged view from the objective truth about things. Freud's claim that dreams fulfilled wishes rather than telling the truth described only the most obvious of several possible distortions resulting from such regression.

In dreams, not only does the wishful imperative merge with the factual statement ("You must finish the book, Freud!" becomes a dream in which the book is finished). The subjective also merges with factual statement ("If Irma had been a better patient, then my reputation would be better" becomes a dream in which Irma *is* a better patient). Finally, subjective, metaphorical versions of reality are presented as if they were literally true. For the most part, as in the examples I have just mentioned, this means returning to the child's concrete, physical way of "grasping" ideas: "the ego was first a body ego," as Freud says. So Freud dreams that he is dissecting his own pelvis when he feels that he is "spilling out his guts" to the readers of his dream book; or in his dream of the "Botanical Monograph," the difficult intellectual achievement of finishing the book becomes the physical achievement of turning its pages. The dreamer is not bothered by this conflation while he sleeps; the wakened dreamer, however, finds that his commonsense, literal-minded insistence on one of the meanings gets him into trouble. Like the dim-witted poet Chaucer exploring his own dream world, he cannot tell the difference between a literal and a figurative game of chess when the man in black talks about losing his queen.

Simple regression like this, however, is not always enough to explain the dream's concrete imagery. In the second case, the dream's pictures, rather than reproducing infantile impressions, are used for some other nonmimetic and even coded presentation of experience. Rather than being used primitively, as direct portrayals of experience, the pictures are put to secondary use as diagrams or emblems or hieroglyphs. Instead of returning to primitive infantile visual experience, these images reflect intellectual schemata which no infant could understand. In other words, the dream draws not only on the infantile consciousness but also on intellectual and sophisticated ways of seeing and thinking about things—on all the modes of consciousness which sort things out, which make judgments and diagrams and hierarchies and anatomies, which see things from all sides, "as they really are," rather than subjectively. These sophisticated modes conflict with a natural, subjective view because they depend on acquired skills and knowledge, on familiarity with all the inherited social, literary, and linguistic conventions that gradually come to organize a child's "natural" and immediate consciousness. Allegories draw, in other words, on both the "savage" and the "bookish" views of the world, as C. S. Lewis has called them. These may seem opposite, but what is important for our purposes here is that they nonetheless meet in their common indifference to reality as we ordinarily perceive it. The regressive modes may ignore the conventions of realism the way a freshman does, out of ignorance; this more intellectual mode ignores the conventions the way a pedant or a philosopher does, out of another order of preconception altogether. But both ignore them.

The interplay among these different modes imposes more than a simple uncertainty about not knowing how to interpret a given dream symbol. It is a more basic disorientation, something like every child's reorientation when he first moves from his picture-books to books with nothing but printed words to look at, and he has to learn the artificial conventions that will turn those black marks into meaningful communications. We all had to learn to use our senses—our primary connection with the world—for secondary purposes. We have all had the experience of constraining our natural responses to fit the artifices of language. We have all had to resee our more impulsive and natural ways of understanding experience in terms of civilization's artificial conventions—had to learn them so thoroughly that the artifices finally became "second nature,"[4] the schemata were taken for reality, and the child's confusions were forgotten. Only in moments of alienation, disorientation, and sleepiness do we once more slip back so that we are unsure of the rules again. Only at threshold moments can we regain the old while retaining the new modes, and see their interplay, feel the old dizziness.

Freud's description of a simple, unambiguous regression to infantile wishes, or a simple, unambiguous use of regressive mechanisms for solely adult purposes, then, applies only to the sleeping dreamer—with whom, of course, we have no contact. For the wakened dreamer looking at his own dream, however, the situation is always more confusing. He straddles the two worlds of remembered dream and waking consciousness, and for him there is always a play between two different ways of reading the dream—as a picture or as a code. This play is what I want to examine now in a sample dream analysis, and then in literary texts, where it takes somewhat different form and is put to rather different use.

4. James Nohrnberg's phrase, describing how the reader's experience of internalizing Spenser's conventions in *The Faerie Queene* repeats the child's original experience (*The Analogy of "The Faerie Queene,"* p. 655).

A Sample: The "Dream of the Botanical Monograph"

Rather than describing the mixture of strange and familiar in dreams, Freud's interpretations were primarily meant to surprise us and show us only something new about how strange dreams really were. Of course, everyone had always thought dreams strange, but Freud was getting at a different kind of strangeness. Traditionally, dreams had been thought of as prophetic, otherworldly, perhaps surrealistic—and this is the way they are portrayed in literature. But the literary dream is more often a symbol for some other extraordinary experience than it is a realistic representation of dreams; there are very few damsels with dulcimers or talking flowers in most people's dreams. Some dreams, if not visionary, are still "strange" in that they are physically or psychologically impossible. But in most cases, rather than being flagrantly impossible, the dream is just a little odd, and it doesn't *seem* to need special interpretation at all. It may simply give the wrong details with an irritating insistence on them (why a *"botanical"* monograph?), or it leaves the right details out ("I couldn't see his face to tell who it was"). It may disappoint ordinary pictorial and narrative conventions, even if it doesn't flout them ("Then, somehow, it was not Berlin but Rome . . ."). It may go too fast or too slow, or fail to locate itself firmly in time and space. Finally, it may just be too ridiculously *un*strange ("I dreamt about having the piano tuned, which is just exactly what happened yesterday . . .").

Freud tried to distract attention away from the surface of all these dreams, whether outrightly ridiculous or suspiciously innocuous. His stated aim was to get to the real meaning behind the dream, to decode its clever language and find its hidden "message"—the wish behind it. But he did not follow his stated program. In fact, Freud's search for the infantile wish, the one hallucinatory image "misrepresented" and distorted in the dream, is replaced by his search for and demonstration of a different *way of reading* the surface. Freud's point was that whether the dream was extravagantly ridiculous or trivially ordinary, he had to ignore its obvious meaning and read it in a special way to discover the dream thoughts encoded in it. What

360 DREAMS AND ALLEGORIES

we can go on to notice is that Freud also makes use of the obvious reading, and that the final interpretation of the dream depends on the play between the two kinds of reading.

The sample dream itself is quite unassuming; indeed, an obvious reading does not go far:

> *I had written a monograph on a certain plant. The book lay before me and I was at the moment turning over a . . . coloured plate. Bound up in each copy there was a dried specimen of the plant, as though it had been taken from a herbarium.* [5]

As Freud asks, Why should he dream about just this bit of trivia? Ultimately, he promises, the thoughts behind the dream deal with profound concerns about work and love, but the surface gives no clue to these if it is read in the ordinary way. Instead, he says, we have to read it like a code, and see how the elements work together in unexpected ways. The dream consists of separate pieces like "botanical," "monograph," "turning pages," and these have been cleverly glued together to form a scene (as in some parlor game, where you are given three words and must make them into a sentence). But the real meaning is elsewhere, and we will not find it unless we are willing to follow strange associational paths very different from any intuitive ones. These associations first take Freud through a strand of "botanical" thoughts. Starting with a perfectly indifferent experience yesterday morning when he happened to notice a botanical monograph in a window, there is the woman whose husband "forgot" to bring her flowers on her birthday; there is Freud's own failure to bring his wife flowers, though she remembers to bring him his favorite "flowers," artichokes, from the market; there is the conversation last night in which the forgotten lady was mentioned, and so were those important topics in the dream-thoughts, work and love—although these

5. 1900–01, pp. 169–76, 180 n. 3, 191, 281–84, 305, 467. Freud refers to the dream several times, each time making different points about it. My analysis is based both on his interpretations and on several biographers' suggestions, particularly about referring to Freud's less discreetly edited paper on "Screen Memories" (1899) as an association to the dream. I have indicated in the text where my interpretation (but not the facts on which it is based) differs from both these sources.

had nothing whatsoever to do with flowers, except in a ridiculously tenuous way, since they concerned his monograph on
cocaine, a "flower" of sorts; there is, finally, Professor Gärtner
and his "blooming" wife, who interrupted that conversation.
The other memories that come to mind are just as tenuously
connected, it would seem.

Freud tries to make the connections between the associations
sound as superficial as he can, but it turns out that elements in
the questionable category—which include artichokes to eat,
bouquets to bring to his wife, cocaine, and Professor Gärtner's
blooming wife—are connected in more important and familiar
ways as well. What Freud has done is to stress the superficial
links and to ignore others. These, it is true, may sometimes be
the only ones to emerge past the patient's resistance in analysis;
but the others are always there. It is as if a reader were to
collect the liquid images in *Twelfth Night* and present them as
the play's only organizing device, without explaining the role
that oceans, rain, urine, and tears have in the rest of the action.
For it turns out that the tenuous string of botanical references
plays a more essential role than Freud gave it in organizing the
dream-thoughts.

In fact, the associations reveal nothing less than a series of
crises in Freud's life, all of which have to do with having to
choose between self-indulgence and discipline, between sensual
pleasure (or favorite hobby) and hard work. They begin with a
very early one, a scene of infantile masturbation and its forbidden fantasies; this is represented by a more innocent memory
in which Freud and his sister are mischievously pulling apart a
book with colored leaves or plates ("like an artichoke," Freud
says)—but with their father's unexpected encouragement.[6]
Later adult crises develop out of Freud's subsequent love of
monographs and failures in botany. Freud used to spend his

6. The connection between masturbation and pulling apart a book or an artichoke is suggested by the phrase "Sich einen herunterreissen" or "ausreissen,"
"to pull one out," and its dream symbol of breaking off a branch. Freud discusses the symbolism both in his autobiographical paper in "Screen Memories"
(1899, p. 319)—to which he directs the reader in his analysis of the Botanical
Monograph—and in *The Interpretation of Dreams* (pp. 348 n. 2, 388).

time doing things like cleaning out bookworms from the school herbarium, and in fact he was himself a "bookworm," collecting expensive monographs with colored plates—much to his father's disapproval. He could not marry his cousin in the flowery countryside because he had to spend his time studying— this is the girl he remembers visiting and stealing flowers from—or "deflowering." Much later, when he did once interrupt his study (of cocaine) in order to visit his fiancée, he paid by missing out on an important discovery. Finally, there is Freud's latest "botanical monograph," the book on dreams itself, which was causing him trouble. Freud was discouraged about finishing it, and his friend Fliess had just written encouragingly that he could see himself "turning over its pages" already—even though Freud had as yet sent only "pieces" of the manuscript. The dream book was the latest "flower of his invention," we might say without fetching too far for the associations. Dreams are not flowers, but Freud himself calls his sample dream at the beginning of his book a "specimen" dream, like the "specimens" in the herbarium.

The crises, when seen together, present an interesting and paradoxical pattern in which the dichotomy between self-indulgence and hard work is partly resolved as Freud turns away from flowers to "analyze" them in his work. The manifest dream then becomes not only a hermeneutical puzzle but a quietly symbolic image of Freud's lifelong conflict. There he is, turning over the dead leaves of a botanical monograph. The flowers are alive in the fields but they only come into his dry-as-dust academic book as dead things, "dried specimens." Freud's study has taken him away from life, courtship, flowers, deflowering, and eating artichokes. However, the opposite is true too. Freud is unfolding a colored plate; his books in a way have become his flowers, and he takes sensual pleasure in their colored leaves—and in possessing them. He may have pulled the flower apart but he has also thereby created it again in the book. He may analyze dreams but he recreates them in his book—he pulls them apart to treasure them.

What we can see now is that although the dream, too, destroys the original thoughts—does not reproduce them literally—it also creates something new, despite what Freud says. As T. S. Eliot says of poetry, dreams

> communicate—if it is communication, for the word may beg the question—an experience which is not an experience in the ordinary sense, for it may only exist, formed out of many personal experiences ordered in some way which may be very different from the way of valuation of practical life, in the expression of it. . . . that which is to be communicated is the [dream] itself, and only incidentally the experience and the thought which have gone into it. [1933]

Freud slighted the "dream itself" because he expected it to communicate "the experience and thought which have gone into it" in a very direct and literal way. He looked for the reproduction of a single, explanatory wish—and saw only censorship if he failed to find that wish. We, however, can see that the dream's indirections do not always disguise but sometimes express something otherwise inexpressible. The dream is not about a single wish (which it has failed to represent), but about a whole network of associations, thoughts, and images related to each other and represented in the dream in the strangest, most diverse ways. Freud thought he discovered the "meaning" of the dream in a single wish behind it, but what he really discovered was the existence of strange connections between ideas which create the illusion of a single source or wish when psychoanalyzed, and which create other "meanings" when approached in another mode of consciousness. In other words, Freud discovered that we all resort to these strange ways of seeing and representing things—and that we do so every night.

Dreams and Literature

Despite Freud's claim that the dream-work was entirely different from mature, well-shaped, and purposeful communication—let alone from the poet's art—others have claimed, on the basis of the same data, that the dream-work is no different from poetic thinking. Freud gave us, they say, a "science of tropes" (Kenneth Burke); his is the one psychology that "makes poetry indigenous in the human mind" (Lionel Trilling); and the two fundamental dream mechanisms are equivalent to the two kinds of figural language: "condensation" and "displacement" are other names for metaphor and metonymy (Jacques Lacan). Or, from a somewhat different perspective, Freud's list of defensive distortions can be mapped onto our poetic tropes (Harold Bloom).

Surely the equation is not quite this simple, whether we want to equate poetry to the primitive thought processes, as Lacan does, or to the censor, as Bloom does. Dream thinking includes elements closer to schizophrenic language than to poetry, and the dream rhetoric includes figures so devious that no handbook has a name for them. Along with the poetic floral fantasies, it encompasses, for example, the ashtray one man said represented his fellow patients because it was six-sided or "sick-sided" (Searles, 1963, pp. 35–36). But there is a connection between dreams and certain kinds of literature which, like the dream, insist on a gap between what the text seems to mean and the extra meaning it seems to imply. I am not thinking of what might seem to be the obvious parallel in the symbolists or surrealists, who claimed to write directly from "the unconscious." The surrealists' famous "chance encounter" of a sewing machine and an umbrella is too disjointed; we stop expecting it to make sense and so we lose the special tension between the promise of sense and the dumbness of events which characterizes dreams. The literary parallels are not in these "artless" modes where all logic and ordinary representation break down, but rather in the more highly wrought, emblematic, and "artificial" modes such as allegory. Sophisticated, consciously shaped, and publicly available art may seem to be at the other end of the scale of human productions from the unsophisticated, unconsciously shaped, private dream. But dreams too use artifice, and the artifices in both cases turn out to be strikingly similar.

Before turning to purely literary examples, consider for a moment one that, though not quite literature, is even more obviously similar to dreams: the medieval and renaissance Memory Systems which Frances Yates has described in *The Art of*

Memory (1966). These are constructs in the service of memory, which produce images like those Freud attributed to the dream's censorship or its artful "forgetting." The Memory Systems were visual devices for holding long lists and arguments in one's head by inserting them, piece by piece, into a perfectly memorized mental picture of some complicated scene or building. To remember, for example, a list of virtues and vices—say, if your memory building were the campus library—you would insert Pride shoving his way into the entry, Lust in the catalogue bank doing something appropriate, and Envy in the form of an old hag at the circulation desk (perhaps with eyes painted on her dress, to signal her Latin etymology). The more details in each case—and the more exact they are—the better the system works. My point is that the result looks very like a scene out of a dream—although the Memory System is a hard-won, consciously organized achievement in the service of communicating, and the dream, in Freud's description, is a regressive escape distorted in the service of censorship. The dichotomies of remembering and censoring, mature and regressed, do not hold; both the Memory System and the dream come out of the attempt to translate ideas into pictures and to reconcile two different ways of seeing and representing things, neither of which is pure "memory" or pure censorship. In both cases the created image hovers uncertainly between picture and diagram, or between narrative and hieroglyphic; and in both cases what matters is the interpreter's movement between the two ways of seeing it.

A similar ambivalence, though in more subtle form, provides the parallel between the dream and allegory. Allegory, like a dream, depends on "the gap between what it means and what we'd normally expect it to mean," as Rosamund Tuve has described it in her study of the genre (1966, p. 397). Interestingly enough, the history of allegorical theory parallels the history of psychoanalytic attitudes toward the dream. Literary theorists first tried to explain allegory's contradictory quality as a simple play between open expression and censorship battling for control of the picture. Allegory presented a transcendent revelatory truth, and the "veil of allegory" shrouded its "misteries

. . . lest by prophane wits it should be abused," as Sir Philip
Sidney explained—just as the dream's censor was supposed to
veil its taboo visions.

And, besides the moral tone, until recently there has been a
curious consistency which emerges in both allegorical and
dream interpretation when interpreters in both realms try to
cross the gap by stripping away the sensuous surface and get
down to (or up to?) the simple abstractions which supposedly
generate it. True allegory is assumed to be about the ultimate
truths and values in our lives (whether seen from a medieval or
a Kafkaesque point of view), and the particular events in any
allegorical story are always seen to point beyond themselves to
their divine source or metaphysical ground. No wonder Tuve
finds that so many allegories "mean the same thing." Actually,
Freud's claim that every dream fulfilled a repressed wish was
also, as he knew, a claim that all dreams mean "the same
thing"—draw on the same tedious reservoir of original infantile
concerns, the ultimate things which are the source and ground
for the rest of our lives. Freud's ultimate truths are psychological rather than metaphysical ones, but of course he would
make no distinction between the two. Whatever the nature of
the ultimate truths, in any case, both Freud and the allegorical
theorists often saw such a gap between the ultimate meaning of
a text and its surface, that the surface seemed no more than a
form of writing or a code. The seeming picture was really a hi-
eroglyph or a rebus recording a prior truth in convenient (if
regressive) pictures, and its surface story could mislead all but
the truly wise who knew the special rules for reading it.

But the "gap" in allegory—like the gap in dreams—is not between the surface and some other, truer meaning but between
different ways of reading the surface. Earlier theorists had
each chosen one way of reading allegories and claimed that *it*
led to the ultimate truth: naïve readers chose literal reading
(Sir Guyon is just a Knight); the moralists chose to see the action as an illustrated lesson (Sir Guyon's adventures in Spenser's *Book of Temperance* show the rewards for adhering to that
virtuous behavior and the punishments for failing). A third

group of more learned theorists followed Dante and the biblical interpreters to look at the surface story for analogies not only to our own lives but also to the New Testament and to divine truths. Sometimes this meant translating the surface story into symbols (Guyon resisting Mammon's temptations is like Christ in the wilderness resisting Satan). At other times it meant translating the surface into a rebuslike sentence in which each allegorical character represents a word, and their interaction is determined more by grammar than by dramatic truth (so Guyon [Temperance] overcomes Pyrocles [Angry Passion] by resisting the old lady [Occasion]). But until recently, all these different kinds of theorists were more interested in the ultimate "message" contained than in the particular means of expression. Lately, however, critics have begun to be more interested in the relation between surface and meaning—and in the particular *way* in which meanings were expressed. They have pointed out a more supple and sophisticated play between language and picture and have explored the "secret wit"[7] of allegory's varied puns.

Most recently, critics have even been suggesting that it is the *interplay between* these various ways of reading allegory that makes it work as it does.[8] Unless the allegory is as simple and uninteresting as Freud's ideal dream of convenience, no one method of reading is enough, because the allegory draws on more than one mode of representation. Not even the traditional search for four "levels" of interpretation is enough, because each of these "levels" is just one more example of the same analogical or symbolic representation; and a sheerly symbolic interpretation is no more appropriate here than in

7. Martha Craig's dissertation on the centrality of Spenser's puns, part of which was published as "The Secret Wit of Spenser's Language" (1967), has been evoked and elaborated by nearly every critic of Spenser's allegory.

8. See, for example, Paul Alpers, *The Poetry of The Faerie Queene* (Princeton, N.J.: Princeton University Press, 1967); Harry Berger, *The Allegorical Temper: Vision and Reality in Book II of Spenser's Faerie Queene* (New Haven, Conn.: Yale University Press, 1957), and his several articles on Spenser's other Books; and, similarly, other critics concerned with "reader response" or the reader's experience of reading the text.

Freud's dream; the "associations" to allegory cannot be lined up as a simple series of analogies any more than Freud's associations can all be lined up.

What we can learn from a comparison with dreams is that, first of all, allegorical representation is not "unnatural" or artificial, as it has always seemed to be, even in the most recent descriptions. It simply draws on the resources of another kind of thinking from the one in which we make a mimetic picture of reality. Like dreams, allegories make use of pictorial narratives for nonmimetic but perfectly natural purposes. And even more important, like dreams, they use the pictures in contradictory ways. In both cases the reader is disoriented at first— and even for some time afterward; but the disorientation in allegory is no more due to its artificiality than it is in a dream. It is due to the clash of rules for understanding and confusion about how to read. Allegories, like dreams, make both regressive and intellectual use of their images. On the one hand the allegory recreates the simplest, most concrete infantile form of thinking. It creates a House of Fame or a House of Pride in order to bring home the intellectual abstraction in familiar, physical terms. Allegory is often described as a story dominated by ideas, but in these instances it is actually presenting ideas directly and tangibly as a child feels them.

On the other hand it does use its pictorial surface in a more artificial way to encode ideas. It draws on intellectual modes that, again, are not mimetic, but go in the opposite direction, away from regressive concretizing imagination to a highly abstract way of conceptualizing. In the familiar multiple presentations of Pride, for example, in Spenser's *Faerie Queene*, Lucifera's House of Pride is an abstraction made visible so that its qualities take tangible form in the glittering, overbearing architecture and its glittering, overbearing owner. But this simple "regressive" concretization becomes more like an intellectual diagram as we hear about parts of the house whose meaning is not so immediately and sensibly obvious: the various compartments or categories of pride, or the various stages of pridefulness whose identification is not a matter of feeling and perception but a matter of disciplined thought.

Like the dream, allegory presents experience from several different points of view apart from the objective mimetic one. It gives us the feel of Pride, its source, its effect, its relation to other qualities—the aspects of an abstraction corresponding to the variety of ways we become aware of it and represent it to ourselves. Allegory includes a range of ways of moving from text to "meaning," just as dreams require a range of ways of moving from surface to its associations. And, as in the dream, part of what we mean by "allegorical" is the temptation to move in the wrong way.

What is the difference, then, between dreams and allegories? How do we distinguish between one man's private, tendentious dream about his predicament and the poet's portrayal of more pervasive contradictions in the human predicament—except to say that the poet's is somehow "better"? Freud's classic statement in "Creative Writers and Day-dreaming" (1908) was that the poet first of all softens the egoistic character of his wish-fulfillment and makes it more publicly available; and then he gives us a bonus of esthetic pleasure. This doesn't take us very far. It has the virtue of not reducing art to wish-fulfillment, but puts us tautologically back where we were by seeing a poem as the simple sum of its esthetic and its wish-fulfilling aspects.

I would like to suggest that we can learn something more than this from the comparison, and that—in the case of dreams and allegories at least—we can better define what is special about the literary text if we compare the different ways in which dream and allegory embody the switch of representational modes that I have just been describing. In the last part of this essay I want to look at two allegorical scenes that present a conflict not unlike the one Freud was dreaming about in "The Botanical Monograph": a scene from Chaucer's Prologue to the *Legend of Good Women,* and one from Spenser's *Legend of Temperance.* By comparing them to Freud's dream, we can see both some specific differences between the representational play in dreams and allegories, and a much more general and more important difference in the degree of self-consciousness about the play.

Chaucer's *Legend of Good Women* is a series of stories about good women introduced by a Prologue in which he explains their "origin in a dream" as an act of penance to the God of Love for having withdrawn from love to write books—books about not-so-good women. The Prologue contains both dream and associations. It begins with Chaucer describing himself as torn between his bookish pursuits and the attractions of Nature when birds perform the rites of love and his favorite flower is blooming. Chaucer's flower is the daisy, not the cyclamen or compositae or cruciferae which haunt Freud's dream, but its traditional associations are similarly natural and amorous, and he plays with them just as Freud does, though in a somewhat different way. One morning in May, he tells us, he left his books to pay observance to the daisy; and the old conflict must have been restimulated because it manifests itself in his dream that night, when the God of Love himself, accompanied by the daisy in the form of a queenly virgin, appears to chide Chaucer. The woman—Marguerite—comes to Chaucer's defense, and the solution to his conflict, like the solution to Freud's, is a compromise: he will continue to write books, but these will be dedicated to praising the women from whom he had turned.

A reader may extract logically statable paraphrases from both Freud's dream and Chaucer's poem. For Freud there were two: "If you had accepted any of the floral or feminine temptations your life would be much more pleasant," but also, "Every time you turn away from your books to these attractive hobbies, you have been punished." For Chaucer, "Because you have sinned against the floral and feminine world to write your books, you must atone." Neither Freud's dream nor Chaucer's "dream" is a mimetically accurate portrayal of the experiences described in these paraphrases, but the first difference we notice between them is that Chaucer's comes closer to portraying its significant center in a recognizable way. Chaucer's conflict takes a phenomenologically appropriate form in the verbal debate with its logical arguments on each side. Freud's dream is more like an emblem of conflict, the tension between flowers and books can be *understood* in it but not *felt,* as it is in Chaucer's personified drama. Freud presents the static solution while Chaucer presents the drama leading up to it.

Not only is the play between readings in Chaucer less contradictory than in Freud (the literal reading is closer to the others required); it is also more firmly tied to a rational, adult point of view: the debate takes verbal form, in which the claims on each side are neatly separated and analyzed. The dominance of an adult point of view is related to another difference between the two passages—one which, as far as I can tell, holds for other dreams and allegories as well: there are no personifications in the dream like the ones carrying on the debate in Chaucer's allegory. Dreams hardly ever portray either specific people actually representing themselves, or any personified abstractions like "love" which exist entirely apart from the dreamer's experience of them. The dream always falls somewhere between Dante's realistic gossip and the degenerate allegories in political cartoons, with their personifications of "socialism" and "poverty." The dream is dominated by the dreamer's relation to or subjective view of some experience or abstraction—not by the thing itself. It is as if the dreamer, unlike the allegorist, does not abstract the *essence* from several different things or people—although he may abstract the essence of their special relation to himself. Instead, he combines his images in another way.

Chaucer's allegorical daisy, for example, is also the loyal and loving Queen Alceste and the Virgin Mary, both of whom share the traits important in his allegory. Compare the little girl with yellow flowers who appears in a screen memory behind Freud's dream. (Freud remembers taking them away from her or "deflowering" her in his childhood.) The girl is his cousin, and the yellow flowers represent the yellow dress of another young woman Freud once loved madly—so that deflowering the little girl represents pulling the petal-dress from the older one. This is metonymy, not metaphor. Chaucer's associations are between things alike in nature; Freud's are between things alike in time and space and superficial sensual details (yellow). Chaucer's is an objective category (beautiful, loving women);

Freud's is a subjective category: "I have seen both women in the country, where I have also seen yellow flowers."[9]

The most interesting difference between Freud's dream and Chaucer's allegory, however, lies neither in the obvious accessibility of the poem nor even in the specific technique of personification, but in Chaucer's self-consciousness about the allegory's play of different kinds of representation. Both dream and allegory require similar shifts in reading, but in the allegory, the very fact of the shifting becomes part of the experience being portrayed.

We can see this first in the nature of Chaucer's debate with Love. The medieval *débat* was an established genre on which all allegories drew (and which has been seen as a protoallegorical mode out of which allegory developed) (Muscatine, 1953). But if we compare, for example, the debate between the lover and the God of Love in *The Romance of the Rose*, it is clear that Chaucer not only has cast his conflict into the form of a debate (the traditional way of portraying it), but also has given us a delightful sketch of just what kind of lover *would* think of his love in this way—rationalizing its tensions and turning them into a perfectly civilized, sublimated conversation. There is no equivalent self-consciousness about its tactics in Freud's dream.

Even more intriguing, Chaucer has purposefully prevented any easy symbolic translation of his experience by making the dream in its way *more* realistic, according to most people's standards, than the experience which prompted it. While Freud's dream finally presents a flower as a relatively traditional symbol of the women in his life (however complicated the relation between specific remembered women and flowers may be), Chaucer reverses the tradition and presents a woman as a symbol of the flower in his life. The reader becomes pleasantly giddy trying to sort out the priorities: the dream-daisy-personified represents the "real" daisy—but of course the real

9. In marginal cases, of course, the distinction between objective and subjective, or between metaphor and metonymy, is questionable ("objective by *whose* standards?"), but the general difference is clear. It has been offered by psychoanalytic theorist Pinchas Noy as the defining difference between "primary-process" thinking and secondary-process thinking (1969).

daisy itself represents just such qualities in "real" women as those the dream-woman displays. The impossibility of any easy separation between the experience and its representation is part of what the poem is about: even the most modest of poets knows that his books about love do not merely imitate it falsely but somehow come closer to the heart of love than random experience can. While Freud's dream, of course, required us to switch the way we understood "flower," the switch was not itself part of the dream's content as it is in Chaucer's poem.

There is a similar and even more pervasive self-consciousness about switching modes in the scene from Spenser's *Legend of Temperance*. Once again the book, like Freud's dream, is about a conflict between sensual dissipation and spiritual or intellectual discipline, as the hero of the legend, Sir Guyon, learns what true temperance is. Interestingly, Guyon's temptations—like Freud's—include not only the obvious ones of sloth and self-indulgence, but their opposites: "Prays-Desire" or proud ambition. Freud had to resist not only sensual distractions but also the proud ambition to triumph in botany exams, in writing the cocaine monograph and the dream-book. Guyon must resist not only the loose delights in Acrasia's false Eden but also the ambitious pride and possessiveness in great Mammon's cave. For Guyon the conflict is not presented so directly in terms of flowers and books, but this imagery is woven into the story nonetheless. Guyon's assigned task is to destroy Acrasia's Bower of Bliss and its floral attractions, and the image of temptation that recurs throughout the legend, though not embodied in a flower, is often in a fruit: apples golden and black, or gold and purple grapes. And in the scene I am interested in, these false temptations are indeed countered by the true one in the form of a history book, which Guyon reaches down from its shelf.

Both in itself and in the context of the two surrounding sections that belong with it, this scene demonstrates Spenser's self-conscious control of the switches in reading necessary to understand it. The scene itself—we might call it the scene of the historical monographs—is the climax of Guyon's adventure. He has endured six cantos of trials and temptations through his own efforts and with the help of the more perfect Sir Arthur; now the two knights have finally arrived at the House of Alma, the achieved state of temperance. They are led through the house in an obvious tour of the temperate body: through the stomach-kitchen and parlor-heart to the turret brain, itself neatly divided into three chambers of fantasy, judgment, and memory. In the last of these, a book-lined chamber where old man Eumenestes tosses constantly in his chair sifting through the volumes, Guyon and Arthur happen on the two historical accounts of their respective nations, and take them down to read.

The action in Alma's house has an obvious literal sense: the dramatic action of looking at, discovering, and exchanging words with the people in Alma's house. It also has an almost equally obvious symbolic meaning as a representation of the state of being "in" a well-tempered body. The drama and the symbolism do not quite coincide, of course: one is a narrative about discovery and the other is a static diagram or chart of temperance, which has nothing to do with *discovering* how to be temperate; and as Spenser's critics have pointed out, there are interesting ways in which the two modes, literal drama and symbolic chart, interact. Nonetheless, for the most part this section of the legend has been generally taken to be primarily a simple symbolic representation of temperance—so simple as to be simple-minded. It has been criticized for being literal-minded, a kind of Spenserian "Hemo the Magnificent" for a citizenship education class. The symbolism is so natural that it hardly requires any effort to make the translation from house to body—or indeed, to a temperate state of mind. All three are naturally conceived in spatial terms; the "goodly frame of temperance" naturally makes us think about not only our physical frame but also our frame of mind, and the highest and most important part of the house, the mind, is appropriately represented by the three chambers, a body-in-little, which is the way we actually think about our minds.

The complaints about the allegory here might hold for Spenser's other symbolic houses as well, but this seems to be an even more extreme case of simple symbolism. Unlike the House of

Holiness or the House of Pride, for example, it represents not something more abstract but something even more concrete; it represents something more familiar, not less familiar; something more directly available to the senses and not less. The body is so close to us—remember Freud's "the ego was first a body ego"—so much a part of our sense of things, that it provides the first measure by which we accustom ourselves to the world and some of the lasting metaphors by which we continue to know the arms of sleep, the head of state, the heart of the matter. It is odd that the source of metaphor should here be metaphorized—but that is precisely the point of Spenser's passage. The state of temperance is a state of perfect harmony in which the "tenor" and "vehicle" can switch places without loss: the perfect body could just as easily have been used to symbolize the "House of Temperance" in a spiritual sense (as indeed, the body already does). Body and mind are in perfect harmony, and so are the literal and figurative meanings of the experience. The very effortlessness of the switch in modes from literal to symbolic readings is part of what the passage is about.

The harmonious perception doesn't last very long, however, for immediately after this scene ends with the two knights opening their books, the next follows with the contents of each book. Suddenly we are swept from this introspective exploration to the outward and impersonal flow of history, from the detailed and static image of a single symbolic place to the sweep of generations—from the ideal to the actual laboratory of temperance.

But there is an even more unsettling switch of perspective required after the two historical narratives are finished. The achievement of temperance seems perfect, at last, and the episode at Alma's house seems over. In fact, Guyon actually does leave the house, finally prepared to undertake his assigned quest. But it is just at this point that Alma's house is attacked by Maleger and an army of villains, and we begin a new scene in an entirely different—and more difficult—mode of representation, as Arthur fights them off. The scene begins as if it were in the same mode as the visit to Alma's house, where abstract and concrete, figurative and literal significances of the action merge into one another, so that intellectual and physical—or "practical"—apprehension work together. As soon as Guyon (the "temperate soul") leaves, the ragged army assaults Alma's house, just as temptations to sin assault the body. Seven of Maleger's troops attack the main gate, suggesting the general threat of the seven deadly sins, and five other troops take on the "outposts" of sight, hearing, smell, taste, and touch. But we notice a discrepancy in this simple symbolism almost immediately: the temptations include not only deceptive attractions such as wealth and flattery, but outrightly repulsive ones such as the toads assaulting the gate of lustful touch. This is the discrepancy between the temptations as *judged* by the intellect and as *felt* by the senses—and it soon grows more obvious. The army, we hear, is both a mighty force and a flock of insubstantial shadows. Temptation feels like a battle with a mighty army, though we know the temptations would evaporate if only we could judge them properly. So, too, sins are powerful enough when felt as impulses, though theologically considered, they are nothings, the mere absence of good.

The discrepancy erupts into flagrant paradox when Maleger appears. We have just been hearing about the army of sins and now we expect its captain to be the Captain of Sin—if not Satan, then he ought at least to have some direct relation to the sins he leads; just as Alma is the spirit of her house so he should be the spirit of his army. But though Alma is manifestly temperate, Maleger shows no literal sinfulness and certainly embodies no obvious temptation. He may fleetingly invite the identifying tags of "Satan" or "Original Sin" which have hung on him, but on the whole he resists interpretation. He is there and not there, fights by running away, is strongest in his weakness. Apart from his tiger, he has no comfortably familiar iconographic details, and even the tiger is not so readily interpreted.

What Maleger represents is not sin itself but a sick desire ("evil eagerness") for sin; or the sickness of desire; or someone sick of desire, who hates the thing he most desires. The weakness that is strength is the weakness of the flesh, which someone like the modest, quiet Guyon can resist in Mammon's

Cave but which someone like "forward" and ambitious Arthur finds so hard to fight because it doesn't take the form of the usual outward physical enemies he knows how to handle. Maleger, then, neither personifies sinful temptation nor enacts it, but represents a different relation to temptation from the one we had been shown before. We must change our perspective to understand the scene; the dramatic story no longer works so harmoniously with its intellectual significance. In fact, if the House of Alma was the archetype of simple allegorical representation, this scene is its antitype. Alma's house represents one almost sheerly physical presence with another; Maleger represents only an absence. Whether we see him as a failure of temperance (with Guyon's departure from the house), or as an absence of will, he does not exist physically; he is an intellectual category, a mental symbol only.[10] He exists on another metaphysical plane from the one on which the house is built, and is an example of a different kind of representation. We have to switch our way of reading as we move from one canto to the next, and switch from expecting a natural symbolism to a rather uncomfortable and unnatural one.

The discrepancy between the two kinds of understanding is also a discrepancy in our relation to temperance. Temperance is a passive virtue; Guyon's heroic achievement in Mammon's Cave is to do nothing—a trial, as one critic has noted, that would have been only awkwardly represented by a battle. But temperance is also an active virtue, and in Arthur's confrontation with Maleger, Spenser purposely chose a battle to represent what is objectively very inappropriate for such representation. The switching is necessary to distinguish passivity from passivity of another kind, activity from the wrong kind of activity, and easy versions of temperance from the seemingly more contradictory and difficult but truer versions.

In a much-quoted comment, Northrop Frye has claimed that allegory interprets itself. If it does, it interprets itself in the way that the wakened dreamer interprets his own dream: by presenting it in different ways, using different modes of represen-

10. See James Nohrnberg's discussion of this episode as an allegory of allegorizing, pp. 320–22.

tation and different points of view. In the case of the dream
and the dreamer, the switch takes place when we move from
the isolated dream-as-dreamt to the larger network of associations and contexts. This is a move from the naïveté of the
sleeping dreamer to the wariness of the wide-awake interpreter; it is a move from one kind of reading to another. The allegory, by contrast, encompasses the clues for the switch within
the bounds of the text; but the switch is the same. The real difference between dream and allegory is not so much that the latter is more artful but that it is more self-conscious. While in the
dream the need to switch just makes understanding more difficult, in the allegory this difficulty is part of what the text is
about.

REFERENCES

Craig, M. "The Secret Wit of Spenser's Language." In P. J. Alpers,
    ed., *Elizabethan Poetry: Modern Essays in Criticism.* New York: Oxford
    University Press, 1967.
de Man, P. *Blindness and Insight.* New York: Oxford University Press,
    1971.
Eliot, T. S. *The Use of Poetry and the Use of Criticism.* London, 1933.
Fairbairn, W. R. D. "Object-Relationships and Dynamic Structure." *In-
    ternational Journal of Psycho-Analysis* 27 (1946) : 30–37.
Freud, S. *Standard Edition of the Complete Psychological Works.* London:
    Hogarth, 1953–74.
    "Screen Memories" (1899), vol. 3.
    The Interpretation of Dreams (1900–01), vols. 4, 5.
    "Creative Writers and Day-Dreaming" (1908), vol. 9.
    Introductory Lectures on Psycho-Analysis (1915–16), vol. 15.
    New Introductory Lectures on Psycho-Analysis (1933), vol. 22.
Laplanche, J., and Leclaire, S. "The Unconscious: A Psychoanalytical
    Study" (1966). Translated by P. Coleman. *French Freud: Structural
    Studies in Psychoanalysis. Yale French Studies* 48 (1972) : 118–75.
Muscatine, C. "The Emergence of Psychological Allegory in Old
    French Romance." *PMLA* 68 (1953) : 1160–82.
Nohrnberg, J. *The Analogy of "The Faerie Queene."* Princeton, N.J.:
    Princeton University Press, 1976.
Noy, P. "A Revision of the Psychoanalytic Theory of the Primary Pro-
    cess." *International Journal of Psycho-Analysis* 50 (1969) : 155–78.

Searles, H. "The Differentiation between Concrete and Metaphysical Thinking in the Recovering Schizophrenic Patient." *Journal of the American Psychoanalytic Association* 11 (1963) : 22–49.

Smith J. H. "The Psychoanalytic Understanding of Human Freedom: Freedom From and Freedom For." Lecture, Mark Kanzer Seminar on Psychoanalysis and the Humanities. New Haven: Yale University, 1976.

Tuve, R. *Allegorical Imagery: Some Medieval Books and Their Posterity.* Princeton, N.J.: Princeton University Press, 1966.

Yates, F. *The Art of Memory.* London: Routledge & Kegan Paul, 1966.

Index

Abse, W., 284
Absent addressee, 29–64
Adams, Hazard, 76
Adams, Henry, 242
Aeneid (Virgil), 273
Aesthetics, 152, 153, 259, 301
"Affidavits of Genius" (Alexander), 120
Aggression, 8–9, 11, 270
Alexander, Jean A., 120
Alienation. *See* Isolation
Allegories, 290–91, 365–78
Allen, D., 289
Among School Children (Yeats), 36
Analysis of Sensations (Mach), 220–21, 222–23, 229, 230–35, 237–39
"Analysis Terminable and Interminable" (Freud), 9, 93, 333
Analyst: and absent addressee, 37–53
Analytical effect, 125
Anatomy of Criticism (Frye), 153
Anniversaries (Donne), 300
Anxiety of Influence (Bloom), xvi
Apple Cart (Shaw), 200–01
Archetypes of literature, 70, 75
Areopagitica (Milton), 265
Aristotle, 163, 268, 269
Arms and the Man (Shaw), 190
Ars Amatoria (Ovid), 152
Art of Memory (Yates), 364–65
Ascham, Roger, 271, 272–73
As You Like It (Shakespeare), 179
Atlantis, 243–44
Auden, W. H., 76, 84
Auerbach, Erich, 68
"Auguries of Innocence" (Blake), 88
Augustine, 267–68
Auroras of Autumn (Stevens), 15, 26

"Autobiographical Study" (Freud), 222, 323
Autoeroticism, 10, 31–32

Back to Methuselah (Shaw), 197–200, 201
Bacon, F., 265, 267, 275–76, 288, 292
Baudelaire, Charles, 122–23
Bergler, E., 289
Bernays, Minna, 9
Berryman, John, 218
Beyond the Pleasure Principle (Freud), ix–xi, 231, 279, 323, 333; and death, x–xi, 225–31, 233, 236–37, 258–59; and defense, 4, 6, 8–27, 155, 167; and repetition compulsion, x–xi, 14–15, 17, 19, 21, 135, 225–26, 228, 231, 236–37
Biologism, 16, 227–31
Birth of Tragedy (Nietzsche), 252, 259
Blake, W., 40, 54, 58–63, 67–109. *See also individual works*
Blindness: of Milton, 205–06, 208, 210, 214, 297; Wordsworth and, 205–06, 208, 210, 211, 212, 214
Bloom, Harold, 70–71, 181–84, 348, 364; and Blake, 75, 76, 95, 101; and defense, xiii, xvi–xvii, 1–27, 214; on drive, xiii, xvi, 3–4, 6, 8–10, 17–18, 20–22; and influence, 7, 70, 122, 202–03, 302; and poetic will, ix–xiv, xvi–xvii, 1–27. *See also individual works*
Boccaccio, G., 150–78 passim, 276
Boccaccio on Poetry, 150
Bonaparte, Marie, 125, 129–33, 138–42, 146
Borges, J. L., 70, 71

Boundary creatures, 150–53
Brandes, George, 170
Bridge (Crane), 218–19, 239–56
Brisman, Leslie, 29–64
Brisman, Susan Hawk, 29–64
Brooks, Cleanth, 68–69
Brown, Norman O., 18, 85
Browne, Thomas, 288
Browning, Robert, 45, 64
Bruno, Giordano, 300
Bryant, William Cullen, 239–41, 245–46, 248, 255–56
Buber, Martin, 34
Buffer-layer, 167–68

Caesar and Cleopatra (Shaw), 200
Candida (Shaw), 190–91
Cantos (Pound), 253
Carrion Comfort (Hopkins), 57
Catastrophe, ix–xiii, xvii, 20–21
Censorship of dreams, 351, 352–53, 354–55, 365–66. *See also* Repression
Chaucer, G., 276, 287, 357, 369–73
Chekhov, Anton, 196
Childhood, 13–14, 81–82, 100–01, 108, 269
Chomsky, N., 262
Christianity, 264, 265–66, 267–68, 301. *See also* Original Presence
Cinthio, 272
Civilization and its Discontents (Freud), 93
Classicism, 86
Coleridge, Samuel Taylor, 37–40, 44, 45–53, 55–56, 68, 302. *See also individual works*
Colet, John, 269
Collar (Herbert), 57–58
Collins, William, 45
Comenius, Jan, 275, 276
Comus (Milton), 53
Condensation, 278
Conflict, 346–47, 352, 370–71, 373
Connections, 309–43
Constancy principle, 12–13, 20, 317

"Constructions in Analysis" (Freud), 155
Contradiction, 185
Conversational tone, 37–64
Cooke, P. Pendleton, 122
Copernicus, Nicholas, 292
Copiousness, 270–71, 285
Counterintention, 184–85
Crane, Hart, 42, 217–19, 239–57, 259–60
"Creative Writers and Day-dreaming" (Freud), xi, 369
Creativity. *See* Originality
Criterion, 255
Critias (Plato), 243
Cuddihy, J. M., 160–61

Daemonic sublime, 53–64
Dante (Alighieri), 41, 247–48, 275, 367, 371
Death drive, ix–xviii, 8, 10, 21; Crane and, 217–19, 239–57, 259–60; Freud and, x–xiv, 3, 18, 19, 22–23, 26–27, 217–39, 257–60, 301. *See also* Repetition compulsion
"Deconstruction of the Drive" (Lacan), 8
Defense, 117; Bloom on, xiii, xvi–xvii, 1–27, 214; Boccaccio and, 150–78 passim; of Crane, 254–55; Freud and, xiii, xvi, 4–27, 103, 149–79; of Poe, 132; Shelley and, 1–2, 150, 151, 153, 157, 159, 171–75; Sidney and, 150–79 passim; in Wordsworth, 205–15
Defense of Poetry (Shelley), 1–2, 150, 171–75
Dejection: An Ode (Coleridge), 37–40, 45–53, 55–56, 302
Delusion, 94
Dependency, 80–81, 102–05
Derrida, Jacques, 11, 181, 182
Dervin, Daniel, 194
Descartes, René, 265–66, 275, 299
Devil's Disciple (Shaw), 191–92

Dickstein, Morris, 67–109
Diction: in Wordsworth, 205–15
Diderot, Denis, 84, 108
Dillon, John, 120
Displacement, 278
Divine Weeks (Du Bartas), 291
Donne, John, 57, 104, 159, 276, 300
Dostoevsky, F., 106
Doubling, 219–20, 231, 232–34, 238–39
Dreams, 175–76, 278, 298, 313–18, 345–78
Drive: Bloom on, xiii, xvi, 3–4, 6, 8–10, 17–18, 20–22. *See also* Death drive; Poetic will; Sexuality
Drury, Elizabeth, 276
Dryden, John, 56
Du Bartas, Guillaume de Salluste, 291
Duncan, Isadora, 254
"Dynamics of Transference" (Freud), 329, 332

Edelson, Marshall, 113–18
Edgar Allan Poe (Dillon), 120
Edgar Allan Poe (Krutch), 120, 125
Edgar Poe (Bonaparte), 125
Education, 268–75, 284–86
Ego, linguistic, 277–90, 303
Ego and the Id (Freud), 12
Einige Ideen (Fechner), 230
Einstein, Albert, 263
Elemente der Psychophysik (Fechner), 230
Eliot, T. S., 40, 70–71, 253, 363; and Blake, 75, 76; Crane and, 247–50, 252, 253, 255–56; and Poe, 121, 122–23
Elizabeth I, 162, 171, 271, 287
Emblem book, 266
Emerson, Ralph Waldo, 109
English Renaissance, 264–77, 284–304
Erasmus, 269, 270–71
Eros. *See* Sexuality
Europe: A Prophecy (Blake), 77–78
Excess, praise of, 88
Exegesis, 264, 266–67

Faerie Queene (Spenser), 291, 368
Fairbairn, W. R. D., 350
"Family Romances" (Freud), 337
Fantasy, 19
Fearful Symmetry (Frye), 74
Fechner, Gustave T., 222–23, 229–30, 313
Felman, Shoshana, 119–48
Fenichel, O., 295
Ferenczi, S., 197, 225, 279
Ferguson, Margaret W., 149–79
Fermor, Arabella, 45
Fixation, 341
Fletcher, Angus, 24
Fletcher, Phineas, 291, 297
Fliess, W., 221, 222, 229, 233, 362
Flight, xiii–xiv, 5
Fludd, Robert, 266–67, 291
Foucault, Michel, 278
"Fountain" (Bryant), 240
Four Ages of Poetry (Peacock), 1, 172–73
Fowre Hymnes (Spenser), 300
Fracastoro, Girolamo, 291
Frank, Waldo, 250, 253
Frazer, James, 278
Free association, 328–29, 331
Freud, Anna, 9, 12–13, 103
Freud, Sigmund, 3–4, 29–30, 31, 129, 280–81, 301; and analysis of signifier, 140, 141; Blake and, 67–109; and connection, 309–43; and death, x–xiv, 3, 18, 19, 22–23, 26–27, 217–39, 257–60, 301; and defense, xiii, xvi, 4–27, 103, 149–79; and dreams, 175–76, 278, 298, 313–18, 345–78; and interpretation, 145, 154–55, 175–77, 178–79, 345–78; and Medusa, 197; and oceanic feeling, 42; and Poe, 132–33, 145, 146; and repression, 5, 7–8, 9–10, 16, 19, 23–24, 99, 103, 239; and science, 16, 154, 220–25, 227–31, 233–35; and sexuality, xi, xiii–xv, 3, 8–10, 19, 21–24, 27, 301, 336–43, 346; and transference, 15,

Freud, Sigmund (*continued*)
46–47, 54, 311–17, 324–25, 327–32; and unconscious, 29, 41, 72–73, 84, 182, 278–79. *See also individual works*
"Freud and Literature" (Trilling), 106
"Freud and the Poetic Sublime" (Bloom), xiii
Frye, Northrop, 153, 154; and allegory, 377; archetypes of literature of, 70, 75; and Blake, 74, 75, 76
Future of an Illusion (Freud), 237

Galen, 294
Galloway, David, 132
"Garden" (Marvell), 31
Genealogia Deorum Gentilium (Boccaccio), 150, 166
Geneva (Shaw), 201
Génie d'Edgar Poe (Mauclair), 120
Genius, ix, 120–21, 132–33
Genius and Character of Edgar Allan Poe (Thompson), 120
Genius and Disaster (Marks), 120
"Genius of Poe" (Robertson), 120
Gerusalemme Liberata (Tasso), xiii
Gesner, Conrad, 293
Gilbert, William, 293
Goethe, J. W. von, 3, 175
Gombrich, Sir Ernst, 263
Gordon, David J., 73, 181–203
Group Psychology and the Analysis of the Ego (Freud), 46–47
Guilt, 143, 147, 209–10

Happiness, 29, 30
Hardison, O. B., 152–53
Hartman, Geoffrey, 205–15
Harvey, William, 268, 293
Heartbreak House (Shaw), 195–97, 201
Hegel, G. W. F., 33–34
Heraclitus, 2
Herbert, George, 57–58, 290
Hering, E., 228–29, 230
Hermes Trismegistus, 292–93
Heroic realism, 186, 187, 188–90, 194
Higginson, Thomas W., 120

Hirsch, E. D., Jr., 76, 78, 104
Historians, 163–64
Historie of Life and Death (Bacon), 276
History, 43; of creativity, 264–304
History of the Royal Society (Sprat), 275
Hobbes, Thomas, 288
Hoffman, E. T. A., 72
Hölderlin, Friedrich, xvi
Homer, 48, 273
Hopkins, Gerard Manley, 57
"Horatian Ode" (Marvell), 45
Hugh Selwyn Mauberley (Pound), 253
Humanism, 268–77, 284–89
Hume, David, 292, 301
Husserl, Edmund, 304
Hutchinson, Sara, 37
Huxley, Aldous, 123
"Hymn to Death" (Bryant), 255
Hypnosis, 331

Idealists, 186
Il Penseroso (Milton), 48
Imaginary Other, 40–64
Imagination, 211, 303; in Renaissance, 298, 302; Wordsworth and, 211, 213
Imitation, 268–77, 285–87
Immortality, 277, 288
Incest, 209
Infantilism, 1, 2, 30, 31; in allegories, 368; dreams and, 347–48, 349, 351–52, 355, 359
Inferiority, 175–76
Inferno (Dante), 247–48
Influence, 67, 70, 71, 202–03, 302; Freud and, 7, 74, 222, 258–59; imitation and, 273; Mach and, 222–23; Poe and, 122–23
Inhibition, 23–24, 323
Inhibitions, Symptoms and Anxiety (Freud), 12, 99, 157
Intention, 184–85
Interpretation, 114–15, 146, 177–79; Freud and, 145, 154–55, 175–77, 178–79, 345–78; Poe and, 145
Interpretation of Dreams (Freud), 175, 339; and memory, 315–16, 333; and

representations, 313–14, 315, 321, 323, 342; and unconscious, 72–73; and wishes, 351
"Intimations of Immortality" (Wordsworth), 34–35, 40, 81
Introductory Lectures (Freud), 74
Irony, 78–79, 94–98, 106
Irreplaceability, 331–32
Irwin, John T., 217–60
Isolation, 14–15, 29–64

Jakobson, R., 9, 272, 277, 278
James, Henry, 94
Jameson, Fredric, 43
Jarrell, Randall, 93, 94
Jeffers, Robinson, 23
Jews, 160–61, 176
John Bull's Other Island (Shaw), 195
Jonson, Ben, 267, 287
Jung, C. G., 9, 18, 75

Kafka, Franz, 71
"Kafka and His Precursors" (Borges), 71
Kahn, Otto, 255
Kant, Immanuel, 303–04
Kaplan, B., 284
Kee, Weldon, 218
Kekulé von Stradonitz, F. A., 263
Kerrigan, William, 261–304
Kierkegaard, S., xi–xii
King Lear (Shakespeare), 212–13, 215, 300
Klein, M., 298, 306
Kohut, M., 282
Kris, Ernst, 263
Krutch, Joseph Wood, 120, 125, 126–29

Lacan, Jacques, 5, 37, 299, 309, 364; and drive, 8; and Imaginary Other, 40, 42–43; and narcissism, 9, 10–11, 31–32, 282–83, 289–90; on Poe, 125, 133–46; and Real Other, 40, 43, 44; and recognition desire, 30, 33–34; *stade du miroir* of, 10, 31–33, 35, 61,

281–83; and Symbolic Other, 40–41, 42–43, 51; and unconscious, 35, 40–41, 49, 53, 145, 146, 182, 261, 262, 278–79. *See also individual works*
L'Allegro (Milton), 48
Lamb (Blake), 59–61, 62
Lang, Fritz, 107
Laplanche, Jean, 8, 9, 10–11, 19, 278–79, 280, 350
Latin, 268–74, 285–89
Lawrence, T. E., 201
Leavis, F. R., 75–76
Leclaire, Serge, 350
Legend of Good Women (Chaucer), 369–73
Legend of Temperance (Spenser), 369, 373–77
Lewis, C. S., 357
Lewis, R. W. B., 240
Libido, 3, 10–11
Life and Death in Psychoanalysis (Laplanche), 9
Life and Works of Edgar Allan Poe (Bonaparte), 125
Life of Coriolanus (Plutarch), 165
Literary Art and the Unconscious (Gordon), 73
Locke, John, 301
Lorin, Jean de, 268
Lovelace, Richard, 300
Lowell, James Russell, 121, 122
Lucy Gray (Wordsworth), 48, 49, 50, 51
Lycidas (Milton), 61
Lyrical Ballads (Wordsworth), 48, 89–90

Mach, Ernst, 217–18, 219–21, 222–24, 229, 230–36, 237–39
Magic, 121–22, 278
Major Barbara (Shaw), 194–95
Mallarmé, S., 120–21, 122–23
Man and Superman (Shaw), 192–94, 195, 197
Manic-depressive psychosis, xviii
Map of Misreading (Bloom), 13
Marks, Jeannet A., 120

Marriage of Heaven and Hell (Blake), 76, 84–85, 86, 87, 90, 108
Marvell, Andrew, 31, 45
Marx, Karl, 107
Masochism, 14, 22–23, 84
Mauclair, Camille, 120, 131
Medicine, Renaissance, 293–96
Medusa, 197–98
Melville, Herman, 244
Memory, 48–49, 315–16, 319, 327–35, 340–41, 364–65
Menenius Agrippa, 165–66, 171
Metaphor, 9, 272–98 passim, 312–13, 323–35, 371, 375
Metonymy, 9, 272–90 passim, 335, 371
Microcosm/macrocosm correspondence, 7, 290–301
Millionairess (Shaw), 201, 202
Milton, John, 265, 267, 270, 274, 276, 300; and absent addressee, 45, 53, 54, 56, 61, 64; Blake and, 87; blindness of, 205–06, 208, 210, 214, 297; Coleridge and, 48, 51; and death, 13; and flight, 5; Shelley and, 174; Wordsworth and, 183, 205, 208, 210, 213, 214, 215. *See also individual works*
Mimesis (Auerbach), 68
Mind over reality, 7–8
Mirror-image. *See* Doubling; *Stade du miroir*
Moby-Dick (Melville), 244
More, Thomas, 269
Morris, Humphrey, 309–43
Moses and Monotheism (Freud), 155, 178–79, 338–41, 342
Mother-of-separation, 116
Mrs. Warren's Profession (Shaw), 188–90
Munroe, Ruth L., 73–74
Munson, Gorham, 249
Muses, 41–42
Mutabilitie Cantos (Spenser), 300
Mysticism, Renaissance, 266–67

Nabokov, Vladimir, 289
Narcissism, 15, 22–23, 31–32, 289–90,

298, 303; Blake and, 84, 105; Freud on, 9–11, 23, 105, 281; and imitation, 275–76; Lacan and, 9, 10–11, 31–32, 282–83, 289–90
Nature, 48, 88–93
"Negation" (Freud), 154–55
Neoplatonism, 298–300
Neurosis, 13–14, 126, 129
New Atlantis (Bacon), 276
New Criticism, 68, 69–71
New Introductory Lectures (Freud), 158, 167, 169–70, 315
Newton, Isaac, 261, 301, 303
Nicolson, M., 301
Nietzsche, F., 70, 84, 252; Freud and, 6, 72, 222, 223, 224, 236–38, 258–59; Mach and, 224, 237–38; and poetic will, 2–3, 6
Nobilitas Literata (Sturm), 271, 272
Notes from Underground (Dostoevsky), 106
Notes toward a Supreme Fiction (Stevens), 63
Nouvelle Héloïse (Rousseau), 108

"Observations on Transference-Love" (Freud), 331
Oceanic feeling, 42
Ode on the Poetical Character (Collins), 45
Oedipus, xii–xiii; Wordsworth and, 205, 207, 209–10
Oedipus at Colonus (Sophocles), 205, 207, 210–11
"Of Mere Being" (Stevens), 29
Ong, Walter, 152
"On Narcissism" (Freud), 9, 11, 23, 105, 281
On the Morning of Christ's Nativity (Milton), 53
On the Power of Sound (Wordsworth), 208
On the Rocks (Shaw), 201
Ordeal of Civility (Cuddihy), 160
"Ordinary Evening in New Haven" (Stevens), xvi

Originality, 19–20, 182, 222, 235–36, 261–304. *See also* Poetic will; Priority
Original Presence, 31–37, 38–62 passim
Original Sin, 93
Otway, Thomas, 49
Outline of Psycho-Analysis (Freud), 4, 21
Ovid, 10, 152

Pagel, Walter, 293
Paracelsus, P. A., 293
Paradise Lost (Milton), 45, 87, 208, 270, 297, 300
Paradise Regained (Milton), 208
Pater, Walter, 252
Paternity, 336–43
Pauline (Browning), 64
Peacock, Thomas Love, 1, 172–73, 174
Petrarch, 41, 166, 275
Phenomenology (Hegel), 33–34
Philosophy of Rhetoric (Richards), 312
Plato, 163, 243, 263
Pleasure principle, x–xi, 12–13, 15–16, 230–352 passim
Pliny the Elder, 293
Plutarch, 165, 171
Poe, Edgar Allan, 119–48; Crane and, 239, 245, 246, 248, 253–54
"Poe at Home and Abroad" (Wilson), 126–27
Poetic effect, 120–25, 146–48
Poetics (Aristotle), 268
Poetic will, ix–xviii, 1–27
Poetry and Repression (Bloom), 181, 184
Poincaré, J. H., 263
Pope, Alexander, 45, 56
Pound, Ezra, 253
Powell, Mary, 297
Pragmatic realism, 186, 194
Pragmatic rhetoric, 152
Preconscious, 73
Prejudice, 158, 160
Prelude (Wordsworth), 44, 82, 207–08, 211, 215, 302
Price, Martin, 76, 78

Primary process, 320–22, 323–27, 333, 341–43
Printing, 330, 332–33, 335
Priority, 6–7, 222, 223, 235, 238, 275. *See also* Originality
Project for a Scientific Philosophy (Freud), 313
Psychopathology of Everyday Life (Freud), 26–27
"Pulley" (Herbert), 290
"Purloined Letter" (Poe), 125, 133–45
Purple Island (Fletcher), 291

Question of Lay Analysis (Freud), 54
Quintessence of Ibsenism (Shaw), 186

Ralegh, Walter, 276
Rank, Otto, 219
Reaction-formation, 12–13, 21
Realism: of Shaw, 186, 187, 188–90, 194
Reality principle, xi, 259, 285
Real Other, 40–45, 51, 52, 53, 61, 63
Reason: Blake and, 86–87
Recognition: and absent addressee, 30, 31, 33–34, 42, 49–50, 51, 52, 64; and defense, 159, 166, 169, 171, 174
Regression, 347–49, 355, 356–58, 368. *See also* Infantilism
Religieuse (Diderot), 84
"Remembering, Repeating and Working-Through" (Freud), 327
Renaissance, English, 264–77, 284–304
Renaissance (Pater), 252
Repetition compulsion, 21; Freud and, x–xi, 14–15, 17, 19, 135, 225–26, 228, 231, 236–37, 327–35; Poe and, 135–40
Representation, 314, 316–43
Repression, 181–86; Blake and, 73–74, 84–85, 90, 95, 103, 105, 108; by Crane, 245–46, 255–56; Freud on, 5, 7–8, 9–10, 16, 19, 23–24, 99, 103, 239; Poe and, 136–38; primal, xiv, 19; Shaw and, 185–203

Resolution and Independence (Words-worth), 214
Reynolds, Joshua, 86
Rhetoric (Aristotle), 268
Richards, I. A., 115–16, 312
Richardson, Samuel, 108
Ricoeur, Paul, 280, 346
Rieff, P., 4, 7, 14, 19, 67, 81–82
Rig-Veda, 290
Ritch Storehouse or Treasurie for Nobilitye and Gentlemen (Sturm), 272
Robert, King of Naples, 166–67
Robertson, J. M. S., 120
Rodman, Selden, 249
Rossetti manuscript (Blake), 77, 90, 93, 94
Rourke, Constance M., 120
Rousseau, Jean-Jacques, 45, 81, 93, 108
Russell, Bertrand, 328

Saint Joan (Shaw), 200
Samson Agonistes (Milton), 205, 208
Satire, 301
Saussure, H. B. de, 272
Schizophrenics, 309
Schopenhauer, Arthur: Freud and, 7–8, 13, 21, 222, 223, 224, 228
Schorer, Mark, 76
Science: Freud and, 16, 154, 220–25, 227–31, 233–35; origins of, 292–94, 301–02, 303–04
Secondary process, 323–27, 341–43, 348–49
"The Seminar on *The Purloined Letter*" (Lacan), 125, 133–46
Sexuality, 8–9, 10, 21–24; Blake and, 77–78, 82–88, 91–93, 103, 104–06, 108; Freud and, xi, xiii–xv, 3, 8–10, 19, 21–24, 27, 301, 336–43, 346; Poe and, 126, 130, 132; in Shakespeare, 213; Shaw and, 187, 188, 189–93, 194, 195–99; and vision, 295–96; Wordsworth and, 82, 209–10
Shakespeare, William, 179, 212–13, 215, 276, 300

Shaw, George Bernard, 121, 122, 185–203. *See also individual works*
Shelley, P. B., 44, 45, 55, 190; and defense, 1–2, 150, 151, 153, 157, 159, 171–75. *See also individual works*
Sidney, Philip, 150–79 passim, 366
Signifier: analysis of, 140–42
Skura, Meredith Anne, 345–78
Smith, John, 268
Smith, Joseph H., ix–xviii
"Song of Liberty" (Blake), 77
Song of Myself (Whitman), 10
Songs of Experience (Blake), 58–59, 71–109 passim
Songs of Innocence (Blake), 58–59, 75–109 passim
Sophocles, 205, 210
Sordello (Browning), 45
"Special Type of Choice of Object Made by Men" (Freud), 330
Spenser, E., 267, 276, 287, 300; allegories of, 291, 368, 369, 373–77. *See also individual works*
Sprat, Thomas, 275
Stade du miroir, 10, 31–33, 35, 61, 281–83
Stevens, Wallace, xvi, 15, 26, 29, 30, 63–64. *See also individual works*
Stone, L., 116
Stovall, Floyd, 131–32
Strachey, James, 330
Structuralism, 62
Studies on Hysteria (Freud), 311–12, 315
Sturm, Johann, 271, 272
Sublimation, 21, 23
Sublime, xiii, 7–8, 15–16; daemonic, 53–64
Superiority, 175–76
Supplement to Bougainville's "Voyage" (Diderot), 84
Surrealism, 364
Surrogates, 330–32
Swift, Jonathan, 95
Swinburne, A. Charles, 23, 120
Symbolic Other, 40–64 passim
Symbolism, 169; in allegories, 367,

374-75; in Renaissance, 264-67, 297, 303
Synecdoche, 328, 335
Szasz, Thomas, 220-21

Taboo, 23-24
Taine, H. A.,69
Tasso, Torquato, xiii, 15
Tate, Allen, 131
Terry, Ellen, 191
Textuality, 70, 142, 181-83
Thalassa (Ferenczi), 279
"Thanatopsis" (Bryant), 239-40, 246, 248, 255
Thanatos. See Death drive
Theologians, 163
Theory of Literature (Wellek and Warren), 69
Thompson, John R., 120
Thoreau, Henry David, 286
Thought identity, 323-24, 326
Three Essays on Sexuality (Freud), 321, 336
Thus Spoke Zarathustra (Nietzsche), 2-3, 236-37
Tintern Abbey (Wordsworth), 44, 183
Tiriel (Blake), 77
"To a Junior Soph, at Cambridge" (Coleridge), 52-53
To a Lady (Pope), 56
"To a Skylark" (Shelley), 44
Too True to Be Good (Shaw), 200-01
Totem and Taboo (Freud), 23, 225
Transference, 30-31; Blake and, 54, 106; Coleridge and, 47-48, 53; Freud and, 15, 46-47, 54, 311-17, 324-25, 327-32; literary history as, 147
Transumption, poetic, 1, 24-25, 26
Trilling, Lionel, 106
Tristia (Ovid), 152
Triumph of Life (Shelley), 45
Trousdale, Marion, 271
Tuve, Rosamund, 365, 366
Tyger (Blake), 54, 59, 60-63

"Uncanny" (Freud), 72, 217-38 passim, 333
Unconscious, 183-84, 261-63; Blake and, 72-73, 84, 94; Freud and, 29, 41, 72-73, 84, 182, 278-79; Lacan and, 35, 40-41, 49, 53, 145, 146, 182, 261, 262, 278-79; Poe and, 131-32, 136-38, 145, 146, 147-48; Wordsworth and, 213
"Unconscious" (Freud), 324
Undecidability, 332, 334, 335, 337, 338, 342
Understanding, 336
Unity, 299-300

Valéry, Paul, 122-23
Valon, Caroline (Wordsworth's illegitimate daughter), 205, 209
Van den Berg, J. H., 9-10
Vico, Giambattista, 25
Virgil, 9-10, 166, 273
Vision, 295-96. See also Blindness
Visions of the Daughters of Albion (Blake), 77, 82-83, 90
Voices, 207-09, 214-15
Voltaire, 93
"Vulgarity in Literature" (Huxley), 123

Waller, Edmund, 288
Warren, Austin, 69
Waste Land (Eliot), 247-49, 252, 253, 255, 256
Weinstock, Herbert, 253
Weismann, August, 227-28, 230-31
Wellek, René, 69
Well Wrought Urn (Brooks), 68
Werner, H., 284
Whitehead, Alfred North, 292
Whitman, Walt, 10, 42, 239, 245
Why She Would Not (Shaw), 201-02
Widowers' Houses (Shaw), 188
Will: to die, 258-60; poetic, ix-xviii, 1-27
Wilson, Edmund, 126-27
Winters, Ivor, 123-24

Wisdom of the Ancients (Bacon), 267
Wishes: and allegories, 369; in dreams,
    175–76, 249–52, 254–55, 256, 259,
    363, 366
Wordsworth, Dora, 205, 209–10
Wordsworth, Dorothy, 44, 209
Wordsworth, William, 109, 205–15,
    302; absent addressee of, 32–33,

34–35, 37, 38–40, 44, 47, 48, 49, 50,
    51, 52; and Blake, compared, 81, 82,
    89–90; and Milton, 183, 205, 208,
    210, 213, 214, 215

Yates, Frances, 364–65
Yeats, William Butler, 36

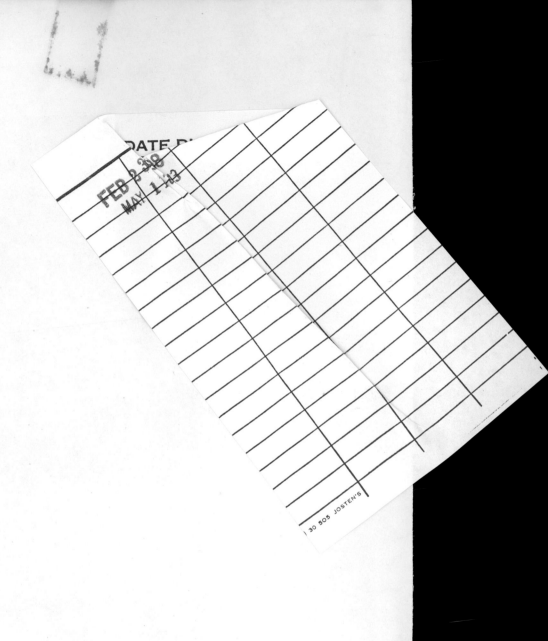